THE PENGUIN POETS

THE PENGUIN BOOK OF ENGLISH VERSE

THE PENGUIN BOOK
OF
ENGLISH VERSE

EDITED BY JOHN HAYWARD

* *

*

PENGUIN BOOKS

Penguin Books Ltd, Harmondsworth, Middlesex, England
Penguin Books, 625 Madison Avenue, New York, New York 10022, U.S.A.
Penguin Books Australia Ltd, Ringwood, Victoria, Australia
Penguin Books Canada Ltd, 2801 John Street, Markham, Ontario, Canada L3R 1B4
Penguin Books (N.Z.) Ltd, 182–190 Wairau Road, Auckland 10, New Zealand

—

First published 1956
Reprinted 1958, 1960, 1962, 1963, 1964, 1966, 1968 (twice), 1970, 1971, 1972, 1973, 1974, 1975, 1976, 1977, 1978 (twice), 1979, 1980, 1981

—

—

Set, printed and bound in Great Britain by
Cox & Wyman Ltd, Reading
Set in Monotype Bembo

A cloth-bound edition of this book
is published by
Faber and Faber Ltd

CONTENTS

[*Titles in square brackets have been supplied by the editor. Titles in italics are those of works originally published separately*]

TO THE READER xxiii

SIR THOMAS WYATT (?1503–1542)
The lover sheweth how he is forsaken . . . 1
Comparison of love to a streame falling . . . 1
The lover rejoiceth . . . 2
The lover complayneth . . . 2
A renouncing of love 3
Of his returne from Spaine 4

HENRY HOWARD, EARL OF SURREY (?1517–1547)
A complaint by night . . . 4
Prisoned in Windsor . . . 5
Of the death of sir T[homas]. W[yatt]. 6

THOMAS SACKVILLE, EARL OF DORSET (1536–1608)
[A Vision of War] (Induction. *A Myrroure for Magistrates*) 7

GEORGE GASCOIGNE (?1542–1577)
'And if I did what then?' 10

SIR EDWARD DYER (?1540–1607)
'The lowest Trees have tops' 11

NICHOLAS BRETON (?1545–?1626)
The Plowmans Song 11

SIR PHILIP SIDNEY (1554–1586)
From *Astrophel and Stella* 12
['Just Exchange'] 13
['Farewell World'] 13

EDMUND SPENSER (?1552–1599)
From *The Faerie Queene* 14
From *Amoretti* 21
Prothalamion 22

GEORGE PEELE (1556–1596)
[The Voice from the Well] (*The Old Wives Tale*) 26
'When as the Rie . . .' (*The Old Wives Tale*) 27
A Sonet 27

Contents

FULKE GREVILLE, LORD BROOKE (1554–1628)
Chorus Sacerdotum (*Mustapha*) 27

THOMAS LODGE (?1558–1625)
Rosalindes Madrigall 28

ROBERT SOUTHWELL (?1561–1595)
Tymes goe by Turnes 29
The Burning Babe 30

HENRY CONSTABLE (1562–1613)
Damelus' Song to his Diaphenia 31

CHRISTOPHER MARLOWE (1564–1593)
The Passionate Sheepheard to his love 31
From *Hero and Leander* 32

SIR WALTER RALEGH (?1552–1618)
Farewell to the Court 34
From 'The Last Booke of the Ocean to Scinthia' 35
[A Lover's Complaint] 37
The Author's Epitaph 38

THOMAS NASHE (1567–1601)
Song from *Summer's Last Will and Testament* 39

SAMUEL DANIEL (1562–1601)
Sonnets from *Delia* 40
From 'To the Countesse of Cumberland' 41

SIR JOHN DAVIES (1569–1626)
From *Orchestra: A Poem of Dauncing* 42

MICHAEL DRAYTON (1563–1631)
The Sheepheards Daffadill 45
Sonnets from *Idea* 47
[Last Verses] 48

THOMAS CAMPION (1567–1620)
Lyrics from Campion's *Bookes of Ayres* 48
['A Pilgrimage towards Loves Holy Land'] 52

GEORGE CHAPMAN (?1559–1634)
['Presage of Storme'] (*Eugenia*) 53
['Natures naked Jem'] (*Ovid's Banquet of Sence*) 55

JOSEPH HALL (1574–1656)
Satire XII: ['The love-sicke Poet'] 57

WILLIAM SHAKESPEARE (1564–1616)

From *Sonnets* 58
[Age and Youth] 65
The Phoenix and the Turtle 65
Songs from Plays 67

JOHN WEBSTER (?1580–1638)

[Summons to Execution] (*The Dutchesse of Malfy*) 70
[Dirge] (*The White Divel*) 70

BEN JONSON (1572–1637)

'Come my Celia . . .' 71
'Drinke to me onely . . .' 71
On my first Sonne 72
Epitaph on S[alomon].P[avy]. 72
From 'To Penshurst' 73
That Women are but Mens Shaddowes 73
From 'An Epistle to Lady Rutland' 74
From 'A Celebration of Charis' 74
An Ode. To Himselfe 75
[Proportion] 76
'Slow, slow, fresh fount' (*Cynthia's Revels*) 77

JOHN DONNE (1572–1631)

The Good-Morrow 77
Lovers Infinitenesse 78
'Sweetest Love I do not goe' 79
A Nocturnall upon S. Lucies Day 80
A Valediction: Forbidding mourning 81
The Extasie 82
Elegie: His Picture 84
From *The Second Anniversarie* 85
Holy Sonnets 86
A Hymne to Christ 87
Hymne to God my God, in my Sicknesse 88

FRANCIS BEAUMONT (1584–1616) & JOHN FLETCHER (1579–1625)

Songs from Plays 89

LORD HERBERT OF CHERBURY (1583–1648)

Elegy over a Tomb 93

WILLIAM DRUMMOND OF HAWTHORNDEN (1585–1649)
'Like the *Idalian* Queene' 94
'Sweet *Spring*, thou turn'st . . .' 94
'As in a duskie and tempestuous Night' 95
['The World a Hunting is'] 95

FRANCIS QUARLES (1592–1644)
Canticle 96

HENRY KING (1592–1669)
The Exequy 97

JAMES SHIRLEY (1596–1666)
Song from *Cupid & Death* 100
Song from *The Contention of Ajax & Ulysses* 101

WILLIAM STRODE (?1602–1645)
On Westwall Downes 102

WILLIAM HABINGTON (1605–1654)
Song from *The Queene of Arragon* 103

THOMAS RANDOLPH (1605–1635)
An Ode to Mr Anthony Stafford 104

GEORGE HERBERT (1593–1633)
From 'Easter' 106
Jordan 106
Even-Song 107
Deniall 108
Vertue 109
The Pearl 109
The Collar 110
The Pulley 111
The Flower 112
Love 113

RICHARD CRASHAW (?1613–1649)
A Hymn to . . . Sainte Teresa 114
On a Young Married Couple 119
From 'M. Crashaws Answer for Hope' 119

HENRY VAUGHAN (1622–1695)
The Retreate 120
Corruption 121

Man 122
The World 123
[Friends Departed] 124
['I walkt the other day'] 125

THOMAS TRAHERNE (?1636–1674)
From 'The Salutation' 127
From 'Solitude' 128
From 'Christendom' 128
On News 130

ABRAHAM COWLEY (1618–1667)
The Change 132

EDWARD BENLOWES (?1603–1676)
From *Theophila* 132

ANDREW MARVELL (1621–1678)
Bermudas 134
To his Coy Mistress 135
The Definition of Love 136
The Garden 137
[The Kingfisher] ('Upon Appleton House') 139

SIR WILLIAM D'AVENANT (1606–1668)
From *Gondibert* 139
'The Lark now leaves his watry Nest' 140
To the Queen, entertain'd at night 141
The Philosopher and the Lover 141

JOHN MILTON (1608–1674)
[On his 24th Birthday] 142
Lycidas 142
[On his Blindness] 147
[Katherine Milton: died MDCLVIII] 148
From *Paradise Lost* 148
[Epilogue] (Samson Agonistes) 155

SAMUEL BUTLER (1612–1680)
From *Hudibras* 156

ROBERT HERRICK (1591–1674)
To the Virgins, to make much of Time 158
Delight in Disorder 159

ROBERT HERRICK – *cont.*
To Dianeme 159
To Meddowes 160
To Daffadills 160
His Poetrie his Pillar 161

THOMAS CAREW (?1595–?1639)
The Spring 162
'Aske me no more . . .' 162

SIR JOHN SUCKLING (1609–1642)
'Oh for some honest Lovers ghost' 163
Loving and Beloved 164

RICHARD LOVELACE (1618–1657)
To Lucasta going beyond the Seas 165
To Lucasta going to the Warres 166
The Grasse-Hopper 166
To Althea, from Prison 167

THOMAS STANLEY (1625–1678)
La Belle Confidente 168

JOHN HALL (1627–1656)
The Call 169

SIR JOHN DENHAM (1615–1669)
[The Thames] (*Cooper's Hill*) 170

EDMUND WALLER (1608–1687)
'Goe lovely Rose' 171
The Selfe Banished 172
Of the Last Verses in the Book 172

CHARLES COTTON (1630–1687)
To Mr Isaac Walton 173
Laura sleeping 174

EDWARD TAYLOR (?1644–1729)
Upon a Wasp chilled with Cold 175

JOHN DRYDEN (1631–1700)
[The Fire of London] (*Annus Mirabilis*) 176
From *Absalom and Achitophel* 177
A Song for St Cecilia's Day, 1687 180

To the University of Oxford, 1674 181
To the Memory of Mr Oldham 182
Songs from Plays 183

SIR CHARLES SEDLEY (?1639–1701)
'Not *Celia*, that I juster am' 186
'Love still has something of the Sea' 187

RICHARD LEIGH (*b.* 1649)
Sleeping on her Couch 188

JOHN WILMOT, EARL OF ROCHESTER (1647–1680)
Love and Life 188
'Absent from thee' 189
From *A Satyr against Mankind* 189

MATTHEW PRIOR (1664–1721)
A Better Answer 192
A Simile 193
An English Padlock 194

ANNE FINCH, COUNTESS OF WINCHILSEA (1661–1720)
A Nocturnal Reverie 196

WILLIAM CONGREVE (1670–1729)
'False though she be . . .' 197

AMBROSE PHILIPS (1674–1749)
To Miss Charlotte Pulteney 198

JONATHAN SWIFT (1667–1745)
A Description of the Morning 199
The Day of Judgement 199
From *Verses on the Death of Dr Swift* 200

ALEXANDER POPE (1688–1744)
From *Windsor Forest* 202
From *An Essay on Criticism* 203
From *The Rape of the Lock* 205
[Epitaph] Intended for Sir Isaac Newton 206
To Mrs M[artha]. B[lount]. on her Birthday 207
From *An Essay on Man* 207
From *Of the Characters of Women* 208

Contents

JOHN GAY (1685–1732)
'Sleep, O Sleep' 212
'Love in her Eyes sits playing' (*Acis & Galatea*) 212

JOHN DYER (?1700–1758)
From 'Grongar Hill' 213

JAMES THOMSON (1700–1748)
From *Winter* 214

WILLIAM SHENSTONE (1714–1763)
'O'er desert plains, and rushy meers' 217

SAMUEL JOHNSON (1709–1784)
[The Scholar's Life] (*The Vanity of Human Wishes*) 218
[Lines on the Death of Mr Levett] 219

JOSEPH WARTON (1722–1800)
From *The Enthusiast: Or, The Lover of Nature* 220

WILLIAM COLLINS (1721–1759)
Ode to Evening 222
[St Kilda] ('Ode on the Popular Superstitions of the Highlands') 224

THOMAS GRAY (1716–1771)
An Elegy written in a Country Church Yard 225

CHRISTOPHER SMART (1722–1771)
[Adoration] (*A Song to David*) 228

OLIVER GOLDSMITH (?1730–1774)
From *The Deserted Village* 230

CHARLES CHURCHILL (1731–1764)
[A Criticaster] (*The Rosciad*) 234

WILLIAM COWPER (1731–1800)
The Castaway 236
The Shrubbery 237
[Town and Country] (*The Task*) 238

WILLIAM BLAKE (1757–1827)
From *Poetical Sketches*
'How sweet I roam'd' 239
'My silks and fine array' 240
From *Songs of Innocence*
The Divine Image 240

From *Songs of Experience*
The Clod and the Pebble 241
The Sick Rose 241
The Tyger 241
London 242
Infant Sorrow 243
Auguries of Innocence 243
From *The Book of Thel* 246
From *Milton*
[The New Jerusalem] 247
[Birdsong] 247
Epilogue (*The Gates of Paradise*) 248

GEORGE CRABBE (1754–1832)
[The Pauper's Funeral] (*The Village*) 248
[Peter Grimes] (*The Borough*) 249
[Jonas Kindred's Household] (*Tales*) 250
[The Dejected Lover] (*Tales of the Hall*) 251

CHARLOTTE SMITH (1749–1806)
Elegiac Sonnet 252

THOMAS RUSSELL (1762–1788)
Sonnet suppos'd to be written at Lemnos 252

WILLIAM LISLE BOWLES (1762–1850)
Sonnet. July 18th 1787 253

SAMUEL TAYLOR COLERIDGE (1772–1834)
Frost at Midnight 253
Kubla Khan 255
Dejection. An Ode 257

WILLIAM WORDSWORTH (1770–1850)
['My heart leaps up'] 261
'She dwelt among the untrodden ways' 261
'A slumber did my spirit seal' 261
From 'Lines composed . . . above Tintern Abbey' 262
['The world is too much with us'] 263
The Solitary Reaper 263
From 'Intimations of Immortality' 264
[To Catherine Wordsworth] 265
Afterthought 265
From *The Prelude* 266

SAMUEL ROGERS (1763–1855)
Captivity 272

WILLIAM CULLEN BRYANT (1794–1878)
To a Waterfowl 272

WALTER SAVAGE LANDOR (1775–1864)
[The Sea-Nymph's Parting] (*Gebir*) 273
Ianthe 274
Rose Aylmer 274
Dirce 275
[Ternissa] 275
[Envoi] 275

THOMAS MOORE (1779–1852)
'At the mid hour of night' 275

GEORGE GORDON, LORD BYRON (1788–1824)
'She walks in beauty' 276
To Ianthe (Dedication. *Childe Harold*) 276
[The Eve of Waterloo] (*Childe Harold*) 278
['My days of love are over'] (*Don Juan*) 280
['The Isles of Greece'] (*Don Juan*) 281
'So we'll go no more a roving' 283

PERCY BYSSHE SHELLEY (1792–1822)
Ode to the West Wind 284
Chorus from *Hellas* 286
From *Adonais* 287
Sonnet 290
Ozymandias 290
Mutability 291
'One word is too often profaned' 291
On Fanny Godwin 292
'A widow bird sate mourning' (*Charles the First*) 292

JOHN KEATS (1795–1821)
On first looking into Chapman's *Homer* 292
Ode to a Nightingale 293
Ode on a Grecian Urn 295
To Autumn 296
Ode on Melancholy 297
From 'Hyperion' 298
'Bright star, would I were stedfast' 300

GEORGE DARLEY (1795–1846)
The Mermaidens' Vesper Hymn 301
[The Unicorn] 301

THOMAS HOOD (1799–1845)
The Sea of Death 302
Silence 303

JOHN CLARE (1793–1864)
Emmonsail's Heath in Winter 304
Mary 304
I am 305
'Love lives beyond the Tomb' 305

RALPH WALDO EMERSON (1803–1882)
Hamatreya 306
'Give all to love' 308
Merops 309
Concord Hymn 309

THOMAS LOVELL BEDDOES (1803–1849)
'We have bathed, where none have seen us' 310

EDGAR ALLEN POE (1809–1849)
To Helen 311
The City in the Sea 311
Romance 313

ALFRED, LORD TENNYSON (1809–1892)
Tithonus 314
[The Sleeping House] (*Maud*) 316
['There is none like her'] (*Maud*) 316
Songs from *The Princess* 317
[Elaine's Song] ('Lancelot and Elaine') 318
[Vivien's Song] ('Merlin and Vivien') 318
From 'Morte d'Arthur' 319
From *In Memoriam* 320
'Break, break, break' 324
Crossing the Bar 324

HENRY WADSWORTH LONGFELLOW (1807–1882)
From 'To a Child' 325
From 'Evangeline' 325
To the Driving Cloud 326

Contents

ROBERT BROWNING (1812–1889)
The Lost Mistress 327
Meeting at Night 328
Parting at Morning 328
Home-Thoughts, from Abroad 329
Any Wife to any Husband 329
Two in the Campagna 333
Memorabilia 334
My Last Duchess 335
Prospice 336
Epilogue to 'Asolando' 337

EMILY JANE BRONTË (1818–1848)
Remembrance 338
'No coward soul is mine' 339
Stanzas [? by Charlotte Brontë] 340

HENRY DAVID THOREAU (1817–1862)
'I am a parcel of vain strivings' 341
'The moon now rises' 342
'For though the caves were rabitted' 342
'I was made erect and lone' 343

ARTHUR HUGH CLOUGH (1819–1861)
'Say not, the struggle nought availeth' 343

MATTHEW ARNOLD (1822–1888)
To Marguerite 344
Dover Beach 344
Palladium 345
The Scholar Gipsy 346
The Last Word 353

WALT WHITMAN (1819–1892)
The Dalliance of the Eagles 353
'When lilacs last in the dooryard bloom'd' 354
Sparkles from the Wheel 360
Reconciliation 361

DANTE GABRIEL ROSSETTI (1828–1882)
Sonnets from 'The House of Life' 361
Sudden Light 363
The Woodspurge 363

CHRISTINA ROSSETTI (1830–1894)
Remember 364
The Bourne 364
A Pause of Thought 365
Passing and Glassing 365
The Thread of Life 366

EMILY DICKINSON (1830–1886)
'There came a wind like a bugle' 367
'My life closed twice before its close' 367
'Presentiment is that long shadow on the lawn' 367
'Elysium is as far as to' 367
'She rose to his requirement' 368
'After a hundred years' 368
'The sky is low, the clouds are mean' 368
'As imperceptibly as grief' 369

WILLIAM MORRIS (1834–1896)
Prologue to *The Earthly Paradise* 369
From 'October' (*The Earthly Paradise*) 371
Summer Dawn 371

ALGERNON CHARLES SWINBURNE (1837–1909)
A Leave-Taking 372
From 'The Garden of Proserpine' 373
A Forsaken Garden 374
Chorus from *Atalanta in Calydon* 376

JAMES THOMSON B.V. (1834–1882)
From 'The City of Dreadful Night' 378

SIDNEY LANIER (1842–1881)
From 'Sunrise' 380

COVENTRY PATMORE (1823–1896)
A Farewell (*The Unknown Eros*) 382
Saint Valentine's Day (*The Unknown Eros*) 382

GEORGE MEREDITH (1828–1909)
From 'The Thrush in February' 384
From 'Modern Love' 384

GERARD MANLEY HOPKINS (1844–1889)
Heaven-Haven 386
Spring 387

GERARD MANLEY HOPKINS – *cont.*
The Windhover 387
Pied Beauty 388
Felix Randal 388
[Sonnets] 389

ROBERT LOUIS STEVENSON (1850–1894)
To S. R. Crockett 390

ROBERT BRIDGES (1844–1930)
Nightingales 391

THOMAS HARDY (1840–1928)
The Self-Unseeing 391
In Tenebris 392
At Casterbridge Fair: Former Beauties 392
After the Visit 393
Wessex Heights 394
The Voice 395
After a Journey 396
At Castle Boterel 397
Afterwards 398

ALFRED EDWARD HOUSMAN (1859–1936)
'Tell me not here, it needs not saying' 398

FRANCIS THOMPSON (1859–1907)
From 'Contemplation' 399

LIONEL JOHNSON (1867–1902)
From 'In Memory' 400
Dead 401

ERNEST DOWSON (1867–1900)
The Garden of Shadow 401

RUDYARD KIPLING (1865–1936)
'Cities and Thrones and Powers' 402
Harp Song of the Dane Women 402
Gertrude's Prayer 403

EDWIN ARLINGTON ROBINSON (1869–1935)
For a Dead Lady 404
Hillcrest 405
New England 406

William Butler Yeats (1865–1939)
The Rose of the World 407
The Second Coming 407
Sailing to Byzantium 408
Leda and the Swan 409
Among School Children 409
Byzantium 411
Three Things 412
Long-legged Fly 413

Walter de la Mare (1873–1956)
The Moth 414
Estranged 414
Good-bye 415
Solitude 415

Robert Frost (1875–1963)
Tree at my Window 415
Loneliness ('The Hill Wife') 416
Putting in the Seed 416
The Need of being versed in Country Things 417
The Gift Outright 418

John Masefield (1878–1967)
'Up on the downs' 418

Edward Thomas (1878–1917)
The Unknown Bird 419
'Out in the dark' 420

Rupert Brooke (1887–1915)
The Soldier 420

Isaac Rosenberg (1890–1918)
Wedded 421

Wilfred Owen (1893–1918)
Strange Meeting 421

Wallace Stevens (1879–1955)
Sunday Morning 423

William Carlos Williams (1883–1963)
Gulls 426

Contents

MARIANNE MOORE (1887–1972)

A Grave 427

Silence 428

ROBINSON JEFFERS (1887–1963)

The Eye 428

JOHN CROWE RANSOM (1888–1974)

Antique Harvesters 429

EZRA POUND (1885–1972)

The Return 430

Ode pour l'Election de son Sépulcre 421

From *The Pisan Cantos* 431

THOMAS STEARNS ELIOT (1888–1965)

Gerontion 432

Ash-Wednesday VI 434

Rannoch by Glencoe 435

Little Gidding 436

EDWIN MUIR (1887–1959)

The Road 443

The Transmutation 444

DAME EDITH SITWELL (1887–1964)

Still falls the Rain 444

HART CRANE (1899–1932)

Voyages. II 446

To Brooklyn Bridge 446

EDWARD ESSLIN CUMMINGS (1894–1962)

'Somewhere I have never travelled' 448

ROBERT GRAVES (*b.* 1895)

Full Moon 449

Never such love 450

EDMUND BLUNDEN (1896–1974)

Report on Experience 450

CECIL DAY LEWIS (1904–1972)

The Album 451

WILLIAM EMPSON (*b.* 1906)

Missing Dates 452

WYSTAN HUGH AUDEN (1907–1973)
1st September 1939 453
['Lay your sleeping head, my love'] 455
From *New Year Letter* 456

LOUIS MACNEICE (1907–1963)
August 457

STEPHEN SPENDER (*b.* 1909)
'I think continually of those who were truly great' 458
Elegy for Margaret. VI 459

DYLAN THOMAS (1914–1953)
A Refusal to mourn . . . 460
Fern Hill 461

ACKNOWLEDGEMENTS 465
INDEX OF FIRST LINES 469
INDEX OF POETS 483

TO THE READER

The chief, if not the only end of poetry, Dryden said, is to delight. It is with this end always in view that the following selection of English poetry has been made. A choice from all the poetry written in English verse during the past four hundred years necessarily involves compromise of one kind or another if a satisfactory balance is to be maintained between rival claims and interests. In order to achieve this, certain restrictions had to be imposed if, in the first place, the selection was to be contained within a volume of manageable and economic size and, in the second, was to be as well-proportioned and as representative as possible within its limits.

The range in time has therefore been set to exclude poets born before 1500, the upper limit being fixed by the publication in 1557 of Tottel's *Songes and Sonettes* (the first anthology of recognizably modern English verse), and the lower around the year 1940 when the poets who had grown up between the two World Wars of this century were reaching maturity. The field of choice within these dates has been further reduced by the exclusion of anonymous poems, dramatic verse (but not songs from plays), and dialect verse. To have attempted to do justice to traditional ballads, Elizabethan and Jacobean drama, and – to quote the title of Burns's first book – 'poems in the Scottish dialect' – would have left too little room for an adequate representation of poets with a prior claim to inclusion.

Even so, long poems of the first order such as *The Faerie Queene*, *Paradise Lost*, and *The Prelude* have had to be curtailed to a few extracts – a compromise which does at least enable them to be sampled along with all the other kinds of English verse exemplified in this collection. Although this particular form of compromise was unavoidable if a proper balance was to be preserved in the collection as a whole, it is unfortunately bound to do injustice to poets for whom the long poem is the most satisfactory medium of poetic expression. Such, indeed, were the principal poets of the eighteenth century from Pope to Crabbe; but there are also a few in every generation whose characteristic poems are too long to be given in full and lose in selection much of the peculiar value and interest inherent in their length.

Subject to these limitations, I have tried to concentrate in the following pages as much as possible of the richness and variety of intellectual and emotional appeal made by the principal poets – some 150 in all – who have written in English throughout the four centuries dividing the first Elizabethan age from the second.

An anthologist must always be indebted to the accumulated taste and judgement of the many critics of the past and of his own time who have insensibly influenced him, not forgetting what he owes to 'the common sense of readers uncorrupted by literary prejudice' by which, according to Dr Johnson, 'must be finally decided all claim to poetical honours'. I am grateful for the help they have indirectly given me. More particularly I wish to thank Mr W. H. Auden, Mr T. S. Eliot, Mr George Fraser, Miss Helen Gardner, and Miss Kathleen Raine for their advice; Mr J. M. G. Blakiston (Moberly Librarian, Winchester College), Mr David Foxon (The British Museum), and Mr John Sweeney (Harvard College) for their assistance in obtaining texts; the Duke of Bedford for the loan of his unique copy of Chapman's *Eugenia*; and Messrs McLeish, Pickering & Chatto Ltd and Bernard Quaritch Ltd for the loan of other volumes.

JOHN HAYWARD

NOTE ON THE TEXT

The poets represented are in chronological order. The texts reproduced are those of the earliest (usually the first) edition published either with the poet's authority, or, in the case of posthumous publication, from authoritative manuscript sources. Exceptionally, certain texts have been taken from later editions, revised by the poet during his lifetime or subsequently by his editors in the light of additional textual evidence. The original spelling, punctuation &c. of the copy-texts have been preserved, not for their extrinsic quaintness, but because, after due allowance has been made for the quirks and aberrations (not to mention simple carelessness or ignorance) of compositors before the nineteenth century, they serve to point sense and sound and rhythm. They illustrate, moreover, the evolution of the printed word. Obvious misprints have, however, been corrected and confusing archaic usages ('then' for 'than', the long ſ, u for v, and i for j) abandoned.

THE TEXT

WYATT

THE LOVER SHEWETH HOW HE IS FORSAKEN OF SUCH AS HE SOMTIME ENJOYED

They flee from me, that somtime did me seke
With naked fote stalkyng within my chamber.
Once have I seen them gentle, tame, and meke,
That now are wild, and do not once remember
That sometyme they have put them selves in danger,
To take bread at my hand, and now they range,
Busily sekyng in continuall change.
  Thanked be fortune, it hath bene otherwise
Twenty tymes better: but once especiall,
In thinne aray, after a pleasant gyse,
When her loose gowne did from her shoulders fall,
And she me caught in her armes long and small,
And therwithall, so swetely did me kysse,
And softly sayd: deare hart, how like you this?
  It was no dreame: for I lay broade awakyng.
But all is turnde now through my gentlenesse,
Into a bitter fashion of forsakyng:
And I have leave to go of her goodnesse,
And she also to use newfanglenesse.
But, sins that I unkyndly so am served:
How like you this, what hath she now deserved?

COMPARISON OF LOVE TO A STREAME FALLING FROM THE ALPES

From these hie hilles as when a spring doth fall,
It trilleth downe with still and suttle course,
Of this and that it gathers ay and shall,
Till it have just downflowed to streame and force:
Then at the fote it rageth over all.
So fareth love, when he hath tane a sourse.
Rage is his raine. Resistance vayleth none.
The first eschue is remedy alone.

THE LOVER REJOICETH THE ENJOYING OF HIS LOVE

ONCE as me thought, fortune me kist:
And bade me aske, what I thought best:
And I should have it as me list,
Therewith to set my hart in rest.
  I asked but my ladies hart
To have for evermore myne owne:
Then at an end were all my smart:
Then should I nede no more to mone.
  Yet for all that a stormy blast
Had overturnde this goodly day:
And fortune semed at the last,
That to her promise she said nay.
  But like as one out of dispayre
To sodain hope revived I.
Now fortune sheweth her selfe so fayre,
That I content me wondersly.
  My most desire my hand may reach:
My will is alway at my hand.
Me nede not long for to beseche
Her, that hath power me to commaunde.
  What earthly thing more can I crave?
What would I wishe more at my will?
Nothing on earth more would I have,
Save that I have, to have it styll.
  For fortune hath kept her promesse,
In grauntyng me my most desire.
Of my soveraigne I have redresse,
And I content me with my hire.

THE LOVER COMPLAYNETH THE UNKINDNES OF HIS LOVE

MY lute awake performe the last
Labour that thou and I shall waste:
And end that I have now begonne:
And when this song is song and past:
My lute be styll for I have done.

As to be heard where eare is none,
As lead to grave in marble stone:
My song may pearse her hart as sone.
Should we then sigh? or singe, or mone?
No, no, my lute for I have done.
The rockes do not so cruelly
Repulse the waves continually,
As she my sute and affection:
So that I am past remedy,
Wherby my lute and I have done.
Proude of the spoile that thou hast gotte
Of simple hartes through loves shot:
By whom unkinde thou hast them wonne,
Thinke not he hath his bow forgot,
Although my lute and I have done.
Vengeaunce shall fall on thy disdaine
That makest but game on earnest payne.
Thinke not alone under the sunne
Unquit to cause thy lovers plaine:
Although my lute and I have done.
May chance thee lie witherd and olde,
In winter nightes that are so colde,
Playning in vaine unto the mone:
Thy wishes then dare not be tolde.
Care then who list, for I have done.
And then may chance thee to repent
The time that thou hast lost and spent
To cause thy lovers sigh and swowne.
Then shalt thou know beauty but lent,
And wish and want as I have done.
Now cease my lute this is the last
Labour that thou and I shall wast,
And ended is that we begonne.
Now is this song both song and past,
My lute be still for I have done.

A RENOUNCING OF LOVE

FAREWELL, Love, and all thy lawes for ever.
Thy bayted hokes shall tangle me no more.

Senec, and Plato call me from thy lore:
To parfit wealth my wit for to endever.
In blinde errour when I dyd parsever:
Thy sharp repulse, that pricketh aye so sore:
Taught me in trifles that I set no store:
But scape forth thence: since libertie is lever.
Therefore, farewell: go trouble younger hartes:
And in me claime no more auctoritie.
With ydle youth go use thy propartie:
And theron spend thy many brittle dartes.
For, hytherto though I have lost my tyme:
Me lyst no lenger rotten bowes to clime.

OF HIS RETURNE FROM SPAINE

TAGUS farewel that westward with thy stremes
Turnes up the graines of gold already tried,
For I with spurre and saile go seke the Temmes,
Gaineward the sunne that sheweth her welthy pride,
And to the towne that Brutus sought by dreames,
Like bended mo[o]ne that leanes her lusty side.
My king, my countrey, I seke for whom I live,
O mighty Jove the windes for this me geve.

SURREY

A COMPLAINT BY NIGHT OF THE LOVER NOT BELOVED

ALAS so all thinges nowe doe holde their peace.
Heaven and earth disturbed in nothing:
The beastes, the ayer, the birdes their song doe cease:
The nightes chare the starres aboute dothe bring:
Calme is the Sea, the waves worke lesse and lesse:
So am not I, whom love alas doth wring,
Bringing before my face the great encrease
Of my desires, whereat I wepe and syng,

In joye and wo, as in a doutfull ease.
For my swete thoughtes sometyme doe pleasure bring:
But by and by the cause of my disease
Geves me a pang, that inwardly dothe sting,
When that I thinke what griefe it is againe,
To live and lacke the thing should ridde my paine.

PRISONED IN WINDSOR, HE RECOUNTETH HIS PLEASURE THERE PASSED

So cruell prison how coulde betide, alas,
As proude Windsor? where I in lust and joye,
With a kinges sonne, my childishe yeres did passe,
In greater feast than Priams sonnes of Troy:
Where eche swete place returns a taste full sower,
The large grene courtes, where we were wont to hove,
With eyes cast up into the maydens tower.
And easie sighes, suche as folke drawe in love:
The stately seates, the ladies bright of hewe:
The daunces shorte, longe tales of great delight:
With wordes and lokes, that tygers coulde but rewe,
Where eche of us did pleade the others right:
The palme play, where, dispoyled for the game,
With dazed eies oft we by gleames of love,
Have mist the ball, and got sight of our dame,
To baite her eyes, whiche kept the leads above:
The gravell grounde, with sleves tyed on the helme:
On fomynge horse, with swordes and frendlye hartes:
With cheare, as though one should another whelme:
Where we have fought, and chased oft with dartes,
With silver droppes the meade yet spred for ruthe,
In active games of nimblenes, and strength,
Where we did straine, trayned with swarmes of youth,
Our tender lymmes, that yet shot up in length:
The secrete groves, which oft we made resounde
Of pleasaunt playnt, and of our ladies prayse,
Recordyng ofte what grace eche one had founde,
What hope of spede, what dreade of long delayes:
The wilde forest, the clothed holtes with grene:
With rayns availed, and swift ybreathed horse,

With crye of houndes, and mery blastes betwene,
Where we did chase the fearfull harte of force,
The wide vales eke, that harborde us ech night,
Wherwith (alas) reviveth in my brest
The swete accorde: such slepes as yet delight,
The pleasant dreames, the quiet bed of rest:
The secrete thoughtes imparted with such trust:
The wanton talke, the divers change of play:
The frendship sworne, eche promise kept so just:
Wherwith we pass the winter night away.
And, with this thought, the bloud forsakes the face,
The teares berayne my chekes of deadly hewe:
The whiche as sone as sobbyng sighes (alas)
Upsupped have, thus I my plaint renewe:
O place of blisse, renuer of my woes,
Geve me accompt, where is my noble fere:
Whom in thy walles thou doest eche night enclose,
To other leefe, but unto me most dere.
Eccho (alas) that dothe my sorow rewe,
Returns therto a hollow sounde of playnte.
Thus I alone, where all my fredome grewe,
In prison pyne, with bondage and restrainte,
And with remembrance of the greater greefe
To banishe the lesse, I find my chief releefe.

OF THE DEATH OF SIR T[HOMAS]. W[YATT].

W. RESTETH here, that quick could never rest:
  Whose heavenly giftes encreased by disdayn,
And vertue sank the deper in his brest.
Such profit he by envy could obtain.
  A hed, where wisdom misteries did frame:
Whose hammers bet styll in that lively brayn,
As on a stithe: where that some work of fame
Was dayly wrought, to turne to Britaines gayn.
  A visgae, stern, and myld: where bothe did grow,
Vice to contenme, in vertue to rejoyce:
Amid great stormes, whom grace assured so,
To lyve upright, and smile at fortunes choyce.
  A hand, that taught, what might be sayd in ryme:

That reft Chaucer the glory of his wit:
A mark, the which (unparfited, for time)
Some may approche, but never none shall hit.
A toung, that served in forein realmes his king:
Whose courteous talke to vertue did enflame
Eche noble hart: a worthy guide to bring
Our English youth, by travail, unto fame.
An eye, whose judgement none affect could blinde,
Frendes to allure, and foes to reconcile:
Whose persing loke did represent a mynde
With vertue fraught, reposed, voyd of gyle.
A hart, where drede was never so imprest,
To hyde the thought, that might the trouth avance:
In neyther fortune loft, nor yet represt,
To swell in wealth, or yeld unto mischance.
A valiant corps, where force, and beawty met:
Happy, alas, to[o] happy, but for foes:
Lived, and ran the race, that nature set
Of manhodes shape where she the molde did lose.
But to the heavens that simple soule is fled:
Which left with such, as covet Christ to know,
Witnesse of faith, that never shall be ded:
Sent for our helth, but not received so.
Thus, for our gilte, this jewel have we lost:
The earth his bones, the heavens possesse his gost.

SACKVILLE

[A VISION OF WAR]

LASTLIE stode warre in glittering armes yclad,
With visage grim sterne lokes and blacklie hued;
In his right hand a naked sword he had
That to the hiltes was all with blood imbrued
And in his left that kinges and kingdomes rewed
Famine and fire he held, and therwithall
He rased townes and threw doune towres and all.

Cities he sackt and relmes that whilome flowred
In honnor glorie and rule above the best
He overwhelmed and all their fame devoured,
Consumde, destroied, wasted and never cest
Til he their welth their name and al oprest,
His face forhewd with woundes, and by his syde
Their hong his targe with gashes depe and wide.

In midst of which depainted ther we found
Dedlie debate all full of snakie here
That with a blooddie fillet was ybound,
Out breathing nought but discord everie wher,
And round about were portraied here and there
The hugie hostes *Darius* and his power,
His kinges, princes his peres, and all his flowre

Whom grete *Mardo* vanquisht ther in fight
With depe slaughter despoiling all his pride,
Perst through his relmes and daunted al his might;
Duke *Hannibal* beheld I ther beside,
In *Cannas* fell victour how he did ride,
And woful Romans that in vain withstode
And Consull *Paulus* covered all in blood.

Yet saw I more the fight at *Trasimene*
And *Trebeie* feld and eke whan *Hannibal*
And worthy *Scipio* last in armes wer sene
Before *Carthago* gate to trie for all
The worldes empire to whom it shold befall,
Pompeie I saw and Caesar clad in armes,
Their hostes alied and all their civil harmes,

With Conquerors handes forbathd in their owne blood,
And *Caesar* weping over *Pompeies* hed;
Yet saw I *Scilla* and *Marius* wher they stood,
Their grete crueltie and the depe bloodshed
Of frends; *Cirus* I saw and his host ded,
And how the quene with gret despite hath flonge
His hed in blood of them she overcome.

Xerxes the Percian King, yet saw I there
With his huge host that drank the rivers drie,
Dismounted hils and made the vales uprere,

His host and all yet saw I slain perdie,
Thebes I saw all raced down how it did lie
In heapes of stones, and *Tirus* put to spoile
With wals and towers flat evened with the soyle.

But *Troie* alas, me thought above them all
It made mine eies in vearie teres consume
When I beheld the woful werd befall
That by the wrathfull wil of gods was come,
And *Joves* unmoved sentence and fordome
On *Priam* king and on his town so bent,
I cold not lin but I must ther lament.

And that the more, syth destenie was so sterne
As force perforce ther mought no force availe
But she must fall and by her fall we learne
That cities, towres, welth, world, and all shal quaile,
No manhood might nor nothing mought prevaile;
All were ther prest, full mainie a prince and pere
And mainie a knight that sold his dethe ful dere.

Not worthie *Hector* worthiest of them all
Her hope, her joie, his force was now for nought;
O *Troie Troie*, there is no bote but bale,
The hugie horse within thy walles is brought,
Thy turrets fall, thie knightes that whilome fought
In armes amid the field ar slain in bed,
Thie gods defild, and all thine honnour ded.

The flames upspring and cruellie they crepe
From wall to ruf til all to cinders wast,
Some fire the houses wher the wretches slepe,
Some rush in here, some roon in ther as fast,
In everie wher or sword or fire they tast;
The walles ar torne, the towres whurld to ground,
Ther is no mischeif but may ther be found.

Cassandra yet ther saw I how they haled
From *Pallas* hous with spercled tresse undoon,
Her wrestes fast bound and with Grekes rout empaled,
And *Priam* eke in vain how he did roon
To armes, whom Pirrhus with despite hath doon
To cruell dethe and bathd him in the baine
Of his soons blood before the Aulter slaine.

But how can I descrive this dolful sight
That in the sheld so livelike fair did shine
Syth in this world I think was never wight
Could have set furth the half not half so fine;
I can no more but tel how ther is sene
Fair *Ilium* fall in burning red gledes doune,
And from the soyle gulf *Troie Neptunus* towne.

GASCOIGNE

AND if I did what then?
Are you agreev'd therfore?
The Sea hath fishe for every man,
And what would you have more?

Thus did my Mistresse once,
Amaze my mind with doubt:
And popt a question for the nonce,
To beat my braynes about.

Wherto I thus replied,
Eche fisherman can wishe,
That all the Sea at every tyde,
Were his alone to fishe.

And so did I (in vaine),
But since it may not be:
Let such fishe there as find the gaine,
And leave the losse for me.

And with such lucke and losse,
I will content my selfe:
Till tydes of turning time may tosse,
Such fishers on the shelfe.

And when they sticke on sands,
That every man may see:
Then will I laugh and clappe my hands,
As they do now at mee.

DYER

The lowest Trees have tops, the Ante her gall,
The flie her splene, the little sparkes their heate:
The slender haires cast shadowes, though but small,
And Bees have stings, although they be not great:
  Seas have their sourse, & so have shallow springs,
  And love is love, in Beggars, as in Kings.

Where rivers smoothest run, deepe are the foords,
The Diall stirres, yet none perceives it moove:
The firmest faith is in the fewest wordes,
The Turtles cannot sing, and yet they love:
  True Harts have eyes, & eares, no tongs to speake,
  They heare, & see, and sigh, and then they breake.

BRETON

THE PLOWMANS SONG

In the merrie moneth of May,
In a morne, by breake of day,
Forth I walked by the wood side,
When as *May* was in his pride:
There I spied all alone,
Phyllida and *Corydon*.
Much adoe there was God wot,
He would love, and she would not.
She sayd never man was true:
He said, none was false to you.
He said, he had loved her long:
She said, love should have no wrong.
Coridon would kisse her then:
She said, maides must kisse no men,
Till they did for good and all.
Then she made the shepheard call
All the heavens to witnesse truth,
Never lov'd a truer youth.

Thus with many a pretie oath,
Yea and nay, and faith and troth,
Such as silly shepheards use,
When they will not love abuse.
Love, which had beene long deluded,
Was with kisses sweet concluded:
And *Phyllida* with garlands gay,
Was made the Lady of the May.

SIDNEY

from ASTROPHEL AND STELLA

LOVING in truth, and faine in verse my love to show,
That she (deare she) might take some pleasure of my paine:
Pleasure might cause her reade, reading might make her know,
Knowledge might pitie winne, and pitie grace obtaine,
I sought fit words to paint the blackest face of woe,
Studying inventions fine, her wits to entertaine:
Oft turning others leaves, to see if thence would flow
Some fresh and fruitfull showers upon my sunne-burn'd braine.

But words came halting forth, wanting Inventions stay,
Invention Natures child, fled step-dame Studies blowes,
And others feete still seem'd but strangers in my way.
Thus great with child to speake, and helplesse in my throwes
Biting my trewand pen, beating my selfe for spite,
Foole, said my Muse to me, looke in thy heart and write.

*

WITH how sad steps, ô Moone, thou climbst the skies,
How silently, and with how wanne a face,
What, may it be that even in heav'nly place
That busy archer his sharpe arrowes tries?

Sure if that long with *Love* acquainted eyes
Can judge of *Love*, thou feel'st a Lovers case;
I reade it in thy lookes, thy languisht grace
To me that feele the like, thy state descries.

Then ev'n of fellowship, ô Moone, tell me
  Is constant *Love* deem'd there but want of wit?
  Are Beauties there as proud as here they be?

Do they above love to be lov'd, and yet
  Those Lovers scorne whom that *Love* doth possesse?
  Do they call *Vertue* there ungratefulnesse?

['JUST EXCHANGE']

My true love hath my heart and I have his,
By just exchange one for another geven:
I holde his deare, and mine he cannot misse,
There never was a better bargaine driven.
  My true love hath my heart and I have his.
My heart in me keepes him and me in one,
My heart in him his thoughts and sences guides:
He loves my heart, for once it was his owne,
I cherish his because in me it bides.
  My true love hath my heart, and I have his.

['FAREWELL WORLD']

Leave me ô Love, which reachest but to dust,
And thou my mind aspire to higher things:
Grow rich in that which never taketh rust:
What ever fades, but fading pleasure brings.

Draw in thy beames, and humble all thy might,
To that sweet yoke, where lasting freedomes be:
Which breakes the clowdes and opens forth the light,
That doth both shine and give us sight to see.

O take fast hold, let that light be thy guide,
In this small course which birth drawes out to death,
And think how evill becommeth him to slide,
Who seeketh heav'n, and comes of heav'nly breath.
  Then farewell world, thy uttermost I see,
  Eternall Love maintaine thy life in me.

SPENSER

from THE FAERIE QUEENE

[TO BE OR NOT TO BE]

ERE long they come, where that same wicked wight
His dwelling has, low in an hollow cave,
Farre underneath a craggie clift ypight,
Darke, dolefull, drearie, like a greedie grave,
That still for carrion carcases doth crave:
On top whereof aye dwelt the ghastly Owle,
Shrieking his balefull note, which ever drave
Farre from that haunt all other chearefull fowle;
And all about it wandring ghostes did waile and howle.

And all about old stockes and stubs of trees,
Whereon nor fruit, nor leafe was ever seene,
Did hang upon the ragged rocky knees;
On which had many wretches hanged beene,
Whose carcases were scattered on the greene,
And throwne about the cliffs. Arrived there,
That bare-head knight for dread and dolefull teene,
Would faine have fled, ne durst approchen neare,
But th'other forst him stay, and comforted in feare.

That darkesome cave they enter, where they find
That cursed man, low sitting on the ground,
Musing full sadly in his sullein mind;
His griesie lockes, long growen, and unbound,
Disordred hong about his shoulders round,
And hid his face; through which his hollow eyne
Lookt deadly dull, and stared as astound;
His raw-bone cheekes through penurie and pine,
Were shronke into his jawes, as he did never dine.

His garment nought but many ragged clouts,
With thornes together pind and patched was,
The which his naked sides he wrapt abouts;
And him beside there lay upon the gras
A drearie corse, whose life away did pas,
All wallowd in his owne yet luke-warme blood,

That from his wound yet welled fresh alas;
In which a rustie knife fast fixed stood,
And made an open passage for the gushing flood.

Which piteous spectacle, approving trew
The wofull tale that *Trevisan* had told,
When as the gentle *Redcrosse* knight did vew,
With firie zeal he burnt in courage bold,
Him to avenge, before his bloud were cold,
And to the villein said, Thou damned wight,
The author of this fact, we here behold,
What justice can but judge against thee right,
With thine owne bloud to price his bloud, here shed in sight?

What franticke fit (quoth he) hath thus distraught
Thee, foolish man, so rash a doome to give?
What justice ever other judgement taught,
But he should die, who merites not to live?
None else to death this man despayring drive,
But his owne guiltie mind deserving death.
Is then unjust to each his due to give?
Or let him die, that loatheth living breath?
Or let him die at ease, that liveth here uneath?

Who travels by the wearie wandring way,
To come unto his wished home in haste,
And meetes a flood, that doth his passage stay,
Is not great grace to help him over past,
Or free his feet, that in the myre sticke fast?
Most envious man, that grieves at neighbours good,
And fond, that joyest in the woe thou hast,
Why wilt not let him passe, that long hath stood
Upon the banke, yet wilt thy selfe not passe the flood?

He there does now enjoy eternall rest
And happie ease, which thou doest want and crave,
And further from it daily wanderest:
What if some litle paine the passage have,
That makes fraile flesh to feare the bitter wave?
Is not short paine well borne, that brings long ease,
And layes the soule to sleepe in quiet grave?
Sleepe after toyle, port after stormie seas,
Ease after warre, death after life does greatly please.

The knight much wondred at his suddeine wit,
And said, The terme of life is limited,
Ne may a man prolong, nor shorten it;
The souldier may not move from watchfull sted,
Nor leave his stand, untill his Captaine bed.
Who life did limit by almightie doome,
(Quoth he) knowes best the termes established;
And he, that points the Centonell his roome,
Doth license him depart at sound of morning droome.

Is not his deed, whatever thing is donne,
In heaven and earth? did not he all create
To die againe? all ends that was begonne.
Their times in his eternall booke of fate
Are written sure, and have their certaine date.
Who then can strive with strong necessitie,
That holds the world in his still chaunging state,
Or shunne the death ordaynd by destinie?
When houre of death is come, let none aske whence, nor why.

The lenger life, I wote the greater sin,
The greater sin, the greater punishment:
All those great battels, which thou boasts to win,
Through strife, and bloud-shed, and avengement,
Now praysd, hereafter dear thou shalt repent:
For life must life, and bloud must bloud repay.
Is not enough thy evill life forespent?
For he, that once hath missed the right way,
The further he doth goe, the further he doth stray.

[SEA-MONSTERS]

THE waves come rolling, and the billowes rore
Outragiously, as they enraged were,
Or wrathfull *Neptune* did them drive before
His whirling charet, for exceeding feare:
For not one puffe of wind there did appeare,
That all the three thereat woxe much afrayd,
Unweeting, what such horrour straunge did reare.
Eftsoones they saw an hideous hoast arrayd,
Of huge Sea monsters, such as living sence dismayd.

Most ugly shapes, and horrible aspects,
  Such as Dame Nature selfe mote feare to see,
  Or shame, that ever should so fowle defects
  From her most cunning hand escaped bee;
  All dreadfull pourtraicts of deformitee:
  Spring-headed *Hydraes*, and sea-shouldring Whales,
  Great whirlpooles, which all fishes make to flee,
  Bright Scolopendraes, arm'd with silver scales,
Mighty *Monoceroses*, with immeasured tayles.

The dreadfull Fish, that hath deserv'd the name
  Of Death, and like him lookes in dreadfull hew,
  The griesly Wasserman, that makes his game
  The flying ships with swiftnesse to pursew,
  The horrible Sea-satyre, that doth shew
  His fearefull face in time of greatest storme,
  Huge *Ziffius*, whom Mariners eschew
  No lesse, than rockes, (as travellers informe,)
And greedy Rosmarines with visages deforme.

All these, and thousand thousands many more,
  And more deformed Monsters thousand fold,
  With dreadfull noise, and hollow rombling rore,
  Came rushing in the fomy waves enrold,
  Which seem'd to fly for feare, them to behold:
  Ne wonder, if these did the knight appall;
  For all that here on earth we dreadfull hold,
  Be but as bugs to fearen babes withall,
Compared to the creatures in the seas entrall.

[THE BOWER OF BLISS]

EFTSOONES they heard a most melodious sound,
  Of all that mote delight a daintie eare,
  Such as attonce might not on living ground,
  Save in this Paradise, be heard elswhere:
  Right hard it was, for wight, which did it heare,
  To read, what manner musicke that mote bee:
  For all that pleasing is to living eare,
  Was there consorted in one harmonee,
Birdes, voyces, instruments, windes, waters, all agree.

Spenser

The joyous birdes shrouded in chearefull shade,
Their notes unto the voyce attempred sweet;
Th'Angelicall soft trembling voyces made
To th'instruments divine respondence meet:
The silver sounding instruments did meet
With the base murmure of the waters fall:
The waters fall with difference discreet,
Now soft, now loud, unto the wind did call:
The gentle warbling wind low answered to all.

There, whence that Musick seemed heard to bee,
Was the faire Witch her selfe now solacing,
With a new Lover, whom through sorceree
And witchcraft, she from farre did thither bring:
There she had him now layd a slombering,
In secret shade, after long wanton joyes:
Whilst round about them pleasauntly did sing
Many faire Ladies, and lascivious boyes,
That ever mixt their song with light licentious toyes.

And all that while, right over him she hong,
With her false eyes fast fixed in his sight,
As seeking medicine, whence she was stong,
Or greedily depasturing delight:
And oft inclining downe with kisses light,
For feare of waking him, his lips bedewd,
And through his humid eyes did sucke his spright,
Quite molten into lust and pleasure lewd;
Wherewith she sighed soft, as if his case she rewd.

The whiles some one did chaunt this lovely lay;
Ah see, who so faire thing doest faine to see,
In springing flowre the image of thy day;
Ah see the Virgin Rose, how sweetly shee
Doth first peepe forth with bashfull modestee,
That fairer seemes, the lesse ye see her may;
Lo see soone after, how more bold and free
Her bared bosome she doth broad display;
Loe see soone after, how she fades, and falles away.

So passeth, in the passing of a day,
Of mortall life the leafe, the bud, the flowre,
Ne more doth flourish after first decay,

That earst was sought to decke both bed and bowre,
Of many a Ladie, and many a Paramowre:
Gather therefore the Rose, whilest yet is prime,
For soone comes age, that will her pride deflowre:
Gather the Rose of love, whilest yet is time,
Whilest loving thou mayst loved be with equall crime.

[MUTABILITY]

For, all that from her springs, and is ybredde,
How-ever fayre it flourish for a time,
Yet see we soone decay; and, being dead,
To turne again unto their earthly slime:
Yet, out of their decay and mortall crime,
We daily see new creatures to arize;
And of their Winter spring another Prime,
Unlike in forme, and chang'd by strange disguise:
So turne they still about, and change in restlesse wise.

As for her tenants; that is, man and beasts,
The beasts we daily see massacred dy,
As thralls and vassalls unto mens beheasts:
And men themselves doe change continually,
From youth to eld, from wealth to poverty,
From good to bad, from bad to worst of all.
Ne doe their bodies only flit and fly:
But eeke their minds (which they immortall call)
Still change and vary thoughts, as new occasions fall.

Ne is the water in more constant case;
Whether those same on high, or these belowe.
For, th'Ocean moveth stil, from place to place;
And every River still doth ebbe and flowe:
Ne any Lake, that seems most still and slowe,
Ne Poole so small, that can his smoothnesse holde,
When any winde doth under heaven blowe;
With which, the clouds are also tost and roll'd;
Now like great Hills; and, streight, like sluces, them unfold.

So likewise are all watry living wights
Still tost, and turned, with continuall change,
Never abyding in their stedfast plights.

Spenser

The fish, still floting, doe at randon range,
And never rest; but evermore exchange
Their dwelling places, as the streames them carrie:
Ne have the watry foules a certaine grange,
Wherein to rest, ne in one stead do tarry;
But flitting still doe flie, and still their places vary.

Next is the Ayre: which who feeles not by sense
(For, of all sense it is the middle meane)
To flit still? and, with subtill influence
Of his thin spirit, all creatures to maintaine,
In state of life? O weake life! that does leane
On thing so tickle as th'unsteady ayre;
Which every howre is chang'd, and altred cleane
With every blast that bloweth fowle or faire:
The faire doth it prolong; the fowle doth it impaire.

Therein the changes infinite beholde,
Which to her creatures every minute chaunce;
Now, boyling hot: streight, friezing deadly cold:
Now, faire sun-shine, that makes all skip and daunce:
Streight, bitter storms and balefull countenance,
That makes them all to shiver and to shake:
Rayne, hayle, and snowe do pay them sad penance,
And dreadfull thunder-claps (that make them quake)
With flames and flashing lights that thousand changes make.

Last is the fire: which, though it live for ever,
Ne can be quenched quite; yet, every day,
Wee see his parts, so soone as they do sever,
To lose their heat, and shortly to decay;
So, makes himself his owne consuming pray.
Ne any living creatures doth he breed:
But all, that are of others bredd, doth slay;
And, with their death, his cruell life dooth feed;
Nought leaving but their barren ashes, without seede.

Thus, all these fower (the which the ground-work bee
Of all the world, and of all living wights)
To thousand sorts of *Change* we subject see:
Yet are they chang'd (by other wondrous slights)
Into themselves, and lose their native mights;
The Fire to Aire, and th'Ayre to Water sheere,

And Water into Earth: yet Water fights
With Fire, and Aire with Earth approaching neere:
Yet all are in one body, and as one appeare.

from AMORETTI

AFTER long stormes and tempests sad assay,
Which hardly I endured heretofore:
in dread of death and daungerous dismay,
with which my silly barke was tossed sore:
I doe at length descry the happy shore,
in which I hope ere long for to arryve;
fayre soyle it seemes from far and fraught with store
of all that deare and daynty is alyve.
Most happy he that can at last atchyve
the ioyous safety of so sweet a rest:
whose least delight sufficeth to deprive
remembrance of all paines which him opprest.
All paines are nothing in respect of this,
all sorrowes short that gaine eternall blisse.

★

FRESH spring the herald of loves mighty king,
In whose cote armour richly are displayd
all sorts of flowers the which on earth do spring
in goodly colours gloriously arrayd.
Goe to my love, where she is careless layd,
yet in her winters bowre not well awake:
tell her the joyous time will not be staid
unless she doe him by the forelock take.
Bid her therefore her selfe soone ready make,
to wayt on love amongst his lovely crew:
where every one that misseth then her make,
shall be by him amearst with penance dew.
Make hast therefore sweet love, whilest it is prime,
for none can call againe the passed time.

PROTHALAMION

Calme was the day, and through the trembling ayre,
Sweete breathing *Zephyrus* did softly play
A gentle spirit, that lightly did delay
Hot *Titans* beames, which then did glyster fayre:
When I whom sullein care,
Through discontent of my long fruitlesse stay
In Princes Court, and expectation vayne
Of idle hopes, which still doe fly away,
Like empty shaddowes, did aflict my brayne,
Walkt forth to ease my payne
Along the shoare of silver streaming *Themmes*,
Whose rutty Bancke, the which his River hemmes,
Was paynted all with variable flowers,
And all the meades adornd with daintie gemmes,
Fit to decke maydens bowres,
And crowne their Paramours,
Against the Brydale day, which is not long:
  Sweete *Themmes* runne softly, till I end my Song.

There, in a Meadow, by the Rivers side,
A Flocke of *Nymphes* I chaunced to espy,
All lovely Daughters of the Flood thereby,
With goodly greenish locks all loose untyde,
As each had been a Bryde,
And each one had a little wicker basket,
Made of fine twigs entrayled curiously,
In which they gathered flowers to fill their flasket:
And with fine Fingers, cropped full feateously
The tender stalkes on hye.
Of every sort, which in that Meadow grew,
They gathered some; the Violet pallid blew,
The little Dazie, that at evening closes,
The virgin Lillie, and the Primrose trew,
With store of vermeil Roses,
To decke their Bridegromes posies,
Against the Brydale day, which was not long:
  Sweet *Themmes* runne softly, till I end my Song.

With that, I saw two Swannes of goodly hewe,
Come softly swimming downe along the Lee;

Two fairer Birds I yet did never see:
The snow which doth the top of *Pindus* strew,
Did never whiter shew,
Nor *Jove* himselfe when he a Swan would be
For love of *Leda*, whiter did appeare:
Yet *Leda* was they say as white as he,
Yet not so white as these, nor nothing neare;
So purely white they were,
That even the gentle streame, the which them bare,
Seem'd foule to them, and bad his billowes spare
To wet their silken feathers, least they might
Soyle their fayre plumes with water not so fayre,
And marre their beauties bright,
That shone as heavens light,
Against their Brydale day, which was not long:
 Sweete *Themmes* runne softly, till I end my Song.

Eftsoones the *Nymphes*, which now had Flowers their fill,
Ran all in haste, to see that silver brood,
As they came floating on the Christal Flood.
Whom when they sawe, they stood amazed still,
Their wondring eyes to fill,
Them seem'd they never saw a sight so fayre,
Of Fowles so lovely, that they sure did deeme
Them heavenly borne, or to be that same payre
Which through the Skie draw *Venus* silver Teeme,
For sure they did not seeme
To be begot of any earthly Seede,
But rather Angels or of Angels breede:
Yet were they bred of *Somers-heat* they say,
In sweetest Season, when each Flower and weede
The earth did fresh aray,
So fresh they seem'd as day,
Even as their Brydale day, which was not long:
 Sweete *Themmes* run softly, till I end my Song.

Then forth they all out of their baskets drew,
Great store of Flowers, the honour of the field,
That to the sense did fragrant odours yeild,
All which upon those goodly Birds they threw,
And all the Waves did strew,
That like old *Peneus* Waters they did seeme,

Spenser

When downe along by pleasant *Tempes* shore
Scattred with Flowres, through *Thessaly* they streeme,
That they appeare through Lillies plenteous store,
Like a Brydes Chamber flore:
Two of those *Nymphes* meane while, two Garlands bound,
Of freshest Flowres which in that Mead they found,
The which presenting all in trim Array,
Their snowy Foreheads therewithall they crownd,
Whil'st one did sing this Lay,
Prepar'd against that Day,
Against their Brydale day, which was not long:
  Sweete *Themmes* runne softly, till I end my Song.

Ye gentle Birdes, the worlds faire ornament,
And heavens glorie, whom this happie hower
Doth leade unto your lovers blisfull bower,
Joy may you have and gentle hearts content
Of your loves couplement:
And let faire *Venus*, that is Queene of love,
With her heart-quelling Sonne upon you smile,
Whose smile they say, hath vertue to remove
All Loves dislike, and friendships faultie guile
For ever to assoile.
Let endlesse Peace your steadfast hearts accord,
And blessed Plentie wait upon your bord,
And let your bed with pleasures chast abound,
That fruitfull issue may to you afford,
Which may your foes confound,
And make your joyes redound,
Upon your Brydale day, which is not long:
  Sweet *Themmes* run softlie, till I end my Song.

So ended she; and all the rest around
To her redoubled that her undersong,
Which said, their bridale daye should not be long.
And gentle Eccho from the neighbour ground,
Their accents did resound.
So forth those joyous Birdes did passe along,
Adowne the Lee, that to them murmurde low,
As he would speake, but that he lackt a tong
Yeat did by signes his glad affection show,
Making his streame run slow.

And all the foule which in his flood did dwell
Gan flock about these twaine, that did excell
The rest, so far, as *Cynthia* doth shend
The lesser starres. So they enranged well,
Did on those two attend,
And their best service lend,
Against their wedding day, which was not long:
Sweete *Themmes* run softly, till I end my song.

At length they all to mery *London* came,
To mery London, my most kyndly Nurse,
That to me gave this Lifes first native sourse:
Though from another place I take my name,
An house of auncient fame.
There when they came, whereas those bricky towres,
The which on *Themmes* brode aged backe doe ryde,
Where now the studious Lawyers have their bowers
There whylome wont the Templer Knights to byde,
Till they decayd through pride:
Next whereunto there standes a stately place,
Where oft I gayned giftes and goodly grace
Of that great Lord, which therein wont to dwell,
Whose want too well now feeles my freendles case:
But Ah here fits not well
Olde woes but joyes to tell
Against the bridale daye, which is not long:
Sweete *Themmes* runne softly, till I end my Song.

Yet therein now doth lodge a noble Peer,
Great *Englands* glory and the Worlds wide wonder,
Whose dreadfull name, late through all *Spaine* did thunder,
And *Hercules* two pillors standing neere,
Did make to quake and feare:
Faire branch of Honor, flower of Chevalrie,
That fillest *England* with thy triumphs fame,
Joy have thou of thy noble victorie,
And endlesse happinesse of thine owne name
That promiseth the same:
That through thy prowesse and victorious armes,
Thy country may be freed from forraine harmes:
And great *Elisaes* glorious name may ring

Through al the world, fil'd with thy wide Alarmes,
Which some brave muse may sing
To ages following,
Upon the Brydale day, which is not long:
Sweete *Themmes* runne softly, till I end my Song.

From those high Towers, this noble Lord issuing,
Like Radiant *Hesper* when his golden hayre
In th'*Ocean* billowes he hath Bathed fayre,
Descended to the Rivers open vewing,
With a great traine ensuing.
Above the rest were goodly to bee seene
Two gentle Knights of lovely face and feature
Beseeming well the bower of anie Queene,
With gifts of wit and ornaments of nature,
Fit for so goodly stature:
That like the twins of *Jove* they seem'd in sight,
Which decke the Bauldricke of the Heavens bright.
They two forth pacing to the Rivers side,
Received those two faire Brides, their Loves delight,
Which at th'appointed tyde,
Each one did make his Bryde,
Against their Brydale day, which is not long:
Sweete *Themmes* runne softly, till I end my Song.

PEELE

[THE VOICE FROM THE WELL]

Gently dip: but not too deepe;
For feare you make the goulden beard to weepe.
Faire maiden white and red,
Combe me smoothe, and stroke my head:
And thou shalt have some cockell bread.
Gently dippe, but not too deepe,
For feare thou make the goulden beard to weep.
Faire maide, white, and redde,
Combe me smooth, and stroke my head;
And every haire, a sheave shall be,
And every sheave a goulden tree.

SONG

When as the Rie reach to the chin,
And chopcherrie chopcherrie ripe within,
Strawberries swimming in the creame,
And schoole boyes playing in the streame:
Then O, then O, then O my true love said,
Till that time come againe,
Shee could not live a maid.

A SONET

His Golden lockes, Time hath to Silver turn'd,
O Time too swift, ô Swiftnesse never ceasing:
His Youth gainst Time and Age hath ever spurn'd
But spurn'd in vain, Youth waineth by increasing.
Beauty, Strength, Youth, are flowers, but fading seen,
Dutie, Faith, Love are roots, and ever greene.

His Helmet now, shall make a hive for Bees,
And Lovers Sonets, turn'd to holy Psalmes:
A man at Armes must now serve on his knees,
And feede on praiers, which are Age his almes.
But though from Court to Cottage he depart,
His Saint is sure of his unspotted heart.

And when he saddest sits in homely Cell,
Heele teach his Swaines this Carroll for a Song,
Blest be the heartes that wish my Soveraigne well,
Curst be the soules that thinke her any wrong.
Goddesse, allow this aged man his right,
To be your Beads-man now, that was your Knight.

GREVILLE

CHORUS SACERDOTUM

Oh wearisome Condition of Humanity!
Borne under one Law, to another, bound:
Vainely begot, and yet forbidden vanity,
Created sicke, commanded to be sound:

What meaneth Nature by these diverse Lawes?
Passion and Reason, self-division cause:
Is it the marke, or Majestie of Power
To make offences that it may forgive?
Nature herselfe, doth her owne selfe defloure,
To hate these errors she herselfe doth give.
For how should man thinke that he may not doe
If Nature did not faile, and punish too?
Tyrant to others, to her selfe unjust,
Onely commands things difficult and hard.
Forbids us all things, which it knowes we lust,
Makes easie paines, impossible reward.
If Nature did not take delight in blood,
She would have made more easie wayes to good.
We that are bound by vowes, and by Promotion,
With pompe of holy Sacrifice and rites,
To teach beliefe in good and still devotion
To preach of Heavens wonders, and delights:
Yet when each of us, in his owne heart lookes,
He findes the God there, farre unlike his Bookes.

LODGE

ROSALINDES MADRIGALL

Love in my bosome like a Bee,
  dooth suck his sweete:
Now with his wings he playes with me,
  now with his feete.
Within mine eyes he makes his nest,
His bed amidst my tender brest,
My kisses are his daily feast,
And yet he robs me of my rest.
  Ah wanton will ye?

And if I sleepe, then pearcheth he,
  with prettie slight:
And makes his pillow of my knee,
  the live-long night.

Strike I my Lute, he tunes the string,
He musique playes if I but sing,
He lends me every lovely thing,
Yet cruell he my hart dooth sting.
    Whist wanton, still ye.

Else I with Roses every day
    will whip you hence:
And binde you when you long to play,
    for your offence.
Ile shut mine eyes to keepe you in,
Ile make you fast it for your sinne,
Ile count your power not woorth a pin.
Alas, what heereby shall I winne
    If he gaine-say me?

What if I beate the wanton boy
    with many a rod?
He will repay me with annoy,
    because a God.
Then sit thou safely on my knee,
And let thy bower my bosome be:
Lurke in mine eyes, I like of thee.
O *Cupid*, so thou pitty me,
    Spare not, but play thee.

SOUTHWELL

TYMES GOE BY TURNES

THE lopped tree in tyme may grow agayne;
Most naked plants renew both frute and floure;
The soriest wight may find release of payne,
The dryest soyle sucke in some moystning shoure;
Tymes go by turnes and chaunces chang by course,
From foule to fayre, from better happ to worse.

The sea of Fortune doth not ever floe,
She drawes her favours to the lowest ebb;
Her tyde hath equall tymes to come and goe,

Her loome doth weave the fine and coarsest webb;
No joy so great but runneth to an ende,
No happ so harde but may in fine amende.

Not allwayes fall of leafe nor ever springe,
No endlesse night yet not eternall daye;
The saddest birdes a season find to singe,
The roughest storme a calme may soone alaye;
Thus with succeding turnes God tempereth all,
That man may hope to rise yet feare to fall.

A chaunce may wynne that by mischance was lost;
The nett that houldes no greate, takes little fishe;
In some thinges all, in all thinges none are croste,
Fewe all they neede, but none have all they wishe;
Unmedled joyes here to no man befall,
Who least hath some, who most hath never all.

THE BURNING BABE

As I in hoary Winter's night stood shiveringe in the snowe,
Surpris'd I was with sodayne heat, which made my hart to glowe;
And lifting upp a fearefull eye to vewe what fire was nere,
A pretty Babe all burninge bright, did in the ayre appeare,
Who scorched with excessive heate, such floodes of teares did shedd,
As though His floodes should quench His flames which with His teares were fedd;
Alas! quoth He, but newly borne, in fiery heates I frye,
Yet none approch to warme their hartes or feele my fire but I!
My faultles brest the fornace is, the fuell woundinge thornes,
Love is the fire, and sighes the smoke, the ashes shame and scornes;
The fuell Justice layeth on, and Mercy blowes the coales,
The mettall in this fornace wrought are men's defiled soules,
For which, as nowe on fire I am, to worke them to their good,
So will I melt into a bath to wash them in My bloode:
With this He vanisht out of sight, and swiftly shroncke awaye,
And straight I called unto mynde that it was Christmas-daye.

CONSTABLE

DAMELUS' SONG TO HIS DIAPHENIA*

DIAPHENIA like the Daffadown-dillie,
White as the Sunne, faire as the Lillie,
heigh hoe, how I doo love thee?
I doo love thee as my Lambs
Are beloved of their Dams,
how blest were I if thou would'st proove me?

Diaphenia like the spreading Roses,
That in thy sweetes all sweetes incloses,
faire sweete how I doo love thee?
I doo love thee as each flower
Loves the Sunnes life-giving power,
for dead, thy breath to life might moove me.

Diaphenia like to all things blessed,
When all thy praises are expressed,
deare Joy, how I doo love thee?
As the birds doo love the Spring:
Or the Bees their carefull King,
then in requite, sweet Virgin love me.

MARLOWE

THE PASSIONATE SHEEPHEARD TO HIS LOVE

COME live with mee, and be my love,
And we will all the pleasures prove,
That Vallies, groves, hills and fieldes,
Woods, or steepie mountaine yeeldes.

And wee will sit upon the Rocks,
Seeing the Sheepheards feede theyr flocks,
By shallow Rivers, to whose falls,
Melodious byrds sing Madrigalls.

* Also attributed to Henry Chettle.

And I will make thee beds of Roses,
And a thousand fragrant poesies,
A cap of flowers, and a kirtle,
Imbroydred all with leaves of Mirtle.

A gowne made of the finest wooll,
Which from our pretty Lambes we pull,
Fayre lined slippers for the cold:
With buckles of the purest gold.

A belt of straw, and Ivie buds,
With Corall clasps and Amber studs,
And if these pleasures may thee move,
Come live with mee, and be my love.

The Sheepheards Swaines shall daunce & sing,
For thy delight each May-morning,
If these delights thy minde may move;
Then live with mee, and be my love.

from HERO AND LEANDER

['HERO THE FAIRE']

AT *Sestos*, *Hero* dwelt; *Hero* the faire,
Whom young *Apollo* courted for her haire,
And offred as a dower his burning throne,
Where she should sit for men to gaze upon.
The outside of her garments were of lawne,
The lining purple silke, with guilte starres drawne,
Her wide sleeves greene, and bordered with a grove,
Where *Venus* in her naked glory strove,
To please the carelesse and disdainfull eies
Of proud *Adonis* that before her lies.
Her kirtle blew, whereon was many a staine,
Made with the blood of wretched Lovers slaine.
Upon her head she ware a myrtle wreath,
From whence her vaile reacht to the ground beneath.
Her vaile was artificiall flowers and leaves,
Whose workmanship both man and beast deceaves.
Many would praise the sweet smell as she past,

When t'was the odour which her breath forth cast,
And there for honie, bees have sought in vaine,
And beat from thence, have lighted there againe.
About her necke hung chaines of peble stone,
Which lightned by her necke, like Diamonds shone.
She ware no gloves, for neither sunne nor wind
Would burne or parch her hands, but to her minde,
Or warme or coole them, for they tooke delite
To play upon those hands, they were so white.
Buskins of shels all silvered, used she,
And brancht with blushing corall to the knee;
Where sparrowes pearcht, of hollow pearle and gold,
Such as the world would woonder to behold:
Those with sweet water oft her handmaid fils,
Which as she went would cherupe through the bils.
Some say, for her the fairest *Cupid* pyn'd,
And looking in her face, was strooken blind.
But this is true, so like was one the other,
As he imagyn'd *Hero* was his mother.
And oftentimes into her bosome flew,
About her naked necke his bare armes threw,
And laid his childish head upon her brest,
And with still panting rockt, there tooke his rest.

[LOVE AT FIRST SIGHT]

So faire a church as this, had *Venus* none.
The wals were of discoloured *Jasper* stone,
Wherein was *Proteus* carv'd, and overhead,
A lively vine of greene sea agget spread;
Where by one hand, light headed *Bacchus* hung,
And with the other, wine from grapes out wrung.
Of Christall shining faire the pavement was,
The towne of *Sestos* calde it *Venus* glasse.
There might you see the gods in sundrie shapes,
Committing headdie ryots, incest, rapes:
For know, that underneath this radiant flowre
Was *Danaes* statue in a brazen towre,
Jove, slylie stealing from his sisters bed,
To dallie with *Idalian Ganimed*:

And for his love *Europa* bellowing lowd,
And tumbling with the Rainbow in a cloud:
Blood-quaffing *Mars*, heaving the yron net,
Which limping *Vulcan* and his *Cyclops* set:
Love kindling fire, to burne such townes as *Troy*,
Sylvanus weeping for the lovely boy,
That now is turnde into a *Cypres* tree,
Under whose shade the Wood-gods love to bee.
And in the midst a silver altar stood;
There *Hero* sacrificing turtles blood,
Vaild to the ground, vailing her eie-lids close,
And modestly they opened as she rose:
Thence flew Loves arrow with the golden head,
And thus *Leander* was enamoured.
Stone still he stood, and evermore he gazed,
Till with the fire that from his countnance blazed,
Relenting *Hero's* gentle heart was strooke,
Such force and vertue hath an amorous looke.
  It lies not in our power to love, or hate,
For will in us is over-rulde by fate.
When two are stript long ere the course begin,
We wish that one should lose, the other win.
And one especiallie doe we affect
Of two gold Ingots like in each respect.
The reason no man knowes, let it suffise,
What we behold is censur'd by our eies.
Where both deliberat, the love is slight,
Who ever lov'd, that lov'd not at first sight?

RALEGH

FAREWELL TO THE COURT

LIKE truthles dreames, so are my joyes expired,
And past returne, are all my dandled daies:
My love misled, and fancie quite retired,
Of all which past, the sorow onely staies.

My lost delights, now cleane from sight of land,
Have left me all alone in unknowne waies:
My minde to woe, my life in fortunes hand,
Of all which past, the sorow onely staies.

As in a countrey strange without companion,
I onely waile the wrong of deaths delaies,
Whose sweete spring spent, whose sommer wel nie don,
Of all which past, the sorow onely staies.

Whom care forwarnes, ere age and winter colde,
To haste me hence, to finde my fortunes folde.

from THE LAST BOOKE OF THE OCEAN TO SCINTHIA*

To seeke new worlds, for golde, for prayse, for glory,
to try desire, to try love severed farr
when I was gonn shee sent her memory
more stronge than weare ten thowsand shipps of warr
to call mee back, to leve great honors thought,
to leve my frinds, my fortune, my attempte
to leve the purpose I so longe had sought
and holde both cares, and cumforts in contempt.
Such heat in Ize, such fier in frost remaynde
such trust in doubt, such cumfort in dispaire
mich like the gentell Lamm, though lately waynde
playes with the dug though finds no cumfort ther,
But as a boddy violently slayne
retayneath warmth although the spirrit be gonn,
and by a poure in nature moves agayne
till it be layd below the fatall stone
Or as the yearth yeven in cold winter dayes
left for a tyme by her life gevinge soonn,
douth by the poure remayninge of his rayes
produce sume green, though not as it hath dunn,
Or as a wheele forst by the fallinge streame
although the course be turnde sume other way

* The surviving fragments of this mysterious poem were not printed until 1870. The present text is that of Ralegh's autograph manuscript.

douth for a tyme go rounde uppon the beame
till wantinge strenght to move, it stands att stay,
So my forsaken hart, my withered minde
widdow of all the joyes it once possest
my hopes cleane out of sight with forced wind
to kyngdomes strange, to lands farr of addrest
Alone, forsaken, frindless onn the shore
with many wounds, with deaths cold pangs inebrased,
writes in the dust as one that could no more
whom love, and tyme, and fortune had defaced,
of things so great, so long, so manefolde
with meanes so weake, the sowle yeven then departing
the weale, the wo, the passages of olde
and worlds of thoughts discribde by one last sythinge.
As if when after Phebus is dessended
and leves a light mich like the past dayes dawninge,
and every toyle and labor wholy ended
each livinge creature draweth to his restinge
wee should beginn by such a partinge light
to write the story of all ages past
and end the same before th'aprochinge night.

*

With youth, is deade the hope of loves returne
who lookes not back to heare our after cryes
wher hee is not, hee laughs at thos that murne
whence hee is gonn, hee scornes the minde that dyes,
when hee is absent hee beleves no words,
when reason speakes hee careless stopps his ears,
whom hee hath left hee never grace affords
but bathes his wings in our lamentinge teares.

*

The minde and vertue never have begotten
a firmer love, since love on yearth had poure,
a love obscurde, but cannot be forgotten,
too great and stronge for tymes Jawes to devoure.

*

But in my minde so is her love inclosde
and is therof not only the best parte
but into it the essence is disposde . . .
Oh love (the more my wo) to it thow art
yeven as the moysture in each plant that growes
yeven as the soonn unto the frosen ground
yeven as the sweetness to th'incarnate rose
yeven as the Center in each perfait rounde.

[A LOVER'S COMPLAINT]

As you came from the holy land
  of Walsinghame
Mett you not with my tru love
  by the way as you came?

How shall I know your trew love
  That have mett many one
As I went to the holy lande
  That have come that have gone?

She is neyther whyte nor browne
  Butt as the heavens fayre
There is none hathe a forme so divine
  In the earth or the ayre:

Such an one did I meet good Sir
  Suche an Angelyke face
Who lyke a queene lyke a nymph did appere
  by her gate by her grace:

She hath lefte me here all alone
  All allone as unknowne
Who somtymes did me lead with her selfe
  And me lovde as her owne:

Whats the cause that she leaves you alone
  And a new waye doth take:
Who loved you once as her owne
  And her joye did you make?

I have lovde her all my youth
  butt now ould as you see
Love lykes not the fallyng frute
  From the wythered tree:

Know that love is a careless chylld
  And forgets promyse paste:
He is blynd he is deaff when he lyste
  And in faythe never faste:

His desyre is a dureless contente
  And a trustless joye
He is wonn with a world of despayre
  And is lost with a toye:

Of women kynde suche indeed is the love
  Or the word Love abused
Under which many chyldysh desyres
  And conceytes are excusde:

Butt Love is a durable fyre
  In the mynde ever burnynge:
Never sycke never ould never dead
  from itt selfe never turnynge.

THE AUTHOR'S EPITAPH, MADE BY HIMSELFE

EVEN such is Time, which takes in trust
Our Youth, our Joys, and all we have,
And payes us but with age and dust,
Who in the darke and silent grave,
When we have wandred all our wayes,
Shuts up the story of our dayes:
And from which Earth, and Grave, and Dust,
The Lord shall raise me up I trust.

NASHE

SONG

Adieu, farewell earths blisse,
This world uncertaine is,
Fond are lifes lustfull joyes,
Death proves them all but toyes,
None from his darts can flye,
I am sick, I must dye:
Lord have mercy on us.

Rich men, trust not in wealth,
Gold cannot buy you health,
Phisick himselfe must fade.
All things, to end are made,
The plague full swift goes bye,
I am sick, I must dye:
Lord have mercy on us.

Beauty is but a flowre,
Which wrinckles will devoure,
Brightness falls from the ayre,
Queenes have died yong, and faire,
Dust hath closde *Helens* eye.
I am sick, I must dye:
Lord have mercy on us.

Strength stoopes unto the grave,
Wormes feed on *Hector* brave,
Swords may not fight with fate,
Earth still holds ope her gate.
Come, come, the bells do crye.
I am sick, I must dye:
Lord have mercy on us.

Wit with his wantonesse,
Tasteth deaths bitterness:
Hels executioner,
Hath no eares for to heare
What vaine art can reply.
I am sick, I must dye:
Lord have mercy on us.

Haste therefore eche degree,
To welcome destiny:
Heaven is our heritage,
Earth but a players stage,
Mount wee unto the sky.
I am sick, I must dye:
Lord have mercy on us.

DANIEL

[SONNETS TO DELIA]

Beautie, sweet love, is like the morning dewe,
Whose short refresh upon the tender greene,
Cheeres for a time but tyll the Sunne doth shew,
And straight tis gone as it had never beene.
Soone doth it fade that makes the fairest florish,
Short is the glory of the blushing Rose,
The hew which thou so carefully doost nourish,
Yet which at length thou must be forc'd to lose.
When thou surcharg'd with burthen of thy yeeres,
Shalt bend thy wrinkles homeward to the earth:
When tyme hath made a pasport for thy feares,
Dated in age the Kalends of our death.
But ah no more, thys hath beene often tolde,
And women grieve to thinke they must be old.

*

Care-charmer sleepe, sonne of the Sable night,
Brother to death, in silent darknes borne:
Relieve my languish, and restore the light,
With darke forgetting of my cares returne.
And let the day be time enough to morne,
The shipwrack of my ill-adventred youth:
Let waking eyes suffice to wayle theyr scorne,
Without the torment of the nights untruth.
Cease dreames, th'ymagery of our day desires,
To modell foorth the passions of the morrow:

Never let rysing Sunne approve you lyers,
To adde more griefe to aggravat my sorrow.
Still let me sleepe, imbracing clowdes in vaine;
And never wake, to feele the dayes disdayne.

*

Let others sing of Knights and Palladines,
In aged accents, and untimely words:
Paint shadowes in imaginary lines,
Which well the reach of their high wits records;
But I must sing of thee and those faire eyes,
Autentique shall my verse in time to come,
When yet th'unborne shall say, loe where she lyes,
Whose beautie made him speake that els was dombe.
These are the Arkes the Tropheis I erect,
That fortifie thy name against old age,
And these thy sacred vertues must protect,
Against the Darke and times consuming rage.
Though th'error of my youth they shall discover,
Suffice they shew I liv'd and was thy lover.

from TO THE LADY MARGARET COUNTESSE OF CUMBERLAND

Knowing the heart of man is set to be
The centre of his world, about the which
These revolutions of disturbances
Still roule, where all th'aspects of miserie
Predominate, whose strong effects are such
As he must beare, being powrelesse to redresse,
And that unlesse above himselfe he can
Erect himselfe, how poore a thing is man?

And how turmoyld they are that levell lie
With earth, and cannot lift themselves from thence,
That never are at peace with their desires,
But worke beyond their yeares, and even deny
Dotage her rest, and hardly will dispence
With Death: that when ability expires,
Desire lives still, so much delight they have
To carry toile and travaile to the grave.

Whose ends you see, and what can be the best
They reach unto, when they have cast the summe
And recknings of their glory, and you know
This floting life hath but this Port of rest,
A heart prepar'd that feares no ill to come:
And that mans greatnesse rests but in his show;
The best of all whose dayes consumed are,
Eyther in warre, or peace conceiving warre.

DAVIES

from ORCHESTRA OR A POEME OF DAUNCING

DAUNCING (bright Lady) then began to be,
When the first seedes whereof the world did spring,
The Fire, Ayre, Earth, and water – did agree,
By Loves perswasion, – Nature's mighty King, –
To leave their first disordred combating;
  And in a daunce such measure to observe,
  As all the world their motion should preserve.

Since when they still are carried in a round,
And changing, come one in anothers place,
Yet doe they neyther mingle nor confound,
But every one doth keepe the bounded space
Wherein the daunce doth bid it turne or trace:
  This wondrous myracle did Love devise
  For Dauncing is Loves proper exercise.

Like this, he fram'd the Gods' eternall bower,
And of a shapelesse and confused masse
By his through-piercing and digesting power
The turning vault of heaven framed was:
Whose starrie wheeles he hath so made to passe,
  As that their movings doe a musick frame
  And they themselves, still daunce unto the same.

*

For that brave Sunne the Father of the Day,
Doth love this Earth, the Mother of the Night,
And like a revellour in rich array,
Doth daunce his Galliard in his Lemmans sight,
Both back, and forth, and side-wayes, passing light,
  His gallant grace doth so the Gods amaze,
  That all stand still and at his beautie gaze.

But see the Earth, when he approcheth neere,
How she for joy doth spring and sweetly smile;
But see againe her sad and heavie cheere
When changing places he retires a while:
But those black clouds he shortly will exile,
  And make them all before his presence flye,
  As mists consum'd before his cheerefull eye.

Who doth not see the measures of the Moone
Which thirteene times she daunceth every yeare?
And ends her pavine thirteene times as soone
As doth her brother, of whose golden heire
She borroweth part and proudly doth it weare.
  Then doth she coylie turne her face aside,
  Then halfe her cheeke is scarse sometimes discride.

Next her, the pure, subtile, and cleansing Fire
Is swiftly carried in a circle even:
Though *Vulcan* be pronounst by many a lyer
The onely halting God that dwells in heaven.
But that foule name may be more fitly given
  To your false fier, that far from heav'n is fall
  And doth consume, wast, spoile, disorder all.

And now behold your tender Nurse the Ayre
And common neighbour that ay runns around,
How many pictures and impressions faire
Within her emptie regions are there found,
Which to your sences Dauncing doe propound?
  For what are breath, speech, Ecchos, musick, winds,
  But Dauncings of the Ayre in sundry kinds?

For when you breath, the Ayre in order moves,
Now in, now out, in time and measure trew;
And when you speake, so well she dauncing loves,

That doubling oft, and oft redoubling new,
With thousand formes she doth her selfe endew:
For all the words that from your lips repaire,
Are naught but tricks and turnings of the aire.

Hence is her pratling daughter Eccho borne,
That daunces to all voyces she can heare;
There is no sound so harsh that shee doth scorne,
Nor any time wherein shee will forbeare
The aiery pavement with her feet to weare.
And yet her hearing sence is nothing quick,
For after time she endeth every trick.

And thou sweet Musicke, Dauncings only life,
The eares sole happines, the ayres best speach,
Loadstone of fellowship, charming-rod of strife,
The soft minds Paradice, the sick mans Leach,
With thine own tongue, thou trees and stones canst teach
That when the Aire doth daunce her finest measure,
Then art thou borne, the Gods and mens sweet pleasure.

Lastly, where keepe the winds their revelry,
Their violent turnings and wild whirling hayes?
But in the Ayres tralucent gallery?
Where she herselfe is turnd a hundreth wayes,
While with those Maskers wantonly she playes;
Yet in this misrule, they such rule embrace,
As two at once encomber not the place.

If then fier, ayre, wandring and fixed lights
In every province of th' imperiall skye,
Yeeld perfect formes of dauncing to your sights,
In vaine I teach the eare, that which the eye
With certaine view already doth descrie.
But for your eyes perceive not all they see,
In this I will your sences maister bee.

For loe the Sea that fleets about the Land,
And like a girdle clips her solide waist,
Musick and measure both doth understand:
For his great Chrystall eye is alwayes cast
Up to the Moone, and on her fixed fast.
And as she daunceth in her pallid spheere,
So daunceth he about the Center heere.

Sometimes his proud greene waves in order set,
One after other flow unto the shore,
Which when they have with many kisses wet,
They ebb away in order as before;
And to make knowne his Courtly Love the more,
  He oft doth lay aside his three-forkt Mace,
  And with his armes the timerous Earth embrace.

Onely the Earth doth stand for ever still,
Her rocks remove not, nor her mountaines meete,
(Although some witts enricht with Learnings skill
Say heav'n stands firme, and that the Earth doth fleete
And swiftly turneth underneath their feete)
  Yet though the Earth is ever stedfast seene,
  On her broad breast hath Dauncing ever beene.

For those blew vaines that through her body spred,
Those saphire streames which from great hils do spring,
(The Earths great duggs: for every wight is fed
With sweet fresh moisture from them issuing):
Observe a daunce in their wild wandering:
  And still their daunce begets a murmur sweete,
  And still the murmur with the daunce doth meete.

DRAYTON

THE SHEEPHEARDS DAFFADILL

GORBO, as thou cam'st this way
By yonder little hill,
Or as thou through the fields didst stray,
Saw'st thou my *Daffadill*?

Shee's in a frock of Lincolne greene,
The colour of Maydes delight,
And never hath her Beauty seene
But through a vayle of white.

Than Roses riper to behold,
That dresse up Lovers Bowers,
The Pansie and the Marigold
Are *Phœbus* Paramoures.

Drayton

Thou well describ'st the *Daffadill*,
It is not full an hower
Since by the Spring neere yonder hill
I saw that lovely flower.

Yet with my flower thou didst not meete,
Nor newes of her doest bring,
Yet is my *Daffadill* more sweete
Than that by yonder Spring.

I saw a Sheepheard that doth keepe
In yonder field of Lillies,
Was making (as he fed his sheepe)
A wreath of Daffadillies.

Yet *Gorbo*: thou delud'st me still,
My flower thou didst not see.
For know; my pretty *Daffadill*
Is worne of none but mee.

To shew it selfe but neere her seate
No Lilly is so bold,
Except to shade her from the heate,
Or keepe her from the cold.

Through yonder vale as I did passe
Descending from the hill,
I met a smerking Bonny-lasse,
They call her *Daffadill*.

Whose presence as a-long she went
The pretty flowers did greete,
As though their heads they downe-ward bent,
With homage to her feete.

And all the Sheepheards that were nie,
From top of every hill;
Unto the Vallies loud did crie,
There goes sweet *Daffadill*.

I gentle Sheepheard now with joy
Thou all my flock doest fill:
Come goe with me thou Sheepheards boy,
Let us to *Daffadill*.

Deere, why should you commaund me to my rest,
When now the night doth summon all to sleepe?
Me thinks this time becommeth lovers best;
Night was ordaind together friends to keepe.
How happy are all other living things,
Which though the day disjoyne by severall flight,
The quiet evening yet together brings,
And each returnes unto his love at night.
O thou that art so curteous unto all,
Why shouldst thou, Night, abuse me onely thus,
That every creature to his kind doost call,
And yet tis thou doost onely sever us?
  Well could I wish it would be ever day,
  If when night comes, you bid me goe away.

*

Since ther's no helpe, Come let us kisse and part,
Nay, I have done: You get no more of Me,
And I am glad, yea glad with all my heart,
That thus so cleanly, I my Selfe can free,
Shake hands for ever, Cancell all our Vowes,
And when We meet at any time againe,
Be it not seene in either of our Browes,
That We one jot of former Love reteyne;
Now at the last gaspe, of Loves latest Breath,
When his Pulse fayling, Passion speechlesse lies,
When Faith is kneeling by his bed of Death,
And Innocence is closing up his Eyes,
  Now if thou would'st, when all have given him over,
  From Death to Life, thou might'st him yet recover.

[LAST VERSES]*

These verses weare made by Michaell Drayton Esquier
Poett Lawreatt
the night before hee dyed

Soe well I love thee, as without thee I
Love Nothing; yf I might Chuse, I'de rather dye
Than bee one day debarde thy companye.

Since Beasts, and plantes doe growe, and live and move,
Beastes are those men, that such a life approve:
Hee onlye Lives, that Deadly is in Love.

The Corne that in the grownd is sowen first dies
And of one seed doe manye Eares arise:
Love this worldes Corne, by dying Multiplies.

The seeds of Love first by thy eyes weare throwne
Into a grownd untild, a harte unknowne
To beare such fruitt, tyll by thy handes t'was sowen.

Looke as thy Looking glass by Chance may fall
Devyde and breake in manye peyces smale
And yett shewes forth, the selfe same face in all;

Proportions, Features, Graces just the same
And in the smalest peyce as well the name
Of Fayrest one deserves, as in the richest frame.

Soe all my Thoughts are peyces but of you
Whiche put together makes a Glass soe true
As I therin noe others face but yours can Veiwe.

CAMPION

from A BOOKE OF AYRES

Follow your Saint, follow with accents sweet;
Haste you, sad noates, fall at her flying feete:
There, wrapt in cloude of sorrowe pitie move,

* First printed 1905. The present text is from a MS copy in the Bodleian Library.

And tell the ravisher of my soule I perish for her love.
But if she scorns my never-ceasing paine,
Then burst with sighing in her sight and nere returne againe.

All that I soong still to her praise did tend,
Still she was first; still she my songs did end.
Yet she my love and Musicke both doeth flie,
The Musicke that her Eccho is and beauties simpathie;
Then let my Noates pursue her scornfull flight:
It shall suffice that they were breath'd and dyed for her delight.

*

WHEN thou must home to shades of under ground,
And there ariv'd, a newe admired guest,
The beauteous spirits do ingirt thee round,
White Iope, blith Hellen, and the rest,
To heare the stories of thy finisht love
From that smoothe toong whose musicke hell can move;

Then wilt thou speake of banqueting delights,
Of masks and revels which sweete youth did make,
Of Turnies and great challenges of knights,
And all these triumphes for thy beauties sake:
When thou has told these honours done to thee,
Then tell, O tell, how thou didst murther me.

*

WHAT then is love but mourning?
   What desire, but a selfe-burning?
Till shee that hates doth love returne,
Thus will I mourne, thus will I sing,
   Come away, come away, my darling.

Beautie is but a blooming,
   Youth in his glorie entombing;
Time hath a wheel, which none can stay:
Then come away, while thus I sing,
   Come away, come away, my darling.

Sommer in winter fadeth;
   Gloomie night heav'nly light shadeth:

Like to the morne are Venus flowers;
Such are her howers: then will I sing,
  Come away, come away, my darling.

from THE THIRD BOOKE OF AYRES

OFT have I sigh'd for him that heares me not;
Who absent hath both love and mee forgot.
O yet I languish still through his delay:
Dayes seeme as yeares when wisht friends breake their day.

Had hee but lov'd as common lovers use,
His faithlesse stay some kindnesse would excuse:
O yet I languish still, still constant mourne
For him that can breake vowes but not returne.

*

  KINDE are her answeres,
  But her performance keeps no day;
Breaks time, as dancers
  From their own Musicke when they stray:
  All her free favors and smooth words,
Wing my hopes in vaine.
O did ever voice so sweet but only fain?
  Can true love yeeld such delay,
  Converting joy to pain?

  Lost is our freedome,
  When we submit to women so:
Why doe wee neede them,
  When in their best they worke our woe?
  There is no wisedome
Can alter ends, by Fate prefixt.
O why is the good of man with evill mixt?
  Never were days yet cal'd two,
  But one night went betwixt.

*

SHALL I come, sweet Love, to thee,
  When the ev'ning beames are set?

Shall I not excluded be?
Will you finde no fained lett?
Let me not, for pitty, more,
Tell the long houres at your dore.

Who can tell what theefe or foe,
In the covert of the night,
For his prey will worke my woe,
Or through wicked foule despight:
So may I dye unredrest,
Ere my long love be possest.

But to let such dangers passe,
Which a lovers thoughts disdaine,
'Tis enough in such a place
To attend loves joyes in vaine.
Do not mocke me in thy bed,
While these cold nights freeze me dead.

from *THE FOURTH BOOKE OF AYRES*

THERE is a Garden in her face,
Where Roses and white Lillies grow;
A heav'nly paradice is that place,
Wherein all pleasant fruits doe flow.
There Cherries grow, which none may buy
Till Cherry ripe themselves doe cry.

Those Cherries fayrely doe enclose
Of Orient Pearle a double row;
Which when her lovely laughter showes,
They look like Rose-buds fill'd with snow.
Yet them nor Peere nor Prince can buy,
Till Cherry ripe themselves doe cry.

Her Eyes like Angels watch them still;
Her Browes like bended bowes doe stand,
Threatning with piercing frownes to kill
All that attempt with eye or hand
Those sacred Cherries to come nigh,
Till Cherry ripe themselves doe cry.

*

YOUNG and simple though I am,
I have heard of *Cupids* name:
Guesse I can what thing it is
Men desire when they doe kisse.
  Smoake can never burne, they say,
  But the flames that follow may.

I am not so foule or fayre
To be proud, nor to despayre;
Yet my lips have oft observed:
Men that kiss them press them hard,
  As glad lovers use to do
  When their new-met loves they woo.

Faith, 'tis but a foolish minde,
Yet me thinkes, a heate I finde,
Like thirstlonging, that doth bide
Ever on my weaker side,
  Where they say my heart doth move.
  Venus, grant it be not love.

If it be, alas, what then?
Were not women made for men?
As good 'twere a thing were past,
That must needes be done at last.
  Roses that are over-blowne,
  Growe lesse sweet, then fall alone.

Yet nor Churle, nor silken Gull,
Shall my Mayden blossome pull:
Who shall not I soone can tell;
Who shall, would I could as well:
  This I know, who ere hee be,
  Love hee must, or flatter me.

['A PILGRIMAGE TOWARDS LOVES HOLY LAND']

WHAT faire pompe have I spide of glittering Ladies;
With locks sparckled abroad, and rosie Coronet
On their yvorie browes, trackt to the daintie thies

With roabs like *Amazons*, blew as Violet,
With gold Aiglets adornd, some in a changeable
Pale; with spangs wavering taught to be moveable.

Then those Knights that a farre off with dolorous viewing
Cast their eyes hetherward; loe, in an agonie,
All unbrac'd, crie aloud, their heavie state ruing:
Moyst cheekes with blubbering, painted as *Ebonie*
Blacke; their feltred haire torne with wrathful hand:
And whiles astonied, starke in a maze they stand.

But hearke! what merry sound! what sodaine harmonie!
Looke looke neere the grove where the Ladies do tread
With their Knights the measures waide by the melodie.
Wantons! whose travesing makes men enamoured;
Now they faine an honor, now by the slender wast
He must lift hir aloft, and seale a kisse in hast.

Streight downe under a shadow for wearines they lie
With pleasant daliance, hand knit with arme in arme,
Now close, now set aloof, they gaze with an equall eie,
Changing kisses alike; streight with a false alarme,
Mocking kisses alike, powt with a lovely lip.
Thus drownd with jollities, their merry daies doe slip.

But stay! now I discerne they goe on a Pilgrimage
Towards Loves holy land, faire *Paphos* or *Cyprus*.
Such devotion is meete for a blithesome age;
With sweet youth, it agrees well to be amorous.
Let olde angrie fathers lurke in an Hermitage:
Come, weele associate this jolly Pilgrimage!

CHAPMAN

['PRESAGE OF STORME']

THEY saw the sun looke pale, and cast through aire,
Discoullor'd beames; nor could he paint so faire,
Heavens bow in dewie vapors, but he left
The greater part unform'd; the circle cleft,

Chapman

And like a buls necke shortned; no hews seene,
But onely one, and that was watrish greene:
His heate was chok't up, as in ovens comprest
Halfe stifeling men; heavens drooping face was droot
In gloomy thunderstocks: earth, seas, arrai'd
In all presage of storme: The Bittours plaid
And met in flocks; the Herons set clamours gone,
That ratteled up aires triple Region.
The Cormorants to drie land did addresse,
And cried away, all soules that us'd the seas.
The wanton Swallow Jirckt the standing springs,
Met in dull lakes; and flew so close, their wings
Shav'd the top waters: Frogs crokt; the Swart crow
Measur'd the sea-sands, with pace passing slow,
And often souc't her ominous heat of blood
Quite over head and shoulders in the flood,
Still scoulding at the Rains so slow accesse:
The trumpet throated, the *Naupliades*,
Their claugers threw about, and summond up,
All cloudes to crowne imperious tempests cup:
The erring *Dolphin* puft the fomie maine
Hither and thither, and did upwards raine:
The Raven sat belching out his funerall din,
Venting his voice, with sucking of it in.
The patient of all labours, the poore Ant
Her egges to caves brought: Molehils proofe did want
To keepe such teares out, as heav'n now would weepe.
The hundred-footed Canker-wormes did creepe
Thicke on the wet wals. The slow Crab did take
Pibbles into her mouth, and ballas make
Of gravell, for her stay, against the Gales,
Close clinging to the shore. Sea-Giant whales
The watrie mountaines darted at the skie.
And (no lesse ominous) the petulant Flie
Bit bitterly for blood, as then most sweet.
The loving Dog dig'd earth up with his feete,
The Asse (as weather wise) confirm'd these feares,
And never left shaking his flaggie eares.
Th'ingenious Bee wrought ever neere her hive.
The Cloddie Ashes, kept coales long alive,
And Dead Coales quickn'd; both transparent cleere:

The Rivers crownd with Swimming feathers were.
The Trees greene fleeces flew about the aire
And Aged thistles lost their downie haire;
Cattaile would run from out their sheds undriven,
To th'ample pastures: Lambes were sprightly given,
And all in jumpes about the short leas borne:
Rammes fiercely butted, locking horne in horne.
The storme now neere: those cattel that abroade
Undriven ranne from their shelter; undriven, trod
Homewards as fast: the large bond Oxen lookt
Oft on the broad Heaven and the soft aire suckt,
Smelling it in; their reeking nostrils still
Sucking the cleere Dew from the Daffadill:
Bow'd to their sides their broad heads, and their haire
Lickt smooth at all parts; lov'd their rightside laire:
And late in night, did bellow from the stall,
As thence the tempest would his blasts exhale.
The Swine, her never-made-bed now did plie
And with her Snowt strow'd every way her stie;
The wolfe hould in her den; th'insatiate beast,
Now fearing no man, met him brest to brest,
And like a murtherous begger, him allur'd,
Haunting the home-groves husbandmen manur'd.
Then night her circle closd; and shut in day,
Her silver spangles shedding every way
And earths poore starres (the Glowormes) lay abroad
As thicke as Heav'ns; that now no twinckle showd,
Sodainstly plucking in their guilty heads.
And forth the Windes brake, from their brasen beds
That strooke the mountaines so, they cried quite out.
The Thunder child; the lightning leapt about;
And cloudes so gusht, as *Iris* nere were showne
But in fresh deluge, Heav'n it selfe came downe.

['NATURES NAKED JEM']

In a loose robe of Tynsell foorth she came,
Nothing but it betwixt her nakednes
And envious light. The downward burning flame,
Of her rich hayre did threaten new accesse,

Chapman

Of ventrous *Phaeton* to scorch the fields:
And thus to bathing came our Poets Goddesse,
Her handmaides bearing all things pleasure yeelds
To such a service; Odors most delighted,
And purest linnen which her lookes had whited.

Then cast she off her robe, and stood upright,
As lightning breakes out of a laboring cloude;
Or as the Morning heaven casts off the Night,
Or as that heaven cast off it selfe, and showde
Heavens upper light, to which the brightest day
Is but a black and melancholy shroude:
Or as when *Venus* striv'd her soveraine sway
Of charmfull beautie, in yong Troyes desire,
So stood *Corynna* vanishing her tire.

A soft enflowred banck embrac'd the founte;
Of *Chloris* ensignes, an abstracted field;
Where grew Melanthy, great in Bees account,
Amareus, that precious Balme dooth yeeld,
Enameld Pansies, us'd at Nuptials still,
Dianas arrow, *Cupid's* crimson shielde,
Ope-morne, night-shade, and *Venus* navill,
Solemne Violets, hanging head as shamed,
And verdant Calaminth, for odor famed;

Sacred Nepenthe, purgative of care,
And soveraine Rumex that doth rancor kill,
Sya, and Hyacinth, that Furies weare,
White and red Jessamines, Merry, Melliphill:
Fayre Crowne-imperiall, Emperor of Flowers,
Immortall Amaranth, white Aphrodill,
And cup-like Twillpants, stroude in *Bacchus* Bowres,
These cling about this Natures naked Jem,
To taste her sweetes, as Bees doe swarme on them.

And now shee usde the Founte, where *Niobe*,
Toomb'd in her selfe, pourde her lost soule in teares,
Upon the bosome of this Romaine *Phoebe*;
Who, bathd and Odord, her bright lyms she rears,
And drying her on that disparent rounde,
Her Lute she takes t'enamoure heavenly eares,

And try if with her voyces vitall sounde,
She could warme life through those colde statues spread,
And cheere the Dame that wept when she was dead.

And thus she sung, all naked as she sat,
Laying the happy Lute upon her thigh,
Not thinking any neere to wonder at
The blisse of her sweete brests divinitie.

HALL

['THE LOVE-SICKE POET']

GREAT is the folly of a feeble braine,
Ore-ruld with love, and tyrannous disdaine:
For love, how-ever in the basest brest
It breeds high thoughts that feede the fancy best,
Yet is he blinde, and leades poore fooles awrie,
While they hang gazing on their mistresse eye.
The love-sicke Poet, whose importune prayer
Repulsed is with resolute dispayre,
Hopeth to conquer his disdainfull dame,
With publique plaints of his conceived flame.
Then poures he forth in patched *Sonettings*
His love, his lust, and loathsome flatterings:
As tho the staring world hangd on his sleeve,
When once he smiles, to laugh: and when he sighs, to grieve.
Careth the world, thou love, thou live, or die?
Careth the world how fayre thy fayre one bee?
Fond wit-old, that would'st lode thy wit-lesse head
With timely hornes, before thy Bridall bed.
Then can he terme his durtie ill-fac'd bride
Lady and Queene, and virgin deifide:
Be shee all sootie-blacke, or bery-browne,
Shee's white as morrows milk, or flakes new blowne.
And tho she be some dunghill drudge at home,
Yet can he her resigne some refuse roome
Amids the well-knowne stars: or if not there,
Sure will he Saint her in his Calendere.

SHAKESPEARE

SONNETS

From fairest creatures we desire increase,
That thereby beauties *Rose* might never die,
But as the riper should by time decease,
His tender heire might beare his memory:
But thou contracted to thine owne bright eyes,
Feed'st thy lights flame with selfe substantiall fewell,
Making a famine where aboundance lies,
Thy selfe thy foe, to thy sweet selfe too cruell:
Thou that art now the worlds fresh ornament,
And only herauld to the gaudy spring,
Within thine owne bud buriest thy content,
And tender chorle makst wast in niggarding:
Pitty the world, or else this glutton be,
To eate the worlds due, by the grave and thee.

*

But wherefore do not you a mightier waie
Make warre uppon this bloudie tirant time?
And fortifie your selfe in your decay
With meanes more blessed than my barren rime?
Now stand you on the top of happie houres,
And many maiden gardens yet unset,
With vertuous wish would beare your living flowers,
Much liker than your painted counterfeit:
So should the lines of life that life repaire
Which this (Times pensel or my pupill pen)
Neither in inward worth nor outward faire
Can make you live your selfe in eies of men,
To give away yourselfe, keeps your selfe still,
And you must live drawne by your owne sweet skill.

*

Shake-speare

SHALL I compare thee to a Summers day?
Thou art more lovely and more temperate:
Rough windes do shake the darling buds of Maie,
And Sommers lease hath all too short a date:
Sometime too hot the eye of heaven shines,
And often is his gold complexion dimm'd,
And every faire from faire some-time declines,
By chance, or natures changing course untrim'd:
But thy eternall Sommer shall not fade,
Nor loose possession of that faire thou ow'st,
Nor shall death brag thou wandr'st in his shade,
When in eternall lines to time thou grow'st,
   So long as men can breath or eyes can see,
   So long lives this, and this gives life to thee.

*

WHEN in disgrace with Fortune and mens eyes,
I all alone beweepe my out-cast state,
And trouble deafe heaven with my bootlesse cries,
And looke upon my selfe and curse my fate.
Wishing me like to one more rich in hope,
Featur'd like him, like him with friends possest,
Desiring this mans art, and that mans skope,
With what I most injoy contented least,
Yet in these thoughts my selfe almost despising,
Haplye I thinke on thee, and then my state,
(Like to the Larke at breake of daye arising)
From sullen earth sings himns at Heavens gate,
   For thy sweet love remembred such welth brings,
   That then I skorne to change my state with Kings.

*

WHEN to the Sessions of sweet silent thought,
I sommon up remembrance of things past,
I sigh the lacke of many a thing I sought,
And with old woes new waile my deare times waste:
Then can I drowne an eye (un-us'd to flow)
For precious friends hid in deaths dateles night,
And weepe afresh loves long since canceld woe,
And mone th'expence of many a vannisht sight.

*Shake-
speare*

Then can I greeve at greevances fore-gon,
And heavily from woe to woe tell ore
The sad account of fore-bemoned mone,
Which I new pay, as if not payd before.
  But if the while I thinke on thee (deare friend)
  All losses are restord, and sorrowes end.

*

FULL many a glorious morning have I seene,
Flatter the mountaine tops with soveraine eie,
Kissing with golden face the meddowes greene;
Guilding pale streames with heavenly alcumy:
Anon permit the basest cloudes to ride,
With ougly rack on his celestiall face,
And from the for-lorne world his visage hide
Stealing unseene to west with this disgrace:
Even so my Sunne one early morne did shine,
With all triumphant splendor on my brow,
But out alack, he was but one houre mine,
The region cloude hath mask'd him from me now.
  Yet him for this, my love no whit disdaineth,
  Suns of the world may staine, when heavens sun staineth.

*

NOT marble, nor the guilded monument,
Of Princes shall out-live this powrefull rime,
But you shall shine more bright in these contents
Than unswept stone, besmeer'd with sluttish time.
When wastefull warre shall *Statues* over-turne,
And broiles roote out the worke of masonry,
Nor *Mars* his sword, nor warres quick fire shall burne
The living record of your memory.
Gainst death, and all oblivious enmity
Shall you pace forth, your praise shall stil finde roome,
Even in the eyes of all posterity
That weare this world out to the ending doome.
  So til the judgement that your selfe arise,
  You live in this, and dwell in lovers eies.

*

If their bee nothing new, but that which is,
Hath beene before, how are our braines beguild,
Which laboring for invention beare amisse
The second burthen of a former child?
Oh that record could with a back-ward looke,
Even of five hundreth courses of the Sunne,
Show me your image in some antique booke,
Since minde at first in carrecter was done.
That I might see what the old world could say,
To this composed wonder of your frame,
Whether we are mended, or where better they,
Or whether revolution be the same.
Oh sure I am the wits of former daies,
  To subjects worse have given admiring praise.

*

Like as the waves make towards the pibled shore,
So do our minuites hasten to their end,
Each changing place with that which goes before,
In sequent toile all forwards do contend.
Nativity once in the maine of light
Crawles to maturity, wherewith being crown'd,
Crooked eclipses gainst his glory fight,
And time that gave, doth now his gift confound.
Time doth transfixe the florish set on youth,
And delves the paralels in beauties brow,
Feedes on the rarities of natures truth,
And nothing stands but for his sieth to mow.
  And yet to times in hope, my verse shall stand
  Praising thy worth, dispight his cruell hand.

*

That time of yeeare thou maist in me behold,
When yellow leaves, or none, or few doe hange
Upon those boughes which shake against the could,
Bare ruin'd quiers, where late the sweet birds sang.
In me thou seest the twi-light of such day,
As after Sun-set fadeth in the West,
Which by and by blacke night doth take away,
Deaths second selfe that seals up all in rest.

Shake-speare

In me thou seest the glowing of such fire,
That on the ashes of his youth doth lye,
As the death-bed, whereon it must expire,
Consum'd with that which it was nurrisht by.
This thou percev'st, which makes thy love more strong,
To love that well, which thou must leave ere long.

★

They that have powre to hurt, and will doe none,
That doe not do the thing, they most do showe,
Who moving others, are themselves as stone,
Unmooved, could, and to temptation slow:
They rightly do inherrit heavens graces,
And husband natures ritches from expence,
They are the Lords and owners of their faces,
Others, but stewards of their excellence:
The sommers flowre is to the sommer sweet,
Though to it selfe, it onely live and die,
But if that flowre with base infection meete,
The basest weed out-braves his dignity:
For sweetest things turne sowrest by their deedes,
Lillies that fester, smell far worse than weeds.

★

How like a Winter hath my absence beene
From thee, the pleasure of the fleeting yeare?
What freezings have I felt, what darke daies seene?
What old Decembers barenesse every where?
And yet this time remov'd was sommers time,
The teeming Autumne big with ritch increase,
Bearing the wanton burthen of the prime,
Like widdowed wombes after their Lords decease:
Yet this aboundant issue seem'd to me,
But hope of Orphans, and un-fathered fruite,
For Sommer and his pleasures waite on thee,
And thou away, the very birds are mute.
Or if they sing, tis with so dull a cheere,
That leaves looke pale, dreading the Winters neere.

★

Shakespeare

To me faire friend you never can be old,
For as you were when first your eye I eyde,
Such seemes your beautie still: Three Winters colde,
Have from the forrests shooke three summers pride,
Three beautious springs to yellow *Autumne* turn'd,
In processe of the seasons have I seene,
Three Aprill perfumes in three hot Junes burn'd,
Since first I saw you fresh which yet are greene.
Ah yet doth beauty like a Dyall hand,
Steale from his figure, and no pace perceiv'd,
So your sweete hew, which me thinkes still doth stand
Hath motion, and mine eye may be deceaved.
For feare of which, heare this thou age unbred,
Ere you were borne was beauties summer dead.

*

When in the Chronicle of wasted time,
I see discriptions of the fairest wights,
And beautie making beautifull old rime,
In praise of Ladies dead, and lovely Knights,
Then in the blazon of sweet beauties best,
Of hand, of foote, of lip, of eye, of brow,
I see their antique Pen would have exprest,
Even such a beauty as you maister now.
So all their praises are but prophesies
Of this our time, all you prefiguring,
And for they look'd but with devining eyes,
They had not skill enough your worth to sing:
For we which now behold these present dayes,
Have eyes to wonder, but lack toungs to praise.

*

Let me not to the marriage of true mindes
Admit impediments, love is not love
Which alters when it alteration findes,
Or bends with the remover to remove.
O no, it is an ever fixed marke
That lookes on tempests and is never shaken;
It is the star to every wandring barke,
Whose worths unknowne, although his higth be taken.

Shake-speare

Lov's not Times foole, though rosie lips and cheeks
Within his bending sickles compasse come,
Love alters not with his breefe houres and weekes,
But beares it out even to the edge of doome:
  If this be error and upon me proved,
  I never writ, nor no man ever loved.

*

Th'expence of Spirit in a waste of shame
Is lust in action, and till action, lust
Is perjurd, murdrous, blouddy, full of blame,
Savage, extreame, rude, cruell, not to trust,
Injoyd no sooner but dispised straight,
Past reason hunted, and no sooner had
Past reason hated as a swollowed bayt,
On purpose layd to make the taker mad.
Mad in pursut and in possession so,
Had, having, and in quest, to have extreame,
A blisse in proofe and proud and very wo,
Before, a joy proposd, behind, a dreame,
  All this the world well knowes yet none knowes well,
  To shun the heaven that leads men to this hell.

*

Poore soule the center of my sinfull earth,
My sinfull earth these rebbell powres that thee array,
Why dost thou pine within and suffer dearth
Painting thy outward walls so costlie gay?
Why so large cost having so short a lease,
Dost thou upon thy fading mansion spend?
Shall wormes inheritors of this excesse
Eate up thy charge? is this thy bodies end?
Then soule live thou upon thy servants losse,
And let that pine to aggravat thy store;
Buy tearmes divine in selling houres of drosse:
Within be fed, without be rich no more,
  So shalt thou feed on death, that feeds on men,
  And death once dead, ther's no more dying then.

['AGE AND YOUTH']

Crabbed age and youth cannot live together,
Youth is full of pleasance, Age is full of care,
Youth like summer morne, Age like winter weather,
Youth like summer brave, Age like winter bare.
Youth is full of sport, Ages breath is short,
Youth is nimble, Age is lame
Youth is hot and bold, Age is weake and cold,
Youth is wild, and Age is tame.
  Age I doe abhor thee, Youth I doe adore thee,
    O my love my love is young:
  Age I doe defie thee. Oh sweet Shepheard hie thee:
    For me thinks thou staies too long.

THE PHOENIX AND TURTLE

Let the bird of lowdest lay,
On the sole *Arabian* tree,
Herauld sad and trumpet be:
To whose sound chaste wings obay.

But thou shriking harbinger,
Foule precurrer of the fiend,
Augour of the fevers end,
To this troupe come thou not neere.

From this Session interdict
Every foule of tyrant wing,
Save the Eagle feath'red King,
Keepe the obsequie so strict.

Let the Priest in Surples white,
That defunctive Musicke can,
Be the death-devining Swan,
Lest the *Requiem* lacke his right.

And thou treble dated Crow,
That thy sable gender mak'st,
With the breath thou giv'st and tak'st,
Mongst our mourners shalt thou go.

*Shake-
speare*

Here the Antheme doth commence,
Love and Constancie is dead,
Phoenix and the *Turtle* fled,
In a mutuall flame from hence.

So they loved as love in twaine,
Had the essence but in one,
Two distincts, Division none,
Number there in love was slaine.

Hearts remote, yet not asunder;
Distance and no space was seene,
Twixt this *Turtle* and his Queene;
But in them it were a wonder.

So betweene them Love did shine,
That the *Turtle* saw his right,
Flaming in the *Phoenix* sight;
Either was the others mine.

Propertie was thus appalled,
That the selfe was not the same:
Single Natures double name,
Neither two nor one was called.

Reason in it selfe confounded,
Saw Division grow together,
To themselves yet either neither,
Simple were so well compounded.

That it cried, how true a twaine,
Seemeth this concordant one,
Love hath Reason, Reason none,
If what parts, can so remaine.

Whereupon it made this *Threne*,
To the *Phoenix* and the *Dove*,
Co-supremes and starres of Love,
As *Chorus* to their Tragique Scene.

THRENOS

Beautie, Truth, and Raritie,
Grace in all simplicitie,
Here enclosde, in cinders lie.

Death is now the *Phoenix* nest,
And the *Turtles* loyall brest,
To eternitie doth rest. *Shake-speare*

Leaving no posteritie,
Twas not their infirmitie,
It was married Chastitie.

Truth may seeme, but cannot be,
Beautie bragge, but tis not she,
Truth and Beautie buried be.

To this urne let those repaire,
That are either true or faire,
For these dead Birds, sigh a prayer.

SONGS FROM PLAYS

[ARIEL'S SONG *from* *THE TEMPEST*]

FULL fadom five thy Father lies,
Of his bones are Corrall made:
Those are pearles that were his eyes,
Nothing of him that doth fade,
But doth suffer a Sea-change
Into something rich, & strange:
Sea-Nimphs hourly ring his knell.
Harke now I heare them, ding-dong bell.

[WINTER'S SONG *from* *LOVE'S LABOUR'S LOST*]

WHEN Isicles hang by the wall,
And Dicke the Sheepheard blowes his naile;
And Tom beares Logges into the hall,
And Milke comes frozen home in paile:
When blood is nipt, and wayes be fowle
Then nightly sings the staring Owle
Tu-whit to-who.
A merrie note,
While greasie Jone doth keele the pot.

When all aloud the winde doth blow,
And coffing drownes the Parsons saw:
And birds sit brooding in the snow,
And Marrians nose looks red and raw:
When roasted Crabs hisse in the bowle,
Then nightly sings the staring Owle,
Tu-whit to-who:
    A merrie note,
    While greasie Jone doth keele the pot.

[CLOWN'S SONG *from* *TWELFTH NIGHT*]

O MISTRIS mine where are you roming?
O stay and heare, your true loves coming,
That can sing both high and low.
Trip no further prettie sweeting.
Journeys end in lovers meeting,
Every wise mans sonne doth know.

What is love, tis not heereafter,
Present mirth, hath present laughter:
What's to come, is still unsure
In delay there lies no plentie,
Then come kisse me sweet and twentie:
Youths a stuffe will not endure.

[AUTOLICUS'S SONG *from* *THE WINTER'S TALE*]

WHEN Daffadils begin to peere,
With heigh the Doxy over the dale,
Why then comes in the sweet o' the yeere,
For the red blood raigns in the winters pale.

The white sheete bleaching on the hedge,
With hey the sweet birds, O how they sing:
Doth set my pugging tooth an edge,
For a quart of Ale is a dish for a King.

The Larke, that tirra-Lyra chaunts,
With heigh, with heigh, the thrush and the jay:
Are Summer songs for me and my Aunts
While we lye tumbling in the hay.

Shake-speare

[LAMENT OF GUIDERIUS AND ARVIRAGUS *from* CYMBELINE]

FEARE no more the heate o' th' Sun,
Nor the furious Winters rages,
Thou thy worldly task hast don,
Home art gon, and tane thy wages.
Golden Lads, and Girles all must,
As Chimney-Sweepers come to dust.

Feare no more the frowne o' th' Great,
Thou art past the Tirants stroake,
Care no more to cloath and eate,
To thee the Reede is as the Oake:
The Scepter, Learning, Physicke must,
All follow this and come to dust.

Feare no more the Lightning flash.
Nor th'all-dreaded Thunderstone.
Feare not Slander, Censure rash.
Thou hast finish'd Joy and mone.
All Lovers young, all Lovers must,
Consigne to thee and come to dust.

No Exorciser harme thee,
Nor no witch-craft charme thee.
Ghost unlaid forbeare thee.
Nothing ill come neere thee.
Quiet consumation have,
And renowned be thy grave.

WEBSTER

[SUMMONS TO EXECUTION]

HEARKE, now every thing is still –
The Schritch-Owle, and the whistler shrill,
Call upon our Dame, aloud,
And bid her quickly don her shrowd:
Much you had in Land and rent,
Your length in clay's now competent.
A long war disturb'd your minde,
Here your perfect peace is sign'd –
Of what is't fooles make such vaine keeping?
Sin their conception, their birth weeping:
Their life, a generall mist of error,
Their death, a hideous storme of terror –
Strew your haire, with powders sweete:
Don cleane linnen, bath your feete,
And (the foule feend more to checke)
A crucifixe let blesse your necke,
'Tis now full tide, 'tweene night, and day,
End your groane, and come away.

[DIRGE]

CALL for the Robin-Red-brest and the wren,
Since ore shadie groves they hover,
And with leaves and flowres doe cover
The friendlesse bodies of unburied men.
Call unto his funerall Dole
The Ante, the field-mouse, and the mole
To reare him hillockes, that shall keepe him warme,
And (when gay tombes are rob'd) sustaine no harme,
But keepe the wolfe far thence, that's foe to men,
For with his nailes hee'l dig them up agen.

JONSON

TO CELIA

COME my CELIA, let us prove,
While we may, the sports of love;
Time will not be ours, for ever:
He, at length, our good will sever.
Spend not then his guifts in vaine.
Sunnes, that set, may rise againe:
But if once we loose this light,
'Tis, with us, perpetuall night.
Why should we deferre our joyes?
Fame, and rumor are but toyes.
Cannot we delude the eyes
Of a few poor houshold spyes?
Or his easier eares beguile,
So removed by our wile?
'Tis no sinne, loves fruit to steale,
But the sweet theft to reveale:
To be taken, to be seene,
These have crimes accounted beene.

TO CELIA

DRINKE to me, onely, with thine eyes,
  And I will pledge with mine;
Or leave a kisse but in the cup,
  And Ile not looke for wine.
The thirst, that from the soule doth rise,
  Doth aske a drinke divine:
But might I of JOVE'S *Nectar* sup,
  I would not change for thine.
I sent thee, late, a rosie wreath,
  Not so much honoring thee,
As giving it a hope, that there
  It could not withered bee.
But thou thereon did'st onely breath,
  And sent'st it back to mee:
Since when it growes, and smells, I sweare,
  Not of it selfe, but thee.

ON MY FIRST SONNE

FAREWELL, thou child of my right hand, and joy;
My sinne was too much hope of thee, lov'd boy,
Seven yeeres tho'wert lent to me, and I thee pay,
Exacted by thy fate, on the just day.
O, could I loose all father, now. For why
Will man lament the state he should envie?
To have so soone scap'd worlds, and fleshes rage,
And, if no other miserie, yet age?
Rest in soft peace, and, ask'd, say here doth lye
BEN. JONSON his best piece of *poetrie*.
For whose sake, hence-forth, all his vowes be such,
As what he loves may never like too much.

EPITAPH ON S[ALOMON]. P[AVY]. A CHILD OF Q. EL[IZABETHS] CHAPPEL

WEEPE with me all you that read
This little storie:
And know, for whom a teare you shed,
Death's selfe is sorry.
'Twas a child, that so did thrive
In grace, and feature,
As *Heaven* and *Nature* seem'd to strive
Which own'd the creature.
Yeeres he numbred scarse thirteene
When *Fates* turn'd cruell,
Yet three fill'd *Zodiackes* had he beene
The stages jewell;
And did act (what now we mone)
Old men so duely,
As, sooth, the *Parcæ* thought him one,
He plai'd so truely.
So, by error, to his fate
They all consented;
But viewing him since (alas, too late)
They have repented.
And have sought (to give new birth)
In bathes to steepe him;
But, being so much too good for earth,
Heaven vowes to keepe him.

THOU hast thy ponds, that pay thee tribute fish,
Fat, aged carps, that runne into thy net.
And pikes, now weary their owne kinde to eat,
As loth, the second draught, or cast to stay,
Officiously, at first, themselves betray.
Bright eeles, that emulate them, and leape on land,
Before the fisher, or into his hand.
Then hath thy orchard fruit, thy garden flowers,
Fresh as the ayre, and new as are the houres.
The earely cherry, with the later plum,
Fig, grape, and quince, each in his time doth come:
The blushing apricot, and woolly peach
Hang on thy walls, that every child may reach.
And though thy walls be of the countrey stone,
They'are rear'd with no mans ruine, no mans grone,
There's none, that dwell about them, wish them downe;
But all come in, the farmer, and the clowne:
And no one empty-handed, to salute
Thy lord, and lady, though they have no sute.
Some bring a capon, some a rurall cake,
Some nuts, some apples; some that thinke they make
The better cheeses, bring 'hem; or else send
By their ripe daughters, whom they would commend
This way to husbands; and whose baskets beare
An embleme of themselves, in plum, or peare.
But what can this (more than expresse their love)
Adde to thy free provisions, farre above
The neede of such? whose liberall boord doth flow,
With all, that hospitalitie doth knowe!

SONG

THAT WOMEN ARE BUT MENS SHADDOWES

FOLLOW a shaddow, it still flies you;
Seeme to flye it, it will pursue:
So court a mistris, shee denyes you;
Let her alone, shee will court you.
Say, are not women truely, then,
Stil'd but the shaddowes of us men?

At morne, and even, shades are longest;
At noone, they are or short, or none:
So men at weakest, they are strongest,
But grant us perfect, they're not knowne.
Say, are not women truely, then,
Stil'd but the shaddowes of us men?

from AN EPISTLE TO LADY RUTLAND

Beautie, I know, is good, and bloud is more;
Riches thought most: But, *Madame*, thinke what store
The world hath seene, which all these had in trust,
And now lye lost in their forgotten dust.
It is the *Muse*, alone, can raise to heaven,
And, at her strong armes end, hold up, and even,
The soules, shee loves. Those other glorious notes,
Inscrib'd in touch or marble, or the cotes
Painted, or carv'd upon our great-mens tombs,
Or in their windowes; doe but prove the wombs,
That bred them, graves: when they were borne, they di'd
That had no *Muse* to make their fame abide.
How many equall with the *Argive* Queene,
Have beautie knowne, yet none so famous seene?

from A CELEBRATION OF CHARIS

HER TRIUMPH

See the Chariot at hand here of Love,
Wherein my Lady rideth!
Each that drawes, is a Swan, or a Dove,
And well the Carre Love guideth.
As she goes, all hearts doe duty
Unto her beauty;
And enamour'd, doe wish, so they might
But enjoy such a sight,
That they still were to run by her side,
Th⟨o⟩rough Swords, th⟨o⟩rough Seas, whether she would ride.

Doe but looke on her eyes, they doe light
  All that Loves world compriseth!
Doe but looke on her Haire, it is bright
  As Loves starre when it riseth!
Doe but marke, her forehead's smoother
        Than words that sooth her!
And from her arched browes, such a grace
        Sheds it selfe through the face,
  As alone there triumphs to the life
All the Gaine, all the Good, of the Elements strife.

Have you seene but a bright Lillie grow,
  Before rude hands have touch'd it?
Have you mark'd but the fall of the Snow
  Before the soyle hath smutch'd it?
Have you felt the wooll o' the Bever?
        Or Swans Downe ever?
Or have smelt o'the bud o'the Brier?
        Or the Nard i' the fire?
  Or have tasted the bag o'the Bee?
O so white! O so soft! O so sweet is she!

AN ODE. TO HIMSELFE

WHERE do'st thou carelesse lie,
  Buried in ease and sloth?
Knowledge, that sleepes, doth die;
And this Securitie,
  It is the common Moath,
That eats on wits, and Arts, and [oft] destroyes
    them both.

Are all th'*Aonian* springs
  Dri'd up? lyes *Thespia* wast?
Doth *Clarius* Harp want strings,
That not a Nymph now sings?
  Or droop they as disgrac't,
To see their Seats and Bowers by chattring
    Pies defac't?

If hence thy silence be,
As 'tis too just a cause;
Let this thought quicken thee,
Minds that are great and free,
Should not on fortune pause,
'Tis crowne enough to vertue still, her owne applause.

What though the greedie Frie
Be taken with false Baytes
Of worded Balladrie,
And thinke it Poësie?
They die with their conceits,
And only pitious scorne, upon their folly waites.

Then take in hand thy Lyre,
Strike in thy proper straine,
With *Japhets* lyne, aspire
Sols Chariot for new fire,
To give the world againe:
Who aided him, will thee, the issue of *Joves* braine.

And since our Daintie age,
Cannot indure reproofe,
Make not thy selfe a Page,
To that strumpet the Stage,
But sing high and aloofe,
Safe from the wolves black jaw, and the dull Asses hoofe.

[PROPORTION]

It is not growing like a tree
In bulke, doth make man better bee;
Or standing long an Oake, three hundred yeare,
To fall a logge at last, dry, bald, and seare:
A Lillie of a Day,
Is fairer farre, in May,

Although it fall, and die that night;
It was the Plant, and flowre of light.
In small proportions, we just beautie see:
And in short measures, life may perfect bee.

[SONG *from* CYNTHIA'S REVELS]

SLOW, slow, fresh fount, keepe time with my salt teares;
Yet slower, yet, ô faintly gentle springs:
List to the heavy part the musique beares,
Woe weepes out her division, when shee sings.
Droupe hearbs, and flowres;
Fall griefe in showres;
Our beauties are not ours:
O, I could still
(Like melting snow upon some craggie hill,)
drop, drop, drop, drop,
Since natures pride is, now, a wither'd daffodill.

DONNE

THE GOOD-MORROW

I WONDER by my troth, what thou, and I
Did, till we lov'd? were we not wean'd till then?
But suck'd on countrey pleasures, childishly?
Or snorted we in the seaven sleepers den?
T'was so; But this, all pleasures fancies bee.
If ever any beauty I did see,
Which I desir'd, and got, t'was but a dreame of thee.

And now good morrow to our waking soules,
Which watch not one another out of feare;
For love, all love of other sights controules,
And makes one little roome, an every where.
Let sea-discoverers to new worlds have gone,
Let Maps to other, worlds on worlds have showne,
Let us possesse one world, each hath one, and is one.

My face in thine eye, thine in mine appeares,
And true plaine hearts doe in the faces rest,
Where can we finde two better hemispheares
Without sharpe North, without declining West?
What ever dyes, was not mixt equally;
If our two loves be one, or, thou and I
Love so alike, that none doe slacken, none can die.

LOVERS INFINITENESSE

If yet I have not all thy love,
Deare, I shall never have it all,
I cannot breath one other sigh, to move,
Nor can intreat one other teare to fall,
And all my treasure, which should purchase thee,
Sighs, teares, and oathes, and letters I have spent.
Yet no more can be due to mee,
Than at the bargaine made was ment,
If then thy gift of love were partiall,
That some to mee, some should to others fall,
  Deare, I shall never have Thee All.

Or if then thou gavest mee all,
All was but All, which thou hadst then;
But if in thy heart, since, there be or shall,
New love created bee, by other men,
Which have their stocks intire, and can in teares,
In sighs, in oathes, and letters outbid mee,
This new love may beget new feares,
For, this love was not vowed by thee.
And yet it was, thy gift being generall,
The ground, thy heart is mine, what ever shall
  Grow there, deare, I should have it all.

Yet I would not have all yet,
Hee that hath all can have no more,
And since my love doth every day admit
New growth, thou shouldst have new rewards in store;
Thou canst not every day give me thy heart,
If thou canst give it, then thou never gavest it:
Loves riddles are, that though thy heart depart,

It stayes at home, and thou with losing savest it:
But wee will have a way more liberall,
Than changing hearts, to joyne them, so wee shall
Be one, and one anothers All.

SONG

Sweetest love, I do not goe,
For weariness of thee,
Nor in hope the world can show
A fitter Love for mee;
But since that I
Must dye at last, 'tis best,
To use my selfe in jest
Thus by fain'd deaths to dye;

Yesternight the Sunne went hence,
And yet is here to day,
He hath no desire nor sense,
Nor halfe so short a way:
Then feare not mee,
But beleeve that I shall make
Speedier journeyes, since I take
More wings and spurres than hee.

O how feeble is mans power,
That if good fortune fall,
Cannot adde another houre,
Nor a lost houre recall!
But come bad chance,
And wee joyne to' it our strength,
And wee teach it art and length,
It selfe o'r us to'advance.

When thou sigh'st, thou sigh'st not winde,
But sigh'st my soule away,
When thou weep'st, unkindly kinde,
My lifes blood doth decay.
It cannot bee
That thou lov'st mee, as thou say'st,
If in thine my life thou waste,
That art the best of mee.

Let not thy divining heart
  Forethinke me any ill,
Destiny may take thy part,
  And may thy feares fulfill;
    But thinke that wee
Are but turn'd aside to sleepe;
They who one another keepe
  Alive, ne'r parted bee.

A NOCTURNALL UPON S. LUCIES DAY,

BEING THE SHORTEST DAY

Tis the yeares midnight, and it is the dayes,
Lucies, who scarce seaven houres herself unmaskes,
  The Sunne is spent, and now his flasks
  Send forth light squibs, no constant rayes;
    The worlds whole sap is sunke:
The generall balme th'hydroptique earth hath drunk,
Whither, as to the beds-feet, life is shrunke,
Dead and enterr'd; yet all these seeme to laugh,
Compar'd with mee, who am their Epitaph.

Study me then, you who shall lovers bee
At the next world, that is, at the next Spring:
  For I am every dead thing,
  In whom love wrought new Alchimie.
    For his art did expresse
A quintessence even from nothingnesse,
From dull privations, and leane emptinesse
He ruin'd mee, and I am re-begot
Of absence, darknesse, death; things which are not.

All others, from all things, draw all that's good,
Life, soule, forme, spirit, whence they beeing have;
  I, by loves limbecke, am the grave
  Of all, that's nothing. Oft a flood
    Have wee two wept, and so
Drownd the whole world, us two; oft did we grow
To be two Chaosses, when we did show
Care to ought else; and often absences
Withdrew our soules, and made us carcasses.

But I am by her death, (which word wrongs her)
Of the first nothing, the Elixer grown;
  Were I a man, that I were one,
  I needs must know; I should preferre,
    If I were any beast,
Some ends, some means; Yea plants, yea stones detest,
And love; All, all some properties invest;
If I an ordinary nothing were,
As shadow, a light, and body must be here.

But I am None; nor will my Sunne renew.
You lovers, for whose sake, the lesser Sunne
  At this time to the Goat is runne
  To fetch new lust, and give it you,
    Enjoy your summer all;
Since shee enjoyes her long nights festivall,
Let mee prepare towards her, and let mee call
This houre her Vigill, and her Eve, since this
Both the yeares, and the dayes deep midnight is.

A VALEDICTION: FORBIDDING MOURNING

As virtuous men passe mildly away,
  And whisper to their soules, to goe,
Whilst some of their sad friends doe say,
  The breath goes now, and some say, no:

So let us melt, and make no noise,
  No teare-floods, nor sigh-tempests move,
T'were prophanation of our joyes
  To tell the layetie our love.

Moving of th'earth brings harmes and feares,
  Men reckon what it did and meant,
But trepidation of the spheares,
  Though greater farre, is innocent.

Dull sublunary lovers love
  (Whose soule is sense) cannot admit
Absence, because it doth remove
  Those things which elemented it.

But we by a love, so much refin'd,
  That our selves know not what it is,
Inter-assured of the mind,
  Care lesse, eyes, lips, and hands to misse.

Our two soules therefore, which are one,
  Though I must goe, endure not yet
A breach, but an expansion,
  Like gold to ayery thinnesse beate.

If they be two, they are two so
  As stiffe twin compasses are two,
Thy soule the fixt foot, makes no show
  To move, but doth, if the'other doe.

And though it in the center sit,
  Yet when the other far doth rome,
It leanes, and hearkens after it,
  And growes erect, as that comes home.

Such wilt thou be to mee, who must
Like th'other foot, obliquely runne;
Thy firmnes drawes my circle just,
  And makes me end, where I begunne.

THE EXTASIE

Where, like a pillow on a bed,
  A Pregnant banke swel'd up, to rest
The violets reclining head,
  Sat we two, one anothers best.
Our hands were firmely cimented
  With a fast balme, which thence did spring,
Our eye-beames twisted, and did thred
  Our eyes, upon one double string;
So to'entergraft our hands, as yet
  Was all the meanes to make us one,
And pictures in our eyes to get
  Was all our propagation.
As 'twixt two equall Armies, Fate
  Suspends uncertaine victorie,
Our soules, (which to advance their state,

Were gone out,) hung 'twixt her, and mee.
And whil'st our soules negotiate there,
Wee like sepulchrall statues lay;
All day, the same our postures were,
And wee said nothing, all the day.
If any, so by love refin'd,
That he soules language understood,
And by good love were growen all minde,
Within convenient distance stood,
He (though he knew not which soul spake,
Because both meant, both spake the same)
Might thence a new concoction take,
And part farre purer than he came.
This Extasie doth unperplex
(We said) and tell us what we love,
Wee see by this, it was not sexe,
Wee see, we saw not what did move:
But as all severall soules containe
Mixture of things, they know not what,
Love, these mixt soules, doth mixe againe,
And makes both one, each this and that.
A single violet transplant,
The strength, the colour, and the size,
(All which before was poore, and scant,)
Redoubles still, and multiplies.
When love, with one another so
Interinanimates two soules,
That abler soule, which thence doth flow,
Defects of lonelinesse controules.
Wee then, who are this new soule, know,
Of what we are compos'd, and made,
For, th'Atomies of which we grow,
Are soules, whom no change can invade.
But O alas, so long, so farre
Our bodies why doe wee forbeare?
They are ours, though they are not wee, Wee are
The intelligences, they the spheares.
We owe them thankes, because they thus,
Did us, to us, at first convay,
Yeelded their forces, sense, to us,
Nor are drosse to us, but allay.

On man heavens influence workes not so,
  But that it first imprints the ayre,
Soe soule into the soule may flow,
  Though it to body first repaire.
As our blood labours to beget
  Spirits, as like soules as it can,
Because such fingers need to knit
  That subtile knot, which makes us man:
So must pure lovers soules descend
  T'affections, and to faculties,
Which sense may reach and apprehend,
  Else a great Prince in prison lies.
To'our bodies turne wee then, that so
  Weake men on love reveal'd may looke;
Loves mysteries in soules doe grow,
  But yet the body is his booke.
And if some lover, such as wee,
  Have heard this dialogue of one,
Let him still marke us, he shall see
  Small change, when we'are to bodies gone.

ELEGIE: HIS PICTURE

HERE take my Picture; though I bid farewell,
Thine, in my heart, where my soule dwels, shall dwell.
'Tis like me now, but I dead, 'twill be more
When wee are shadowes both, than'twas before.
When weather-beaten I come backe; my hand,
Perhaps with rude oares torne, or Sun beams tann'd,
My face and brest of hairecloth, and my head
With cares rash sodaine stormes, being o'rspread,
My body'a sack of bones, broken within,
And powders blew staines scatter'd on my skinne;
If rivall fooles taxe thee to'have lov'd a man,
So foule, and coarse, as, Oh, I may seeme then,
This shall say what I was: and thou shalt say,
Doe his hurts reach mee? doth my worth decay?
Or doe they reach his judging minde, that hee
Should now love lesse, what hee did love to see?
That which in him was faire and delicate,

Was but the milke, which in loves childish state
Did nurse it: who now is growne strong enough
To feed on that, which to disus'd tasts seemes tough.

from THE SECOND ANNIVERSARIE OF THE PROGRESSE OF THE SOULE

FORGET this rotten world; And unto thee
Let thine owne times as an old storie be.
Be not concern'd: studie not why, nor when;
Doe not so much as not beleeve a man.
For though to erre, be worst, to try truths forth,
Is far more busines, than this world is worth.
The world is but a carcasse; thou art fed
By it, but as a worme, that carcas bred;
And why should'st thou, poore worme, consider more,
When this world will grow better than before,
Than those thy fellow-wormes doe thinke upon
That carcasses last resurrection.
Forget this world, and scarse thinke of it so,
As of old cloaths, cast off a yeere agoe.
To be thus stupid is Alacrity;
Men thus lethargique have best Memory.
Look upward; that's towards her, whose happy state
We now lament not, but congratulate.
Shee, to whom all this world was but a stage,
Where all sat harkning how her youthfull age
Should be emploid, because in all shee did,
Some Figure of the Golden times was hid.
Who could not lacke, what ere this world could give,
Because shee was the forme, that made it live;
Nor could complaine, that this world was unfit
To be staid in, then when shee was in it;
Shee that first tried indifferent desires
By vertue, and vertue by religious fires,
Shee to whose person Paradise adhear'd,
As Courts to Princes, shee whose eyes ensphear'd
Star-light enough, t'have made the South controll,
(Had shee beene there) the Star-full Northerne Pole,
Shee, shee is gone; shee is gone; when thou knowest this,

What fragmentary rubbidge this world is
Thou knowest, and that it is not worth a thought;
He honors it too much that thinkes it nought.
Thinke then, my soule, that death is but a Groome,
Which brings a Taper to the outward roome,
Whence thou spiest first a little glimmering light,
And after brings it nearer to thy sight:
For such approches doth heaven make in death.
Thinke thy selfe labouring now with broken breath,
And thinke those broken & soft Notes to bee
Division, and thy happiest Harmonie.
Thinke thee laid on thy death-bed, loose and slacke;
And thinke that, but unbinding of a packe,
To take one precious thing, thy soule from thence.
Thinke thy selfe parch'd with fevers violence,
Anger thine ague more, by calling it
Thy Physicke; chide the slacknes of the fit.
Thinke that thou hear'st thy knell, and thinke no more,
But that, as Bels cal'd thee to Church before,
So this, to the Triumphant Church, cals thee.

HOLY SONNETS

Thou hast made me, And shall thy worke decay?
Repaire me now, for now mine end doth haste,
I runne to death, and death meets me as fast,
And all my pleasures are like yesterday;
I dare not move my dimme eyes any way,
Despaire behind, and death before doth cast
Such terrour, and my feebled flesh doth waste
By sinne in it, which it t'wards hell doth weigh;
Onely thou art above, and when towards thee
By thy leave I can looke, I rise againe;
But our old subtle foe so tempteth me,
That not one houre my selfe I can sustaine;
Thy Grace may wing me to prevent his art,
And thou like Adamant draw mine iron heart.

*

At the round earths imagin'd corners, blow
Your trumpets, Angells, and arise, arise
From death, you numberlesse infinities
Of soules, and to your scattred bodies goe,
All whom the flood did, and fire shall o'erthrow,
All whom warre, dearth, age, agues, tyrannies,
Despaire, law, chance, hath slaine, and you whose eyes,
Shall behold God, and never tast deaths woe.
But let them sleepe, Lord, and mee mourne a space,
For, if above all these, my sinnes abound,
'Tis late to aske abundance of thy grace,
When wee are there; here on this lowly ground,
Teach mee how to repent; for that's as good
As if thou'hadst seal'd my pardon, with thy blood.

*

Death be not proud, though some have called thee
Mighty and dreadfull, for, thou art not soe,
For, those, whom thou think'st, thou dost overthrow,
Die not, poore death, nor yet canst thou kill mee.
From rest and sleepe, which but thy pictures bee,
Much pleasure, then from thee, much more must flow,
And soonest our best men with thee doe goe,
Rest of their bones, and soules deliverie.
Thou art slave to Fate, Chance, kings, and desperate men,
And dost with poyson, warre, and sicknesse dwell,
And poppie, or charmes can make us sleepe as well,
And better than thy stroake; why swell'st thou then?
One short sleepe past, wee wake eternally,
And death shall be no more; death, thou shalt die.

A HYMNE TO CHRIST,

AT THE AUTHORS LAST GOING INTO GERMANY

In what torne ship soever I embarke,
That ship shall be my embleme of thy Arke;
What sea soever swallow mee, that flood
Shall be to mee an embleme of thy blood;
Though thou with clouds of anger do disguise

Thy face; yet through that maske I know those eyes,
Which, though they turne away sometimes,
They never will despise.

I sacrifice this Iland unto thee,
And all whom I lov'd there, and who lov'd mee;
When I have put our seas twixt them and mee,
Put thou thy sea betwixt my sinnes and thee.
As the trees sap doth seeke the root below
In winter, in my winter now I goe,
Where none but thee, th'Eternall root
Of true Love I may know.

Nor thou nor thy religion dost controule,
The amorousnesse of an harmonious Soule,
But thou would'st have that love thy selfe: As thou
Art jealous, Lord, so I am jealous now,
Thou lov'st not, till from loving more, thou free
My soule: Who ever gives, takes libertie:
O, if thou car'st not whom I love
Alas, thou lov'st not mee.

Seale then this bill of my Divorce to All,
On whom those fainter beames of love did fall;
Marry those loves, which in youth scattered bee
On Fame, Wit, Hopes (false mistresses) to thee.
Churches are best for Prayer, that have least light:
To see God only, I goe out of sight:
And to scape stormy dayes, I chuse
An Everlasting night.

HYMNE TO GOD MY GOD, IN MY SICKNESSE

SINCE I am comming to that Holy roome,
Where, with thy Quire of Saints for evermore,
I shall be made thy Musique; As I come
I tune the Instrument here at the dore,
And what I must doe then, thinke here before.

Whilst my Physitians by their love are growne
Cosmographers, and I their Mapp, who lie

Flat on this bed, that by them may be showne
  That this is my South-west discoverie
  Per fretum febris, by these streights to die,

I joy, that in these straits, I see my West;
  For, though theire currants yeeld returne to none,
What shall my West hurt me? As West and East
  In all flatt Maps (and I am one) are one,
  So death doth touch the Resurrection.

Is the Pacifique Sea my home? Or are
  The Easterne riches? Is *Jerusalem?*
Anyan, and *Magellan*, and *Gibraltare*,
  All streights, and none but streights, are wayes to them,
  Whether where *Japhet* dwelt, or *Cham*, or *Sem*.

We thinke that *Paradise* and *Calvarie*,
  Christs Crosse, and *Adams* tree, stood in one place;
Looke, Lord, and finde both *Adams* met in me;
  As the first *Adams* sweat surrounds my face,
  May the last *Adams* blood my soule embrace.

So, in his purple wrapp'd receive mee Lord,
  By these his thornes give me his other Crowne;
And as to others soules I preach'd thy word,
  Be this my Text, my Sermon to mine owne,
  Therfore that he may raise the Lord throws down.

BEAUMONT & FLETCHER

SONGS FROM PLAYS

[LOVE SONG *from* VALENTINIAN]

I

Now the lusty Spring is seen,
  Golden yellow, gaudy Blew,
  Daintily invite the view.
Every where, on every Green,

Roses blushing as they blow,
  And enticing men to pull,
Lillies whiter than the snow.
  Woodbines of sweet hony full.
    All Loves Emblems and all cry,
    Ladys, if not pluckt we dye.

Yet the lusty Spring hath staid,
  Blushing red and purest white,
  Daintily to love invite,
Every Woman, every Maid,
Cherries kissing as they grow;
  And inviting men to taste,
Apples even ripe below,
  Winding gently to the waste:
    All loves emblems and all cry,
    Ladies, if not pluckt we dye.

II

Hear ye Ladies that despise
  What the mighty Love has done,
Fear examples, and be wise,
  Fair *Calisto* was a Nun,
Læda sailing on the stream,
  To deceive the hopes of man,
Love accounting but a dream,
  Doted on a silver Swan,
Danæ in a Brazen Tower,
  Where no love was, lov'd a Showr.

Hear ye Ladys that are coy,
  What the mighty Love can do,
Fear the fierceness of the Boy,
  The chaste Moon he makes to wooe:
Vesta kindling holy fires,
  Circles round about with spies,
Never dreaming loose desires,
  Doting at the Altar dies.
    Ilion in a short hour higher
    He can build and once more fire.

[SONG FOR THE SICK EMPEROR *from VALENTINIAN*]

CARE charming sleep, thou easer of all woes,
Brother to death, sweetly thy self dispose
On this afflicted Prince, fall like a cloud
In gentle showrs, give nothing that is lowd,
Or painfull to his slumbers; easie, sweet,
And as a purling stream, thou son of night,
Pass by his troubled senses; sing his pain
Like hollow murmuring wind, or silver Rain,
Into this Prince gently, Oh gently slide,
And kiss him into slumbers like a Bride.

[THE SAD SONG *from THE CAPTAIN*]

AWAY delights, go seek some other dwelling,
    For I must dye:
Farewel false Love, thy Tongue is ever telling
    Lye after Lye.
For ever let me rest now from thy smarts,
    Alas, for pity go,
    And fire their hearts
That have been hard to thee, mine was not so.

Never again deluding Love shall know me,
    For I will dye;
And all those griefs that think to over-grow me,
    Shall be as I:
For ever will I sleep, while poor Maids cry,
    Alas, for pity stay,
    And let us dye
With thee, men cannot mock us in the day.

[‘LOVERS REJOYCE’ *from CUPID’S REVENGE*]

LOVERS rejoyce, your pains shall be rewarded,
  The god of Love himself grieves at your crying:
No more shall frozen honor be regarded,
  Nor the coy faces of a Maids denying.

No more shall Virgins sigh, and say we dare not,
For men are false, and what they do they care not,
All shall be well again, then do not grieve,
Men shall be true, and Women shall believe.

Lovers rejoyce, what you shall say henceforth,
When you have caught your Sweet-hearts in your arms,
It shall be accounted Oracle and Worth:
No more faint-hearted Girls shall dream of harms,
And cry they are too young; the god hath said
Fifteen shall make a Mother of a Maid:
Then wise men, pull your Roses yet unblown,
Love hates the too ripe fruit that falls alone.

[LULLABY *from* *THE WOMAN-HATER*]

COME sleep, and with the sweet deceiving,
Lock me in delight a while,
Let some pleasing Dreams beguile
All my fancies; That from thence,
I may feel an influence,
All my powers of care bereaving.

Though but a shadow, but a sliding,
Let me know some little Joy,
We that suffer long anoy
Are contented with a thought
Through an idle fancie wrought,
O let my joyes, have some abiding.

[LOVE SONG *from* *THE BLOODY BROTHER*]

TAKE, Oh take those lips away
That so sweetly were forsworn,
And those eyes, like break of day,
Lights that do mislead the morn,
But my kisses bring again,
Seals of love, though seal'd in vain.

Hide, Oh hide those hills of Snow,
Which thy frozen bosom bears,
On whose tops the Pinks that grow
Are of those that *April* wears,
But first set my poor heart free,
Bound in those Ivy chains by thee.

HERBERT OF CHERBURY

ELEGY OVER A TOMB

MUST I then see, alas! eternal night
Sitting upon those fairest eyes,
And closing all those beams, which once did rise
So radiant and bright,
That light and heat in them to us did prove
Knowledge and Love?

Oh, if you did delight no more to stay
Upon this low and earthly stage,
But rather chose an endless heritage,
Tell us at least, we pray,
Where all the beauties that those ashes ow'd
Are now bestow'd?

Doth the Sun now his light with yours renew?
Have Waves the curling of your hair?
Did you restore unto the Sky and Air,
The red, and white, and blew?
Have you vouchsafed to flowrs since your death
That sweetest breath?

Had not Heav'ns Lights else in their houses slept,
Or to some private life retir'd?
Must not the Sky and Air have else conspir'd,
And in their Regions wept?
Must not each flower else the earth could breed
Have been a weed?

But thus enrich'd may we not yield some cause
Why they themselves lament no more?
That must have changed the course they held before,
And broke their proper Laws,
Had not your beauties giv'n this second birth
To Heaven and Earth?

Tell us, for Oracles must still ascend,
For those that crave them at your tomb:
Tell us, where are those beauties now become,
And what they now intend:
Tell us, alas, that cannot tell our grief,
Or hope relief.

DRUMMOND

MADRIGAL

LIKE the *Idalian* Queene
Her Haire about her Eyne,
With Necke and Brests ripe Apples to be seene,
At first Glance of the *Morne*
In *Cyprus* Gardens gathering those faire Flowrs
Which of her Bloud were borne,
I saw, but fainting saw, my Paramours.
The *Graces* naked danc'd about the Place,
The *Winds* and *Trees* amaz'd
With Silence on Her gaz'd,
The Flowrs did smile, like those upon her Face,
And as their Aspine Stalkes those Fingers band,
(That Shee might read my Case)
A *Hyacinth* I wisht mee in her Hand.

SONNET

SWEET *Spring*, thou turn'st with all thy goodlie Traine,
Thy Head with Flames, thy Mantle bright with Flowrs,
The *Zephyres* curle the greene Lockes of the Plaine,
The Cloudes for Joy in Pearles weepe down their Showrs.

Thou turn'st (sweet Youth) but *ah* my pleasant Howres, *Drummond*
And happie Dayes, with thee come not againe,
The sad Memorialls only of my Paine
Doe with thee turne, which turne my Sweets in Sowres.
Thou art the same which still thou wast before,
Delicious, wanton, amiable, faire,
But *shee*, whose Breath embaulm'd thy wholesome Aire,
Is gone: nor Gold, nor Gemmes Her can restore.
Neglected *Vertue*, Seasons goe and come,
While thine forgot lie closed in a Tombe.

SONNET

As in a duskie and tempestuous Night,
A Starre is wont to spreade her Lockes of Gold,
And while her pleasant Rayes abroad are roll'd,
Some spitefull Cloude doth robbe us of her Sight:
(Faire Soule) in this black Age so shin'd thou bright,
And made all Eyes with Wonder thee beholde,
Till uglie *Death* depriving us of Light,
In his grimme mistie Armes thee did enfolde.
Who more shall vaunt true Beautie heere to see?
What Hope doth more in any Heart remaine,
That such Perfections shall his *Reason* raine?
If Beautie with thee borne too died with thee?
World, plaine no more of *Love*, nor count his Harmes,
With his pale Trophees *Death* hath hung his Armes.

['THE WORLD A HUNTING IS']

The World a Hunting is,
The prey, poore Man, the *Nimrod* fierce is Death,
His speedy Grey-hounds are
Lust, Sicknesse, Envie, Care,
Strife that ne'er falls amisse,
With all those ills which haunt us while we breathe.
Now if (by chance) wee flie
Of these the eager Chase,
Old Age with stealing Pace
Casts up his Nets, and there wee panting die.

QUARLES

CANTICLE

'My beloved is mine, and I am his; He feedeth among the Lillies'

Ev'n like two little bank-dividing brookes,
  That wash the pebles with their wanton streames,
And having rang'd and search'd a thousand nookes,
  Meet both at length, in silver-brested *Thames*;
    Where, in a greater Current they conjoyne:
So I my Best-Beloveds am; so He is mine.

Ev'n so we met; and after long pursuit,
  Ev'n so we joyn'd; we both became entire;
No need for either to renew a Suit,
  For I was Flax, and he was Flames of fire:
    Our firm united soules did more than twine;
So I my Best-Beloveds am; so He is mine.

If all those glittring Monarchs that command
  The servile Quarters of this earthly Ball,
Should tender, in Exchange, their shares of land,
  I would not change my Fortunes for them all:
    Their wealth is but a Counter to my Coyne;
The world's but theirs; but my Beloved's mine.

Nay, more; If the faire Thespian Ladies, all
  Should heap together their diviner treasure:
That Treasure should be deem'd a price too small
  To buy a minuts Lease of half my Pleasure;
    'Tis not the sacred wealth of all the Nine
Can buy my heart from Him; or His, from being mine.

Nor Time, nor Place, nor Chance, nor Death can bow
  My least desires unto the least remove;
Hee's firmely mine by Oath; I, His, by Vow;
  Hee's mine by Faith; and I am His, by Love;
    Hee's mine by Water; I am His, by Wine;
Thus I my Best-Beloveds am; Thus He is mine.

He is my Altar; I, his Holy Place;
  I am his Guest; and he, my living Food;

I'm his, by Poenitence; He, mine by Grace;
I'm his, by Purchase; He is mine, by Blood;
Hee's my supporting Elme; and I, his Vine:
Thus I my Best-Beloveds am; Thus He is mine.

He gives me wealth: I give him all my Vowes:
I give Him songs; He gives me length of dayes;
With wrethes of Grace he crownes my conq'ring browes:
And I, his Temples, with a Crowne of Praise,
Which he accepts as an everlasting signe,
That I my Best-Beloveds am; that He is mine.

KING

THE EXEQUY

Accept thou Shrine of my dead Saint,
Insteed of Dirges this complaint;
And for sweet flowres to crown thy hearse,
Receive a strew of weeping verse
From thy griev'd friend, whom thou might'st see
Quite melted into tears for thee.

Dear loss! since thy untimely fate
My task hath been to meditate
On thee, on thee: thou art the book,
The library whereon I look
Though almost blind. For thee (lov'd clay)
I languish out not live the day,
Using no other exercise
But what I practise with mine eyes:
By which wet glasses I find out
How lazily time creeps about
To one that mourns: this, onely this
My exercise and bus'ness is:
So I compute the weary houres
With sighs dissolved into showres.

Nor wonder if my time go thus
Backward and most preposterous;

King

Thou hast benighted me, thy set
This Eve of blackness did beget,
Who was't my day, (though overcast
Before thou had'st thy Noon-tide past)
And I remember must in tears,
Thou scarce had'st seen so many years
As Day tells houres. By thy cleer Sun
My love and fortune first did run;
But thou wilt never more appear
Folded within my Hemisphear,
Since both thy light and motion
Like a fled Star is fall'n and gon,
And twixt me and my soules dear wish
The earth now interposed is,
Which such a strange eclipse doth make
As ne're was read in Almanake.

I could allow thee for a time
To darken me and my sad Clime,
Were it a month, a year, or ten,
I would thy exile live till then;
And all that space my mirth adjourn,
So thou wouldst promise to return;
And putting off thy ashy shrowd
At length disperse this sorrows cloud.

But woe is me! the longest date
Too narrow is to calculate
These empty hopes: never shall I
Be so much blest as to descry
A glimpse of thee, till that day come
Which shall the earth to cinders doome,
And a fierce Feaver must calcine
The body of this world like thine,
(My Little World!) that fit of fire
Once off, our bodies shall aspire
To our soules bliss: then we shall rise,
And view our selves with cleerer eyes
In that calm Region, where no night
Can hide us from each others sight.

Mean time, thou hast her, Earth: much good
May my harm do thee. Since it stood
With Heavens will I might not call
Her longer mine, I give thee all
My short-liv'd right and interest
In her, whom living I lov'd best:
With a most free and bounteous grief,
I give thee what I could not keep.
Be kind to her, and prethee look
Thou write into thy Dooms-day book
Each parcell of this Rarity
Which in thy Casket shrin'd doth ly:
See that thou make thy reck'ning streight,
And yield her back again by weight;
For thou must audit on thy trust
Each graine and atome of this dust,
As thou wilt answer *Him* that lent,
Not gave thee my dear Monument.

So close the ground, and 'bout her shade
Black curtains draw, my *Bride* is laid.

Sleep on my *Love* in thy cold bed
Never to be disquieted!
My last good night! Thou wilt not wake
Till I thy fate shall overtake:
Till age, or grief, or sickness, must
Marry my body to that dust
It so much loves; and fills the room
My heart keeps empty in thy Tomb.
Stay for me there; I will not faile
To meet thee in that hollow Vale.
And think not much of my delay;
I am already on the way,
And follow thee with all the speed
Desire can make, or sorrows breed.
Each minute is a short degree,
And ev'ry houre a step towards thee.
At night when I betake to rest,
Next morn I rise neerer my West
Of life, almost by eight houres saile,
Than when sleep breath'd his drowsie gale.

Thus from the Sun my Bottom stears,
And my dayes Compass downward bears:
Nor labour I to stemme the tide
Through which to *Thee* I swiftly glide.

'Tis true, with shame and grief I yield,
Thou like the *Vann* first took'st the field,
And gotten hast the victory
In thus adventuring to dy
Before me, whose more years might crave
A just precedence in the grave.
But heark! My Pulse like a soft Drum
Beats my approch, tells *Thee* I come;
And slow howere my marches be,
I shall at last sit down by *Thee*.

The thought of this bids me go on,
And wait my dissolution
With hope and comfort. *Dear* (forgive
The crime) I am content to live
Divided, with but half a heart,
Till we shall meet and never part.

SHIRLEY

[SONG *from* CUPID AND DEATH]

Victorious men of Earth, no more
Proclame how wide your Empires are;
Though you binde in every shore,
And your triumphs reach as far
as Night or Day,
Yet you proud Monarks must obey,
And mingle with forgotten ashes, when
Death calls yee to the croud of common men.

Devouring Famine, Plague, and War,
Each able to undo man-kind,
Deaths servile Emissaries are,

Nor to these alone confin'd,
He hath at will
More quaint and subtle wayes to kill.
A smile or kiss, as he will use the art,
Shall have the cunning skill to break a heart.

[SONG *from THE CONTENTION OF AJAX AND ULYSSES*]

THE glories of our blood and state,
are shadows, not substantial things,
There is no armour against Fate,
Death lays his icy hand on Kings,
Scepter and Crown,
Must tumble down,
And in the dust be equal made,
With the poor crooked sithe and spade.

Some men with swords may reap the field,
and plant fresh laurels where they kill,
But their strong nerves at last must yield,
They tame but one another still;
Early or late,
They stoop to Fate,
And must give up their murmuring breath,
When they pale Captives creep to death.

The Garlands wither on your brow,
then boast no more your mighty deeds,
Upon Death's purple Altar now,
See where the Victor-victim bleeds,
Your heads must come,
To the cold Tomb,
Onely the actions of the just
Smell sweet, and blossom in their dust.

STRODE

ON WESTWALL DOWNES

When Westwall Downes I gan to tread,
Where cleanely wynds the greene did sweepe,
Methought a landskipp there was spread,
Here a bush and there a sheepe:
  The pleated wrinkles of the face
  Of wave-swolne earth did lend such grace,
  As shadowings in Imag'ry
  Which both deceive and please the eye.

The sheepe sometymes did tread the maze
By often wynding in and in,
And sometymes round about they trace
Which mylkmaydes call a Fairie ring:
  Such semicircles have they runne,
  Such lynes across so trymly spunne
  That sheppeards learne whenere they please
  A new Geometry with ease.

The slender food upon the downe
Is allwayes even, allwayes bare,
Which neither spring nor winter's frowne
Can ought improve or ought impayre:
  Such is the barren Eunuches chynne,
  Which thus doth evermore begynne
  With tender downe to be orecast
  Which never comes to haire at last.

Here and there twoe hilly crests
Amiddst them hugg a pleasant greene,
And these are like twoe swelling breasts
That close a tender fall betweene.
  Here would I sleepe, or read, or pray
  From early morn till flight of day:
  But harke! a sheepe-bell calls mee upp,
  Like Oxford colledge bells, to supp.

HABINGTON

[A SONG *from* *THE QUEENE OF ARRAGON*]

FINE young folly, though you were
That faire beauty I did sweare,
Yet you neere could reach my heart.
For we Courtiers learne at Schoole,
Onely with your sex to foole,
Y'are not worth the serious part.

When I sigh and kisse your hand,
Crosse my Armes and wondring stand:
Holding parley with your eye,
Then dilate on my desires,
Sweare the sunne nere shot such fires,
All is but a handsome lye.

When I eye your curle or Lace,
Gentle soule you thinke your face
Streight some murder doth commit,
And your virtue doth begin
To grow scrupulous of my sinne,
When I talke to shew my wit.

Therefore Madam weare no cloud
Nor to check my love grow proud,
For in sooth I much doe doubt
'Tis the powder in your haire,
Not your breath perfumes the ayre,
And your Cloathes that set you out.

Yet though truth has this confest,
And I vow I love in Jest:
When I next begin to Court
And protest an amorous flame,
You will sweare I in earnest am:
Bedlam! this is pretty sport.

RANDOLPH

AN ODE TO MR ANTHONY STAFFORD TO HASTEN HIM INTO THE COUNTRY

Come spurre away,
I have no patience for a longer stay;
But must goe downe,
And leave the chargeable noise of this great Towne.
I will the country see,
Where old simplicity,
Though hid in gray
Doth looke more gay
Than foppery in plush and scarlat clad.
Farewell you City-wits that are
Almost at Civill warre;
Tis time that I grow wise, when all the world grows mad.

More of my dayes
I will not spend to gaine an Idiots praise;
Or to make sport
For some slight Punie of the Innes of Court.
Then worthy *Stafford* say
How shall we spend the day,
With what delights,
Shorten the nights?
When from this tumult we are got secure;
Where mirth with all her freedome goes,
Yet shall no finger loose;
Where every word is thought, and every thought is pure.

There from the tree
Wee'l cherries plucke, and pick the strawbery.
And every day
Go see the wholesome Country Girles make hay,
Whose browne hath lovlier grace,
Than any painted face
That I doe know
Hide-Parke can show.
Where I had rather gain a kisse than meet,

Though some of them in greater state
Might court my love with plate
The beauties of the *Cheape*, and wives of *Lumbardstreet*.

But thinke upon
Some other pleasures, these to me are none,
Why doe I prate
Of woemen, that are things against my fate?
I never meane to wed,
That torture to my bed.
My Muse is shee
My Love shall bee.
Let Clownes get wealth, and heires; when I am gone,
And the great Bugbeare grisly death
Shall take this idle breath,
If I a Poem leave, that Poem is my Sonne.

Of this no more;
Wee'l rather tast the bright *Pomona's* store,
No fruit shall scape
Our pallats, from the damsen, to the grape.
Then full we'l seek a shade,
And heare what musique's made;
How Philomell
Her tale doth tell:
And how the other Birds doe fill the quire;
The Thrush and Blackbird lend their throats
Warbling melodious notes;
Wee will all sports enjoy, which others but desire.

Ours is the skie,
Where at what fowle we please our Hauke shall flye;
Nor will we spare
To hunt the crafty foxe, or timorous hare,
But let our hounds runne loose
In any ground they'l choose,
The bucke shall fall,
The stagge and all:
Our pleasures must from their owne warrants bee,
For to my *Muse*, if not to mee,
I'me sure all game is free;
Heaven, Earth, are all but parts of her great Royalty.

And when we meane
To tast of *Bacchus* blessings now and then,
And drinke by stealth
A cup or two to noble *Barkleys* health,
I'le take my pipe and try
The *Phrygian* melody;
Which he that heares
Lets through his eares
A madnesse to distemper all the braine.
Then I another pipe will take
And *Dorique* musique make,
To Civilize with graver notes our wits againe.

HERBERT

from EASTER

I GOT me flowers to straw thy way;
I got me boughs off many a tree:
But thou wast up by break of day,
And brought'st thy sweets along with thee.

The Sunne arising in the East,
Though he give light, & th'East perfume;
If they should offer to contest
With thy arising, they presume.

Can there be any day but this,
Though many sunnes to shine endeavour?
We count three hundred, but we misse:
There is but one, and that one ever.

JORDAN

WHO sayes that fictions onely and false hair
Become a verse? Is there in truth no beautie?
Is all good structure in a winding stair?
May no lines passe, except they do their dutie
Not to a true, but painted chair?

Is it no verse, except enchanted groves
And sudden arbours shadow course-spunne lines?
Must purling streams refresh a lovers loves?
Must all be vail'd, while he that reades, divines,
  Catching the sense at two removes?

Shepherds are honest people; let them sing:
Riddle who list, for me, and pull for Prime:
I envie no mans nightingale or spring;
Nor let them punish me with losse of rime,
  Who plainly say, *My God, My King.*

EVEN-SONG

BLEST be the God of love,
Who gave me eyes, and light, and power this day,
Both to be busie, and to play.
But much more blest be God above,
Who gave me sight alone,
Which to himself he did denie:
For when he sees my waies, I dy:
But I have got his sonne, and he hath none.

What have I brought thee home
For this thy love? have I discharg'd the debt,
Which this dayes favour did beget?
I ranne; but all I brought, was fome.
Thy diet, care, and cost
Do end in bubbles, balls of winde;
Of winde to thee whom I have crost,
But balls of wilde-fire to my troubled minde.

Yet still thou goest on,
And now with darknesse closest wearie eyes
Saying to man, *It doth suffice:*
Henceforth repose; your work is done.
Thus in thy ebony box
Thou dost inclose us, till the day
Put our amendment in our way,
And give new wheels to our disorder'd clocks.

I muse, which shows more love,
The day or night: that is the gale, this th'harbour;
That is the walk, and this the arbour;
Or that the garden, this the grove.
My God, thou art all love.
Not one poore minute scapes thy breast,
But brings a favour from above;
And in this love, more than in bed, I rest.

DENIALL

When my devotions could not pierce
Thy silent eares;
Then was my heart broken, as was my verse:
My breast was full of fears
And disorder:

My bent thoughts, like a brittle bow,
Did flie asunder:
Each took his way; some would to pleasures go,
Some to the warres and thunder
Of alarms.

As good go any where, they say,
As to benumme
Both knees and heart, in crying night and day,
Come, come, my God, O come,
But no hearing.

O that thou shouldst give dust a tongue
To crie to thee,
And then not heare it crying! all day long
My heart was in my knee,
But no hearing.

Therefore my soul lay out of sight,
Untun'd, unstrung:
My feeble spirit, unable to look right,
Like a nipt blossome, hung
Discontented.

O cheer and tune my heartlesse breast,
Deferre no time;
That so thy favours granting my request,
They and my minde may chime,
And mend my ryme.

VERTUE

Sweet day, so cool, so calm, so bright,
The bridall of the earth and skie:
The dew shall weep thy fall to night;
For thou must die.

Sweet rose, whose hue angrie and brave
Bids the rash gazer wipe his eye:
Thy root is ever in its grave,
And thou must die.

Sweet spring, full of sweet dayes and roses,
A box where sweets compacted lie;
My musick shows ye have your closes,
And all must die.

Onely a sweet and vertuous soul,
Like season'd timber, never gives;
But though the whole world turn to coal,
Then chiefly lives.

THE PEARL

I know the wayes of Learning; both the head
And pipes that feed the presse, and make it runne;
What reason hath from nature borrowed,
Or of it self, like a good huswife, spunne
In laws and policie; what the starres conspire,
What willing nature speaks, what forc'd by fire;
Both th'old discoveries, and the new-found seas,
The stock and surplus, cause and historie:
All these stand open, or I have the keyes:
Yet I love thee.

I know the wayes of Honour, what maintains
The quick returns of courtesie and wit:
In vies of favours whether partie gains,
When glorie swells the heart, and moldeth it
To all expressions both of hand and eye,
Which on the world a true-love-knot may tie,
And bear the bundle, wheresoe're it goes:
How many drammes of spirit there must be
To sell my life unto my friends or foes:
Yet I love thee.

I know the wayes of Pleasure, the sweet strains,
The lullings and the relishes of it;
The propositions of hot bloud and brains;
What mirth and musick mean; what love and wit
Have done these twentie hundred yeares, and more:
I know the projects of unbridled store:
My stuffe is flesh, not brasse; my senses live,
And grumble oft, that they have more in me
Than he that curbs them, being but one to five:
Yet I love thee.

I know all these, and have them in my hand:
Therefore not sealed, but with open eyes
I flie to thee, and fully understand
Both the main sale, and the commodities;
And at what rate and price I have thy love;
With all the circumstances that may move:
Yet through these labyrinths, not my groveling wit,
But thy silk twist let down from heav'n to me,
Did both conduct and teach me, how by it
To climbe to thee.

THE COLLAR

I STRUCK the board, and cry'd, No more.
I will abroad.
What? shall I ever sigh and pine?
My lines and life are free; free as the rode,
Loose as the winde, as large as store.
Shall I be still in suit?

Have I no harvest but a thorn
To let me bloud, and not restore
What I have lost with cordiall fruit?
Sure there was wine
Before my sighs did drie it: there was corn
Before my tears did drown it.
Is the yeare onely lost to me?
Have I no bayes to crown it?
No flowers, no garlands gay? all blasted?
All wasted?
Not so my heart: but there is fruit,
And thou hast hands.
Recover all thy sigh-blown age
On double pleasures: leave thy cold dispute
Of what is fit, and not. Forsake thy cage,
Thy rope of sands,
Which pettie thoughts have made, and made to thee
Good cable, to enforce and draw,
And be thy law,
While thou didst wink and wouldst not see.
Away; take heed:
I will abroad.
Call in thy deaths head there: tie up thy fears.
He that forbears
To suit and serve his need,
Deserves his load.
But as I rav'd and grew more fierce and wilde
At every worde,
Methought I heard one calling, *Child!*
And I replied, *My Lord.*

THE PULLEY

WHEN God at first made man,
Having a glasse of blessings standing by;
Let us (said he) poure on him all we can:
Let the worlds riches, which dispersed lie,
Contract into a span.

So strength first made a way;
Then beautie flow'd, then wisdome, honour, pleasure:
When almost all was out, God made a stay,
Perceiving that alone of all his treasure
Rest in the bottome lay.

For if I should (said he)
Bestow this jewell also on my creature,
He would adore my gifts in stead of me,
And rest in Nature, not the God of Nature:
So both should losers be.

Yet let him keep the rest,
But keep them with repining restlesnesse:
Let him be rich and wearie, that at least,
If goodnesse leade him not, yet wearinesse
May tosse him to my breast.

THE FLOWER

How fresh, O Lord, how sweet and clean
Are thy returns! ev'n as the flowers in spring;
To which, besides their own demean,
The late-past frosts tributes of pleasure bring.
Grief melts away
Like snow in May,
As if there were no such cold thing.

Who would have thought my shrivel'd heart
Could have recover'd greennesse? It was gone
Quite under ground; as flowers depart
To see their mother-root, when they have blown;
Where they together
All the hard weather,
Dead to the world, keep house unknown.

These are thy wonders, Lord of power,
Killing and quickning, bringing down to hell
And up to heaven in an houre;
Making a chiming of a passing-bell.
We say amisse,
This or that is:
Thy word is all, if we could spell.

O that I once past changing were,
Fast in thy Paradise, where no flower can wither!
Many a spring I shoot up fair,
Offring at heav'n, growing and groning thither:
Nor doth my flower
Want a spring-showre,
My sinnes and I joining together.

But while I grow in a straight line,
Still upwards bent, as if heav'n were mine own,
Thy anger comes, and I decline:
What frost to that? what pole is not the zone,
Where all things burn,
When thou dost turn,
And the least frown of thine is shown?

And now in age I bud again,
After so many deaths I live and write;
I once more smell the dew and rain,
And relish versing: O my onely light,
It cannot be
That I am he
On whom thy tempests fell all night.

These are thy wonders, Lord of love,
To make us see we are but flowers that glide:
Which when we once can finde and prove,
Thou hast a garden for us, where to bide.
Who would be more,
Swelling through store,
Forfeit their Paradise by their pride.

LOVE

LOVE bade me welcome: yet my soul drew back,
Guiltie of dust and sinne.
But quick-ey'd Love, observing me grow slack
From my first entrance in,
Drew nearer to me, sweetly questioning,
If I lack'd any thing.

A guest, I answer'd, worthy to be here:
Love said, You shall be he.
I the unkinde, ungratefull? Ah my deare,
I cannot look on thee.
Love took my hand, and smiling did reply,
Who made the eyes but I?

Truth Lord, but I have marr'd them: let my shame
Go where it doth deserve.
And know you not, sayes Love, who bore the blame?
My deare, then I will serve.
You must sit down, sayes Love, and taste my meat:
So I did sit and eat.

CRASHAW

A HYMN TO THE NAME AND HONOR OF THE ADMIRABLE SAINTE TERESA

LOVE, thou art Absolute sole lord
OF LIFE & DEATH. To prove the word,
Wee'l now appeal to none of all
Those thy old Souldiers, Great & tall,
Ripe Men of Martyrdom, that could reach down
With strong armes, their triumphant crown;
Such as could with lusty breath
Speak lowd into the face of death
Their Great LORD's glorious name, to none
Of those whose spatious Bosomes spread a throne
For LOVE at larg to fill: spare blood & sweat;
And see him take a private seat,
Making his mansion in the mild
And milky soul of a soft child.
Scarse has she learn't to lisp the name
Of Martyr; yet she thinks it shame
Life should so long play with that breath
Which spent can buy so brave a death.
She never undertook to know
What death with love should have to doe;

Nor has she e're yet understood
Why to show love, she should shed blood,
Yet though she cannot tell you why,
She can Love, & she can Dy.
  Scarse has she Blood enough to make
A guilty sword blush for her sake;
Yet has she'a Heart dares hope to prove
How much lesse strong is Death than Love.
  Be love but there; let poor six yeares
Be pos'd with the maturest Feares
Man trembles at, you straight shall find
Love knowes no nonage, nor the Mind.
'Tis Love, not Yeares or Limbs that can
Make the Martyr, or the man.
  Love touch't her Heart, & lo it beates
High, & burnes with such brave heates;
Such thirsts to dy, as dares drink up,
A thousand cold deaths in one cup.
Good reason. For she breathes All fire.
Her weake brest heaves with strong desire
Of what she may with fruitles wishes
Seek for amongst her Mother's Kisses.
  Since 'tis not to be had at home
She'l travail to a Martyrdom.
No home for hers confesses she
But where she may a Martyr be.
  She'l to the Moores; And trade with them,
For this unvalued Diadem.
She'l offer them her dearest Breath,
With Christ's Name in't, in change for death.
She'l bargain with them; & will give
Them God; teach them how to live
In him: or, if they this deny,
For him she'l teach them how to Dy.
So shall she leave amongst them sown
Her Lord's Blood; or at lest her own.
  Farewel then, all the world! Adieu.
Teresa is no more for you.
Farewell, all pleasures, sports, & joyes,
(Never tillnow esteemed toyes)
Farewell what ever deare may bee,

Crashaw

MOTHER's armes or FATHER's knee
Farewell house, & farewell home!
SHE's for the Moores, & MARTYRDOM.
SWEET, not so fast! lo thy fair Spouse,
Whom thou seekst with so swift vowes,
Calls thee back, & bidds thee come
T'embrace a milder MARTYRDOM.
Blest powres forbid, Thy tender life
Should bleed upon a barborous knife;
Or some base hand have power to race
Thy Brest's chast cabinet, & uncase
A soul kept there so sweet, ô no;
Wise heavn will never have it so.
THOU art Love's victime; & must dy
A death more mysticall & high.
Into love's armes thou shalt let fall
A still-surviving funerall.
His is the DART must make the DEATH
Whose stroke shall tast thy hallow'd breath;
A Dart thrice dip't in that rich flame
Which writes thy spouse's radiant Name
Upon the roof of Heav'n; where ay
It shines, & with a soveraign ray
Beates bright upon the burning faces
Of soules which in that name's sweet graces
Find everlasting smiles. So rare,
So spirituall, pure, & fair
Must be th'immortall instrument
Upon whose choice point shall be sent
A life so lov'd; And that there be
Fitt executioners for Thee,
The fair'st & first-born sons of fire
Blest SERAPHIM, shall leave their quire
And turn love's souldiers, upon THEE
To exercise their archerie.
O how oft shalt thou complain
Of a sweet & subtle PAIN.
Of intolerable JOYES;
Of a DEATH, in which who dyes
Loves his death, and dyes again;
And would for ever so be slain.

And lives, & dyes; and knowes not why
To live, But that he thus may never leave to DY.
  How kindly will thy gentle HEART
Kisse the sweetly-killing DART!
And close in his embraces keep
Those delicious Wounds, that weep
Balsom to heal themselves with. Thus
When These thy DEATHS, so numerous,
Shall all at last dy into one,
And melt thy Soul's sweet mansion;
Like a soft lump of incense, hasted
By too hott a fire, & wasted
Into perfuming clouds, so fast
Shalt thou exhale to Heavn at last
In a resolving SIGH, and then
O what? Ask not the Tongues of men.
Angells cannot tell, suffice,
Thy selfe shall feel thine own full joyes
And hold them fast for ever. There
So soon as thou shalt first appear,
The MOON of maiden starrs, thy white
MISTRESSE, attended by such bright
Soules as thy shining self, shall come
And in her first rankes make thee room;
Where 'mongst her snowy family
Immortall wellcomes wait for thee.
  O what delight, when reveal'd LIFE shall stand
And teach thy lipps heav'n with his hand;
On which thou now maist to thy wishes
Heap up thy consecrated kisses.
What joyes shall seize thy soul, when she
Bending her blessed eyes on thee
(Those second Smiles of Heav'n) shall dart
Her mild rayes through thy melting heart!
  Angels, thy old freinds, there shall greet thee
Glad at their own home now to meet thee.
  All thy good WORKES which went before
And waited for thee, at the door,
Shall own thee there; and all in one
Weave a constellation
Of CROWNS, with which the KING thy spouse

Crashaw

Shall build up thy triumphant browes.
All thy old woes shall now smile on thee
And thy paines sitt bright upon thee,
All thy sorrows here shall shine,
All thy SUFFRINGS be divine.
TEARES shall take comfort, & turn gemms
And WRONGS repent to Diademms.
Ev'n thy DEATHS shall live; & new
Dresse the soul that erst they slew.
Thy wounds shall blush to such bright scarres
As keep account of the LAMB's warres.
Those rare WORKES where thou shalt leave writt
Love's noble history, with witt
Taught thee by none but him, while here
They feed our soules, shall cloth THINE there.
Each heavnly word by whose hid flame
Our hard Hearts shall strike fire, the same
Shall flourish on thy browes, & be
Both fire to us & flame to thee;
Whose light shall live bright in thy FACE
By glory, in our hearts by grace.
Thou shalt look round about, & see
Thousands of crown'd Soules throng to be
Themselves thy crown. Sons of thy vowes
The virgin-births with which thy soveraign spouse
Made fruitfull thy fair soul, goe now
And with them all about thee bow
To Him, put on (hee'l say) put on
(My rosy love) That thy rich zone
Sparkling with the sacred flames
Of thousand soules, whose happy names
Heav'n keeps upon thy score. (Thy bright
Life brought them first to kisse the light
That kindled them to starrs.) And so
Thou with the LAMB, thy lord, shalt goe;
And whereso'ere he setts his white
Stepps, walk with HIM those ways of light
Which who in death would live to see,
Must learn in life to dy like thee.

AN EPITAPH

UPON A YOUNG MARRIED COUPLE DEAD AND BURYED TOGETHER

To these, whom DEATH again did wed,
This GRAVE's their second Marriage-bed.
For though the hand of fate could ſorce
'Twixt SOUL & BODY a Divorce,
It could not sunder man & WIFE,
'Cause They Both lived but one life.
Peace, good Reader. Doe not weep.
Peace, The Lovers are asleep.
They, sweet Turtles, folded ly
In the last knott love could ty.

from M. CRASHAWS ANSWER FOR HOPE

FAIR hope! our earlyer heav'n by thee
Young time is taster to eternity
Thy generous wine with age growes strong, not sowre.
Nor does it kill thy fruit, to smell thy flowre.
Thy golden, growing, head never hangs down
Till in the lappe of loves full noone
It falls; and dyes! o no, it melts away
As does the dawn into the day.
As lumpes of sugar loose themselves; and twine
Their supple essence with the soul of wine.
Fortune? alas, above the world's low warres
Hope walks; & kickes the curld heads of conspiring starres.
Her keel cutts not the waves where These winds stirr
Fortune's whole lottery is one blank to her.
Her shafts, and shee fly farre above,
And forrage in the fields of light and love.
Sweet hope! kind cheat! fair fallacy by thee
We are not WHERE nor What we be,
But WHAT & WHERE we would be. Thus art thou
Our absent PRESENCE, and our future Now.
Faith's sister! nurse of fair desire!
Fear's antidote! a wise & well-stay'd fire!
Temper twixt chill despair, & torrid joy!

Queen Regent in yonge love's minority!
    Though the vext chymick vainly chases
    His fugitive gold through all her faces;
Though love's more feirce, more fruitless, fires assay
    One face more fugitive than all they;
True hope's a glorious hunter & her chase,
The GOD of nature in the feilds of grace.

VAUGHAN

THE RETREATE

HAPPY those early dayes! when I
Shin'd in my Angell-infancy.
Before I understood this place
Appointed for my second race,
Or taught my soul to fancy ought
But a white, Celestiall thought,
When yet I had not walkt above
A mile, or two, from my first love,
And looking back (at that short space,)
Could see a glimpse of his bright-face;
When on some *gilded Cloud*, or *flowre*
My gazing soul would dwell an houre,
And in those weaker glories spy
Some shadows of eternity;
Before I taught my tongue to wound
My Conscience with a sinfull sound,
Or had the black art to dispence
A sev'rall sinne to ev'ry sence,
But felt through all this fleshly dresse
Bright *shootes* of everlastingness.
  O how I long to travell back
And tread again that ancient track!
That I might once more reach that plaine,
Where first I left my glorious traine,
From whence th'Inlightned spirit sees
That shady City of Palme trees;

But (ah!) my soul with too much stay
Is drunk, and staggers in the way.
Some men a forward motion love,
But I by backward steps would move,
And when this dust falls to the urn
In that state I came return.

CORRUPTION

SURE, It was so. Man in those early days
Was not all stone, and Earth,
He shin'd a little, and by those weak Rays
Had some glimpse of his birth.
He saw Heaven o'r his head, and knew from whence
He came (condemned,) hither,
And, as first Love draws strongest, so from hence
His mind sure progress'd thither.
Things here were strange unto him: Swet, and till
All was a thorn, or weed,
Nor did those last, but (like himself,) dyed still
As soon as they did *Seed*,
They seem'd to quarrel with him; for that Act
That fel him, foyl'd them all,
He drew the Curse upon the world, and Crackt
The whole frame with his fall.
This made him long for *home*, as loath to stay
With murmurers, and foes;
He sigh'd for *Eden*, and would often say
Ah! what bright days were those?
Nor was Heav'n cold unto him; for each day
The vally, or the Mountain
Afforded visits, and still *Paradise* lay
In some green shade, or fountain.
Angels lay *Leiger* here; Each Bush, and Cel,
Each Oke, and high-way knew them,
Walk but the fields, or sit down at some *wel*,
And he was sure to view them.
Almighty *Love*! where art thou now? mad man
Sits down, and freezeth on,
He raves, and swears to stir nor fire, nor fan,
But bids the threads be spun.

I see, thy Curtains are Close-drawn; Thy bow
Looks dim too in the Cloud,
Sin triumphs still, and man is sunk below
The Center, and his shrowd;
All's in deep sleep, and night; Thick darknes lyes
And hatcheth o'r thy people;
But hark! what trumpets that? what Angel cries
Arise! Thrust in thy sickle.

MAN

WEIGHING the stedfastness and state
Of some mean things which here below reside,
Where birds like watchful Clocks the noiseless date
And Intercourse of times divide,
Where Bees at night get home and hive, and flowrs
Early, aswel as late,
Rise with the Sun, and set in the same howrs;

I would (said I) my God would give
The staidness of these things to man! for these
To his divine appointments ever cleave,
And no new business breaks their peace;
The birds nor sow, nor reap, yet sup and dine,
The flowres without clothes live,
Yet *Solomon* was never drest so fine.

Man hath stil either toyes, or Care,
He hath no root, nor to one place is ty'd,
But ever restless and Irregular
About this Earth doth run and ride,
He knows he hath a home, but scarce knows where,
He sayes it is so far
That he hath quite forgot how to go there.

He knocks at all doors, strays and roams,
Nay hath not so much wit as some stones have
Which in the darkest nights point to their homes,
By some hid sense their Maker gave;
Man is the shuttle, to whose winding quest
And passage through these looms
God order'd motion, but ordain'd no rest.

I SAW Eternity the other night
Like a great *Ring* of pure and endless light,
All calm, as it was bright,
And round beneath it, Time in hours, days, years
Driv'n by the spheres
Like a vast shadow mov'd, In which the world
And all her train were hurl'd;
The doting Lover in his queintest strain
Did their Complain,
Neer him, his Lute, his fancy, and his flights,
Wits sour delights,
With gloves, and knots the silly snares of pleasure
Yet his dear Treasure
All scatter'd lay, while he his eys did pour
Upon a flowr.

The darksome States-man hung with weights and woe
Like a thick midnight-fog mov'd there so slow
He did not stay, nor go;
Condemning thoughts (like sad Ecclipses) scowl
Upon his soul,
And Clouds of crying witnesses without
Pursued him with one shout.
Yet dig'd the Mole, and lest his ways be found
Workt under ground,
Where he did Clutch his prey, but one did see
That policie,
Churches and altars fed him, Perjuries
Were gnats and flies,
It rain'd about him bloud and tears, but he
Drank them as free.

The fearfull miser on a heap of rust
Sate pining all his life there, did scarce trust
His own hands with the dust,
Yet would not place one peece above, but lives
In feare of theeves.
Thousands there were as frantick as himself
And hug'd each one his pelf,

The down-right Epicure plac'd heav'n in sense
And scornd pretence
While others slipt into a wide Excesse
Said little lesse;
The weaker sort slight, triviall wares Inslave
Who think them brave,
And poor, despised truth sat Counting by
Their victory.

Yet some, who all this while did weep and sing,
And sing, and weep, soar'd up into the *Ring*,
But most would use no wing.
O fools (said I,) thus to prefer dark night
Before true light,
To live in grots, and caves, and hate the day
Because it shews the way,
The way which from this dead and dark abode
Leads up to God,
A way where you might tread the Sun, and be
More bright than he.
But as I did their madnes so discusse
One whisper'd thus,
This Ring the Bride-groome did for none provide
But for his Bride.

[FRIENDS DEPARTED]

They are all gone into the world of light!
And I alone sit lingring here;
Their very memory is fair and bright,
And my sad thoughts doth clear.

It glows and glitters in my cloudy brest
Like stars upon some gloomy grove,
Or those faint beams in which this hill is drest,
After the Sun's remove.

I see them walking in an Air of glory,
Whose light doth trample on my days:
My days, which are at best but dull and hoary,
Meer glimering and decays.

O holy hope! and high humility,
High as the Heavens above!
These are your walks, and you have shew'd them me
To kindle my cold love,

Dear, beauteous death! the Jewel of the Just,
Shining no where, but in the dark;
What mysteries do lie beyond thy dust;
Could man outlook that mark!

He that hath found some fledg'd birds nest, may know
At first sight, if the bird be flown;
But what fair Well, or Grove he sings in now
That is to him unknown.

And yet, as Angels in some brighter dreams
Call to the soul, when man doth sleep:
So some strange thoughts transcend our wonted theams,
And into glory peep.

If a star were confin'd into a Tomb
Her captive flames must needs burn there;
But when the hand that lockt her up, gives room,
She'l shine through all the sphære.

O Father of eternal life, and all
Created glories under thee!
Resume thy spirit from this world of thrall
Into true liberty.

Either disperse these mists, which blot and fill
My perspective (still) as they pass,
Or else remove me hence unto that hill,
Where I shall need no glass.

['I WALKT THE OTHER DAY']

I WALKT the other day (to spend my hour,)
Into a field
Where I sometimes had seen the soil to yield
A gallant flowre,
But Winter now had ruffled all the bowre
And curious store
I knew there heretofore.

Yet I whose search lov'd not to peep and peer
I' th' face of things
Thought with my self, there might be other springs
Besides this here
Which, like cold friends, sees us but once a year,
And so the flowre
Might have some other bowre.

Then taking up what I could neerest spie
I digg'd about
That place where I had seen him to grow out,
And by and by
I saw the warm Recluse alone to lie
Where fresh and green
He lived of us unseen.

Many a question Intricate and rare
Did I there strow,
But all I could extort was, that he now
Did there repair
Such losses as befel him in this air
And would e'r long
Come forth most fair and young.

This past, I threw the Clothes quite o'r his head,
And stung with fear
Of my own frailty dropt down many a tear
Upon his bed,
Then sighing whisper'd, *Happy are the dead!*
What peace doth now
Rock him asleep below?

And yet, how few believe such doctrine springs
From a poor root
Which all the Winter sleeps here under foot
And hath no wings
To raise it to the truth and light of things,
But is stil trod
By ev'ry wandring clod.

O thou! whose spirit did at first inflame
And warm the dead,

And by a sacred Incubation fed
With life this frame
Which once had neither being, forme, nor name,
Grant I may so
Thy steps track here below,

That in these Masques and shadows I may see
Thy sacred way,
And by those hid ascents climb to that day
Which breaks from thee
Who art in all things, though invisibly;
Shew me thy peace,
Thy mercy, love, and ease,

And from this Care, where dreams and sorrows raign
Lead me above
Where Light, Joy, Leisure, and true Comforts move
Without all pain,
There, hid in thee, shew me his life again
At whose dumbe urn
Thus all the year I mourn.

TRAHERNE

from THE SALUTATION

From Dust I rise
And out of Nothing now awake;
These brighter Regions which salute mine Eys
A Gift from God I take:
The Earth, the Seas, the Light, the lofty Skies,
The Sun and Stars are mine; if these I prize.

A Stranger here,
Strange things doth meet, strange Glory see,
Strange Treasures lodg'd in this fair World appear,
Strange all and New to me:
But that they *mine* should be who Nothing was,
That Strangest is of all: yet brought to pass.

from SOLITUDE

I DO believ,
The Ev'ning being shady and obscure,
The very Silence did me griev,
And Sorrow more procure:
A secret Want
Did make me think my Fortune scant.
I was so blind, I could not find my Health,
No Joy mine Ey could there espy, nor Wealth.

Nor could I ghess
What kind of thing I long'd for: But that I
Did somwhat lack of Blessedness,
Beside the Earth and Sky,
I plainly found;
It griev'd me much, I felt a Wound
Perplex me sore; yet what my Store should be
I did not know, nothing would shew to me.

Ye sullen Things!
Ye dumb, ye silent Creatures, and unkind!
How can I call you Pleasant Springs
Unless ye eas my Mind!
Will ye not speak
What 'tis I want, nor Silence break?
O pity me, and let me see som Joy;
Som Kindness shew to me, altho a Boy.

They silent stood;
Nor Earth, nor Woods, nor Hills, nor Brooks, nor Skies,
Would tell me where the hidden Good,
Which I did long for, lies:
The shady Trees,
The Ev'ning dark, the humming Bees,
The chirping Birds, mute Springs and Fords, conspire,
While they deny to answer my Desire.

from CHRISTENDOM

THINGS Native sweetly grew,
Which there mine Ey did view,
Plain, simple, cheap, on either side the Street,

Which was exceeding fair and wide;
Sweet Mansions there mine Eys did meet;
Green Trees the shaded Doors did hide:
My chiefest Joys
Were Girls and Boys
That in those Streets still up and down did play,
Which crown'd the Town with constant Holiday.

A sprightly pleasant Time,
(Ev'n Summer in its prime),
Did gild the Trees, the Houses, Children, Skies,
And made the City all divine;
It ravished my wondring Eys
To see the Sun so brightly shine:
The Heat and Light
Seem'd in my sight
With such a dazling Lustre shed on them,
As made me think 'twas th' *New Jerusalem*.

Beneath the lofty Trees
I saw, of all Degrees,
Folk calmly sitting in their doors; while som
Did standing with them kindly talk,
Som smile, som sing, or what was don
Observ, while others by did walk;
They view'd the Boys
And Girls, their Joys,
The Streets adorning with their Angel-faces,
Themselvs diverting in those pleasant Places.

The Streets like Lanes did seem,
Not pav'd with Stones, but green,
Which with red Clay did partly mixt appear;
'Twas Holy Ground of great Esteem;
The Spring's choice Liveries did wear
Of verdant Grass that grew between
The purling Streams,
Which golden Beams
Of Light did varnish, coming from the Sun,
By which to distant Realms was Service don.

In fresh and cooler Rooms
Retir'd they dine: Perfumes
They wanted not, having the pleasant Shade
And Peace to bless their House within,
By sprinkled Waters cooler made,
For those incarnat Cherubin.
This happy Place,
With all the Grace
The Joy and Beauty which did it beseem,
Did ravish me and highten my Esteem.

That here to rais Desire
All Objects do conspire,
Peeple in Years, and Yong enough to play,
Their Streets of Houses, common Peace,
In one continued Holy day
Whose gladsom Mirth shall never cease:
Since these becom
My *Christendom*,
What learn I more than that *Jerusalem*
Is *mine*, as 'tis *my Maker's*, choicest Gem.

ON NEWS

News from a forrein Country came,
As if my Treasure and my Wealth lay there:
So much it did my Heart Enflame!
Twas wont to call my Soul into mine Ear.
Which thither went to Meet
The Approaching Sweet:
And on the Thresh hold stood,
To entertain the Unknown Good.
It Hoverd there
As if twould leav mine Ear.
And was so Eager to Embrace
The Joyfull Tidings as they came,
Twould almost leav its Dwelling Place,
To Entertain the Same.

As if the Tidings were the Things,
My very Joys them selvs, my forrein Treasure,

Or els did bear them on their Wings;
With so much Joy they came, with so much Pleasure.
My Soul stood at the Gate
To recreat
It self with Bliss: And to
Be pleasd with Speed. A fuller View
It fain would take,
Yet Journeys back would make
Unto my Heart: as if twould fain
Go out to meet, yet Stay within
To fit a place, to Entertain,
And bring the Tidings in.

What Sacred Instinct did inspire
My Soul in Childhood with a Hope so Strong?
What Secret Force movd my Desire,
To Expect my Joys beyond the Seas, so Yong?
FELICITY I knew
Was out of view:
And being here alone,
I saw that Happiness was gone
From Me! for this,
I Thirsted Absent Bliss,
And thought that sure beyond the Seas,
Or els in som thing near at hand
I knew not yet, (since nought did pleas
I knew:) my Bliss did stand.

But little did the Infant Dream
That all the Treasures of the World were by:
And that Himself was so the Cream
And Crown of all, which round about did lie.
Yet thus it was. The Gem,
The Diadem,
The Ring Enclosing all
That Stood upon this Earthy Ball;
The Heavenly Ey,
Much Wider than the Skie,
Wher in they all included were
The Glorious Soul that was the King
Made to possess them, did appear
A Small and little thing!

COWLEY

THE CHANGE

LOVE in her Sunny Eyes does basking play;
Love walks the pleasant Mazes of her Hair;
Love does on both her Lips for ever stray;
And *sows* and *reaps* a thousand *kisses* there.
In all her outward parts *Love*'s always seen;
But, oh, He never went within.

Within *Love*'s foes, his greatest foes abide,
Malice, Inconstancy, and Pride.
So the Earths face, Trees, Herbs, and Flowers do dress,
With other beauties numberless:
But at the *Center*, *Darkness* is, and *Hell*;
There wicked *Spirits*, and there the *Damned* dwell.

With me alas, quite contrary it fares;
Darkness and *Death* lies in my weeping eyes,
Despair and Paleness in my face appears,
And Grief, and Fear, Love's greatest Enemies;
But, like the *Persian-Tyrant*, *Love* within
Keeps his proud *Court*, and ne're is seen.

Oh take *my Heart*, and by that means you'll prove
Within too stor'd enough of *Love*:
Give me but Yours, I'll by that change so thrive,
That *Love* in all my parts shall live.
So powerful is this change, it render can,
My *outside Woman*, and your *inside Man*.

BENLOWES

[EVENING PRAYER *from* THEOPHILA]

BUT, hark, 'tis late; the *Whistlers* knock from Plough;
The droyling *Swineheards* Drum beats now;
Maids have their *Cursies* made to th'spungy-teated Cow.

Larks roosted are, the folded *Flocks* are pent
In hurdled Grates, the tir'd *Ox* sent
In loose Trace home, nów *Hesper* lights his Torch in's Tent.

See glimmering Light, the *Pharos* of our Cot;
By *Innocence* protected, not
By *Guards*, we thither tend, where *Ev'n-song*'s not forgot.

O, *Pray'r!* Thou Anchor through the Worldly Sea!
Thou sov'raign Rhet'rick, 'bove the Plea
Of Flesh! that feed'st the fainting Soul, thou art *Heav'ns* Key.

Blest *Season*, when Dayes Eye is clos'd, to win
Our Heart to clear th' *Account*, – when Sin
Has past the *Audit*, Ravishments of Soul begin.

Who never wake to meditate, or weep,
Shall sure be sentenc'd for their *Sleep*;
Night to forepassed Day should still strict Centrie keep.

[LIFE AND DEATH *from* THEOPHILA]

FAMES Plant takes Root from *Vertue*, grows thereby;
Pure *Souls*, though Fortune-trod, stand high,
When mundane shallow-searching *Breath* It self shall die.

O, frail Applause of *Flesh!* swoln Bubbles passe.
Turf-fire more *Smoak* than *Splendor* has;
What *Bulwark* firm on Sand: What Shell for Pearl may passe.

But *Saints* with an attentive *Hope* from *High*,
On HEAV'NS *Paroll* do live and die;
Passing from *Lifes* short Night to *Dayes* ETERNITIE.

Who blessedly so *breathe*, and leave their *Breath*,
Of dying *Life* make living *Death*;
Each Day, spent like the last, does act a HEAV'N beneath.

Death's one long Sleep, and humane *Life* no more
Than one short Watch an Hour before:
World! after thy mad *Tempest* 'tis the landing *Shore*.

MARVELL

BERMUDAS

WHERE the remote *Bermudas* ride
In th'Oceans bosome unespy'd,
From a small Boat, that row'd along,
The listning Winds receiv'd this Song.
  What should we do but sing his Praise
That led us through the watry Maze,
Unto an Isle so long unknown,
And yet far kinder than our own?
Where he the huge Sea-Monsters wracks,
That lift the Deep upon their Backs.
He lands us on a grassy Stage;
Safe from the Storms, and Prelat's rage.
He gave us this eternal Spring,
Which here enamells every thing;
And sends the Fowl's to us in care,
On daily Visits through the Air.
He hangs in shades the Orange bright,
Like golden Lamps in a green Night.
And does in the Pomgranates close,
Jewels more rich than *Ormus* show's.
He makes the Figs our mouths to meet;
And throws the Melons at our feet.
But Apples plants of such a price,
No Tree could ever bear them twice.
With Cedars, chosen by his hand,
From *Lebanon*, he stores the Land.
And makes the hollow Seas, that roar,
Proclaime the Ambergris on shoar.
He cast (of which we rather boast)
The Gospels Pearl upon our Coast.
And in these Rocks for us did frame
A Temple, where to sound his Name.
Oh let our Voice his Praise exalt,
Till it arrive at Heavens Vault:
Which thence (perhaps) rebounding, may
Eccho beyond the *Mexique Bay*.
Thus sung they, in the *English* boat,

An holy and a chearful Note,
And all the way, to guide their Chime,
With falling Oars they kept the time.

TO HIS COY MISTRESS

HAD we but World enough, and Time,
This coyness Lady were no crime.
We would sit down, and think which way
To walk, and pass our long Loves Day.
Thou by the *Indian Ganges* side
Should'st Rubies find: I by the Tide
Of *Humber* would complain. I would
Love you ten years before the Flood:
And you should if you please refuse
Till the Conversion of the *Jews*.
My vegetable Love should grow
Vaster than Empires, and more slow.
An hundred years should go to praise
Thine Eyes, and on thy Forehead Gaze.
Two hundred to adore each Breast:
But thirty thousand to the rest.
An Age at least to every part,
And the last Age should show your Heart.
For Lady you deserve this State;
Nor would I love at lower rate.
But at my back I alwaies hear
Times winged Charriot hurrying near:
And yonder all before us lye
Desarts of vast Eternity.
Thy Beauty shall no more be found,
Nor, in thy marble Vault, shall sound
My ecchoing Song: then Worms shall try
That long preserv'd Virginity:
And your quaint Honour turn to dust;
And into ashes all my Lust.
The Grave's a fine and private place,
But none I think do there embrace.
Now therefore, while the youthful hew
Sits on thy skin like morning dew,

And while thy willing Soul transpires
At every pore with instant Fires,
Now let us sport us while we may;
And now, like am'rous birds of prey,
Rather at once our Time devour,
Than languish in his slow-chapt pow'r.
Let us roll all our Strength, and all
Our sweetness, up into one Ball:
And tear our Pleasures with rough strife,
Thorough the Iron gates of Life.
Thus, though we cannot make our Sun
Stand still, yet we will make him run.

THE DEFINITION OF LOVE

My Love is of a birth as rare
As 'tis for object strange and high:
It was begotten by despair
Upon Impossibility.

Magnanimous Despair alone
Could show me so divine a thing,
Where feeble Hope could ne'r have flown
But vainly flapt its Tinsel Wing.

And yet I quickly might arrive
Where my extended Soul is fixt,
But Fate does Iron wedges drive,
And alwaies crouds it self betwixt.

For Fate with jealous Eye does see
Two perfect Loves; nor lets them close:
Their union would her ruine be,
And her Tyrannick pow'r depose.

And therefore her Decrees of Steel
Us as the distant Poles have plac'd,
(Though Loves whole World on us doth wheel)
Not by themselves to be embrac'd.

Unless the giddy Heaven fall,
And Earth some new Convulsion tear;
And, us to joyn, the World should all
Be cramp'd into a *Planisphere.*

As Lines so Loves *oblique* may well
Themselves in every Angle greet:
But ours so truly *Paralel,*
Though infinite can never meet.

Therefore the Love which us doth bind,
But Fate so enviously debarrs,
Is the conjunction of the Mind,
And Opposition of the Stars.

THE GARDEN

How vainly men themselves amaze
To win the Palm, the Oke, or Bayes;
And their uncessant Labours see
Crown'd from some single Herb or Tree,
Whose short and narrow verged Shade
Does prudently their Toyles upbraid;
While all Flow'rs and all Trees do close
To wave the Garlands of repose.

Fair quiet, have I found thee here,
And Innocence thy Sister dear!
Mistaken long, I sought you then
In busie Companies of Men.
Your sacred Plants, if here below,
Only among the Plants will grow.
Society is all but rude,
To this delicious Solitude.

No white nor red was ever seen
So am'rous as this lovely green.
Fond Lovers, cruel as their Flame,
Cut in these Trees their Mistress name.
Little, Alas, they know, or heed,
How far these Beauties Hers exceed!
Fair Trees! where s'eer your barkes I wound,
No Name shall but your own be found.

When we have run our Passions heat,
Love hither makes his best retreat.
The *Gods*, that mortal Beauty chase,
Still in a Tree did end their race.
Apollo hunted *Daphne* so,
Only that She might Laurel grow.
And *Pan* did after *Syrinx* speed,
Not as a Nymph, but for a Reed.

What wond'rous Life in this I lead!
Ripe Apples drop about my head;
The Luscious Clusters of the Vine
Upon my Mouth do crush their Wine;
The Nectaren, and curious Peach,
Into my hands themselves do reach;
Stumbling on Melons, as I pass,
Insnar'd with Flow'rs, I fall on Grass.

Mean while the Mind, from Pleasure less,
Withdraws into its happiness:
The Mind, that Ocean where each kind
Does streight its own resemblance find;
Yet it creates, transcending these,
Far other Worlds, and other Seas;
Annihilating all that's made
To a green Thought in a green Shade.

Here at the Fountains sliding foot,
Or at some Fruit-trees mossy root,
Casting the Bodies Vest aside,
My Soul into the boughs does glide:
There like a Bird it sits, and sings,
Then whets, and combs its silver Wings;
And, till prepar'd for longer flight,
Waves in its Plumes the various Light.

Such was that happy Garden-state,
While Man there walk'd without a Mate:
After a Place so pure, and sweet,
What other Help could yet be meet!
But 'twas beyond a Mortal's share
To wander solitary there:

Two Paradises 'twere in one
To live in Paradise alone.

How well the skilful Gardner drew
Of flow'rs and herbes this Dial new;
Where from above the milder Sun
Does through a fragrant Zodiack run;
And, as it works, th'industrious Bee
Computes its time as well as we.
How could such sweet and wholsome Hours
Be reckon'd but with herbs and flow'rs!

[THE KINGFISHER]

So when the Shadows laid asleep
From underneath these Banks do creep,
And on the River as it flows
With *Eben Shuts* begin to close;
The modest *Halcyon* comes in sight,
Flying betwixt the Day and Night;
And such an horror calm and dumb,
Admiring Nature does benum.

The viscous Air, wheres'ere She fly,
Follows and sucks her Azure dy;
The gellying Stream compacts below,
If it might fix her shadow so;
The stupid Fishes hang, as plain
As *Flies* in *Chrystal* overt'ane;
And Men the silent *Scene* assist,
Charm'd with the *Saphir-winged Mist.*

D'AVENANT

from GONDIBERT

By what bold passion am I rudely led,
  Like Fame's too curious and officious Spie,
Where I these Rolls in her dark Closet read,
  Where Worthies wrapp'd in Time's disguises lie?

Why should we now their shady Curtains draw,
Who by a wise retirement hence are freed,
And gone to Lands exempt from Nature's Law,
Where Love no more can mourn, nor valor bleed?

Why to this stormy world from their long rest,
Are these recall'd to be again displeas'd,
Where during Nature's reign we are opprest,
Till we by Death's high priviledge are eas'd?

Is it to boast that Verse has Chymick pow'r,
And that its rage (which is productive heat)
Can these revive, as Chymists raise a Flow'r,
Whose scatter'd parts their Glass presents compleat?

Though in these Worthies gone, valor and love
Did chastly as in sacred Temples meet,
Such reviv'd Patterns us no more improve,
Than Flow'rs so rais'd by Chymists make us sweet,

Yet when the souls disease we desp'rate finde,
Poets the old renown'd Physitians are,
Who for the sickly habits of the mind,
Examples as the ancient cure prepare.

And bravely then Physitians honor gain,
When to the World diseases cureless seem,
And they (in Science valiant) ne'er refrain
Art's war with Nature, till they life redeem.

SONG

The Lark now leaves his watry Nest
And climbing, shakes his dewy Wings;
He takes this Window for the East;
And to implore your Light, he Sings,
Awake, awake, the Morn will never rise,
Till she can dress her Beauty at your Eyes.

The Merchant bowes unto the Seamans Star,
The Ploughman from the Sun his Season takes;
But still the Lover wonders what they are,
Who look for day before his Mistress wakes.
Awake, awake, break through your Vailes of Lawne!
Then draw your Curtains, and begin the Dawne.

TO THE QUEEN, ENTERTAIN'D AT NIGHT BY THE COUNTESS OF ANGLESEY

FAIRE as unshaded Light, or as the Day
In its first birth, when all the Year was *May*;
Sweet, as the Altars smoke, or as the new
Unfolded Bud, swell'd by the early dew;
Smooth, as the face of waters first appear'd,
Ere Tides began to strive, or Winds were heard:
Kind as the willing Saints, and calmer farre,
Than in their sleeps forgiven Hermits are:
You that are more, than our discreeter feare
Dares praise, with such full Art, what make you here?
Here, where the summer is so little seen,
That leaves (her cheapest wealth) scarce reach at green,
You come, as if the silver planet were
Misled a while from her much injur'd Sphere,
And t'ease the travailes of her beames to night,
In this small Lanthorn would contract her light.

THE PHILOSOPHER AND THE LOVER: TO A MISTRESS DYING

Lover

YOUR Beauty, ripe, and calm, and fresh
As Eastern Summers are,
Must now, forsaking Time and Flesh,
Add light to some small star.

Philosopher

Whilst she yet lives, were Stars decay'd,
Their light by hers, relief might find:
But Death will lead her to a shade
Where Love is cold, and Beauty blinde.

Lover

Lovers (whose Priests all Poets are)
Think ev'ry Mistress, when she dies,
Is chang'd at least into a Starr:
And who dares doubt the Poets wise?

Philosopher

But ask not Bodies doom'd to die,
  To what abode they go;
Since Knowledge is but sorrows spy,
  It is not safe to know.

MILTON

[ON HIS 24TH BIRTHDAY]

HOW soon hath Time the suttle theef of youth,
  Stoln on his wing my three and twentith yeer!
  My hasting dayes flie on with full career,
  But my late spring no bud or blossom shew'th.
Perhaps my semblance might deceive the truth,
  That I to manhood am arriv'd so near,
  And inward ripenes doth much less appear,
  That som more timely-happy spirits indu'th.
Yet be it less or more, or soon or slow,
  It shall be still in strictest measure eev'n,
  To that same lot, however mean, or high,
Toward which Time leads me, and the will of Heav'n;
  All is, if I have grace to use it so,
  As ever in my great task-Masters eye.

LYCIDAS

In this Monody the Author bewails a learned Friend [Edward King], unfortunatly drown'd in his passage from Chester *on the* Irish *Seas,* 1637. *And by occasion foretels the ruine of our corrupted Clergy then in their height.*

YET once more, O ye Laurels, and once more
Ye Myrtles brown, with Ivy never-sear,
I com to pluck your Berries harsh and crude,
And with forc'd fingers rude,
Shatter your leaves before the mellowing year.
Bitter constraint, and sad occasion dear,

Compels me to disturb your season due:
For *Lycidas* is dead, dead ere his prime
Young *Lycidas*, and hath not left his peer:
Who would not sing for *Lycidas*? he well knew
Himself to sing, and build the lofty rhyme.
He must not flote upon his watry bear
Unwept, and welter to the parching wind,
Without the meed of som melodious tear.
  Begin then, Sisters of the sacred well,
That from beneath the seat of *Jove* doth spring,
Begin, and somwhat loudly sweep the string.
Hence with denial vain, and coy excuse,
So may some gentle Muse
With lucky words favour my destin'd Urn,
And as he passes turn,
And bid fair peace be to my sable shrowd.
For we were nurst upon the self-same hill,
Fed the same flock, by fountain, shade, and rill.
  Together both, ere the high Lawns appear'd
Under the opening eye-lids of the morn,
We drove a field, and both together heard
What time the Gray-fly winds her sultry horn,
Batt'ning our flocks with the fresh dews of night,
Oft till the Star that rose, at Ev'ning, bright
Toward Heav'ns descent had slop'd his westering wheel.
Mean while the Rural ditties were not mute,
Temper'd to th'Oaten Flute,
Rough *Satyrs* danc'd, and *Fauns* with clov'n heel,
From the glad sound would not be absent long,
And old *Damœtas* lov'd to hear our song.
  But O the heavy change, now thou art gon,
Now thou art gon, and never must return!
Thee Shepherd, thee the Woods, and desert Caves,
With wilde Thyme and the gadding Vine o'regrown,
And all their echoes mourn.
The Willows, and the Hazle Copses green,
Shall now no more be seen,
Fanning their joyous Leaves to thy soft layes.
As killing as the Canker to the Rose,
Or Taint-worm to the weanling Herds that graze,
Or Frost to Flowers, that their gay wardrop wear,

Milton

When first the White-thorn blows;
Such, *Lycidas*, thy loss to Shepherds ear.
Where were ye Nymphs when the remorseless deep
Clos'd o're the head of your lov'd *Lycidas*?
For neither were ye playing on the steep,
Where your old *Bards*, the famous *Druids* ly,
Nor on the shaggy top of *Mona* high,
Nor yet where *Deva* spreads her wisard stream:
Ay me, I fondly dream!
Had ye bin there ... for what could that have don?
What could the Muse her self that *Orpheus* bore,
The Muse her self, for her inchanting son
Whom Universal nature did lament,
When by the rout that made the hideous roar,
His goary visage down the stream was sent,
Down the swift *Hebrus* to the *Lesbian* shore.
Alas! What boots it with uncessant care
To tend the homely slighted Shepherds trade,
And strictly meditate the thankles Muse,
Were it not better don as others use,
To sport with *Amaryllis* in the shade,
Or with* the tangles of *Neæra's* hair?
Fame is the spur that the clear spirit doth raise
(That last infirmity of Noble mind)
To scorn delights, and live laborious dayes;
But the fair Guerdon when we hope to find,
And think to burst out into sudden blaze,
Comes the blind *Fury* with th' abhorred shears,
And slits the thin-spun life. But not the praise,
Phœbus repli'd, and touch'd my trembling ears;
Fame is no plant that grows on mortal soil,
Nor in the glistering foil
Set off to th'world, nor in broad rumour lies,

* Milton's MS reads: '... wth Amaryllis ... | Or with the tangles' (a marginal substitution for 'Hid in the tangles', which Milton deleted). It is difficult to believe that he intended a syllepsis here (i.e. one verb – 'to sport' – governing two activities) – an uncharacteristically weak construction. It may be suggested that the second (unabbreviated) 'with' is not, like the first (abbreviated) 'w[th]', a preposition, but the infinitive of the verb 'withe' (the spelling 'with' was also used in the seventeenth century) meaning 'to plait'.

But lives and spreds aloft by those pure eyes, *Milton*
And perfet witnes of all-judging *Jove*;
As he pronounces lastly on each deed,
Of so much fame in Heav'n expect thy meed.
O Fountain *Arethuse*, and thou honour'd floud,
Smooth-sliding Mincius, crown'd with vocall reeds,
That strain I heard was of a higher mood:
But now my Oate proceeds,
And listens to the Herald of the Sea
That came in *Neptune's* plea,
He ask'd the Waves, and ask'd the Fellon Winds,
What hard mishap hath doom'd this gentle swain?
And question'd every gust of rugged wings
That blows from off each beaked Promontory;
They knew not of his story,
And sage *Hippotades* their answer brings,
That not a blast was from his dungeon stray'd,
The Ayr was calm, and on the level brine,
Sleek *Panope* with all her sisters play'd.
It was that fatall and perfidious Bark
Built in th'eclipse, and rigg'd with curses dark,
That sunk so low that sacred head of thine.
Next *Camus*, reverend Sire, went footing slow,
His Mantle hairy, and his Bonnet sedge,
Inwrought with figures dim, and on the edge
Like to that sanguine flower inscrib'd with woe.
Ah! Who hath reft (quoth he) my dearest pledge?
Last came, and last did go,
The Pilot of the *Galilean* lake,
Two massy Keyes he bore of metals twain,
(The Golden opes, the Iron shuts amain)
He shook his Miter'd locks, and stern bespake,
How well could I have spar'd for thee young swain,
Anow of such as for their bellies sake,
Creep and intrude, and climb into the fold?
Of other care they little reck'ning make,
Than how to scramble at the shearers feast,
And shove away the worthy bidden guest;
Blind mouthes! that scarce themselves know how to hold
A Sheep-hook, or have learn'd ought els the least
That to the faithfull Herdmans art belongs!

Milton

What recks it them? What need they? They are sped;
And when they list, their lean and flashy songs
Grate on their scrannel Pipes of wretched straw,
The hungry Sheep look up, and are not fed,
But swoln with wind, and the rank mist they draw,
Rot inwardly, and foul contagion spread:
Besides what the grim Woolf with privy paw
Daily devours apace, and nothing sed,
But that two-handed engine at the door,
Stands ready to smite once, and smite no more.
  Return *Alpheus*, the dread voice is past,
That shrunk thy streams; Return *Sicilian* Muse,
And call the Vales, and bid them hither cast
Their Bels, and Flourets of a thousand hues.
Ye valleys low where the milde whispers use,
Of shades and wanton winds, and gushing brooks,
On whose fresh lap the swart Star sparely looks,
Throw hither all your quaint enameld eyes,
That on the green terf suck the honied showres,
And purple all the ground with vernal flowres.
Bring the rathe Primrose that forsaken dies,
The tufted Crow-toe, and pale Gessamine,
The white Pink, and the Pansie freakt with jeat,
The glowing Violet.
The Musk-rose, and the well-attir'd Woodbine,
With Cowslips wan that hang the pensive hed,
And every flower that sad embroidery wears:
Bid *Amarantus* all his beauty shed,
And Daffadillies fill their cups with tears,
To strew the Laureat Herse where *Lycid* lies.
For so to interpose a little ease,
Let our frail thoughts dally with false surmise.
Ay me! Whilst thee the shores, and sounding Seas
Wash far away, where ere thy bones are hurld,
Whether beyond the stormy *Hebrides*,
Where thou perhaps under the whelming tide
Visit'st the bottom of the monstrous world;
Or whether thou to our moist vows deny'd,
Sleep'st by the fable of *Bellerus* old,
Where the great vision of the guarded Mount
Looks toward *Namancos* and *Bayona's* hold;

Look homeward Angel now, and melt with ruth,
And, O ye *Dolphins*, waft the haples youth.
Weep no more, woful Shepherds weep no more,
For *Lycidas* your sorrow is not dead,
Sunk though he be beneath the watry floar,
So sinks the day-star in the Ocean bed,
And yet anon repairs his drooping head,
And tricks his beams, and with new spangled Ore,
Flames in the forehead of the morning sky:
So *Lycidas* sunk low, but mounted high,
Through the dear might of him that walk'd the waves;
Where other groves, and other streams along,
With *Nectar* pure his oozy Locks he laves,
And hears the unexpressive nuptiall Song,
In the blest Kingdoms meek of joy and love.
There entertain him all the Saints above,
In solemn troops, and sweet Societies
That sing, and singing in their glory move,
And wipe the tears for ever from his eyes.
Now *Lycidas* the Shepherds weep no more;
Henceforth thou art the Genius of the shore,
In thy large recompense, and shalt be good
To all that wander in that perilous flood.
Thus sang the uncouth Swain to th'Okes and rills,
While the still morn went out with Sandals gray,
He touch'd the tender stops of various Quills,
With eager thought warbling his *Dorick* lay:
And now the Sun had stretch'd out all the hills,
And now was dropt into the Western bay;
At last he rose, and twitch'd his Mantle blew:
To morrow to fresh Woods, and Pastures new.

[ON HIS BLINDNESS]

WHEN I consider how my light is spent,
Ere half my days, in this dark world and wide,
And that one Talent which is death to hide,
Lodg'd with me useless, though my Soul more bent
To serve therewith my Maker, and present
My true account, least he returning chide,

Doth God exact day-labour, light deny'd,
I fondly ask; But patience to prevent
That murmur, soon replies, God doth not need
Either man's work or his own gifts, who best
Bear his milde yoak, they serve him best, his State
Is Kingly. Thousands at his bidding speed
And post o're Land and Ocean without rest:
They also serve who only stand and waite.

[KATHERINE MILTON: DIED MDCLVIII]

METHOUGHT I saw my late espoused Saint
Brought to me like *Alcestis* from the grave,
Whom *Joves* great Son to her glad Husband gave,
Rescu'd from death by force though pale and faint.
Mine as whom washt from spot of child-bed taint,
Purification in the old Law did save,
And such, as yet once more I trust to have
Full sight of her in Heaven without restraint,
Came vested all in white, pure as her mind:
Her face was vail'd, yet to my fancied sight,
Love, sweetness, goodness, in her person shin'd
So clear, as in no face with more delight.
But O as to embrace me she enclin'd,
I wak'd, she fled, and day brought back my night.

from PARADISE LOST

[INVOCATION]

OF Mans First Disobedience, and the Fruit
Of that Forbidd'n Tree, whose mortal tast
Brought Death into the World, and all our woe,
With loss of *Eden*, till one greater Man
Restore us, and regain the blissful Seat,
Sing Heav'nly Muse, that on the secret top
Of *Oreb*, or of *Sinai*, didst inspire
That Shepherd, who first taught the chosen Seed,
In the Beginning how the Heav'ns and Earth

Rose out of *Chaos*: or if *Sion* Hill
Delight thee more, and *Siloa's* Brook that flow'd
Fast by the Oracle of God; I thence
Invoke thy aid to my adventrous Song,
That with no middle flight intends to soar
Above th'*Aonian* Mount; while it persues
Things unattempted yet in Prose or Rime.
And chiefly Thou O Spirit, that dost preferr
Before all Temples th'upright heart and pure,
Instruct me, for Thou know'st; Thou from the first
Wast present, and with mighty wings outspred
Dove-like satst brooding on the vast Abyss
And mad'st it pregnant: What in mee is dark
Illumin, what is low raise and support;
That to the highth of this great Argument
I may assert Eternal Providence,
And justifie the wayes of God to men.

[THE FALLEN ANGELS]

Him the Almighty Power
Hurld headlong flaming from th'Ethereal Skie
With hideous ruin and combustion down
To bottomless perdition, there to dwell
In Adamantin Chains and penal Fire,
Who durst defie th'Omnipotent to Arms.
Nine times the Space that measures Day and Night
To mortal men, hee with his horrid crew
Lay vanquisht, rowling in the fiery Gulfe
Confounded though immortal: But his doom
Reserv'd him to more wrauth; for now the thought
Both of lost happiness and lasting pain
Torments him; round he throws his baleful eyes
That witnessd huge affliction and dismay
Mixt with obdurat pride and stedfast hate:
At once as farr as Angels kenn he views
The dismal Situation waste and wilde:
A Dungeon horrible, on all sides round
As one great Furnace flam'd, yet from those flames
No light, but rather darkness visible

Serv'd onely to discover sights of woe,
Regions of sorrow, doleful shades, where peace
And rest can never dwell, hope never comes
That comes to all; but torture without end
Still urges, and a fiery Deluge, fed
With ever-burning Sulfur unconsum'd:
Such place Eternal Justice had prepar'd
For these rebellious, here thir Pris'n ordaind
In utter darkness, and thir portion set
As farr remov'd from God and light of Heav'n
As from the Center thrice to th'utmost Pole.

[SATAN'S ADJURATION]

What though the field be lost?
All is not lost; the unconquerable Will,
And study of revenge, immortal hate,
And courage never to submit or yeild:
And what is else not to be overcome?
That Glory never shall his wrauth or might
Extort from mee. To bow and sue for grace
With suppliant knee, and deifie his power
Who from the terrour of this Arm so late
Doubted his Empire; that were low indeed,
That were an ignominy and shame beneath
This downfall; since by Fate the strength of Gods
And this Empyreal substance cannot fail,
Since through experience of this great event
In Arms not worse, in foresight much advanc't,
We may with more successful hope resolve
To wage by force or guile eternal Warr,
Irreconcileable to our grand Foe,
Who now triumphs, and in th'excess of joy
Sole reigning holds the Tyranny of Heav'n.

[THE PLACE OF THE DAMNED]

Farr off from these a slow and silent stream,
Lethe the River of Oblivion roules
Her watrie Labyrinth, whereof who drinks,

Forthwith his former state and being forgets,
Forgets both joy and grief, pleasure and pain.
Beyond this flood a frozen Continent
Lies dark and wilde, beat with perpetual storms
Of Whirlwind and dire Hail, which on firm land
Thaws not, but gathers heap, and ruin seems
Of ancient pile; all else deep snow and ice,
A gulf profound as that *Serbonian* Bog
Betwixt *Damiata* and Mount *Casius* old,
Where Armies whole have sunk: the parching Air
Burns frore, and cold performs th'effect of Fire.
Thither by harpy-footed Furies haild,
At certain revolutions all the damnd
Are brought; and feel by turns the bitter change
Of fierce extreams, extreams by change more fierce,
From Beds of raging Fire to starve in Ice
Thir soft Ethereal warmth, and there to pine
Immovable, infixt, and frozen round,
Periods of time, thence hurried back to fire.

[HYMN TO LIGHT]

HAIL holy Light, ofspring of Heav'n first-born,
Or of th'Eternal Coeternal beam
May I express thee unblam'd? since God is Light,
And never but in unapproached Light
Dwelt from Eternitie, dwelt then in thee,
Bright effluence of bright essence increate.
Or hear'st thou rather pure Ethereal stream,
Whose Fountain who shall tell? before the Sun,
Before the Heav'ns thou wert, and at the voice
Of God, as with a Mantle didst invest
The rising world of waters dark and deep,
Won from the void and formless infinite.
Thee I re-visit now with bolder wing,
Escap't the *Stygian* Pool, though long detaind
In that obscure sojourn, while in my flight
Through utter and through middle darkness borne
With other notes than to th'*Orphean* Lyre
I sung of *Chaos* and *Eternal Night*,

Taught by that heav'nly Muse to venture down
The dark descent, and up to reascend,
Though hard and rare: thee I revisit safe,
And feel thy sovran vital Lamp; but thou
Revisit'st not these eyes, that rowle in vain
To find thy piercing ray, and find no dawn:
So thick a drop serene hath quencht thir Orbs,
Or dim suffusion veild. Yet not the more
Cease I to wander where the Muses haunt
Cleer Spring, or shadie Grove, or Sunnie Hill,
Smit with the love of sacred Song; but chief
Thee *Sion* and the flowrie Brooks beneath
That wash thy hallowd feet, and warbling flow,
Nightly I visit: nor somtimes forget
Those other two equald with me in Fate,
So were I equald with them in renown,
Blind *Thamyris* and blind *Mæonides*,
And *Tiresias* and *Phineus* Prophets old:
Then feed on thoughts, that voluntarie move
Harmonious numbers; as the wakeful Bird
Sings darkling, and in shadiest Covert hid
Tunes her nocturnal Note. Thus with the Year
Seasons return, but not to mee returns
Day, or the sweet approach of Ev'n or Morn,
Or sight of vernal bloom, or Summers Rose,
Or flocks, or herds, or human face divine;
But cloud in stead, and ever-during dark
Surrounds me, from the chearful waies of men
Cut off, and for the Book of knowledg fair
Presented with a Universal blanc
Of Natures works to mee expung'd and ras'd,
And wisdom at one entrance quite shut out.

[EDEN]

THUS was this place,
A happy rural seat of various view;
Groves whose rich Trees wept odorous Gumms and Balme,
Others whose fruit burnisht with Gold'n Rinde
Hung amiable, *Hesperian* Fables true,

If true, here onely, and of delicious taste:
Betwixt them Lawns, or level Downs, and Flocks
Grasing the tender herb, were interpos'd,
Or palmie hilloc, or the flourie lap
Of som irriguous Valley spred her store,
Flours of all hue, and without Thorn the Rose:
Another side, umbrageous Grots and Caves
Of coole recess, ore which the mantling Vine
Layes forth her purple Grape, and gently creeps
Luxuriant; mean while murmuring waters fall
Down the slope hills, disperst, or in a Lake,
That to the fringed Bank with Myrtle crownd,
Her crystal mirror holds, unite their streams.
The Birds thir quire apply; aires, vernal aires,
Breathing the smell of field and grove, attune
The trembling leaves, while Universal *Pan*
Knit with the *Graces* and the *Hours* in dance
Led on th'Eternal Spring.

[EVENING IN PARADISE]

Now came still Eevning on, and Twilight gray
Had in her sober Liverie all things clad;
Silence accompanied, for Beast and Bird,
They to their grassie Couch, these to thir Nests
Were slunk, all but the wakeful Nightingale;
Shee all night long her amorous descant sung;
Silence was pleas'd: now glowd the Firmament
With living Saphirs: *Hesperus* that led
The starrie Host, rode brightest, till the Moon
Rising in clouded Majestie, at length
Apparent Queen unvaild her peerless light,
And ore the dark her Silver Mantle threw.

[EVE TO ADAM]

With thee conversing I forget all time,
All seasons and thir change, all please alike.
Sweet is the breath of morn, her rising sweet,

With charm of earliest Birds; pleasant the Sun
When first on this delightful Land he spreads
His orient Beams, on herb, tree, fruit and flour,
Glistring with dew; fragrant the fertil earth
After soft showers; and sweet the coming on
Of grateful Eevning milde, then silent Night
With this her solemn Bird and this fair Moon,
And these the Gemms of Heav'n, her starrie train:
But neither breath of Morn when she ascends
With charm of earliest Birds, nor rising Sun
On this delightful land, nor herb, fruit, floure,
Glistring with dew, nor fragrance after showers,
Nor grateful Eevning mild, nor silent Night
With this her solemn Bird, nor walk by Moon,
Or glittering Starr-light without thee is sweet.

[LEAVE TAKING]

WHENCE thou returnst, and whither wentst, I know;
For God is also in sleep, and Dreams advise,
Which he hath sent propitious, some great good
Presaging, since with sorrow and hearts distress
Wearied I fell asleep: but now lead on;
In mee is no delay; with thee to goe,
Is to stay here; without thee here to stay,
Is to go hence unwilling; thou to mee
Art all things under Heav'n, all places thou,
Who for my wilful crime art banisht hence.
This furder consolation yet secure
I carry hence: though all by mee is lost,
Such favour I unworthie am voutsaft,
By mee the Promisd Seed shall all restore.
So spake our Mother *Eve*, and *Adam* heard
Well pleas'd, but answerd not; for now too nigh
Th'Arch-Angel stood, and from the other Hill
To thir fixt Station, all in bright array
The Cherubim descended; on the ground
Gliding meteorous, as Ev'ning Mist
Ris'n from a River ore the marish glides,
And gathers ground fast at the Labourers heel

Homeward returning. High in Front advanc't,
The brandisht Sword of God before them blaz'd
Fierce as a Comet; which with torrid heat,
And vapour as the *Libyan* Air adust,
Began to parch that temperat Clime; whereat
In either hand the hastning Angel caught
Our lingring Parents, and to th'Eastern Gate
Led them direct, and down the Cliff as fast
To the subjected Plaine; then disappeerd.
They looking back, all th'Eastern side beheld
Of Paradise, so late thir happie seat,
Wav'd over by that flaming Brand, the Gate
With dreadful Faces throngd and fierie Armes:
Som natural tears they dropd, but wip'd them soon;
The World was all before them, where to choose
Thir place of rest, and Providence thir guide:
They hand in hand with wandring steps and slow,
Through *Eden* took thir solitarie way.

from SAMSON AGONISTES

[EPILOGUE]

All is best, though we oft doubt,
What th'unsearchable dispose
Of highest wisdom brings about,
And ever best found in the close.
Oft he seems to hide his face,
But unexpectedly returns
And to his faithful Champion hath in place
Bore witness gloriously; whence *Gaza* mourns
And all that band them to resist
His uncontroulable intent;
His servants hee with new acquist
Of true experience from this great event
With peace and consolation hath dismist,
And calm of mind all passion spent.

BUTLER

from HUDIBRAS

[SIR HUDIBRAS'S RELIGION]

For his *Religion* it was fit
To match his Learning and his Wit:
'Twas *Presbyterian* true blew,
For he was of that stubborn Crew
Of Errant Saints, whom all men grant
To be the true Church *Militant*:
Such as do build their Faith upon
The holy Text of *Pike* and *Gun*;
Decide all Controversies by
Infallible *Artillery*;
And prove their Doctrine Orthodox
By Apostolic *Blows* and *Knocks*;
Call Fire and Sword and Desolation,
A *godly-thorough-Reformation*,
Which always must be carry'd on,
And still be doing, never done:
As if Religion were intended
For nothing else but to be mended.
A Sect, whose chief Devotion lies
In odd perverse Antipathies;
In falling out with that or this,
And finding somewhat still amiss:
More peevish, cross, and spleenatick,
Than Dog distract, or Monky sick.
That with more care keep Holy-day
The wrong, than others the right way:
Compound for Sins, they are inclin'd to,
By damning those they have no mind to;
Still so perverse and opposite,
As if they worshipp'd God for spight,
The self-same thing they will abhor
One way, and long another for.
Free-will they one way disavow,
Another, nothing else allow.
All Piety consists therein
In them, in other Men all Sin.

[SIR SIDROPHEL THE CONJUROR]

HE had been long t'wards *Mathematicks*
Opticks, *Philosophy*, and *Staticks*,
Magick, *Horoscopie*, *Astrology*,
And was *old Dog* at *Physiologie*;
But, as a *Dog* that turns the spit,
Bestirs himself, and plys his feet,
To climb the *Wheel*; but all in vain,
His own weight brings him down again;
And still he's in the self-same place
Where at his setting out he was.
So in the *Circle* of the *Arts*,
Did he advance his nat'ral Parts;
Till falling back still, for retreat,
He fell to *Juggle*, *Cant*, and *Cheat*;
For, as those *Fowls* that live in Water
Are never wet, he did but smatter;
What e're he labour'd to appear,
His understanding still was clear.
Yet none a deeper knowledge boasted,
Since old *Hodg* Bacon, and *Bob Grosted.*
Th'*Intelligible world* he knew,
And all, men dream on't, to be true:
That in this *World*, there's not a *Wart*,
That has not there a Counterpart;
Nor can there on the *face* of Ground
An Individual *Beard* be found,
That has not, in that Forrain *Nation*,
A fellow of the self-same fashion;
So *cut*, so color'd, and so *curl'd*,
As those are, in th'*Inferior World.*

[THE ART OF LOVE]

'TIS true, no Lover has that Pow'r,
T'enforce a desperate Amour,
As he that has two *Strings* t'his *Bow*
And burns for *Love*, and *Money* too:
For then he's Brave, and Resolute,

Disdains to render in his Suit,
H'as all his *Flames* and *Raptures* double,
And *Hangs* or *Drowns*, with half the trouble.
While those who sillily pursue
The simple downright way and true,
Make as unlucky Applications,
And steer, against the Stream, their passions:
Some forge their *Mistresses* of *Stars*,
And when the Ladyes prove averse
And more untoward to be won,
Than by *Caligula*, the *Moon*,
Cry out upon the *Stars*, for doing
Ill Offices, to cross their *Wooing*,
When only by themselves, they're hindred
For trusting *those they made her kindred*:
And still the Harsher, and Hide-bounder
The Damsels prove, become the Fonder.
For what Mad Lover ever dy'd,
To gain a soft, and gentle *Bride*?
Or for a Lady tender-hearted,
In *Purling Streams*, or *Hemp* departed?
Leap't headlong int' *Elizium*,
Through th'Windows of a *Dazeling Room*?
But for some cross Ill-natur'd Dame,
The Am'rous Fly burnt in his *flame*.

HERRICK

TO THE VIRGINS, TO MAKE MUCH OF TIME

GATHER ye Rose-buds while ye may,
  Old Time is still a flying:
And this same flower that smiles to day,
  To morrow will be dying.

The glorious Lamp of Heaven, the Sun,
  The higher he's a getting;
The sooner will his Race be run,
  And neerer he's to Setting.

That Age is best, which is the first,
  When Youth and Blood are warmer;
But being spent, the worse, and worst
  Times, still succeed the former.

Then be not coy, but use your time;
  And while ye may, goe marry:
For having lost but once your prime,
  You may for ever tarry.

DELIGHT IN DISORDER

A SWEET disorder in the dresse
Kindles in cloathes a wantonnesse:
A Lawne about the shoulders thrown
Into a fine distraction:
An erring Lace, which here and there
Enthralls the Crimson Stomacher:
A Cuffe neglectfull, and thereby
Ribbands to flow confusedly:
A winning wave (deserving Note)
In the tempestuous petticote:
A carelesse shooe-string, in whose tye
I see a wilde civility:
Doe more bewitch me, than when Art
Is too precise in every part.

TO DIANEME

SWEET, be not proud of those two eyes,
Which Star-like sparkle in their skies:
Nor be you proud, that you can see
All hearts your captives; yours, yet free:
Be you not proud of that rich haire,
Which wantons with the Love-sick aire:
When as that *Rubie*, which you weare,
Sunk from the tip of your soft eare,
Will last to be a precious Stone,
When all your world of Beautie's gone.

TO MEDDOWES

Ye have been fresh and green,
 Ye have been fill'd with flowers:
And ye the Walks have been
 Where Maids have spent their houres.

You have beheld, how they
 With *Wicker Arks* did come
To kisse, and beare away
 The richer Couslips home.

Y'ave heard them sweetly sing,
 And seen them in a Round:
Each Virgin, like a Spring,
 With Hony-succles crown'd.

But now, we see, none here,
 Whose silv'rie feet did tread,
And with dishevell'd Haire,
 Adorn'd this smoother Mead.

Like Unthrifts, having spent,
 Your stock, and needy grown,
Y'are left here to lament
 Your poore estates, alone.

TO DAFFADILLS

Faire Daffadills, we weep to see
 You haste away so soone:
As yet the early-rising Sun
 Has not attain'd his Noone.
  Stay, stay,
 Untill the hasting day
  Has run
 But to the Even-song;
And, having pray'd together, we
 Will goe with you along.

We have short time to stay, as you,
 We have as short a Spring;

As quick a growth to meet Decay,
As you, or any thing.
We die,
As your hours doe, and drie
Away,
Like to the Summers raine;
Or as the pearles of Mornings dew
Ne'r to be found againe.

HIS POETRIE HIS PILLAR

ONELY a little more
I have to write,
Then Ile give o're,
And bid the world Good-night.

'Tis but a flying minute,
That I must stay,
Or linger in it;
And then I must away.

O time that cut'st down all!
And scarce leav'st here
Memoriall
Of any men that were.

How many lye forgot
In Vaults beneath?
And piece-meale rot
Without a fame in death?

Behold this living stone,
I reare for me,
Ne'r to be thrown
Downe, envious Time by thee.

Pillars let some set up,
(If so they please)
Here is my hope,
And my *Pyramides*.

CAREW

THE SPRING

Now that the winter's gone, the earth hath lost
Her snow-white robes, and now no more the frost
Candies the grasse, or castes an ycie creame
Upon the silver Lake, or Chrystall streame:
But the warme Sunne thawes the benummed Earth,
And makes it tender, gives a sacred birth
To the dead Swallow; wakes in hollow tree
The drowzie Cuckow, and the Humble-Bee.
Now doe a quire of chirping Minstrels bring
In tryumph to the world, the youthfull Spring.
The Vallies, hills, and woods, in rich araye,
Welcome the comming of the long'd for May.
Now all things smile; onely my *Love* doth lowre:
Nor hath the scalding Noon-day-Sunne the power,
To melt that marble yce, which still doth hold
Her heart congeald, and makes her pittie cold.
The Oxe which lately did for shelter flie
Into the stall, doth now securely lie
In open fields; and love no more is made
By the fire side; but in the cooler shade
Amyntas now doth with his *Cloris* sleepe
Under a Sycamoure, and all things keepe
Time with the season, only shee doth carry
June in her eyes, in her heart *January*.

A SONG

Aske me no more where *Jove* bestowes,
When *June* is past, the fading rose:
For in your beauties orient deepe,
These Flowers as in their causes sleepe.

Aske me no more whither doe stray
The golden Atomes of the day:
For in pure love heaven did prepare
Those powders to inrich your haire.

Aske me no more whither doth hast
The Nightingale when May is past:
For in your sweet dividing throat
She winters, and keepes warme her note.

Aske me no more where those starres light,
That downewards fall in dead of night:
For in your eyes they sit, and there,
Fixed become as in their sphere.

Aske me no more if East or West,
The Phenix builds her spicy nest:
For unto you at last shee flies,
And in your fragrant bosome dyes.

SUCKLING

SONNET

Oh! for some honest Lovers ghost,
Some kind unbodied post
Sent from the shades below.
I strangely long to know
Whether the nobler Chaplets wear,
Those that their mistresse scorn did bear,
Or those that were us'd kindly.

For what-so-e're they tell us here
To make those sufferings clear
'Twill there I fear be found,
That to the being crown'd
T'have lov'd alone will not suffice,
Unlesse we also have been wise,
And have our Loves enjoy'd.

What posture can we think him in,
That here unlov'd agen
Departs, and's thither gone
Where each sits by his own?

Or how can that *Elizium* be
Where I my Mistresse still must see
Circled in others Armes?

For there the Judges all are just,
And *Sophonisba* must
Be his whom she held dear;
Not his who lov'd her here:
The sweet *Philoclea* since she dy'de
Lies by her *Pirocles* his side,
Not by *Amphialus*.

Some Bayes (perchance) or Myrtle bough
For difference crowns the brow
Of those kind souls that were
The noble Martyrs here;
And if that be the onely odds
(As who can tell) ye kinder Gods,
Give me the Woman here.

LOVING AND BELOVED

There never yet was honest man
That ever drove the trade of love;
It is impossible, nor can
Integrity our ends promove:
For Kings and Lovers are alike in this
That their chief art in reigne dissembling is.

Here we are lov'd, and there we love,
Good nature now and passion strive
Which of the two should be above,
And laws unto the other give.
So we false fire with art sometime discover,
And the true fire with the same art do cover.

What Rack can Fancy find so high?
Here we must Court, and here ingage,
Though in the other place we die.
O! 'tis a torture all, and cozenage;
And which the harder is I cannot tell,
To hide true love, or make false love look well.

Since it is thus, God of desire,
  Give me my honesty again,
And take thy brands back, and thy fire;
  I'me weary of the State I'me in:
Since (if the very best should now befal)
Loves Triumph, must be Honours Funeral.

LOVELACE

TO LUCASTA
GOING BEYOND THE SEAS

IF to be absent were to be
    Away from thee;
  Or that when I am gone,
  You or I were alone;
Then my *Lucasta* might I crave
Pity from blustring winde, or swallowing wave.

But I'le not sigh one blast or gale
    To swell my saile,
  Or pay a teare to swage
  The foaming blew-Gods rage;
For whether he will let me passe
Or no, I'm still as happy as I was.

Though Seas and Land betwixt us both,
    Our Faith and Troth,
  Like separated soules,
  All time and space controules:
Above the highest sphere wee meet
Unseene, unknowne, and greet as Angels greet.

So then we doe anticipate
    Our after-fate,
  And are alive i' th' skies,
  If thus our lips and eyes
Can speake like spirits unconfin'd
In Heav'n, their earthy bodies left behind.

TO LUCASTA

GOING TO THE WARRES

TELL me not (Sweet) I am unkinde,
That from the Nunnerie
Of thy chaste breast, and quiet minde,
To Warre and Armes I flie.

True; a new Mistresse now I chase,
The first Foe in the Field;
And with a stronger Faith imbrace
A Sword, a Horse, a Shield.

Yet this Inconstancy is such,
As you too shall adore;
I could not love thee (Deare) so much,
Lov'd I not Honour more.

THE GRASSE-HOPPER

TO MY NOBLE FRIEND, MR CHARLES COTTON

OH thou that swing'st upon the waving haire
Of some well-filled Oaten Beard,
Drunke ev'ry night with a Delicious teare
Dropt thee from Heav'n, where now th'art reard.

The Joyes of Earth and Ayre are thine intire,
That with thy feet and wings dost hop and flye;
And when thy Poppy workes thou dost retire
To thy Carv'd Acron-bed to lye.

Up with the Day, the Sun thou welcomst then,
Sportst in the guilt-plats of his Beames,
And all these merry dayes mak'st merry men,
Thy selfe, and Melancholy streames.

But ah the Sickle! Golden Eares are Cropt;
Ceres and *Bacchus* bid good night;
Sharpe frosty fingers all your Flowr's have topt,
And what sithes spar'd, Winds shave off quite.

Poore verdant foole! and now green Ice! thy Joys *Lovelace*
Large and as lasting, as thy Peirch of Grasse,
Bid us lay in 'gainst Winter, Raine, and poize
Their flouds, with an o'reflowing glasse.

Thou best of *Men* and *Friends*! we will create
A Genuine Summer in each others breast;
And spite of this cold Time and frosen Fate
Thaw us a warme seate to our rest.

Our sacred harthes shall burne eternally
As Vestall Flames, the North-wind, he
Shall strike his frost-stretch'd Winges, dissolve and flye
This *Ætna* in Epitome.

Dropping *December* shall come weeping in,
Bewayle th'usurping of his Raigne;
But when in show'rs of old Greeke we beginne,
Shall crie, he hath his Crowne againe!

Night as cleare *Hesper* shall our Tapers whip
From the light Casements where we play,
And the darke Hagge from her black mantle strip,
And sticke there everlasting Day.

Thus richer than untempted Kings are we,
That asking nothing, nothing need:
Though Lord of all what Seas imbrace; yet he
That wants himselfe, is poore indeed.

TO ALTHEA, FROM PRISON

WHEN Love with unconfined wings
Hovers within my Gates;
And my divine *Althea* brings
To whisper at the Grates:
When I lye tangled in her haire,
And fetterd to her eye;
The *Gods* that wanton in the Aire,
Know no such Liberty.

When flowing Cups run swiftly round
With no allaying *Thames*,
Our carelesse heads with Roses bound,
Our hearts with Loyall Flames;
When thirsty griefe in Wine we steepe,
When Healths and draughts go free,
Fishes that tipple in the Deepe,
Know no such Libertie.

When (like committed Linnets) I
With shriller throat shall sing
The sweetnes, Mercy, Majesty,
And glories of my King;
When I shall voyce aloud, how Good
He is, how Great should be;
Inlarged Winds that curle the Flood,
Know no such Liberty.

Stone Walls doe not a Prison make,
Nor I'ron bars a Cage;
Mindes innocent and quiet take
That for an Hermitage;
If I have freedome in my Love,
And in my soule am free;
Angels alone that sore above,
Injoy such Liberty.

STANLEY

LA BELLE CONFIDENTE

You earthly Souls that court a wanton flame,
Whose pale weak influence
Can rise no higher than the humble name
And narrow laws of sence,
Learn by our friendship to create
An immaterial fire,
Whose brightnesse Angels may admire,
But cannot emulate.

Sicknesse may fright the roses from her cheek,
Or make the Lilies fade,
But all the subtil wayes that death doth seek
Cannot my love invade:
Flames that are kindled by the eye,
Through time and age expire;
But ours that boast a reach far higher
Can nor decay, nor die.

For when we must resigne our vitall breath,
(Even in divorce delighted)
We by this friendship shall survive in death,
Still in the grave united.
Weak Love through fortune or distrust
In time forgets to burn,
But this pursues us to the Urn,
And marries eithers Dust.

HALL

THE CALL

ROMIRA, stay,
And run not thus like a young Roe away,
No enemie
Pursues thee (foolish girle) tis onely I,
I'le keep off harms,
If thou'l be pleas'd to garrison mine arms;
What dost thou fear
I'le turn a Traitour? may these Roses here
To palenesse shred,
And Lilies stand disguised in new Red,
If that I lay
A snare, wherein thou wouldst not gladly stay;
See see the Sunne
Does slowly to his azure Lodging run,
Come sit but here
And presently hee'l quit our Hemisphere,
So still among

Lovers, time is too short or else too long;
Here will we spin
Legends for them that have Love Martyrs been,
Here on this plain
Wee'l talk *Narcissus* to a flour again;
Come here, and chose
On which of these proud plats thou would repose,
Here maist thou shame
The rusty Violets, with the Crimson flame
Of either cheek,
And Primroses white as thy fingers seek,
Nay, thou maist prove
That mans most Noble Passion is to Love.

DENHAM

[THE THAMES]

THAMES, the most lov'd of all the Oceans sons,
By his old Sire to his embraces runs,
Hasting to pay his tribute to the Sea,
Like mortal life to meet Eternity.
Though with those streams he no resemblance hold,
Whose foam is Amber, and their Gravel Gold;
His genuine, and less guilty wealth t'explore,
Search not his bottom, but survey his shore;
Ore which he kindly spreads his spacious wing,
And hatches plenty for th'ensuing Spring.
Nor then destroys it with too fond a stay,
Like Mothers which their Infants overlay.
Nor with a sudden and impetuous wave,
Like profuse Kings, resumes the wealth he gave.
No unexpected inundations spoyl
The mowers hopes, nor mock the plowmans toyl:
But God-like his unwearied Bounty flows;
First loves to do, then loves the Good he does.
Nor are his Blessings to his banks confin'd,
But free, and common, as the Sea or Wind;

When he to boast, or to disperse his stores
Full of the tribute of his grateful shores,
Visits the world, and in his flying towers
Brings home to us, and makes both *Indies* ours;
Finds wealth where 'tis, bestows it where it wants
Cities in deserts, woods in Cities plants.
So that to us no thing, no place is strange,
While his fair bosom is the worlds exchange.
O could I flow like thee, and make thy stream
My great example, as it is my theme!
Though deep, yet clear, though gentle, yet not dull,
Strong without rage, without ore-flowing full.

WALLER

SONG

Goe lovely Rose,
Tell her that wastes her time and me,
That now she knowes,
When I resemble her to thee
How sweet and faire she seems to be.

Tell her that's young,
And shuns to have her Graces spy'd,
That hadst thou sprung
In Desarts, where no men abide,
Thou must have uncommended dy'd.

Small is the worth
Of Beauty from the light retir'd:
Bid her come forth,
Suffer her selfe to be desir'd,
And not blush so to be admir'd.

Then die, that she
The common fate of all things rare
May read in thee,
How small a part of time they share,
That are so wondrous sweet and fair.

THE SELFE BANISHED

It is not that I love you less
Than when before your feet I lay:
But to prevent the sad increase
Of hopeless love, I keep away.

In vain (alas) for everything
Which I have knowne belong to you,
Your Forme does to my Fancy bring,
And makes my old wounds bleed anew.

Who in the Spring from the new Sun,
Already has a Fever got,
Too late begins these shafts to shun,
Which Phoebus through his veines has shot,

Too late he would the pains assuage,
And to thick shadowes does retire;
About with him he beares the rage,
And in his tainted blood the Fire.

But vow'd I have, and never must
Your banish'd servant trouble you;
For if I breake, you may mistrust
The vow I made to love you too.

OF THE LAST VERSES IN THE BOOK

When we for Age could neither read nor write,
The Subject made us able to indite.
The Soul with Nobler Resolutions deckt,
The Body stooping, does Herself erect:
No Mortal Parts are requisit to raise
Her, that Unbody'd can her Maker praise.

The Seas are quiet, when the Winds give o're;
So calm are we, when Passions are no more:
For then we know how vain it was to boast
Of fleeting Things, so certain to be lost.
Clouds of Affection from our younger Eyes
Conceal that emptiness, which Age descries.

The Soul's dark Cottage, batter'd and decay'd,
Let's in new Light thrô chinks that Time has made.
Stronger by weakness, wiser Men become
As they draw near to their Eternal home:
Leaving the Old, both Worlds at once they view,
That stand upon the Threshold of the New.

COTTON

TO MY DEAR AND MOST WORTHY FRIEND, MR ISAAC WALTON

WHILST in this cold and blust'ring Clime,
  Where bleak winds howl, and Tempests roar,
We pass away the roughest time
  Has been of many years before;

Whilst from the most tempest'ous Nooks
  The chillest Blasts our peace invade,
And by great Rains our smallest Brooks
  Are almost navigable made;

Whilst all the ills are so improv'd
  Of this dead quarter of the year,
That even you, so much belov'd,
  We would not now wish with us here;

In this estate, I say, it is
  Some comfort to us to suppose,
That in a better Clime than this
  You our dear Friend have more repose;

And some delight to me the while,
  Though nature now does weep in Rain,
To think that I have seen her smile,
  And haply may I do again.

If the all-ruling Power please
  We live to see another *May*,
We'll recompence an Age of these
  Foul days in one fine fishing day:

We then shall have a day or two,
  Perhaps a week, wherein to try,
What the best Master's hand can doe
  With the most deadly killing Flie:

A day without too bright a Beam,
  A warm, but not a scorching Sun,
A southern gale to curl the Stream,
  And (Master) half our work is done.

There whilst behind some bush we wait
  The Scaly People to betray,
We'll prove it just with treach'rous Bait
  To make the preying Trout our prey;

And think our selves in such an hour
  Happier than those, though not so high,
Who, like Leviathans, devour
  Of meaner men the smaller Fry.

This (my best Friend) at my poor Home
  Shall be our Pastime and our Theme,
But then should you not deign to come
  You make all this a flatt'ring Dream.

LAURA SLEEPING

WINDS whisper gently whilst she sleeps,
  And fan her with your cooling wings;
Whilst she her drops of Beauty weeps,
  From pure, and yet unrivall'd Springs.

Glide over Beauties Field her Face,
  To kiss her Lip, and Cheek be bold,
But with a calm, and stealing pace;
  Neither too rude; nor yet too cold.

Play in her beams, and crisp her Hair,
  With such a gale, as wings soft *Love*
And with so sweet, so rich an Air,
  As breaths from the *Arabian* Grove.

A Breath as hush't as Lovers sigh;
  Or that unfolds the Morning door:
Sweet, as the Winds, that gently fly,
  To sweep the *Springs* enamell'd Floor.

Murmur soft *Musick* to her Dreams,
  That pure, and unpoluted run,
Like to the new-born Christal Streams,
  Under the bright enamour'd Sun.

But when she waking shall display
  Her light, retire within your bar,
Her Breath is life, her Eyes are day,
  And all Mankind her Creatures are.

TAYLOR

UPON A WASP CHILLED WITH COLD

The Bear that breaks the Northern blast
Did numb, Torpedo-like, a Wasp
Whose stiffend limbs encrampt, lay bathing
In Sol's warm breath and shine as saving,
Which with her hands she chafes and slams
Rubbing her Legs, Shanks, Thighs, and hands.
Her petty toes, and fingers ends
Nipt with this breath, she out extends
Unto the Sun, in greate desire
To warm her digits at that fire:
Doth hold her Temples in this state
Where pulse doth beate, and head doth ake:
Doth turn and stretch her body small,
Doth comb her velvet capitall
As if her little brain-pan were
A Volume of choice precepts cleare:
As if her sattin jacket hot
Contained Apothecaries shop
Of Natures recepts, that prevails
To remedy all her sad ailes,

As if her velvet helmet high
Did turret rationality.
She fans her wing up to the winde
As if her Pettycoate were lin'de
With reasons fleece, and hoises saile
And humming flies in thankfull gaile
Unto her dun curld palace Hall,
Her warm thanks offering all.

Lord, cleare my misted sight that I
May hence view thy Divinity,
Some sparkles whereof thou up dost hasp
Within this little downy Wasp,
In whose small Corporation wee
A school and a schoolmaster see:
Where we may learn, and easily finde
A nimble Spirit, bravely minde
Her worke in ev'ry limb: and lace
It up neate with a vitall grace,
Acting each part though ne'er so small,
Here of this fustian animall,
Till I enravisht climb into
The Godhead on this ladder doe:
Where all my pipes inspir'de upraise
An Heavenly musick, furr'd with praise.

DRYDEN

[THE FIRE OF LONDON]

NIGHT came, but without darkness or repose,
A dismal picture of the gen'ral doom:
Where Souls distracted when the Trumpet blows,
And half unready with their bodies come.

Those who have homes, when home they do repair,
To a last lodging call their wand'ring friends.
Their short uneasie sleeps are broke with care,
To look how near their own destruction tends.

Those who have none sit round where once it was,
  And with full eyes each wonted room require:
Haunting the yet warm ashes of the place,
  As murder'd men walk where they did expire.

Some stir up coals and watch the Vestal fire,
  Others in vain from sight of ruine run:
And, while through burning Lab'rinths they retire,
  With loathing eyes repeat what they would shun.

The most in fields, like herded beasts lie down;
  To dews obnoxious on the grassie floor:
And while their Babes in sleep their sorrows drown,
  Sad Parents watch the remnants of their store.

While by the motion of the flames they ghess
  What streets are burning now, & what are near:
An Infant, waking, to the paps would press,
  And meets, instead of milk, a falling tear.

from ABSALOM AND ACHITOPHEL

[THE EARL OF SHAFTESBURY]

Some had in Courts been Great, and thrown from thence,
Like Fiends, were harden'd in Impenitence.
Some, by their Monarch's fatal mercy grown,
From Pardon'd Rebels, Kinsmen to the Throne;
Were rais'd in Pow'r and publick Office high:
Strong Bands, if Bands ungrateful men coud tie.
Of these the false *Achitophel* was first:
A Name to all succeeding Ages curst.
For close Designs, and crooked Counsels fit;
Sagacious, Bold, and Turbulent of wit:
Restless, unfixt in Principles and Place;
In Pow'r unpleas'd, impatient of Disgrace.
A fiery Soul, which working out its way,
Fretted the Pigmy-Body to decay:
And o'r inform'd the Tenement of Clay.
A daring Pilot in extremity;
Pleas'd with the Danger, when the Waves went high

Dryden

He sought the Storms; but for a Calm unfit,
Would Steer too near the Sands, to boast his Wit.
Great Wits are sure to Madness near alli'd;
And thin Partitions do their Bounds divide:
Else, why should he, with Wealth and Honour blest,
Refuse his Age the needful Hours of Rest?
Punish a Body which he coud not please;
Bankrupt of Life, yet Prodigal of Ease?
And all to leave, what with his Toil he won,
To that unfeather'd, two-legg'd thing, a Son:
Got, while his Soul did huddled Notions trie;
And born a shapeless Lump, like Anarchy.
In friendship false, implacable in Hate:
Resolv'd to Ruine or to Rule the State.
To Compass this, the Triple Bond he broke;
The Pillars of the Publick safety shook:
And fitted *Israel* for a Foreign Yoke.
Then, seiz'd with Fear, yet still affecting Fame,
Usurp'd a Patriot's All-attoning Name.
So easie still it proves in Factious Times,
With publick Zeal to cancel private Crimes:
How safe is Treason, and how sacred ill,
Where none can sink against the Peoples Will:
Where Crouds can wink; and no offence be known,
Since in anothers guilt they find their own.
Yet, Fame deserv'd, no Enemy can grudge;
The Statesman we abhor, but praise the Judge.
In *Israels* Courts ne'r sat an *Abbethdin*
With more discerning Eyes, or Hands more clean:
Unbrib'd, unsought, the Wretched to redress;
Swift of Dispatch and easie of Access.
Oh, had he been content to serve the Crown,
With vertues onely proper to the Gown;
Or, had the rankness of the Soil been freed
From Cockle, that opprest the Noble Seed:
David, for him his tuneful Harp had strung,
And Heav'n had wanted one Immortal Song.
But wild Ambition loves to slide, not stand;
And Fortunes Ice prefers to Vertues Land.

[THE DUKE OF BUCKINGHAM]

A NUMEROUS Host of dreaming Saints succeed;
Of the true old Enthusiastick Breed:
'Gainst Form and Order they their Pow'r imploy;
Nothing to Build, and all things to Destroy.
But far more numerous was the Herd of such,
Who think too little, and who talk too much.
These, out of meer instinct, they knew not why,
Ador'd their Father's God, and Property:
And, by the same blind Benefit of Fate,
The Devil and the *Jebusite* did hate:
Born to be sav'd, even in their own despight;
Because they could not help believing right.
Such were the Tools; but a whole Hydra more
Remains, of sprouting heads too long, to score.
Some of their Chiefs were Princes of the Land:
In the first Rank of these did *Zimri* stand:
A man so various, that he seem'd to be
Not one, but all Mankind's Epitome.
Stiff in Opinions, always in the wrong;
Was Every thing by starts, and Nothing long:
But, in the course of one revolving Moon,
Was Chymist, Fidler, States-Man, and Buffoon:
Then all for Women, Painting, Rhiming, Drinking;
Besides ten thousand Freaks that dy'd in thinking.
Blest Madman, who coud every hour employ,
With something New to wish, or to enjoy.
Railing and praising were his usual Theams;
And both (to shew his Judgment) in Extreams:
So over Violent, or over Civil,
That every Man, with him, was God or Devil.
In squandering Wealth was his peculiar Art:
Nothing went unrewarded, but Desert.
Begger'd by Fools, whom still he found too late:
He had his Jest, and they had his Estate.
He laugh'd himself from Court; then sought Relief
By forming Parties, but could ne'r be Chief:
For, spight of him, the weight of Business fell
On *Absalom* and wise *Achitophel*:
Thus, wicked but in Will, of Means bereft,
He left not Faction, but of that was left.

A SONG FOR ST CECILIA'S DAY, 1687

FROM Harmony, from Heav'nly Harmony
This Universal Frame began.
When Nature underneath a heap
Of jarring Atoms lay,
And cou'd not heave her Head,
The tuneful Voice was heard from high,
Arise ye more than dead.
Then cold, and hot, and moist, and dry
In order to their stations leap,
And MUSICK's Pow'r obey.
From Harmony, from Heav'nly Harmony
This Universal Frame began:
From Harmony to Harmony
Through all the compass of the Notes it ran,
The Diapason closing full in Man.

What Passion cannot MUSICK raise and quell!
When *Jubal* struck the corded Shell,
His list'ning Brethren stood around
And wond'ring, on their Faces fell
To worship that Celestial Sound:
Less than a God they thought there cou'd not dwell
Within the hollow of that Shell
That spoke so sweetly and so well.
What Passion cannot MUSICK raise and quell!

The TRUMPETS loud Clangor
Excites us to Arms
With shrill Notes of Anger
And mortal Alarms.
The double double double beat
Of the thundring DRUM
Cries, heark the Foes come;
Charge, Charge, 'tis too late to retreat.

The soft complaining FLUTE
In dying Notes discovers
The Woes of hopeless Lovers,
Whose Dirge is whisper'd by the Warbling LUTE.

Sharp VIOLINS proclaim
Their jealous Pangs, and Desperation,
Fury, frantick Indignation,
Depth of Pains and height of Passion,
  For the fair, disdainful Dame.

But oh! what Art can teach
  What human Voice can reach
The sacred ORGAN's praise?
Notes inspiring holy Love,
Notes that wing their Heav'nly ways
    To mend the Choires above.

Orpheus cou'd lead the savage race;
And Trees unrooted left their place;
  Sequacious of the *Lyre*:
But bright *CECILIA* rais'd the wonder high'r;
  When to her ORGAN, vocal breath was giv'n,
An Angel heard, and straight appear'd
  Mistaking Earth for Heav'n.

Grand CHORUS

As from the pow'r of Sacred Lays
  The Spheres began to move,
And sung the great Creator's praise
  To all the bless'd above;
So when the last and dreadful hour
This crumbling Pageant shall devour,
The TRUMPET *shall be heard on high,*
The Dead shall live, the Living die,
And MUSICK *shall untune the Sky.*

TO THE UNIVERSITY OF OXFORD, 1674

EPILOGUE

OFT has our Poet wisht, this happy Seat
Might prove his fading Muses last retreat:
I wonder'd at his wish, but now I find
He sought for quiet, and content of mind;
Which noisfull Towns, and Courts can never know,
And onely in the shades like Laurels grow.

Youth, e'er it sees the World, here studies rest,
And Age returning thence concludes it best.
What wonder if we court that happiness
Yearly to share, which hourly you possess,
Teaching ev'n you, (while the vext World we show,)
Your Peace to value more, and better know?
'Tis all we can return for favours past,
Whose holy Memory shall ever last,
For Patronage from him whose care presides
O'er every noble Art, and every Science guides:
Bathurst, a name the learn'd with reverence know,
And scarcely more to his own *Virgil* owe.
Whose Age enjoys but what his Youth deserv'd,
To rule those Muses whom before he serv'd.
His Learning, and untainted Manners too
We find (*Athenians*) are deriv'd to you;
Such Ancient hospitality there rests
In yours, as dwelt in the first *Grecian* Breasts,
Whose kindness was Religion to their Guests.
Such Modesty did to our Sex appear,
As had there been no Laws, we need not fear,
Since each of you was our Protector here.
Converse so chast, and so strict Vertue shown,
As might *Apollo*, with the Muses own.
Till our return we must despair to find
Judges so just, so knowing, and so kind.

TO THE MEMORY OF MR OLDHAM

Farewel, too little and too lately known,
Whom I began to think and call my own;
For sure our Souls were near ally'd; and thine
Cast in the same Poetick mould with mine.
One common Note on either Lyre did strike,
And Knaves and Fools we both abhorr'd alike:
To the same Goal did both our Studies drive,
The last set out the soonest did arrive.
Thus *Nisus* fell upon the slippery place,
While his young Friend perform'd and won the Race.
O early ripe! to thy abundant store

What could advancing Age have added more?
It might (what Nature never gives the young)
Have taught the numbers of thy native Tongue.
But Satyr needs not those, and Wit will shine
Through the harsh cadence of a rugged line.
A noble Error, and but seldom made,
When Poets are by too much force betray'd.
Thy generous fruits, though gather'd ere their prime
Still shew'd a quickness; and maturing time
But mellows what we write to the dull sweets of Rime.
Once more, hail and farewel; farewel thou young,
But ah too short, *Marcellus* of our Tongue;
Thy Brows with Ivy, and with Laurels bound;
But Fate and gloomy Night encompass thee around.

SONGS FROM PLAYS

[*from* THE INDIAN EMPEROR]

AH fading joy, how quickly art thou past?
Yet we thy ruine haste:
As if the cares of Humane Life were few
We seek out new:
And follow Fate that does too fast pursue.

See how on every bough the Birds express
In the sweet notes their happiness.
They all enjoy, and nothing spare;
But on their Mother Nature lay their care:
Why then should Man, the Lord of all below
Such troubles chuse to know
As none of all his Subjects undergo?

Hark, hark, the Waters fall, fall, fall;
And with a Murmuring sound
Dash, dash, upon the ground,
To gentle slumbers call.

[*from* TYRANNICK LOVE]

AH how sweet it is to love,
Ah how gay is young desire!
And what pleasing pains we prove
When we first approach Loves fire!
  Pains of Love be sweeter far
  Than all other pleasures are.

Sighs which are from Lovers blown,
Do but gently heave the Heart;
Ev'n the tears they shed alone
Cure, like trickling Balm their smart.
  Lovers when they lose their breath,
  Bleed away in easie death.

Love and Time with reverence use,
Treat 'em like a parting friend:
Nor the golden gifts refuse
Which in youth sincere they send:
  For each year their price is more,
  And they less simple than before.

Love, like Spring-tides full and high,
Swells in every youthful vein:
But each Tide does less supply,
Till they quite shrink in again:
  If a flow in Age appear,
  'Tis but rain, and runs not clear.

[*from* AN EVENING'S LOVE]

AFTER the pangs of a desperate Lover,
When day and night I have sigh'd all in vain,
Ah what a pleasure it is to discover
In her eyes pity, who causes my pain!

When with unkindness our love at a stand is,
And both have punish'd our selves with the pain,
Ah what a pleasure the touch of her hand is,
Ah what a pleasure to press it again!

When the denyal comes fainter and fainter,
And her eyes give what her tongue does deny,
Ah what a trembling I feel when I venture,
Ah what a trembling does usher my joy!

When, with a Sigh, she accords me the blessing,
And her eyes twinkle 'twixt pleasure and pain;
Ah what a joy 'tis beyond all expressing,
Ah what a joy to hear, shall we again!

[*from* THE SPANISH FRYAR]

Farewell ungratefull Traytor,
  Farewell my perjur'd Swain
Let never injur'd Creature
  Believe a Man again.
The Pleasure of Possessing
Surpasses all Expressing,
But 'tis too short a Blessing,
  And Love too long a Pain.

'Tis easie to deceive us
  In pity of our Pain,
But when we love you leave us
  To rail at you in vain.
Before we have descry'd it
There is no Bliss beside it,
But she that once has try'd it
  Will never love again.

The Passion you pretended
  Was onely to obtain,
But when the Charm is ended
  The Charmer you disdain.
Your Love by ours we measure
Till we have lost our Treasure,
But Dying is a Pleasure,
  When Living is a Pain.

A SONG OF THE RIVER THAMES
[*from* ALBION & ALBANIUS]

Old Father Ocean calls my Tyde:
Come away, come away;
The Barks upon the Billows ride,
The Master will not stay;
The merry Boson from his side,
His Whistle takes to check and chide
The lingring Lads delay,
And all the Crew alowd has Cry'd,
Come away, come away.

See the God of Seas attends Thee,
Nymphs Divine, a Beauteous Train;
All the calmer Gales befriend Thee
In thy passage o're the Main:
Every Maid her Locks is binding,
Every *Triton's* Horn is winding,
Welcome to the watry Plain.

SEDLEY

SONG

Not *Celia*, that I juster am
  Or better than the rest,
For I would change each Hour like them,
  Were not my Heart at rest.

But I am ty'd to very thee,
  By every Thought I have,
Thy Face I only care to see,
  Thy Heart I only crave.

All that in Woman is ador'd,
  In thy dear Self I find,
For the whole Sex can but afford,
  The Handsome and the Kind.

LEIGH

SLEEPING ON HER COUCH

THUS lovely, *Sleep* did *first* appear,
  E're yet it was with *Death* ally'd;
When the first *fair one*, like *her* here,
  Lay down, and for a little *dy'd*.

E're *happy Souls* knew how to *dye*,
  And trod the *rougher Paths* to *Bliss*
Transported in an *Extasie*,
  They *breath'd out* such *smooth waies*, as this.

Her *Hand* bears gently up her *Head*,
  And like a *Pillow*, rais'd doth keep;
But *softer* than her *Couch* is spread,
  Though that be *softer* than her *Sleep*.

Alas! that death-like *Sleep*, or *Night*,
  Should power have to close those *Eyes*,
Vhich once vy'd with the *fairest Light*,
  Or what *gay Colours*, thence did rise.

! that lost *Beams*, thus long have shin'd,
'o them, with *Darkness* over-spread,
een, as *Day breaks*, to the *Blind*,
the *Sun rises*, to the *Dead*.

'un, in all his *Eastern Pride*,
never see a *Shape* so rare,
ht, within its *black Arms* hide
t Beauty, half so *fair*.

OCHESTER

AND LIFE. A SONG

st Life is mine no more,
ing hours are gone;
y Dreams giv'n o're,
s are kept in store,
y alone.

Why then should I seek farther
And still make Love a-new
When Change itself can giv
'Tis easie to be true.

SONG

Love still has som
From whence
No time his Sla
Nor give th

They are be
And in
They wi
Or a

One

S

Ah
T
Uns
Or
That S
Did
Nor Nig
A silen

R

LOVE

All my pa
The fly
Like transito
Whose Imag
By *Memo*

What ever is to come, is not,
 How can it then be mine?
The present *Moment's* all my *Lot*,
And that as fast as it is got,
 Phillis, is wholly thine.

Then talk not of inconstancy,
 False *Hearts*, and broken *Vows*,
If I by *Miracle* can be,
This live-long *Minute* true to thee,
 'Tis all that *Heav'n* allows.

A SONG

ABSENT from thee I languish still,
 Then ask me not, when I return?
The straying Fool 'twill plainly kill,
 To wish all Day, all Night to Mourn.

Dear; from thine Arms then let me flie,
 That my Fantastick mind may prove,
The Torments it deserves to try,
 That tears my fixt Heart from my Love.

When wearied with a world of Woe,
 To thy safe Bosom I retire
Where Love and Peace and Truth does flow,
 May I contented there expire.

Lest once more wandring from that Heav'n
 I fall on some base heart unblest;
Faithless to thee, False, unforgiv'n,
 And lose my Everlasting rest.

from *A SATYR AGAINST MANKIND*

WERE I (who to my cost already am
One of those strange prodigious Creatures *Man*.)
A Spirit free, to choose for my own share,
What Case of Flesh, and Blood, I pleas'd to weare,
I'd be a *Dog*, a *Monkey*, or a *Bear*.

Or any thing but that vain *Animal*,
Who is so proud of being rational.
The senses are too gross, and he'll contrive
A Sixth, to contradict the other Five;
And before certain instinct, will preferr
Reason, which Fifty times for one does err.
Reason, an *Ignis fatuus*, in the *Mind*,
Which leaving light of *Nature*, sense behind;
Pathless and dang'rous wandring ways it takes,
Through errors' Fenny-*Boggs*, and Thorny *Brakes*;
Whilst the misguided follower, climbs with pain,
Mountains of Whimseys, heap'd in his own *Brain*:
Stumbling from thought to thought, falls headlong down,
Into doubts boundless Sea, where like to drown,
Books bear him up awhile, and make him try,
To swim with Bladders of *Philosophy*;
In hopes still t'oretake th'escaping light,
The *Vapour* dances in his dazling sight,
Till spent, it leaves him to eternal Night.
Then Old Age, and experience, hand in hand,
Lead him to death, and make him understand,
After a search so painful, and so long,
That all his Life he has been in the wrong;

*

And 'tis this very reason I despise.
This supernatural gift, that makes a *Myte*,
Think he's the Image of the Infinite:
Comparing his short life, void of all rest,
To the *Eternal*, and the ever blest.
This busie, puzling, stirrer up of doubt,
That frames deep Mysteries, then finds 'em out;
Filling with Frantick Crowds of thinking *Fools*,
Those Reverend *Bedlams*, *Colledges*, and *Schools*,
Borne on whose Wings, each heavy *Sot* can pierce,
The limits of the boundless Universe.
So charming Oyntments, make an Old *Witch* flie,
And bear a Crippled Carcass through the Skie.
'Tis this exalted Pow'r, whose bus'ness lies,
In *Nonsense*, and impossibilities.
This made a Whimsical *Philosopher*,

Before the spacious *World*, his *Tub* prefer.
And we have modern *Cloyster Coxcombs*, who
Retire to think, cause they have naught to do.
But thoughts are giv'n for Actions government,
Where Action ceases, thought's impertinent:
Our *Sphere* of Action, is lifes happiness,
And he who thinks Beyond, thinks like an *Ass*.
Thus, whilst 'gainst false reas'ning I inveigh,
I own right *Reason*, which I wou'd obey:
That *Reason* that distinguishes by sense,
And gives us *Rules*, of good, and ill from thence:
That bounds desires, with a reforming Will,
To keep 'em more in vigour, not to kill.

*

Which is the basest *Creature*, *Man* or *Beast*?
Birds feed on *Birds*, *Beasts* on each other prey,
But Savage *Man* alone, does *Man* betray:
Prest by necessity, they Kill for Food,
Man undoes *Man*, to do himself no good.
With Teeth, & Claws, by Nature arm'd they hunt,
Natures allowance, to supply their want.
But *Man*, with smiles, embraces, Friendships, praise,
Unhumanely his Fellows life betrays;
With voluntary pains, works his distress,
Not through necessity, but wantonness.
For hunger, or for Love, they fight, or tear,
Whilst wretched *Man*, is still in Arms for fear;
For fear he armes, and is of Armes afraid,
By fear, to fear, successively betray'd;
Base fear, the source whence his best passion came,
His boasted Honor and his dear bought Fame.
That lust of Pow'r, to which He's such a *Slave*,
And for the which alone he dares be brave:
To which his various Projects are design'd,
Which makes him gen'rous, affable, and kind.
For which he takes such pains to be thought wise,
And screws his actions, in a forc'd disguise:
Leading a tedious life in Misery,
Under laborious, mean *Hypocrisie*.
Look to the bottom, of his vast design,

Wherein *Mans* Wisdom, Pow'r, and Glory joyn;
The good he'acts, the ill he does endure,
'Tis all for fear, to make himself secure.
Meerly for safety, after Fame we thirst,
For all Men wou'd be *Cowards* if they durst.
And honesty's against all common sense,
Men must be *Knaves*, 'tis in their own defence.
Mankind's dishonest, if you think it fair,
Amongst known *Cheats*, to play upon the square,
You'le be undone –
Nor can weak truth, your reputation save,
The *Knaves* will all agree to call you *Knave*.
Wrong'd shall he live, insulted o're, oppress,
Who dares be less a *Villain*, than the rest.
Thus Sir you see what humane Nature craves,
Most Men are *Cowards*, all Men shou'd be *Knaves*:
The diff'rence lyes (as far as I can see)
Not in the thing it self, but the degree;
And all the subject matter of debate,
Is only who's a *Knave*, of the first *Rate*?

PRIOR

A BETTER ANSWER

DEAR CLOE, how blubber'd is that pretty Face?
  Thy Cheek all on Fire, and Thy Hair all uncurl'd:
Pr'ythee quit this Caprice; and (as Old FALSTAF says)
  Let Us e'en talk a little like Folks of This World.

How canst Thou presume, Thou hast leave to destroy
  The Beauties, which VENUS but lent to Thy keeping?
Those Looks were design'd to inspire Love and Joy:
  More ord'nary Eyes may serve People for weeping.

To be vext at a Trifle or two that I writ,
  Your Judgment at once, and my Passion You wrong:
You take that for Fact, which will scarce be found Wit:
  Od's Life! must One swear to the Truth of a Song?

What I speak, my fair CLOE, and what I write, shews
  The Diff'rence there is betwixt Nature and Art:
I court others in Verse; but I love Thee in Prose:
  And They have my Whimsies; but Thou hast my Heart.

The God of us Verse-men (You know Child) the SUN,
  How after his Journeys He sets up his Rest:
If at Morning o'er Earth 'tis his Fancy to run;
  At Night he reclines on his THETIS's Breast.

So when I am weary'd with wand'ring all Day;
  To Thee my Delight in the Evening I come:
No Matter what Beauties I saw in my Way:
  They were but my Visits; but Thou art my Home.

The finish, Dear CLOE, this Pastoral War;
  And let us like HORACE and LYDIA agree:
For Thou art a Girl as much brighter than Her,
  As He was a Poet sublimer than Me.

A SIMILE

DEAR THOMAS, didst Thou never pop
Thy Head into a Tin-man's Shop?
There, THOMAS, didst Thou never see
('Tis but by way of Simile;)
A SQUIRREL spend his little Rage,
In jumping round a rowling Cage?
The Cage, as either Side turn'd up,
Striking a Ring of Bells a-top – ?

  Mov'd in the Orb; pleas'd with the Chimes;
The foolish Creature thinks he climbs:
But here or there, turn Wood or Wire,
He never gets two Inches higher.

  So fares it with those merry Blades,
That frisk it under PINDUS' Shades.
In noble Songs, and lofty Odes,
They tread on Stars, and talk with Gods.
Still Dancing in an airy Round:
Still pleas'd with their own Verses Sound.
Brought back, how fast soe'er they go:
Always aspiring; always low.

AN ENGLISH PADLOCK

Miss Danae, when Fair and Young
(As Horace has divinely sung)
Could not be kept from Jove's Embrace
By Doors of Steel, and Walls of Brass.
The Reason of the Thing is clear;
Would Jove the naked Truth aver:
Cupid was with Him of the Party;
And show'd himself sincere and hearty:
For, give That Whipster but his Errand;
He takes my Lord Chief Justice' Warrant:
Dauntless as Death away He walks;
Breaks the Doors open; snaps the Locks;
Searches the Parlour, Chamber, Study;
Nor stops, 'till He has Culprit's Body.

Since This has been Authentick Truth,
By Age deliver'd down to Youth;
Tell us, mistaken Husband, tell us,
Why so Mysterious, why so Jealous?
Does the Restraint, the Bolt, the Bar
Make Us less Curious, Her less Fair?
The Spy, which does this Treasure keep,
Does She ne'er say her Pray'rs, nor sleep?
Does She to no Excess incline?
Does She fly Musick, Mirth, and Wine?
Or have not Gold and Flatt'ry Pow'r,
To purchase One unguarded Hour?

Your Care does further yet extend:
That Spy is guarded by your Friend. –
But has This Friend nor Eye, nor Heart?
May He not feel the cruel Dart,
Which, soon or late, all Mortals feel?
May He not, with too tender Zeal,
Give the Fair Pris'ner Cause to see,
How much He wishes, She were free?
May He not craftily infer
The Rules of Friendship too severe,
Which chain Him to a hated Trust;
Which make Him Wretched, to be Just?

And may not She, this Darling She,
  Youthful and healthy, Flesh and Blood,
Easie with Him, ill us'd by Thee,
  Allow this Logick to be good?

  Sir, Will your Questions never end?
I trust to neither Spy nor Friend.
In short, I keep Her from the Sight
Of ev'ry Human Face. – She'll write. –
From Pen and Paper She's debarr'd. –
Has She a Bodkin and a Card?
She'll prick her Mind. – She will, You say:
But how shall She That Mind convey?
I keep Her in one Room: I lock it:
The Key (look here) is in this Pocket.
The Key-hole, is That left? Most certain.
She'll thrust her Letter thro' – Sir MARTIN.

  Dear angry Friend, what must be done?
Is there no Way? – There is but One.
Send Her abroad; and let Her see,
That all this mingled Mass, which She
Being forbidden longs to know,
Is a dull Farce, an empty Show,
Powder, and Pocket-Glass, and Beau;
A Staple of Romance and Lies,
False Tears, and real Perjuries:
Where Sighs and Looks are bought and sold;
And Love is made but to be told:
Where the fat Bawd, and lavish Heir
The Spoils of ruin'd Beauty share:
And Youth seduc'd from Friends and Fame,
Must give up Age to Want and Shame.
Let Her behold the Frantick Scene,
The Women wretched, false the Men:
And when, these certain Ills to shun,
She would to Thy Embraces run;
Receive Her with extended Arms:
Seem more delighted with her Charms:
Wait on Her to the Park and Play:
Put on good Humour; make Her gay:
Be to her Virtues very kind:

Be to her Faults a little blind:
Let all her Ways be unconfin'd:
And clap your PADLOCK – on her Mind.

ANNE WINCHILSEA

A NOCTURNAL REVERIE

IN such a *Night*, when every louder Wind
Is to its distant Cavern safe confin'd;
And only gentle *Zephyr* fans his Wings,
And lonely *Philomel*, still waking, sings;
Or from some Tree, fam'd for the *Owl's* delight,
She, hollowing clear, directs the Wand'rer right:
In such a *Night*, when passing Clouds give place,
Or thinly vail the Heav'ns mysterious Face;
When in some River, overhung with Green,
The waving Moon and trembling Leaves are seen;
When freshen'd Grass now bears it self upright,
And makes cool Banks to pleasing Rest invite,
Whence springs the *Woodbind*, and the *Bramble*-Rose,
And where the sleepy *Cowslip* shelter'd grows;
Whilst now a paler hue the *Foxglove* takes,
Yet checquers still with Red the dusky brakes:
When scatter'd *Glow-worms*, but in Twilight fine,
Shew trivial Beauties watch their Hour to shine;
Whilst *Salisb'ry* stands the Test of every Light,
In perfect Charms, and perfect Virtue bright:
When Odours, which declin'd repelling Day,
Thro' temp'rate Air uninterrupted stray;
When darken'd Groves their softest Shadows wear,
And falling Waters we distinctly hear;
When thro' the Gloom more venerable shows
Some ancient Fabrick, awful in Repose,
While Sunburnt Hills their swarthy Looks conceal,
And swelling Haycocks thicken up the Vale:
When the loos'd *Horse* now, as his Pasture leads,
Comes slowly grazing thro' th'adjoining Meads,
Whose stealing Pace, and lengthen'd Shade we fear,

Till torn up Forage in his Teeth we hear:
When nibbling *Sheep* at large pursue their Food,
And unmolested Kine rechew the Cud;
When *Curlews* cry beneath the Village-walls,
And to her straggling Brood the *Partridge* calls;
Their shortliv'd Jubilee the Creatures keep,
Which but endures, whilst Tyrant-*Man* do's sleep:
When a sedate Content the Spirit feels,
And no fierce Light disturbs, whilst it reveals;
But silent Musings urge the Mind to seek
Something, too high for Syllables to speak;
Till the free Soul to a compos'dness charm'd,
Finding the Elements of Rage disarm'd,
O'er all below a solemn Quiet grown,
Joys in th'inferiour World, and thinks it like her Own:
In such a *Night* let Me abroad remain,
Till Morning breaks, and All's confus'd again;
Our Cares, our Toils, our Clamours are renew'd,
Or Pleasures, seldom reach'd, again pursu'd.

CONGREVE

[SONG]

False though she be to me and Love,
I'll ne'er pursue Revenge;
For still the Charmer I approve,
Tho' I deplore her Change.

In Hours of Bliss we oft have met,
They could not always last;
And though the present I regret,
I'm grateful for the past.

PHILIPS

TO MISS CHARLOTTE PULTENEY IN HER MOTHER'S ARMS

TIMELY blossom, infant fair,
Fondling of a happy pair,
Every morn, and every night,
Their solicitous delight,
Sleeping, waking, still at ease,
Pleasing, without skill to please,
Little gossip, blithe and hale,
Tatling many a broken tale,
Singing many a tuneless song,
Lavish of a heedless tongue,
Simple maiden, void of art,
Babbling out the very heart,
Yet abandon'd to thy will,
Yet imagining no ill,
Yet too innocent to blush,
Like the linlet in the bush,
To the Mother-linnet's note
Moduling her slender throat,
Chirping forth thy petty joys,
Wanton in the change of toys,
Like the linnet green, in *May*,
Flitting to each bloomy spray,
Wearied then, and glad of rest,
Like the linlet in the nest.
This thy present happy lot,
This, in time, will be forgot:
Other pleasures, other cares,
Ever-busy Time prepares.
And thou shalt in thy daughter see,
This picture, once, resembled thee.

SWIFT

A DESCRIPTION OF THE MORNING

Now hardly here and there an Hackney-Coach
Appearing, show'd the Ruddy Morn's Approach.
Now *Betty* from her Master's Bed had flown,
And softly stole to discompose her own.
The Slipshod 'Prentice from his Master's Dore,
Had par'd the Street, and Sprinkled round the Floor.
Now *Moll* had whirl'd her Mop with dext'rous Airs,
Prepar'd to scrub the Entry and the Stairs.
The Youth with broomy Stumps began to trace
The Kennel Edge, where Wheels had worn the Place.
The Smallcoal-Man was heard with Cadence deep,
Till drown'd in shriller Notes of Chimney-sweep.
Duns at his Lordship's Gate began to meet;
And Brickdust *Moll* had scream'd through half a Street.
The Turn-key now his Flock returning sees,
Duly let out a'Nights to steal for Fees.
The watchful Bayliffs take their silent Stands;
And School-boys lag with Satchels in their Hands.

THE DAY OF JUDGEMENT

With a Whirl of Thought oppress'd,
I sink from Reverie to Rest.
An horrid Vision seiz'd my Head,
I saw the Graves give up their Dead.
Jove, arm'd with Terrors, burst the Skies,
And Thunder roars, and Light'ning flies!
Amaz'd, confus'd, its Fate unknown,
The World stands trembling at his Throne.
While each pale Sinner hangs his Head,
Jove, nodding, shook the Heav'ns, and said,
'Offending Race of Human Kind,
By Nature, Reason, Learning, blind;
You who thro' Frailty step'd aside,
And you who never fell – *thro' Pride*;
You who in different Sects have shamm'd,

And come to see each other damn'd;
(So some Folks told you, but they knew
No more of Jove's Designs than you)
The World's mad Business now is o'er,
And I resent these Pranks no more,
I to such Blockheads set my Wit!
I damn such Fools! – Go, go, you're bit.'

from VERSES ON THE DEATH OF Dr SWIFT

The Dean, if we believe Report,
Was never ill receiv'd at Court:
As for his Works in Verse and Prose,
I own my self no Judge of those:
Nor, can I tell what Criticks thought 'em;
But, this I know, all People bought 'em;
As with a moral View design'd
To cure the Vices of Mankind:
His Vein, ironically grave,
Expos'd the Fool, and lash'd the Knave:
To steal a Hint was never known,
But what he writ, was all his own.

He never thought an Honour done him,
Because a Duke was proud to own him:
Would rather slip aside, and chuse
To talk with Wits in dirty Shoes:
Despis'd the Fools with Stars and Garters,
So often seen caressing *Chartres*:
He never courted Men in Station,
Nor Persons had in Admiration;
Of no Man's Greatness was afraid,
Because he sought for no Man's Aid.
Though trusted long in great Affairs,
He gave himself no haughty Airs:
Without regarding private Ends,
Spent all his Credit for his Friends:
And, only chose the Wise and Good;
No Flatt'rers; no Allies in Blood;
But succour'd Virtue in Distress,

And seldom fail'd of good Success;
As Numbers in their Hearts must own,
Who, but for him, had been unknown.

*

Had he but spar'd his Tongue and Pen,
He might have rose like other Men:
But, Power was never in his Thought;
And, Wealth he valu'd not a Groat:
Ingratitude he often found,
And pity'd those who meant the Wound:
But, kept the Tenor of his Mind,
To merit well of human Kind:
Nor made a Sacrifice of those
Who still were true, to please his Foes.
He labour'd many a fruitless Hour
To reconcile his Friends in Power;
Saw Mischief by a Faction brewing,
While they pursu'd each others Ruin.
But, finding vain was all his Care,
He left the Court in meer Despair.

*

Perhaps I may allow, the Dean
Had too much Satyr in his Vein;
And seem'd determin'd not to starve it,
Because no Age could more deserve it.
Yet, Malice never was his Aim;
He lash'd the Vice but spar'd the Name.
No Individual could resent,
Where Thousands equally were meant.
His Satyr points at no Defect,
But what all Mortals may correct;
For he abhorr'd that senseless Tribe,
Who call it Humour when they jibe:
He spar'd a Hump or crooked Nose,
Whose Owners set not up for Beaux.
True genuine Dulness mov'd his Pity,
Unless it offer'd to be witty.
Those, who their Ignorance confess'd,

He ne'er offended with a Jest;
But laugh'd to hear an Idiot quote,
A Verse from *Horace*, learn'd by Rote.

He knew an hundred pleasant Stories,
With all the Turns of *Whigs* and *Tories*:
Was chearful to his dying Day,
And Friends would let him have his Way.

He gave the little Wealth he had,
To build a House for Fools and Mad:
And shew'd by one satyric Touch,
No Nation wanted it so much:
*That Kingdom he hath left his Debtor,
I wish it soon may have a Better.

POPE

from WINDSOR-FOREST

SEE! from the brake the whirring Pheasant springs,
And mounts exulting on triumphant wings:
Short is his joy; he feels the fiery wound,
Flutters in blood, and panting beats the ground.
Ah! what avail his glossy, varying dyes,
His purple crest, and scarlet-circled eyes,
The vivid green his shining plumes unfold,
His painted wings, and breast that flames with gold?
Nor yet, when moist *Arcturus* clouds the sky,
The woods and fields their pleasing toils deny.
To plains with well-breath'd beagles we repair,
And trace the mazes of the circling hare.
(Beasts, taught by us, their fellow beasts pursue,
And learn of man each other to undo.)
With slaught'ring guns th' unweary'd fowler roves,
When frosts have whiten'd all the naked groves;
Where doves in flocks the leafless trees o'ershade,
And lonely woodcocks haunt the wat'ry glade.

* *Meaning* Ireland, *where he now lives, and probably may dye.*

He lifts the tube, and levels with his eye;
Strait a short thunder breaks the frozen sky.
Oft', as in airy rings they skim the heath,
The clam'rous Plovers feel the leaden death:
Oft', as the mounting Larks their notes prepare,
They fall, and leave their little lives in air.

from AN ESSAY ON CRITICISM

'Tis hard to say, if greater want of skill
Appear in writing or in judging ill;
But, of the two, less dang'rous is th' offence
To tire our patience, than mislead our sense.
Some few in that, but numbers err in this,
Ten censure wrong for one who writes amiss;
A fool might once himself alone expose,
Now one in verse makes many more in prose.
'Tis with our judgments as our watches, none
Go just alike, yet each believes his own.
In Poets as true Genius is but rare,
True Taste as seldom is the Critic's share;
Both must alike from heav'n derive their light,
These born to judge, as well as those to write.
Let such teach others who themselves excell,
And censure freely who have written well.
Authors are partial to their wit, 'tis true,
But are not Critics to their judgment too?
Yet if we look more closely, we shall find
Most have the seeds of judgment in their mind:
Nature affords at least a glimm'ring light;
The lines, tho' touch'd but faintly, are drawn right.
But as the slightest sketch, if justly trac'd,
Is by ill colouring but the more disgrac'd,
So by false learning is good sense defac'd:
Some are bewilder'd in the maze of schools,
And some made coxcombs Nature meant but fools.
In search of wit these lose their common sense,
And then turn Critics in their own defence:
Those hate as rivals all that write; and others
But envy wits, as eunuchs envy lovers.

All such have still an itching to deride,
And fain would be upon the laughing side.
If *Maevius* scribble in *Apollo's* spight,
There are, who judge still worse than he can write.
  Some have at first for Wits, then Poets past,
Turn'd Critics next, and prov'd plain fools at last.
Some neither can for Wits nor Critics pass,
As heavy mules are neither horse nor ass.
Those half-learn'd witlings, numerous in our isle,
As half-form'd insects on the banks of *Nile*;
Unfinish'd things, one knows not what to call,
Their generation's so equivocal:
To tell 'em, would a hundred tongues require,
Or one vain Wit's, that might a hundred tire.
  But you who seek to give and merit fame,
And justly bear a Critic's noble name,
Be sure your self and your own reach to know,
How far your genius, taste, and learning go;
Launch not beyond your depth, but be discreet,
And mark that point where sense and dulness meet.

*

Of all the causes which conspire to blind
Man's erring judgment, and misguide the mind,
What the weak head with strongest biass rules,
Is Pride, the never-failing vice of fools.
Whatever Nature has in worth deny'd,
She gives in large recruits of needful pride;
For as in bodies, thus in souls, we find
What wants in blood and spirits, swell'd with wind:
Pride, where Wit fails, steps in to our defence,
And fills up all the mighty void of sense!
If once right reason drives that cloud away,
Truth breaks upon us with resistless day;
Trust not your self; but your defects to know,
Make use of ev'ry friend – and ev'ry foe.
  A little learning is a dang'rous thing;
Drink deep, or taste not the *Pierian* spring:
There shallow draughts intoxicate the brain,
And drinking largely sobers us again.

Fir'd at first sight with what the Muse imparts,
In fearless youth we tempt the heights of Arts,
While from the bounded level of our mind,
Short views we take, nor see the lengths behind;
But more advanc'd, behold with strange surprize
New distant scenes of endless science rise!
So pleas'd at first the tow'ring *Alps* we try,
Mount o'er the vales, and seem to tread the sky,
Th' eternal snows appear already past,
And the first clouds and mountains seem the last:
But, those attain'd, we tremble to survey
The growing labours of the lengthen'd way,
Th' increasing prospect tires our wand'ring eyes,
Hills peep o'er hills, and *Alps* on *Alps* arise!

from THE RAPE OF THE LOCK

NOT with more glories, in th' etherial plain,
The Sun first rises o'er the purpled main,
Than, issuing forth, the rival of his beams
Launch'd on the bosom of the silver *Thames*.
Fair nymphs, and well-drest youths around her shone,
But ev'ry eye was fix'd on her alone.
On her white breast a sparkling Cross she wore,
Which Jews might kiss, and Infidels adore.
Her lively looks a sprightly mind disclose,
Quick as her eyes, and as unfix'd as those:
Favours to none, to all she smiles extends,
Oft' she rejects, but never once offends.
Bright as the sun, her eyes the gazers strike,
And, like the sun, they shine on all alike.
Yet graceful ease, and sweetness void of pride,
Might hide her faults, if *Belles* had faults to hide:
If to her share some female errors fall,
Look on her face, and you'll forget 'em all.
This nymph, to the destruction of mankind,
Nourish'd two Locks, which graceful hung behind
In equal curls, and well conspir'd to deck
With shining ringlets the smooth iv'ry neck.
Love in these labyrinths his slaves detains,

And mighty hearts are held in slender chains.
With hairy sprindges we the birds betray,
Slight lines of hair surprize the finny prey,
Fair tresses man's imperial race insnare,
And beauty draws us with a single hair.
  Th' advent'rous Baron the bright locks admir'd;
He saw, he wish'd, and to the prize aspir'd:
Resolv'd to win, he meditates the way,
By force to ravish, or by fraud betray;
For when success a Lover's toil attends,
Few ask, if fraud or force attain'd his ends.
  For this, ere *Phœbus* rose, he had implor'd
Propitious heav'n, and ev'ry pow'r ador'd,
But chiefly Love – to Love an altar built,
Of twelve vast French Romances, neatly gilt.
There lay three garters, half a pair of gloves;
And all the trophies of his former loves;
With tender Billet-doux he lights the pyre,
And breathes three am'rous sighs to raise the fire.
Then prostrate falls, and begs with ardent eyes
Soon to obtain, and long possess the prize:
The Pow'rs gave ear, and granted half his pray'r,
The rest, the winds dispers'd in empty air.
  But now secure the painted vessel glides,
The sun-beams trembling on the floating tydes,
While melting music steals upon the sky,
And soften'd sounds along the waters die.
Smooth flow the waves, the zephyrs gently play,
Belinda smil'd, and all the world was gay.

INTENDED FOR SIR ISAAC NEWTON IN WESTMINSTER-ABBEY

NATURE and Nature's Laws lay hid in Night.
GOD said, *Let Newton be!* and All was *Light*.

TO MRS M[ARTHA]. B[LOUNT]. ON HER BIRTHDAY

Oh be thou blest with all that Heav'n can send,
Long Health, long Youth, long Pleasure, and a Friend:
Not with those Toys the female world admire,
Riches that vex, and Vanities that tire.
With added years if Life bring nothing new,
But like a Sieve let ev'ry blessing thro',
Some joy still lost, as each vain year runs o'er,
And all we gain, some sad Reflection more;
Is that a Birth-day? 'tis alas! too clear,
'Tis but the Fun'ral of the former year.
Let Joy or Ease, let Affluence or Content,
And the gay Conscience of a life well spent,
Calm ev'ry thought, inspirit ev'ry Grace,
Glow in thy heart, and smile upon thy face.
Let day improve on day, and year on year,
Without a Pain, a Trouble, or a Fear;
Till Death unfelt that tender frame destroy,
In some soft Dream, or Extasy of joy:
Peaceful sleep out the Sabbath of the Tomb,
And wake to Raptures in a Life to come.

from AN ESSAY ON MAN

Who sees with equal eye, as God of all,
A hero perish, or a sparrow fall,
Atoms or systems into ruin hurl'd,
And now a bubble burst, and now a world.
Hope humbly then; with trembling pinions soar;
Wait the great teacher Death, and God adore!
What future bliss, he gives not thee to know,
But gives that Hope to be thy blessing now.
Hope springs eternal in the human breast:
Man never Is, but always To be blest:
The soul, uneasy and confin'd from home,
Rests and expatiates in a life to come.
Lo! the poor Indian, whose untutor'd mind
Sees God in clouds, or hears him in the wind;

His soul proud Science never taught to stray
Far as the solar walk, or milky way;
Yet simple Nature to his hope has giv'n,
Behind the cloud-topt hill, an humbler heav'n,
Some safer world in depth of woods embrac'd,
Some happier island in the watry waste,
Where slaves once more their native land behold,
No fiends torment, no Christians thirst for gold!
To Be, contents his natural desire,
He asks no Angel's wing, no Seraph's fire;
But thinks, admitted to that equal sky,
His faithful dog shall bear him company.

from OF THE CHARACTERS OF WOMEN

Nothing so true as what you once let fall,
'Most Women have no Characters at all.'
Matter too soft a lasting mark to bear,
And best distinguish'd by black, brown, or fair.
How many pictures of one Nymph we view,
All how unlike each other, all how true!
Arcadia's Countess, here, in ermin'd pride,
Is there, Pastora by a fountain side.
Here Fannia, leering on her own good man,
And there, a naked Leda with a Swan.
Let then the Fair one beautifully cry,
In Magdalen's loose hair and lifted eye,
Or drest in smiles of sweet Cecilia shine,
With simp'ring Angels, Palms, and Harps divine;
Whether the Charmer sinner it, or saint it,
If Folly grows romantic, I must paint it.
Come then, the colours and the ground prepare!
Dip in the Rainbow, trick her off in Air,
Chuse a firm Cloud, before it fall, and in it
Catch, ere she change, the Cynthia of this minute.
Rufa, whose eye quick-glancing o'er the Park,
Attracts each light gay meteor of a Spark,
Agrees as ill with Rufa studying Locke,
As Sappho's diamonds with her dirty smock,
Or Sappho at her toilet's greazy task,

With Sappho fragrant at an evening Mask:
So morning Insects that in muck begun,
Shine, buzz, and fly-blow in the setting-sun.
How soft is Silia! fearful to offend;
The Frail one's advocate, the Weak one's friend:
To her, Calista prov'd her conduct nice,
And good Simplicius asks of her advice.
Sudden, she storms! she raves! You tip the wink,
But spare your censure; Silia does not drink.
All eyes may see from what the change arose,
All eyes may see – a Pimple on her nose.
Papillia, wedded to her donating spark,
Sighs for the shades! – 'How charming is a Park!'
A Park is purchas'd, but the Fair he sees
All bath'd in tears – 'Oh odious, odious Trees!'
Ladies, like variegated Tulips, show,
'Tis to their Changes half their charms we owe;
Their happy Spots the nice admirer take,
Fine by defect, and delicately weak.
'Twas thus Calypso once each heart alarm'd,
Aw'd without Virtue, without Beauty charm'd;
Her Tongue bewitch'd as odly as her Eyes,
Less Wit than Mimic, more a Wit than wise;
Strange graces still, and stranger flights she had,
Was just not ugly, and was just not mad;
Yet ne'er so sure our passion to create,
As when she touch'd the brink of all we hate.

*

But what are these to great Atossa's mind?
Scarce once herself, by turns all Womankind!
Who, with herself, or others, from her birth
Finds all her life one warfare upon earth:
Shines, in exposing Knaves, and painting Fools,
Yet is, whate'er she hates and ridicules.
No Thought advances, but her Eddy Brain
Whisks it about, and down it goes again.
Full sixty years the World has been her Trade,
The wisest Fool much Time has ever made.
From loveless youth to unrespected age,

No Passion gratify'd, except her Rage.
So much the Fury still out-ran the Wit,
The Pleasure miss'd her, and the Scandal hit.
Who breaks with her, provokes Revenge from Hell,
But he's a bolder man who dares be well:
Her ev'ry turn with Violence pursu'd,
Nor more a storm her Hate than Gratitude.
To that each Passion turns, or soon or late;
Love, if it makes her yield, must make her hate:
Superiors? death! and Equals? what a curse!
But an Inferior not dependent? worse.
Offend her, and she knows not to forgive;
Oblige her, and she'll hate you while you live:
But die, and she'll adore you – Then the Bust
And Temple rise – then fall again to dust.
Last night, her Lord was all that's good and great,
A Knave this morning, and his Will a Cheat.
Strange! by the Means defeated of the Ends,
By Spirit robb'd of Pow'r, by Warmth of Friends,
By Wealth of Follow'rs! without one distress,
Sick of herself through very selfishness!
Atossa, curs'd with ev'ry granted pray'r,
Childless with all her Children, wants an Heir.
To Heirs unknown descends th' unguarded store,
Or wanders, Heav'n-directed, to the Poor.
  Pictures like these, dear Madam, to design,
Asks no firm hand, and no unerring line;
Some wand'ring touches, some reflected light,
Some flying stroke alone can hit 'em right:
For how should equal Colours do the knack?
Chameleons who can paint in white and black?
  'Yet Cloe sure was form'd without a spot' –
Nature in her then err'd not, but forgot.
'With ev'ry pleasing, ev'ry prudent part,
Say, what can Cloe want?' – She wants a Heart.
She speaks, behaves, and acts just as she ought;
But never, never reach'd one gen'rous Thought.
Virtue she finds too painful an endeavour,
Content to dwell in Decencies for ever.
So very reasonable, so unmov'd,
As never yet to love, or to be lov'd.

Pope

She, while her Lover pants upon her breast,
Can mark the figures on an Indian chest;
And when she sees her Friend in deep despair,
Observes how much a Chintz exceeds Mohair.
Forbid it Heav'n, a Favour or a Debt
She e'er should cancel – but she may forget.
Safe is your Secret still in Cloe's ear;
But none of Cloe's shall you ever hear.
Of all her Dears she never slander'd one,
But cares not if a thousand are undone.
Would Cloe know if you're alive or dead?
She bids her Footman put it in her head.
Cloe is prudent – would you too be wise?
Then never break your heart when Cloe dies.

*

Men, some to Bus'ness, some to Pleasure take;
But ev'ry Woman is at heart a Rake;
Men, some to Quiet, some to public Strife;
But ev'ry Lady would be Queen for life.
Yet mark the fate of a whole Sex of Queens!
Pow'r all their end, but Beauty all the means.
In Youth they conquer, with so wild a rage,
As leaves them scarce a Subject in their Age:
For foreign glory, foreign joy, they roam;
No thought of Peace or Happiness at home.
But Wisdom's Triumph is well-tim'd Retreat,
As hard a science to the Fair as Great!
Beauties, like Tyrants, old and friendless grown,
Yet hate Repose, and dread to be alone,
Worn out in public, weary ev'ry eye,
Nor leave one sigh behind them when they die.
Pleasures the sex, as children Birds, pursue,
Still out of reach, yet never out of view,
Sure, if they catch, to spoil the Toy at most,
To covet flying, and regret when lost:
At last, to follies Youth could scarce defend,
It grows their Age's prudence to pretend;
Asham'd to own they gave delight before,
Reduc'd to feign it, when they give no more:

As Hags hold Sabbaths, less for joy than spight,
So these their merry, miserable Night;
Still round and round the Ghosts of Beauty glide,
And haunt the places where their Honour dy'd.
  See how the World its Veterans rewards!
A Youth of Frolics, an old Age of Cards,
Fair to no purpose, artful to no end,
Young without Lovers, old without a Friend,
A Fop their Passion, but their Prize a Sot,
Alive, ridiculous, and dead, forgot!

GAY

SONG

Sleep, O Sleep,
With thy Rod of Incantation,
Charm my Imagination,
Then, only then, I cease to weep.

By thy Power,
The Virgin, by Time o'ertaken,
For Years forlorn, forsaken,
Enjoys the happy Hour.

What's to sleep?
'Tis a visionary Blessing;
A Dream that's past expressing;
Our utmost Wish possessing:
So may I always keep.

SONG

Love in her Eyes sits playing,
  And sheds delicious Death;
Love in her Lips is straying,
  And warbling in her Breath;
Love on her Breast sits panting,
  And swells with soft Desire;
Nor Grace, nor Charm, is wanting
To set the Heart on Fire.

DYER

from GRONGAR HILL

BELOW me Trees unnumber'd rise,
Beautiful in various Dies:
The gloomy Pine, the Poplar blue,
The yellow Beech, the sable Yew,
The slender Firr, that taper grows,
The sturdy Oak with broad-spread Boughs;
And beyond the purple Grove,
Haunt of *Phillis*, Queen of Love!
Gawdy as the op'ning Dawn,
Lies a long and level Lawn,
On which a dark Hill, steep and high,
Holds and charms the wand'ring Eye!
Deep are his Feet in *Towy's* Flood,
His sides are cloath'd with waving Wood
And antient towers crown his brow,
That cast an awful Look below;
Whose ragged Walls the Ivy creeps,
And with her Arms from falling keeps;
So both a Safety from the Wind
On mutual dependance find.
'Tis now the Raven's bleak Abode;
'Tis now th'Apartment of the Toad;
And there the Fox securely feeds;
And there the pois'nous Adder breeds,
Conceal'd in Ruins, Moss and Weeds:
While, ever and anon, there falls,
Huge heaps of hoary moulder'd Walls.
Yet Time has seen, that lifts the low,
And level lays the lofty Brow,
Has seen this broken Pile compleat,
Big with the Vanity of State;
But transient is the Smile of Fate!
A little Rule, little Sway,
A Sun-beam in a Winter's day
Is all the Proud and Mighty have,
Between the Cradle and the Grave.

THOMSON

from WINTER

Now, solitary, and in pensive Guise,
Oft, let me wander o'er the russet Mead,
Or thro' the pining Grove; where scarce is heard
One dying Strain, to chear the *Woodman's* Toil:
Sad *Philomel*, perchance, pours forth her Plaint,
Far, thro' the withering Copse. Mean while, the Leaves,
That, late, the Forest clad with lively Green,
Nipt by the drizzly Night, and Sallow-hu'd,
Fall, wavering, thro' the Air; or shower amain,
Urg'd by the Breeze, that sobs amid the Boughs.
Then list'ning *Hares* forsake the rusling Woods,
And, starting at the frequent Noise, escape
To the rough Stubble, and the rushy Fen.
Then *Woodcocks*, o'er the fluctuating Main,
That glimmers to the Glimpses of the Moon,
Stretch their long Voyage to the woodland Glade:
Where, wheeling with uncertain Flight, they mock
The nimble *Fowler's* Aim. – Now Nature droops;
Languish the living Herbs, with pale Decay:
And all the *various Family* of Flowers
Their sunny Robes resign. The falling Fruits,
Thro' the still Night, forsake the Parent-Bough,
That, in the first, grey, Glances of the Dawn,
Looks wild, and wonders at the wintry Waste.

*

Late, in the louring Sky, red, fiery, Streaks
Begin to flush about; the reeling Clouds
Stagger with dizzy Aim, as doubting yet
Which Master to obey: while rising, slow,
Sad, in the Leaden-colour'd East, the Moon
Wears a bleak Circle round her sully'd Orb.
Then issues forth the Storm, with loud Control,
And the thin Fabrick of the pillar'd Air
O'erturns, at once. Prone, on th'uncertain Main,
Descends th'Etherial Force, and plows its Waves,

With dreadful Rift: from the mid-Deep, appears,
Surge after Surge, the rising, wat'ry, War.
Whitening, the angry Billows rowl immense,
And roar their Terrors, thro' the shuddering Soul
Of feeble Man, amidst their Fury caught,
And, dash'd upon his Fate: Then o'er the Cliff,
Where dwells the *Sea-Mew*, unconfin'd, they fly,
And, hurrying, swallow up the steril Shore.

The Mountain growls; and all its sturdy *Sons*
Stoop to the Bottom of the Rocks they shade:
Lone, on its Midnight-Side, and all aghast,
The dark, way-faring, *Stranger*, breathless, toils,
And climbs against the Blast –
Low, waves the rooted Forest, vex'd, and sheds
What of its leafy Honours yet remains.
Thus, struggling thro' the dissipated Grove,
The whirling Tempest raves along the Plain;
And, on the Cottage thacht, or lordly Dome,
Keen-fastening, shakes 'em to the solid Base.
Sleep, frighted, flies; the hollow Chimney howls,
The Windows rattle, and the Hinges creak.

*

Lo! from the livid East, or piercing North,
Thick Clouds ascend, in whose capacious Womb,
A vapoury Deluge lies, to Snow congeal'd:
Heavy, they roll their fleecy World along;
And the Sky saddens with th'impending Storm.
Thro' the hush'd Air, the whitening Shower descends,
At first, thin-wavering; till, at last, the Flakes
Fall broad, and wide, and fast, dimming the Day,
With a continual Flow. See! sudden, hoar'd,
The Woods beneath the stainless Burden bow,
Blackning, along the mazy Stream it melts;
Earth's universal Face, deep-hid, and chill,
Is all one, dazzling, Waste. The Labourer-Ox
Stands cover'd o'er with Snow, and then demands
The Fruit of all his Toil. The Fowls of Heaven,
Tam'd by the cruel Season, croud around

Thomson

The winnowing Store, and claim the little Boon,
That *Providence* allows. The foodless Wilds
Pour forth their brown *Inhabitants*; the Hare,
Tho' timorous of Heart, and hard beset
By Death, in various Forms, dark Snares, and Dogs,
And more unpitying Men, the Garden seeks,
Urg'd on by *fearless* Want. The bleating Kind
Eye the bleak Heavens, and next, the glistening Earth,
With Looks of dumb Despair; then sad, dispers'd,
Dig, for the wither'd Herb, thro' Heaps of Snow.

*

Clear Frost succeeds, and thro' the blew Serene,
For Sight too fine, th' Ætherial Nitre flies,
To bake the Glebe, and bind the slip'ry Flood.
This of the wintry Season is the Prime;
Pure are the Days, and lustrous are the Nights,
Brighten'd with starry Worlds, till then unseen.
Mean while, the Orient, darkly red, breathes forth
An Icy Gale, that, in its mid Career,
Arrests the bickering Stream. The nightly Sky,
And all her glowing Constellations pour
Their rigid Influence down: It freezes on
Till Morn, late-rising, o'er the drooping World,
Lifts her pale Eye, unjoyous: then appears
The various Labour of the silent Night,
The pendant Isicle, the Frost-Work fair,
Where thousand Figures rise, the crusted Snow,
Tho' white, made whiter, by the fining North.
On blithsome Frolics bent, the youthful Swains,
While every Work of Man is laid at Rest,
Rush o'er the watry Plains, and, shuddering, view
The fearful Deeps below: or with the Gun,
And faithful Spaniel, range the ravag'd Fields,
And, adding to the Ruins of the Year,
Distress the Feathery, or the Footed *Game*.

But hark! the nightly Winds, with hollow Voice,
Blow, blustering, from the South – the Frost subdu'd,
Gradual, resolves into a weeping Thaw.

Spotted, the Mountains shine: loose Sleet descends,
And floods the Country round: the Rivers swell,
Impatient for the Day. – Those sullen Seas,
That wash th'ungenial Pole, will rest no more,
Beneath the Shackles of the mighty North;
But, rousing all their Waves, resistless heave, –
And hark! – the length'ning Roar, continuous, runs
Athwart the rifted Main; at once, it bursts,
And piles a thousand Mountains to the Clouds!
Ill fares the Bark, the Wretches' last Resort,
That, lost amid the floating Fragments, moors
Beneath the Shelter of an Icy Isle;
While Night o'erwhelms the Sea, and Horror looks
More horrible. Can human Hearts endure
Th'assembled *Mischiefs*, that besiege them round:
Unlist'ning *Hunger*, fainting *Weariness*,
The *Roar* of Winds, and Waves, the *Crush* of Ice,
Now, ceasing, now, renew'd, with louder Rage,
And bellowing round the Main: Nations remote,
Shook from their Midnight-Slumbers, deem they hear
Portentous Thunder, in the troubled Sky.
More to embroil the Deep, Leviathan,
And his unweildy Train, in horrid Sport,
Tempest the loosen'd Brine; while, thro' the Gloom,
Far, from the dire, unhospitable Shore,
The Lyon's Rage, the Wolf's sad Howl is heard,
And all the fell Society of Night.

SHENSTONE

SONG

O'ER desert plains, and rushy meers,
  And wither'd heaths I rove;
Where tree, nor spire, nor cot appears,
  I pass to meet my love.

But, tho' my path were damask'd o'er
With beauties e'er so fine;
My busy thoughts would fly before,
To fix alone – on thine.

No fir-crown'd hills cou'd give delight,
No palace please mine eye;
No pyramid's aërial height,
Where mouldering monarchs lie.

Unmov'd, should Eastern kings advance;
Could I the pageant see:
Splendour might catch one scornful glance,
Not steal one thought from thee.

JOHNSON

[THE SCHOLAR'S LIFE]

WHEN first the College Rolls receive his Name,
The young Enthusiast quits his Ease for Fame;
Thro' all his Veins the Fever of Renown
Burns from the strong Contagion of the Gown;
O'er *Bodley's* Dome his future Labours spread,
And *Bacon's* Mansion trembles o'er his Head;
Are these thy Views? proceed, illustrious Youth,
And Virtue guard thee to the Throne of Truth.
Yet should thy Soul indulge the gen'rous Heat
Till captive Science yields her last Retreat;
Should Reason guide thee with her brightest Ray,
And pour on misty Doubt resistless Day;
Should no false Kindness lure to loose Delight,
Nor Praise relax, nor Difficulty fright;
Should tempting Novelty thy Cell refrain,
And Sloth effuse her opiate Fumes in Vain;
Should Beauty blunt on Fops her fatal Dart,
Nor claim the triumph of a letter'd Heart;
Should no Disease thy torpid Veins invade,
Nor Melancholy's Phantoms haunt thy shade;

Yet hope not Life from Grief or Danger free,
Nor think the Doom of Man revers'd for thee.
Deign on the passing World to turn thine Eyes
And pause awhile from Letters to be wise;
There mark what Ills the Scholar's Life assail,
Toil, Envy, Want, the Patron, and the Jail.
See Nations slowly wise, and meanly just,
To buried Merit raise the tardy Bust.
If Dreams yet flatter, once again attend,
Hear *Lydiat's* Life, and *Galileo's* End.

[LINES ON THE DEATH OF MR LEVETT]

CONDEMN'D to Hope's delusive mine,
As on we toil from day to day,
By sudden blast or slow decline,
Our social comforts drop away.

Well try'd through many a varying year,
See *Levett* to the grave descend;
Officious, innocent, sincere,
Of ev'ry friendless name the friend.

Yet still he fills Affection's eye,
Obscurely wise, and coarsely kind,
Nor, letter'd arrogance, deny
Thy praise to merit unrefin'd.

When fainting Nature call'd for aid,
And hov'ring Death prepar'd the blow,
His vigorous remedy display'd
The pow'r of art without the show.

In Misery's darkest caverns known,
His ready help was ever nigh,
Where hopeless Anguish pours his groan,
And lonely want retir'd to die.

No summons mock'd by chill delay,
No petty gains disdain'd by pride;
The modest wants of ev'ry day
The toil of ev'ry day supply'd.

His virtues walk'd their narrow round,
Nor made a pause, nor left a void;
And sure th'Eternal Master found
His single talent well employ'd.

The busy day, the peaceful night,
Unfelt, uncounted, glided by;
His frame was firm, his powers were bright,
Though now his eightieth year was nigh.

Then, with no throbs of fiery pain,
No cold gradations of decay,
Death broke at once the vital chain,
And freed his soul the nearest way.

WARTON

from *THE ENTHUSIAST: OR, THE LOVER OF NATURE*

Ye green-rob'd *Dryads*, oft' at dusky Eve
By wondering Shepherds seen, to Forests brown,
To unfrequented Meads, and pathless Wilds,
Lead me from Gardens deckt with Art's vain Pomps.
Can gilt Alcoves, can Marble-mimic Gods,
Parterres embroider'd, Obelisks, and Urns
Of high Relief; can the long, spreading Lake,
Or Vista lessening to the Sight; can *Stow*
With all her *Attic* Fanes, such Raptures raise,
As the Thrush-haunted Copse, where lightly leaps
The fearful Fawn the rustling Leaves along,
And the brisk Squirrel sports from Bough to Bough,
While from an hollow Oak the busy Bees
Hum drowsy Lullabies? The Bards of old,
Fair Nature's Friends, sought such Retreats, to charm
Sweet *Echo* with their Songs; oft' too they met,
In Summer Evenings, near sequester'd Bow'rs,
Or Mountain-Nymph, or Muse, and eager learnt
The moral Strains she taught to mend Mankind.

As to a secret Grot *Ægeria* stole
With Patriot *Numa*, and in silent Night
Whisper'd him sacred Laws, he list'ning sat
Rapt with her virtuous Voice, old *Tyber* leant
Attentive on his Urn, and husht his Waves.

Rich in her weeping Country's Spoils *Versailles*
May boast a thousand Fountains, that can cast
The tortur'd Waters to the distant Heav'ns;
Yet let me choose some Pine-topt Precipice
Abrupt and shaggy, whence a foamy Stream,
Like *Anio*, tumbling roars; or some bleak Heath,
Where straggling stand the mournful Juniper,
Or Yew-tree scath'd; while in clear Prospect round,
From the Grove's Bosom Spires emerge, and Smoak
In bluish Wreaths ascends, ripe Harvests wave,
Herds low, and Straw-rooft Cotts appear, and Streams
Beneath the Sun-beams twinkle – The shrill Lark,
That wakes the Wood-man to his early Task,
Or love-sick *Philomel*, whose luscious Lays
Sooth lone Night-wanderers, the moaning Dove
Pitied by listening Milkmaid, far excell
The deep-mouth'd Viol, the Soul-lulling Lute,
And Battle-breathing Trumpet. Artful Sounds!
That please not like the Choristers of Air,
When first they hail th'Approach of laughing *May*.

*

Happy the first of Men, ere yet confin'd
To smoaky Cities; who in sheltering Groves,
Warm Caves, and deep-sunk Vallies liv'd and lov'd,
By Cares unwounded; what the Sun and Showers,
And genial Earth untillag'd could produce,
They gather'd grateful, or the Acorn brown,
Or blushing Berry; by the liquid Lapse
Of murm'ring Waters call'd to slake their Thirst,
Or with fair Nymphs their Sun-brown Limbs to bathe;
With Nymphs who fondly clasp'd their fav'rite Youths,
Unaw'd by Shame, beneath the Beechen Shade,
Nor Wiles, nor artificial Coyness knew.

*

Oft' near some crowded City would I walk,
Listening the far-off Noises, rattling Carrs,
Loud Shouts of Joy, sad Shrieks of Sorrow, Knells
Full slowly tolling, Instruments of Trade,
Striking mine Ears with one deep-swelling Hum.
Or wandering near the Sea, attend the Sounds
Of hollow Winds, and ever-beating Waves.

★

But let me never fail in cloudless Nights,
When silent *Cynthia* in her silver Car
Thro' the blue Concave slides, when shine the Hills,
Twinkle the Streams, and Woods look tipt with Gold,
To seek some level Mead, and there invoke
Old Midnight's Sister Contemplation sage,
(Queen of the rugged Brow, and stern-fixt Eye)
To lift my Soul above this little Earth,
This Folly-fetter'd World; to purge my Ears,
That I may hear the rolling Planets Song,
And tuneful-turning Spheres: If this debarr'd,
The little *Fayes* that dance in neighbouring Dales,
Sipping the Night-dew, while they laugh and love,
Shall charm me with aërial Notes.

COLLINS

ODE TO EVENING

If ought of Oaten Stop, or Pastoral Song,
May hope, chaste Eve, to soothe thy modest Ear,
    Like thy own solemn Springs,
    Thy Springs, and dying Gales,
O Nymph reserv'd, while now the bright-hair'd Sun
Sits in yon western Tent, whose cloudy Skirts,
    With Brede ethereal wove,
    O'erhang his wavy Bed:
Now Air is hush'd, save where the weak-ey'd Bat,
With short shrill Shriek flits by on leathern Wing,

Or where the Beetle winds
His small but sullen Horn,
As oft he rises 'midst the twilight Path,
Against the Pilgrim born in heedless Hum:
Now teach me, Maid compos'd,
To breathe some soften'd Strain,
Whose Numbers stealing thro' thy darkning Vale,
May not unseemly with its Stillness suit,
As musing slow, I hail
Thy genial lov'd Return!
For when thy folding Star arising shews
His paly Circlet, at his warning Lamp
The fragrant Hours, and Elves
Who slept in Flow'rs the Day,
And many a Nymph who wreaths her Brows with Sedge,
And sheds the fresh'ning Dew, and lovelier still,
The Pensive Pleasures sweet
Prepare thy shadowy Car.

Then lead, calm Vot'ress, where some sheety Lake,
Cheers the lone Heath, or some time-hallow'd Pile,
Or up-land Fallows grey
Reflect it's last cool Gleam.
But when chill blust'ring Winds, or driving Rain,
Forbid my willing Feet, be mine the Hut,
That from the Mountain's Side,
Views Wilds, and swelling Floods,
And Hamlets brown, and dim-discover'd Spires,
And hears their simple Bell, and marks o'er all
The Dewy Fingers draw
The gradual dusky Veil.

While Spring shall pour his Show'rs, as oft he wont,
And bathe thy breathing Tresses, meekest Eve!
While Summer loves to sport,
Beneath thy ling'ring Light:
While sallow Autumn fills thy Lap with Leaves,
Or Winter yelling thro' the troublous Air,
Affrights thy shrinking Train,
And rudely rends thy Robes,
So long sure-found beneath thy sylvan Shed,

Shall Fancy, Friendship, Science, rose-lip'd Health,
  Thy gentlest Influence own,
  And hymn thy fav'rite Name!

[ST KILDA]

But oh! o'er all, forget not Kilda's race,
  On whose bleak rocks, which brave the wasting tides,
Fair Nature's daughter, Virtue, yet abides.
  Go, just, as they, their blameless manners trace!
Then to my ear transmit some gentle song
  Of those whose lives are yet sincere and plain,
Their bounded walks the rugged cliffs along,
  And all their prospect but the wintry main.
With sparing temperance, at the needful time,
  They drain the sainted spring, or, hunger-prest,
Along the Atlantic rock undreading climb,
  And of its eggs despoil the solan's nest.
Thus blest in primal innocence they live,
  Suffic'd and happy with that frugal fare
Which tasteful toil and hourly danger give.
  Hard is their shallow soil, and bleak and bare;
Nor ever vernal bee was heard to murmur there!

Unbounded is thy range; with varied stile
  Thy Muse may, like those feathery tribes which spring
From their rude rocks, extend her skirting wing
  Round the moist marge of each cold Hebrid isle,
To that hoar pile which still its ruins shows:
  In whose small vaults a pigmy-folk is found,
Whose bones the delver with his spade upthrows,
  And culls them, wondering, from the hallow'd ground!
Or thither where beneath the showery west
  The mighty kings of three fair realms are laid:
Once foes, perhaps, together now they rest.
  No slaves revere them, and no wars invade:
Yet frequent now, at midnight solemn hour,
  The rifted mounds their yawning cells unfold,
And forth the Monarchs stalk with sovereign power
  In pageant robes, and wreath'd with sheeny gold,
And on their twilight tombs aerial council hold.

GRAY

AN ELEGY WRITTEN IN A COUNTRY CHURCH YARD

The *Curfeu* tolls the Knell of parting Day,
The lowing Herd winds slowly o'er the Lea,
The Plow-man homeward plods his weary Way,
And leaves the World to Darkness, and to me.

Now fades the glimmering Landscape on the Sight,
And all the Air a solemn Stillness holds;
Save where the Beetle wheels his droning Flight,
And drowsy Tinklings lull the distant Folds.

Save that from yonder Ivy-mantled Tow'r
The mopeing Owl does to the Moon complain
Of such as, wand'ring near her secret Bow'r,
Molest her ancient solitary Reign.

Beneath whose rugged Elms, that Yew-Tree's Shade,
Where heaves the Turf in many a mould'ring Heap,
Each in his narrow Cell for ever laid,
The rude Forefathers of the Hamlet sleep.

The breezy Call of Incense-breathing Morn,
The Swallow twitt'ring from the Straw-built Shed,
The Cock's shrill Clarion, or the ecchoing Horn,
No more shall rouse them from their lowly Bed.

For them no more the blazing Hearth shall burn,
Or busy Houswife ply her Evening Care:
No Children run to lisp their Sire's Return,
Or climb his Knees the envied Kiss to share.

Oft did the Harvest to their Sickle yield,
Their Furrow oft the stubborn Glebe has broke;
How jocund did they drive their Team afield!
How bow'd the Woods beneath their sturdy Stroke!

Let not Ambition mock their useful Toil,
Their homely Joys and Destiny obscure;
Nor Grandeur hear with a disdainful Smile,
The short and simple Annals of the Poor.

The Boast of Heraldry, the Pomp of Pow'r,
And all that Beauty, all that Wealth e'er gave,
Awaits alike th'inevitable Hour.
The Paths of Glory lead but to the Grave.

Nor you, ye Proud, impute to these the Fault,
If Mem'ry o'er their Tomb no Trophies raise,
Where thro' the long-drawn Isle and fretted Vault
The pealing Anthem swells the Note of Praise.

Can storied Urn or animated Bust
Back to its Mansion call the fleeting Breath?
Can Honour's Voice provoke the silent Dust,
Or Flatt'ry sooth the dull cold Ear of Death?

Perhaps in this neglected Spot is laid
Some Heart once pregnant with celestial Fire,
Hands that the Rod of Empire might have sway'd,
Or wak'd to Extacy the living Lyre.

But Knowledge to their Eyes her ample Page
Rich with the Spoils of Time did ne'er unroll;
Chill Penury repress'd their noble Rage,
And froze the genial Current of the Soul.

Full many a Gem of purest Ray serene,
The dark unfathom'd Caves of Ocean bear:
Full many a Flower is born to blush unseen,
And waste its Sweetness on the desart Air.

Some Village-*Hampden* that with dauntless Breast
The little Tyrant of his Fields withstood;
Some mute inglorious *Milton* here may rest,
Some *Cromwell* guiltless of his Country's Blood.

Th'Applause of list'ning Senates to command,
The Threats of Pain and Ruin to despise,
To scatter Plenty o'er a smiling Land,
And read their Hist'ry in a Nation's Eyes

Their Lot forbad: nor circumscrib'd alone
Their growing Virtues, but their Crimes confin'd;
Forbad to wade through Slaughter to a Throne,
And shut the Gates of Mercy on Mankind,

The struggling Pangs of conscious Truth to hide,
To quench the Blushes of ingenuous Shame,
Or heap the Shrine of Luxury and Pride
With Incense, kindled at the Muse's Flame.

Far from the madding Crowd's ignoble Strife,
Their sober Wishes never learn'd to stray;
Along the cool sequester'd Vale of Life
They kept the noiseless Tenor of their Way.

Yet ev'n these Bones from Insult to protect

Some frail Memorial still erected nigh,
With uncouth Rhimes and shapeless Sculpture deck'd,
Implores the passing Tribute of a Sigh.

Their Name, their Years, spelt by th'unletter'd Muse,
The Place of Fame and Elegy supply:
And many a holy Text around she strews,
That teach the rustic Moralist to dye.

For who to dumb Forgetfulness a Prey,
This pleasing anxious Being e'er resign'd,
Left the warm Precincts of the chearful Day,
Nor cast one longing ling'ring Look behind?

On some fond Breast the parting Soul relies,
Some pious Drops the closing Eye requires;
Ev'n from the Tomb the Voice of Nature cries,
Ev'n in our Ashes live their wonted Fires.

For thee, who mindful of th'unhonour'd Dead
Dost in these Lines their artless Tale relate;
If chance, by lonely Contemplation led,
Some kindred Spirit shall inquire thy Fate,

Haply some hoary-headed Swain may say,
'Oft have we seen him at the Peep of Dawn
'Brushing with hasty Steps the Dews away
'To meet the Sun upon the upland Lawn.

'There at the Foot of yonder nodding Beech
'That wreathes its old fantastic Roots so high,
'His listless Length at Noontide wou'd he stretch,
'And pore upon the Brook that babbles by.

'Hard by yon Wood, now smiling as in Scorn,
'Mutt'ring his wayward Fancies he wou'd rove,
'Now drooping, woeful wan, like one forlorn,
'Or craz'd with Care, or cross'd in hopeless Love.

'One Morn I miss'd him on the custom'd Hill,
'Along the Heath, and near his fav'rite Tree;
'Another came; nor yet beside the Rill,
'Nor up the Lawn, nor at the Wood was he.

'The next with Dirges due in sad Array
'Slow thro' the Church-way Path we saw him born.
'Approach and read (for thou can'st read) the Lay,
'Grav'd on the Stone beneath yon aged Thorn.'

(There scatter'd oft, the earliest of the Year,
By Hands unseen, are Show'rs of Violets found:

The Red-breast loves to bill* and warble there,
And little Footsteps lightly print the Ground.)

THE EPITAPH

Here rests his Head upon the Lap of Earth
A Youth to Fortune and to Fame unknown:
Fair Science frown'd not on his humble Birth,
And Melancholy mark'd him for her own.
Large was his Bounty, and his Soul sincere,
Heav'n did a Recompence as largely send:
He gave to Mis'ry all he had, a Tear:
He gain'd from Heav'n ('twas all he wish'd) a Friend.
No farther seek his Merits to disclose,
Or draw his Frailties from their dread Abode,
(There they alike in trembling Hope repose)
The Bosom of his Father and his God.

SMART

[ADORATION]

For Adoration seasons change,
And order, truth and beauty range,
Adjust, attract, and fill:
The grass the polyanthus cheques;
And polish'd porphyry reflects,
By the descending rill.

Rich almonds colour to the prime
For Adoration; tendrils climb,
And fruit-trees pledge their gems;
And Ivis, with her gorgeous vest,
Builds for her eggs her cunning nest,
And bell-flowers bow their stems.

* All the printed texts read 'build'. The emendation 'bill' preferable both poetically and ornithologically, occurs in Gray's autograph of this stanza in his own copy of the 1753 edition with Bentley's 'Designs'.

With vinous syrup cedars spout;
From rocks pure honey gushing out,
  For ADORATION springs:
All scenes of painting croud the map
Of nature; to the mermaid's pap
  The scaled infant clings.

The spotted ounce and playsome cubs
Run rustling 'mongst the flow'ring shrubs,
  And lizards feed the moss;
For ADORATION beasts embark,
While waves upholding halcyon's ark
  No longer roar and toss.

While Israel sits beneath his fig,
With coral root and amber sprig
  The wean'd advent'rer sports;
Where to the palm the jasmin cleaves,
For ADORATION 'mongst the leaves
  The gale his peace reports.

Increasing days their reign exalt,
Nor in the pink and mottled vault
  The opposing spirits tilt;
And, by the coasting reader spied,
The silverlings and crusions glide
  For ADORATION gilt.

For ADORATION rip'ning canes,
And cocoa's purest milk detains
  The western pilgrim's staff;
Where rain in clasping boughs inclos'd,
And vines with oranges dispos'd,
  Embow'r the social laugh.

Now labour his reward receives,
For ADORATION counts his sheaves,
  To peace, her bounteous prince;
The nectarine his strong tint imbibes,
And apples of ten thousand tribes,
  And quick peculiar quince.

The wealthy crops of whit'ning rice,
'Mongst thyine woods and groves of spice,
  For ADORATION grow;
And, marshall'd in the fenced land,
The peaches and pomegranates stand,
  Where wild carnations blow.

The laurels with the winter strive;
The crocus burnishes alive
  Upon the snow-clad earth:
For ADORATION myrtles stay
To keep the garden from dismay,
  And bless the sight from dearth.

The pheasant shows his pompous neck;
And ermine, jealous of a speck,
  With fear eludes offence:
The sable with his glossy pride,
For ADORATION is descried,
  Where frosts the waves condense.

The cheerful holly, pensive yew,
And holy thorn, their trim renew;
  The squirrel hoards his nuts:
All creatures batten o'er their stores,
And careful nature all her doors
  For ADORATION shuts.

GOLDSMITH

from THE DESERTED VILLAGE

SWEET was the sound when oft at evening's close,
Up yonder hill the village murmur rose;
There as I past with careless steps and slow,
The mingling notes came softened from below;
The swain responsive as the milk-maid sung,
The sober herd that lowed to meet their young;
The noisy geese that gabbled o'er the pool,
The playful children just let loose from school;

The watch-dog's voice that bayed the whispering wind, *Goldsmith*
And the loud laugh that spoke the vacant mind,
These all in soft confusion sought the shade,
And filled each pause the nightingale had made.
But now the sounds of population fail,
No chearful murmurs fluctuate in the gale,
No busy steps the grass-grown foot-way tread,
But all the bloomy flush of life is fled.
All but yon widowed, solitary thing
That feebly bends beside the plashy spring;
She, wretched matron, forced, in age, for bread,
To strip the brook with mantling cresses spread,
To pick her wintry faggot from the thorn,
To seek her nightly shed, and weep till morn;
She only left of all the harmless train,
The sad historian of the pensive plain.

Near yonder copse, where once the garden smil'd,
And still where many a garden flower grows wild;
There, where a few torn shrubs the place disclose,
The village preacher's modest mansion rose.
A man he was, to all the country dear,
And passing rich with forty pounds a year;
Remote from towns he ran his godly race,
Nor ere had changed, nor wish'd to change his place;
Unskilful he to fawn, or seek for power,
By doctrines fashioned to the varying hour;
Far other aims his heart had learned to prize,
More bent to raise the wretched than to rise.
His house was known to all the vagrant train,
He chid their wanderings, but relieved their pain;
The long remembered beggar was his guest,
Whose beard descending swept his aged breast;
The ruined spendthrift, now no longer proud,
Claimed kindred there, and had his claims allowed;
The broken soldier, kindly bade to stay,
Sate by his fire, and talked the night away;
Wept o'er his wounds, or tales of sorrow done,
Shouldered his crutch, and shewed how fields were won.
Pleased with his guests, the good man learned to glow,
And quite forgot their vices in their woe;

Careless their merits, or their faults to scan,
His pity gave ere charity began.

Thus to relieve the wretched was his pride,
And even his failings leaned to Virtue's side;
But in his duty prompt at every call,
He watched and wept, he prayed and felt, for all.
And, as a bird each fond endearment tries,
To tempt its new fledged offspring to the skies;
He tried each art, reproved each dull delay,
Allured to brighter worlds, and led the way.

Beside the bed where parting life was layed,
And sorrow, guilt, and pain, by turns dismayed,
The reverend champion stood. At his control,
Despair and anguish fled the struggling soul;
Comfort came down the trembling wretch to raise,
And his last faultering accents whispered praise.

At church, with meek and unaffected grace,
His looks adorned the venerable place;
Truth from his lips prevailed with double sway,
And fools, who came to scoff, remained to pray.
The service past, around the pious man,
With ready zeal each honest rustic ran;
Even children followed with endearing wile,
And plucked his gown, to share the good man's smile.
His ready smile a parent's warmth exprest,
Their welfare pleased him, and their cares distrest;
To them his heart, his love, his griefs were given,
But all his serious thoughts had rest in Heaven.
As some tall cliff that lifts its awful form
Swells from the vale, and midway leaves the storm,
Tho' round its breast the rolling clouds are spread,
Eternal sunshine settles on its head.

Beside yon straggling fence that skirts the way,
With blossomed furze unprofitably gay,
There, in his noisy mansion, skill'd to rule,
The village master taught his little school;
A man severe he was, and stern to view,
I knew him well, and every truant knew;
Well had the boding tremblers learned to trace

The day's disasters in his morning face;
Full well they laugh'd with counterfeited glee,
At all his jokes, for many a joke had he;
Full well the busy whisper circling round,
Conveyed the dismal tidings when he frowned;
Yet he was kind, or if severe in aught,
The love he bore to learning was in fault;
The village all declared how much he knew;
'Twas certain he could write, and cypher too;
Lands he could measure, terms and tides presage,
And even the story ran that he could gauge.
In arguing too, the parson owned his skill,
For e'en tho' vanquished, he could argue still;
While words of learned length, and thundering sound,
Amazed the gazing rustics ranged around,
And still they gazed, and still the wonder grew,
That one small head could carry all he knew.

But past is all his fame. The very spot
Where many a time he triumphed, is forgot.
Near yonder thorn, that lifts its head on high,
Where once the sign-post caught the passing eye,
Low lies that house where nut-brown draughts inspired,
Where grey-beard mirth and smiling toil retired,
Where village statesmen talked with looks profound,
And news much older than their ale went round.
Imagination fondly stoops to trace
The parlour splendours of that festive place;
The white-washed wall, the nicely sanded floor,
The varnished clock that clicked behind the door;
The chest contrived a double debt to pay,
A bed by night, a chest of drawers by day;
The pictures placed for ornament and use,
The twelve good rules, the royal game of goose;
The hearth, except when winter chill'd the day,
With aspen boughs, and flowers, and fennel gay,
While broken tea-cups, wisely kept for shew,
Ranged o'er the chimney, glistened in a row.

Vain transitory splendours! Could not all
Reprieve the tottering mansion from its fall!
Obscure it sinks, nor shall it more impart

An hour's importance to the poor man's heart;
Thither no more the peasant shall repair
To sweet oblivion of his daily care;
No more the farmer's news, the barber's tale,
No more the wood-man's ballad shall prevail;
No more the smith his dusky brow shall clear,
Relax his ponderous strength, and lean to hear;
The host himself no longer shall be found
Careful to see the mantling bliss go round;
Nor the coy maid, half willing to be prest,
Shall kiss the cup to pass it to the rest.

CHURCHILL

[A CRITICASTER]

WITH that *low* CUNNING, which in fools supplies,
And amply too, the place of being wise,
Which Nature, kind indulgent parent, gave
To qualify the Blockhead for a Knave;
With that *smooth* FALSHOOD, whose appearance charms,
And reason of each wholsome doubt disarms,
Which to the lowest depth of guile descends,
By vilest means pursues the vilest ends,
Wears Friendship's mask for purposes of spite,
Fawns in the day, and Butchers in the night;
With that *malignant* ENVY, which turns pale,
And sickens, even if a friend prevail,
Which merit and success pursues with hate,
And damns the worth it cannot imitate;
With the *cold* CAUTION of a coward's spleen,
Which fears not guilt, but always seeks a screen,
Which keeps this maxim ever in her view –
What's *basely* done, should be done *safely* too;
With that *dull, rooted, callous* IMPUDENCE,
Which, dead to shame, and ev'ry nicer sense,
Ne'er blushed, unless, in spreading VICE's snares,
She blunder'd on some VIRTUE unawares;

With all these blessings, which we seldom find
Lavish'd by Nature on *one* happy mind,
A Motley Figure, of the FRIBBLE Tribe,
Which Heart can scarce conceive, or pen describe,
Came *simp'ring* on; to ascertain whose sex
Twelve, sage, *impanell'd* Matrons would perplex.
Nor *Male*, nor *Female*; *Neither*, and yet both;
Of *Neuter* Gender, tho' of *Irish* growth;
A six-foot suckling, mincing in *Its* gait;
Affected, peevish, prim, and delicate;
Fearful *It* seem'd, tho' of Athletic make,
Lest *brutal breezes* should too roughly shake
Its tender form, and *savage* motion spread,
O'er *Its* pale cheeks, the horrid manly red.
    Much did *It* talk, in *Its* own pretty phrase,
Of Genius and of Taste, of Play'rs and Plays;
Much too of writings, which *Itself* had wrote,
Of special merit, tho' of little note;
For Fate, in a strange humour, had decreed
That what *It* wrote, none but *Itself* should read;
Much too *It* chatter'd of *Dramatic* Laws,
Misjudging Critics, and misplac'd applause,
Then, with a self-complacent jutting air,
It smil'd, It smirk'd, It wriggled to the chair;
And, with an aukward briskness not its own,
Looking around, and *perking* on the throne,
Triumphant seem'd, when that strange savage Dame,
Known but to few, or only known by name,
Plain COMMON SENSE appear'd, by Nature there
Appointed with plain TRUTH to guard the Chair.
The Pageant saw, and blasted with her frown,
To *Its* first state of Nothing melted down.

COWPER

THE CASTAWAY

OBSCUREST night involv'd the sky,
  Th'Atlantic billows roar'd,
When such a destin'd wretch as I,
  Wash'd headlong from on board,
Of friends, of hope, of all bereft,
His floating home for ever left.

No braver chief could Albion boast
  Than he with whom he went,
Nor ever ship left Albion's coast,
  With warmer wishes sent.
He lov'd them both, but both in vain,
Nor him beheld, nor her again.

Not long beneath the whelming brine,
  Expert to swim, he lay;
Nor soon he felt his strength decline,
  Or courage die away;
But wag'd with death a lasting strife,
Supported by despair of life.

He shouted: nor his friends had fail'd
  To check the vessel's course,
But so the furious blast prevail'd,
  That, pitiless perforce,
They left their outcast mate behind,
And scudded still before the wind.

Some succour yet they could afford;
  And such as storms allow,
The cask, the coop, the floated cord,
  Delay'd not to bestow.
But he (they knew) nor ship, nor shore,
Whate'er they gave, should visit more.

Nor, cruel as it seemed, could he
  Their haste himself condemn,
Aware that flight, in such a sea,
  Alone could rescue them;

Yet bitter felt it still to die
Deserted, and his friends so nigh.

He long survives, who lives an hour
  In ocean, self-upheld;
And so long he, with unspent pow'r,
  His destiny repell'd;
And ever, as the minutes flew,
Entreated help, or cried – Adieu!

At length, his transient respite past,
  His comrades, who before
Had heard his voice in ev'ry blast,
  Could catch the sound no more.
For then, by toil subdued, he drank
The stifling wave, and then he sank.

No poet wept him: but the page
  Of narrative sincere,
That tells his name, his worth, his age,
  Is wet with Anson's tear.
And tears by bards or heroes shed
Alike immortalize the dead.

I therefore purpose not, or dream,
  Descanting on his fate,
To give the melancholy theme
  A more enduring date:
But misery still delights to trace
Its 'semblance in another's case.

No voice divine the storm allay'd,
  No light propitious shone;
When, snatch'd from all effectual aid,
  We perished, each alone:
But I beneath a rougher sea,
And whelm'd in deeper gulphs than he.

THE SHRUBBERY

WRITTEN IN A TIME OF AFFLICTION

OH happy shades! to me unblest,
  Friendly to peace, but not to me,

How ill the scene that offers rest,
  And heart that cannot rest, agree!

This glassy stream, that spreading pine,
  Those alders quiv'ring to the breeze,
Might sooth a soul less hurt than mine,
  And please, if any thing could please.

But fixt unalterable care
  Foregoes not what she feels within,
Shows the same sadness ev'ry where,
  And slights the season and the scene.

For all that pleas'd in wood or lawn,
  While peace possess'd these silent bow'rs,
Her animating smile withdrawn,
  Has lost its beauties and its pow'rs.

The saint or moralist should tread
  This moss-grown alley, musing, slow;
They seek, like me, the secret shade,
  But not, like me, to nourish woe.

Me fruitful scenes and prospects waste
  Alike admonish not to roam;
These tell me of enjoyments past,
  And those of sorrows yet to come.

[TOWN & COUNTRY]

GOD made the country, and man made the town.
What wonder then that health and virtue, gifts
That can alone make sweet the bitter draught
That life holds out to all, should most abound
And least be threaten'd in the fields and groves?
Possess ye, therefore, ye, who, borne about
In chariots and sedans, know no fatigue
But that of idleness, and taste no scenes
But such as art contrives, possess ye still
Your element; there only can ye shine;
There only minds like yours can do no harm.
Our groves were planted to console at noon

The pensive wanderer in their shades. At eve
The moonbeam, sliding softly in between
The sleeping leaves, is all the light they wish,
Birds warbling all the music. We can spare
The splendour of your lamps; they but eclipse
Our softer satellite. Your songs confound
Our more harmonious notes: the thrush departs
Scar'd, and th'offended nightingale is mute.
There is a public mischief in your mirth;
It plagues your country. Folly such as yours,
Grac'd with a sword, and worthier of a fan,
Has made, which enemies could ne'er have done,
Our arch of empire, steadfast but for you,
A mutilated structure, soon to fall.

BLAKE

SONG

How sweet I roam'd from field to field,
  And tasted all the summer's pride,
'Till I the prince of love beheld,
  Who in the sunny beams did glide!

He shew'd me lilies for my hair,
  And blushing roses for my brow;
He led me through his gardens fair,
  Where all his golden pleasures grow.

With sweet May dews my wings were wet,
  And Phœbus fir'd my vocal rage;
He caught me in his silken net,
  And shut me in his golden cage.

He loves to sit and hear me sing,
  Then, laughing, sports and plays with me;
Then stretches out my golden wing,
  And mocks my loss of liberty.

SONG

My silks and fine array,
  My smiles and languish'd air,
By love are driv'n away;
  And mournful lean Despair
Brings me yew to deck my grave:
Such end true lovers have.

His face is fair as heav'n,
  When springing buds unfold;
O why to him was't giv'n,
  Whose heart is wintry cold?
His breast is love's all worship'd tomb,
Where all love's pilgrims come.

Bring me an axe and a spade,
  Bring me a winding sheet;
When I my grave have made,
  Let winds and tempests beat:
Then down I'll lie, as cold as clay.
True love doth pass away!

THE DIVINE IMAGE

To Mercy, Pity, Peace, and Love
All pray in their distress;
And to these virtues of delight
Return their thankfulness.

For Mercy, Pity, Peace, and Love
Is God, our father dear,
And Mercy, Pity, Peace, and Love
Is Man, his child and care.

For Mercy has a human heart,
Pity a human face,
And Love, the human form divine,
And Peace, the human dress.

Then every man, of every clime,
That prays in his distress,
Prays to the human form divine,
Love, Mercy, Pity, Peace.

And all must love the human form,
In heathen, turk, or jew;
Where Mercy, Love, & Pity dwell
There God is dwelling too.

THE CLOD AND THE PEBBLE

'Love seeketh not Itself to please,
Nor for itself hath any care,
But for another gives its ease,
And builds a Heaven in Hell's despair.'

So sung a little Clod of Clay
Trodden with the cattle's feet,
But a Pebble of the brook
Warbled out these metres meet:

'Love seeketh only Self to please,
To bind another to Its delight,
Joys in another's loss of ease,
And builds a Hell in Heaven's despite.'

THE SICK ROSE

O Rose, thou art sick!
The invisible worm
That flies in the night,
In the howling storm,

Has found out thy bed
Of crimson joy,
And his dark secret love
Does thy life destroy.

THE TYGER

Tyger! Tyger! burning bright
In the forests of the night,
What immortal hand or eye
Could frame thy fearful symmetry?

In what distant deeps or skies
Burnt the fire of thine eyes?
On what wings dare he aspire?
What the hand dare sieze the fire?

And what shoulder, & what art,
Could twist the sinews of thy heart?
And when thy heart began to beat,
What dread hand? & what dread feet?

What the hammer? what the chain?
In what furnace was thy brain?
What the anvil? what dread grasp
Dare its deadly terrors clasp?

When the stars threw down their spears,
And water'd heaven with their tears,
Did he smile his work to see?
Did he who made the Lamb make thee?

Tyger! Tyger! burning bright
In the forests of the night,
What immortal hand or eye,
Dare frame thy fearful symmetry?

LONDON

I WANDER thro' each charter'd street,
Near where the charter'd Thames does flow,
And mark in every face I meet
Marks of weakness, marks of woe.

In every cry of every Man,
In every Infant's cry of fear,
In every voice, in every ban,
The mind-forg'd manacles I hear.

How the Chimney-sweeper's cry
Every black'ning Church appalls;
And the hapless Soldier's sigh
Runs in blood down Palace walls.

But most thro' midnight streets I hear
How the youthful Harlot's curse
Blasts the new born Infant's tear,
And blights with plagues the Marriage hearse.

INFANT SORROW

My mother groan'd! my father wept.
Into the dangerous world I leapt:
Helpless, naked, piping loud:
Like a fiend hid in a cloud.

Struggling in my father's hands,
Striving against my swadling bands,
Bound and weary I thought best
To sulk upon my mother's breast.

AUGURIES OF INNOCENCE

To see a World in a Grain of Sand
And a Heaven in a Wild Flower,
Hold Infinity in the palm of your hand
And Eternity in an hour.

A Robin Red breast in a Cage
Puts all Heaven in a Rage.
A dove house fill'd with doves & Pigeons
Shudders Hell thro 'all its regions.
A dog starv'd at his Master's Gate
Predicts the ruin of the State.
A Horse misus'd upon the Road
Calls to Heaven for Human blood.
Each outcry of the hunted Hare
A fibre from the Brain does tear.
A Skylark wounded in the wing,
A Cherubim does cease to sing.
The Game Cock clip'd & arm'd for fight
Does the Rising Sun affright.
Every Wolf's & Lion's howl
Raises from Hell a Human Soul.

The wild deer, wandr'ing here & there,
Keeps the Human Soul from Care.
The Lamb misus'd breeds Public strife
And yet forgives the Butcher's Knife.
The Bat that flits at close of Eve
Has left the Brain that won't Believe.
The Owl that calls upon the Night
Speaks the Unbeliever's fright.
He who shall hurt the little Wren
Shall never be belov'd by Men.
He who the Ox to wrath has mov'd
Shall never be by Woman lov'd.
The wanton Boy that kills the Fly
Shall feel the Spider's enmity.
He who torments the Chafer's sprite
Weaves a Bower in endless Night.
The Catterpiller on the Leaf
Repeats to thee thy Mother's grief.
Kill not the Moth nor Butterfly,
For the Last Judgment draweth nigh.
He who shall train the Horse to War
Shall never pass the Polar Bar.
The Begger's Dog & Widow's Cat,
Feed them & thou wilt grow fat.
The Gnat that sings his Summer's song
Poison gets from Slander's tongue.
The poison of the Snake & Newt
Is the sweat of Envy's Foot.
The Poison of the Honey Bee
Is the Artist's Jealousy.
The Prince's Robes & Beggar's Rags
Are Toadstools on the Miser's Bags.
A truth that's told with bad intent
Beats all the Lies you can invent.
It is right it should be so;
Man was made for Joy & Woe;
And when this we rightly know
Thro' the World we safely go.
Joy & Woe are woven fine,
A Clothing for the Soul divine;
Under every grief & pine

Runs a joy with silken twine.
The Babe is more than swadling Bands;
Throughout all these Human Lands
Tools were made, & Born were hands,
Every Farmer Understands.
Every Tear from Every Eye
Becomes a Babe in Eternity;
This is caught by Females bright
And return'd to its own delight.
The Bleat, the Bark, Bellow & Roar
Are Waves that Beat on Heaven's Shore.
The Babe that weeps the Rod beneath
Writes Revenge in realms of death.
The Beggar's Rags, fluttering in Air,
Does to Rags the Heavens tear.
The Soldier, arm'd with Sword & Gun,
Palsied strikes the Summer's Sun.
The poor Man's Farthing is worth more
Than all the Gold on Afric's Shore.
One Mite wrung from the Labrer's hands
Shall buy & sell the Miser's Lands:
Or, if protected from on high,
Does that whole Nation sell & buy.
He who mocks the Infant's Faith
Shall be mock'd in Age & Death.
He who shall teach the Child to Doubt
The rotting Grave shall ne'er get out.
He who respects the Infant's faith
Triumphs over Hell & Death.
The Child's Toys & the Old Man's Reasons
Are the Fruits of the Two seasons.
The Questioner, who sits so sly,
Shall never know how to Reply.
He who replies to words of Doubt
Doth put the Light of Knowledge out.
The Strongest Poison ever known
Came from Caesar's Laurel Crown.
Nought can deform the Human Race
Like to the Armour's iron brace.
When Gold & Gems adorn the Plow
To peaceful Arts shall Envy Bow.

A Riddle or the Cricket's Cry
Is to Doubt a fit Reply.
The Emmet's Inch & Eagle's Mile
Make Lame Philosophy to smile.
He who Doubts from what he sees
Will ne'er Believe, do what you Please.
If the Sun & Moon should doubt,
They'd immediately Go out.
To be in a Passion you Good may do,
But no Good if a Passion is in you.
The Whore & Gambler, by the State
Licenc'd, build that Nation's Fate.
The Harlot's cry from Street to Street
Shall weave Old England's winding Sheet.
The Winner's Shout, the Loser's Curse,
Dance before dead England's Hearse.
Every Night & every Morn
Some to Misery are Born.
Every Morn & every Night
Some are Born to sweet delight.
Some are Born to sweet delight,
Some are Born to Endless Night.
We are led to Believe a Lie
When we see not Thro' the Eye
Which was Born in a Night to perish in a Night
When the Soul Slept in Beams of Light.
God Appears & God is Light
To those poor Souls who dwell in Night,
But does a Human Form Display
To those who Dwell in Realms of day.

from THE BOOK OF THEL

WHY cannot the Ear be closed to its own destruction?
Or the glist'ning Eye to the poison of a smile?
Why are the Eyelids stor'd with arrows ready drawn,
Where a thousand fighting men in ambush lie?
Or an Eye of gifts & graces show'ring fruits & coined gold?
Why a Tongue impress'd with honey from every wind?
Why an Ear, a whirlpool fierce to draw creations in?

Why a Nostril wide inhaling terror, trembling, & affright?
Why a tender curb upon the youthful burning boy?
Why a little curtain of flesh on the bed of our desire?

[THE NEW JERUSALEM]

AND did those feet in ancient time
Walk upon England's mountains green?
And was the holy Lamb of God
On England's pleasant pastures seen?

And did the Countenance Divine
Shine forth upon our clouded hills?
And was Jerusalem builded here
Among these dark Satanic Mills?

Bring me my Bow of burning gold:
Bring me my Arrows of desire:
Bring me my Spear: O clouds unfold!
Bring me my Chariot of fire.

I will not cease from Mental Fight,
Nor shall my Sword sleep in my hand
Till we have built Jerusalem
In England's green & pleasant Land.

[BIRDSONG]

THOU hearest the Nightingale begin the Song of Spring.
The Lark sitting upon his earthy bed, just as the morn
Appears, listens silent; then springing from the waving Corn-field, loud
He leads the Choir of Day: trill, trill, trill, trill,
Mounting upon the wings of light into the Great Expanse,
Reechoing against the lovely blue & shining heavenly Shell,
His little throat labours with inspiration; every feather
On throat & breast & wings vibrates with the effluence Divine.
All Nature listens silent to him, & the awful Sun
Stands still upon the Mountain looking on this little Bird
With eyes of soft humility & wonder, love & awe,

Then loud from their green covert all the Birds begin their Song:
The Thrush, the Linnet & the Goldfinch, Robin & the Wren
Awake the Sun from his sweet reverie upon the Mountain.
The Nightingale again assays his song, & thro' the day
And thro' the night warbles luxuriant, every Bird of Song
Attending his loud harmony with admiration & love.

EPILOGUE

TO THE ACCUSER WHO IS THE GOD OF THIS WORLD

TRULY, My Satan, thou art but a Dunce,
And dost not know the Garment from the Man.
Every Harlot was a Virgin once,
Nor can'st thou ever change Kate into Nan.

Tho' thou art Worship'd by the Names Divine
Of Jesus & Jehovah, thou art still
The Son of Morn in weary Night's decline,
The lost Traveller's Dream under the Hill.

CRABBE

[THE PAUPER'S FUNERAL]

NOW once again the gloomy scene explore,
Less gloomy now; the bitter hour is o'er,
The man of many sorrows sighs no more. –
Up yonder hill, behold how sadly slow
The bier moves winding from the vale below;
There lie the happy dead, from trouble free,
And the glad parish pays the frugal fee:
No more, O Death! thy victim starts to hear
Churchwarden stern, or kingly overseer;
No more the farmer claims his humble bow,
Thou art his lord, the best of tyrants thou!
  Now to the church behold the mourners come,
Sedately torpid and devoutly dumb;
The village children now their games suspend,

To see the bier that bears their ancient friend;
For he was one in all their idle sport,
And like a monarch ruled their little court.
The pliant bow he form'd, the flying ball,
The bat, the wicket, were his labours all;
Him now they follow to his grave, and stand
Silent and sad, and gazing, hand in hand;
While bending low, their eager eyes explore
The mingled relics of the parish poor:
The bell tolls late, the moping owl flies round,
Fear marks the flight and magnifies the sound;
The busy priest, detain'd by weightier care,
Defers his duty till the day of prayer;
And, waiting long, the crowd retire distress'd,
To think a poor man's bones should lie unbless'd.

[PETER GRIMES]

THUS by himself compell'd to live each day,
To wait for certain hours the tide's delay;
At the same times the same dull views to see,
The bounding marsh-bank and the blighted tree;
The water only, when the tides were high,
When low, the mud half cover'd and half-dry;
The sun-burnt tar that blisters on the planks,
And bank-side stakes in their uneven ranks;
Heaps of entangled weeds that slowly float,
As the tide rolls by the impeded boat.
When tides were neap, and, in the sultry day,
Through the tall bounding mud-banks made their way,
Which on each side rose swelling, and below
The dark warm flood ran silently and slow;
There anchoring, Peter chose from man to hide,
There hang his head, and view the lazy tide
In its hot slimy channel slowly glide;
Where the small eels that left the deeper way
For the warm shore, within the shallows play;
Where gaping muscles, left upon the mud,
Slope their slow passage to the fallen flood; –
Here dull and hopeless he'd lie down and trace

How sidelong crabs had scrawl'd their crooked race;
Or sadly listen to the tuneless cry
Of fishing gull or clanging golden eye;
What time the sea-birds to the marsh would come,
And the loud bittern from the bull-rush home,
Gave from the salt-ditch side the bellowing boom:
He nursed the feelings these dull scenes produce,
And loved to stop beside the opening sluice;
Where the small stream, confined in narrow bound,
Ran with a dull, unvaried, sadd'ning sound;
Where all, presented to the eye or ear,
Oppress'd the soul with misery, grief, and fear.

[JONAS KINDRED'S HOUSEHOLD]

Fix'd were their habits; they arose betimes,
Then pray'd their hour, and sang their party-rhymes:
Their meals were plenteous, regular, and plain;
The trade of Jonas brought him constant gain;
Vender of hops and malt, of coals and corn –
And, like his father, he was merchant born:
Neat was their house; each table, chair, and stool,
Stood in its place, or moving moved by rule;
No lively print or picture graced the room;
A plain brown paper lent its decent gloom;
But here the eye, in glancing round, survey'd
A small recess that seem'd for china made;
Such pleasing pictures seem'd this pencill'd ware,
That few would search for nobler objects there –
Yet, turn'd by chosen friends, and there appear'd
His stern strong features, whom they all revered;
For there in lofty air was seen to stand
The bold protector of the conquer'd land;
Drawn in that look with which he wept and swore,
Turn'd out the members, and made fast the door,
Ridding the house of every knave and drone,
Forced, though it grieved his soul, to rule alone.
The stern still smile each friend approving gave,
Then turn'd the view, and all again were grave.
 There stood a clock, though small the owner's need,

For habit told when all things should proceed;
Few their amusements, but when friends appear'd,
They with the world's distress their spirits cheer'd;
The nation's guilt, that would not long endure
The reign of men so modest and so pure:
Their town was large, and seldom pass'd a day
But some had fail'd, and others gone astray;
Clerks had absconded, wives eloped, girls flown
To Gretna-Green, or sons rebellious grown;
Quarrels and fires arose; – and it was plain
The times were bad; the saints had ceased to reign!
A few yet lived to languish and to mourn
For good old manners never to return.

[THE DEJECTED LOVER]

THAT evening all in fond discourse was spent,
When the sad lover to his chamber went,
To think on what had past, to grieve and to repent:
Early he rose, and look'd with many a sigh
On the red light that fill'd the eastern sky;
Oft had he stood before, alert and gay,
To hail the glories of the new-born day:
But now dejected, languid, listless, low,
He saw the wind upon the water blow,
And the cold stream curl'd onward as the gale
From the pine-hill blew harshly down the dale;
On the right side the youth a wood survey'd,
With all its dark intensity of shade;
Where the rough wind alone was heard to move,
In this, the pause of nature and of love,
When now the young are rear'd, and when the old,
Lost to the tie, grow negligent and cold –
Far to the left he saw the huts of men,
Half hid in mist, that hung upon the fen;
Before him swallows, gathering for the sea,
Took their short flights, and twitter'd on the lea;
And near the bean-sheaf stood, the harvest done,
And slowly blacken'd in the sickly sun;
All these were sad in nature, or they took

Sadness from him, the likeness of his look,
And of his mind – he ponder'd for a while,
Then met his Fanny with a borrow'd smile.

CHARLOTTE SMITH

ELEGIAC SONNET

WRITTEN AT THE CLOSE OF SPRING

THE garlands fade that Spring so lately wove,
Each simple flower, which she had nurs'd in dew,
Anemonies that spangled every grove,
The primrose wan, and hare-bell, mildly blue.
No more shall violets linger in the dell,
Or purple orchis variegate the plain,
Till Spring again shall call forth every bell,
And dress with humid hands, her wreaths again.
Ah! poor humanity! so frail, so fair,
Are the fond visions of thy early day,
Till tyrant passion, and corrosive care,
Bid all thy fairy colours fade away!
Another May new buds and flowers shall bring;
Ah! why has happiness – no second spring?

RUSSELL

SONNET

SUPPOS'D TO BE WRITTEN AT LEMNOS

ON this lone Isle, whose rugged rocks affright
The cautious pilot, ten revolving years
Great Paean's Son, unwonted erst to tears,
Wept o'er his wound: alike each rolling light
Of heaven he watch'd, and blam'd its lingering flight.
By day the sea-mew screaming round his cave
Drove slumber from his eyes, the chiding wave,

And savage howlings chas'd his dreams by night.
HOPE still was his: in each low breeze, that sigh'd
Thro' his rude grot, he heard a coming oar,
In each white cloud a coming sail he spied;
Nor seldom listen'd to the fancied roar
Of Octa's torrents, or the hoarser tide
That parts ſam'd Trachis ſrom th'Euboic shore.

BOWLES

SONNET

JULY 18TH 1787

O TIME! who know'st a lenient hand to lay
Softest on sorrow's wounds, and slowly thence,
(Lulling to sad repose the weary sense)
The faint pang stealest unperceiv'd away;
On Thee I rest my only hope at last,
And think, when thou hast dried the bitter tear
That flows in vain o'er all my soul held dear,
I may look back on many sorrows past,
And meet life's peaceful evening with a smile –
As some lone bird, at day's departing hour,
Sings in the sunbeam of the transient shower,
Forgetful, tho' its wings are wet the while: –
Yet ah! how much must that poor heart endure,
Which hopes from thee, and thee alone, a cure!

COLERIDGE

FROST AT MIDNIGHT

THE Frost performs its secret ministry,
Unhelped by any wind. The owlet's cry
Came loud – and hark, again! loud as before.

The inmates of my cottage, all at rest,
Have left me to that solitude, which suits
Abstruser musings: save that at my side
My cradled infant slumbers peacefully.
'Tis calm indeed! so calm, that it disturbs
And vexes meditation, with its strange
And extreme silentness. Sea, hill, and wood,
This populous village! Sea, and hill, and wood,
With all the numberless goings-on of life,
Inaudible as dreams! the thin blue flame
Lies on my low-burnt fire, and quivers not;
Only that film, which fluttered on the grate,
Still flutters there, the sole unquiet thing.
Methinks, its motion in this hush of nature
Gives it dim sympathies with me who live,
Making it a companionable form,
Whose puny flaps and freaks the idling Spirit
By its own moods interprets, every where
Echo or mirror seeking of itself,
And makes a toy of Thought.
But O! how oft,
How oft, at school, with most believing mind,
Presageful, have I gazed upon the bars,
To watch that fluttering *stranger*! and as oft
With unclosed lids, already had I dreamt
Of my sweet birth-place, and the old church-tower,
Whose bells, the poor man's only music, rang
From morn to evening, all the hot Fair-day,
So sweetly, that they stirred and haunted me
With a wild pleasure, falling on mine ear
Most like articulate sounds of things to come!
So gazed I, till the soothing things, I dreamt,
Lulled me to sleep, and sleep prolonged my dreams!
And so I brooded all the following morn,
Awed by the stern preceptor's face, mine eye
Fixed with mock study on my swimming book:
Save if the door half-opened, and I snatched
A hasty glance, and still my heart leaped up,
For still I hoped to see the *stranger's* face,
Townsman, or aunt, or sister more beloved,
My play-mate when we both were clothed alike!

Dear Babe, that sleepest cradled by my side,
Whose gentle breathings, heard in this deep calm,
Fill up the interspersed vacancies
And momentary pauses of the thought!
My babe so beautiful! it thrills my heart
With tender gladness, thus to look at thee,
And think that thou shalt learn far other lore,
And in far other scenes! For I was reared
In the great city, pent 'mid cloisters dim,
And saw nought lovely but the sky and stars.
But *thou*, my babe! shalt wander like a breeze
By lakes and sandy shores, beneath the crags
Of ancient mountain, and beneath the clouds,
Which image in their bulk both lakes and shores
And mountain crags: so shalt thou see and hear
The lovely shapes and sounds intelligible
Of that eternal language, which thy God
Utters, who from eternity doth teach
Himself in all, and all things in himself.
Great universal Teacher! he shall mould
Thy spirit, and by giving make it ask.

Therefore all seasons shall be sweet to thee,
Whether the summer clothe the general earth
With greenness, or the redbreast sit and sing
Betwixt the tufts of snow on the bare branch
Of mossy apple-tree, while the nigh thatch
Smokes in the sun-thaw; whether the eave-drops fall
Heard only in the trances of the blast,
Or if the secret ministry of frost
Shall hang them up in silent icicles,
Quietly shining to the quiet Moon.

KUBLA KHAN

IN Xanadu did KUBLA KHAN
A stately pleasure-dome decree:
Where ALPH, the sacred river, ran
Through caverns measureless to man
Down to a sunless sea.

So twice five miles of fertile ground
With walls and towers were girdled round:
And there were gardens bright with sinuous rills,
Where blossomed many an incense-bearing tree;
And here were forests ancient as the hills,
Enfolding sunny spots of greenery.

But oh! that deep romantic chasm which slanted
Down the green hill athwart a cedarn cover!
A savage place! as holy and inchanted
As e'er beneath a waning moon was haunted
By woman wailing for her demon-lover!
And from this chasm, with ceaseless turmoil seething,
As if this earth in fast thick pants were breathing,
A mighty fountain momently was forced:
Amid whose swift half-intermitted Burst
Huge fragments vaulted like rebounding hail,
Or chaffy grain beneath the thresher's flail:
And 'mid these dancing rocks at once and ever
It flung up momently the sacred river.
Five miles meandering with a mazy motion
Through wood and dale the sacred river ran,
Then reached the caverns measureless to man,
And sank in tumult to a lifeless ocean:
And 'mid this tumult Kubla heard from far
Ancestral voices prophesying war!

The shadow of the dome of pleasure
Floated midway on the waves;
Where was heard the mingled measure
From the fountain and the caves.
It was a miracle of rare device,
A sunny pleasure-dome with caves of ice!

A damsel with a dulcimer
In a vision once I saw:
It was an Abyssinian maid,
And on her dulcimer she play'd,
Singing of Mount Abora.
Could I revive within me
Her symphony and song,
To such a deep delight 'twould win me,

That with music loud and long,
I would build that dome in air,
That sunny dome! those caves of ice!
And all who heard should see them there,
And all should cry, Beware! Beware!
His flashing eyes, his floating hair!
Weave a circle round him thrice,
And close your eyes with holy dread:
For he on honey-dew hath fed,
And drunk the milk of Paradise.

DEJECTION

AN ODE

Late, late yestreen I saw the new Moon,
With the old Moon in her arms;
And I fear, I fear, my Master dear!
We shall have a deadly storm.

Ballad of Sir PATRICK SPENCE

WELL! If the Bard was weather-wise, who made
The grand old ballad of Sir Patrick Spence,
This night, so tranquil now, will not go hence
Unrous'd by winds, that ply a busier trade
Than those which mould yon clouds in lazy flakes,
Or the dull sobbing draft, that moans and rakes
Upon the strings of the Æolian lute,
Which better far were mute.
For lo! the New-moon winter-bright!
And overspread with phantom-light,
(With swimming phantom-light o'erspread
But rimm'd and circled by a silver thread)
I see the old Moon in her lap, foretelling
The coming on of rain and squally blast.
And oh! that even now the gust were swelling,
And the slant night-shower driving loud and fast!
Those sounds which oft have raised me, whilst they awed,
And sent my soul abroad,
Might now perhaps their wonted impulse give,
Might startle this dull pain, and make it move and live!

A grief without a pang, void, dark, and drear,
A stifled, drowsy, unimpassion'd grief,

Which finds no natural outlet, no relief,
In word, or sigh, or tear—
O Lady! in this wan and heartless mood,
To other thoughts by yonder throstle woo'd,
All this long eve, so balmy and serene,
Have I been gazing on the western sky,
And it's peculiar tint of yellow green:
And still I gaze – and with how blank an eye!
And those thin clouds above, in flakes and bars,
That give away their motion to the stars;
Those stars, that glide behind them or between,
Now sparkling, now bedimm'd, but always seen;
Yon crescent Moon, as fix'd as if it grew
In its own cloudless, starless lake of blue;
I see them all so excellently fair,
I see, not feel how beautiful they are!

My genial spirits fail,
And what can these avail,
To lift the smoth'ring weight from off my breast?
It were a vain endeavor,
Though I should gaze for ever
On that green light that lingers in the west:
I may not hope from outward forms to win
The passion and the life, whose fountains are within.

O Lady! we receive but what we give,
And in our life alone does nature live:
Ours is her wedding garment, ours her shroud!
And would we aught behold, of higher worth,
Than that inanimate cold world allow'd
To the poor loveless ever-anxious crowd,
Ah! from the soul itself must issue forth,
A light, a glory, a fair luminous cloud
Enveloping the Earth –
And from the soul itself must there be sent
A sweet and potent voice, of its own birth,
Of all sweet sounds the life and element!

O pure of heart! thou need'st not ask of me
What this strong music in the soul may be!
What, and wherein it doth exist,

This light, this glory, this fair luminous mist,
This beautiful and beauty-making power.
  Joy, virtuous Lady! Joy that ne'er was given,
Save to the pure, and in their purest hour,
Life, and life's effluence, cloud at once and shower,
Joy, Lady! is the spirit and the power,
Which wedding Nature to us gives in dow'r
  A new Earth and new Heaven,
Undreamt of by the sensual and the proud –
Joy is the sweet voice, Joy the luminous cloud –
    We in ourselves rejoice!
And thence flows all that charms or ear or sight,
  All melodies the echoes of that voice,
All colours a suffusion from that light.

There was a time when, though my path was rough,
  This joy within me dallied with distress,
And all misfortunes were but as the stuff
  Whence Fancy made me dreams of happiness:
For hope grew round me, like the twining vine,
And fruits, and foliage, not my own, seem'd mine.
But now afflictions bow me down to earth:
Nor care I that they rob me of my mirth;
    But oh! each visitation
Suspends what nature gave me at my birth,
  My shaping spirit of Imagination.
For not to think of what I needs must feel,
  But to be still and patient, all I can;
And haply by abstruse research to steal
  From my own nature all the natural Man –
  This was my sole resource, my only plan:
Till that which suits a part infects the whole,
And now is almost grown the habit of my Soul.

Hence, viper thoughts, that coil around my mind,
    Reality's dark dream!
I turn from you, and listen to the wind,
  Which long has rav'd unnotic'd. What a scream
Of agony by torture lengthen'd out
That lute sent forth! Thou Wind, that rav'st without,
  Bare crag, or mountain-tairn, or blasted tree,
Or pine-grove whither woodman never clomb,

Coleridge

Or lonely house, long held the witches' home,
Methinks were fitter instruments for thee,
Mad Lutanist! who in this month of show'rs,
Of dark brown gardens, and of peeping flow'rs,
Mak'st Devils' yule, with worse than wintry song,
The blossoms, buds, and tim'rous leaves among.
Thou Actor, perfect in all tragic sounds!
Thou mighty Poet, e'en to Frenzy bold!
What tell's thou now about?
'Tis of the rushing of an Host in rout,
With groans of trampled men, with smarting wounds –
At once they groan with pain, and shudder with the cold!
But hush! there is a pause of deepest silence!
And all that noise, as of a rushing crowd,
With groans, and tremulous shudderings – all is over –
It tells another tale, with sounds less deep and loud!
A tale of less affright,
And temper'd with delight,
As Otway's self had fram'd the tender lay –
'Tis of a little child
Upon a lonesome wild,
Not far from home, but she hath lost her way:
And now moans low in bitter grief and fear,
And now screams loud, and hopes to make her mother hear.

'Tis midnight, but small thoughts have I of sleep:
Full seldom may my friend such vigils keep!
Visit her, gentle Sleep! with wings of healing,
And may this storm be but a mountain-birth,
May all the stars hang bright above her dwelling,
Silent as though they watch'd the sleeping Earth!
With light heart may she rise,
Gay fancy, cheerful eyes,
Joy lift her spirit, joy attune her voice:
To her may all things live, from Pole to Pole,
Their life the eddying of her living soul!
O simple spirit, guided from above,
Dear Lady! friend devoutest of my choice,
Thus may'st thou ever, evermore rejoice.

['MY HEART LEAPS UP']

My heart leaps up when I behold
   A rainbow in the sky:
So was it when my life began;
So is it now I am a man;
So be it when I shall grow old,
   Or let me die!
The Child is father of the Man;
And I could wish my days to be
Bound each to each by natural piety.

[LUCY]

She dwelt among the untrodden ways
  Beside the springs of Dove,
A Maid whom there were none to praise
  And very few to love:

A violet by a mossy stone
  Half hidden from the eye!
– Fair as a star, when only one
  Is shining in the sky.

She lived unknown, and few could know
  When Lucy ceased to be;
But she is in her grave, and, oh,
  The difference to me!

★

A slumber did my spirit seal;
  I had no human fears:
She seemed a thing that could not feel
  The touch of earthly years.

No motion has she now, no force;
  She neither hears nor sees;
Rolled round in earth's diurnal course,
  With rocks, and stones, and trees.

Wordsworth

from LINES COMPOSED A FEW MILES ABOVE TINTERN ABBEY ... 13 JULY 1798

THE sounding cataract
Haunted me like a passion: the tall rock,
The mountain, and the deep and gloomy wood,
Their colours and their forms, were then to me
An appetite; a feeling and a love,
That had no need of a remoter charm,
By thought supplied, nor any interest
Unborrowed from the eye. – That time is past,
And all its aching joys are now no more,
And all its dizzy raptures. Not for this
Faint I, nor mourn nor murmur; other gifts
Have followed; for such loss, I would believe,
Abundant recompense. For I have learned
To look on nature, not as in the hour
Of thoughtless youth; but hearing oftentimes
The still, sad music of humanity,
Nor harsh nor grating, though of ample power
To chasten and subdue. And I have felt
A presence that disturbs me with the joy
Of elevated thoughts; a sense sublime
Of something far more deeply interfused,
Whose dwelling is the light of setting suns,
And the round ocean and the living air,
And the blue sky, and in the mind of man:
A motion and a spirit, that impels
All thinking things, all objects of all thought,
And rolls through all things. Therefore am I still
A lover of the meadows and the woods,
And mountains; and of all that we behold
From this green earth; of all the mighty world
Of eye, and ear, – both what they half create,
And what perceive; well pleased to recognise
In nature and the language of the sense
The anchor of my purest thoughts, the nurse,
The guide, the guardian of my heart, and soul
Of all my moral being.

THE world is too much with us; late and soon,
Getting and spending, we lay waste our powers:
Little we see in Nature that is ours;
We have given our hearts away, a sordid boon!
This Sea that bares her bosom to the moon;
The winds that will be howling at all hours,
And are up-gathered now like sleeping flowers;
For this, for everything, we are out of tune;
It moves us not. – Great God! I'd rather be
A Pagan suckled in a creed outworn;
So might I, standing on this pleasant lea,
Have glimpses that would make me less forlorn;
Have sight of Proteus rising from the sea;
Or hear old Triton blow his wreathèd horn.

THE SOLITARY REAPER

BEHOLD her, single in the field,
Yon solitary Highland Lass!
Reaping and singing by herself;
Stop here, or gently pass!
Alone she cuts and binds the grain,
And sings a melancholy strain;
O listen! for the Vale profound
Is overflowing with the sound.

No Nightingale did ever chaunt
More welcome notes to weary bands
Of travellers in some shady haunt,
Among Arabian sands:
A voice so thrilling ne'er was heard
In spring-time from the Cuckoo-bird,
Breaking the silence of the seas
Among the farthest Hebrides.

Will no one tell me what she sings? –
Perhaps the plaintive numbers flow
For old, unhappy, far-off things,
And battles long ago:

Or is it some more humble lay,
Familiar matter of to-day?
Some natural sorrow, loss, or pain,
That has been, and may be again?

Whate'er the theme, the Maiden sang
As if her song could have no ending;
I saw her singing at her work,
And o'er the sickle bending; –
I listened, motionless and still;
And, as I mounted up the hill,
The music in my heart I bore,
Long after it was heard no more.

from INTIMATIONS OF IMMORTALITY FROM RECOLLECTIONS OF EARLY CHILDHOOD

OUR birth is but a sleep and a forgetting:
The Soul that rises with us, our life's Star,
Hath had elsewhere its setting,
And cometh from afar:
Not in entire forgetfulness,
And not in utter nakedness,
But trailing clouds of glory do we come
From God, who is our home:
Heaven lies about us in our infancy!
Shades of the prison-house begin to close
Upon the growing Boy,
But He beholds the light, and whence it flows,
He sees it in his joy;
The Youth, who daily farther from the east
Must travel, still is Nature's Priest,
And by the vision splendid
Is on his way attended;
At length the Man perceives it die away,
And fade into the light of common day.

*

And O, ye Fountains, Meadows, Hills, and Groves,
Forebode not any severing of our loves!

Yet in my heart of hearts I feel your might;
I only have relinquished one delight
To live beneath your more habitual sway.
I love the Brooks which down their channels fret,
Even more than when I tripped lightly as they;
The innocent brightness of a new-born Day
Is lovely yet;
The Clouds that gather round the setting sun
Do take a sober colouring from an eye
That hath kept watch o'er man's mortality;
Another race hath been, and other palms are won.
Thanks to the human heart by which we live,
Thanks to its tenderness, its joys, and fears,
To me the meanest flower that blows can give
Thoughts that do often lie too deep for tears.

[TO CATHERINE WORDSWORTH 1808–1812]

SURPRISED by joy – impatient as the Wind
I turned to share the transport – Oh! with whom
But Thee, deep buried in the silent tomb,
That spot which no vicissitude can find?
Love, faithful love, recalled thee to my mind –
But how could I forget thee? Through what power,
Even for the least division of an hour,
Have I been so beguiled as to be blind,
To my most grievous loss! – That thought's return
Was the worst pang that sorrow ever bore,
Save one, one only, when I stood forlorn,
Knowing my heart's best treasure was no more;
That neither present time, nor years unborn
Could to my sight that heavenly face restore.

AFTERTHOUGHT

I THOUGHT of Thee, my partner and my guide,
As being past away. – Vain sympathies!
For, backward, Duddon! as I cast my eyes
I see what was, and is, and will abide;

Still glides the Stream, and shall for ever glide;
The Form remains, the Function never dies;
While we, the brave, the mighty, and the wise,
We Men, who in our morn of youth defied
The elements, must vanish; – be it so!
Enough, if something from our hands have power
To live, and act, and serve the future hour;
And if, as toward the silent tomb we go,
Through love, through hope, and faith's transcendent [dower,
We feel that we are greater than we know.

from THE PRELUDE

CHILDHOOD AND SCHOOL-TIME

FAIR seed-time had my soul, and I grew up
Foster'd alike by beauty and by fear;
Much favour'd in my birthplace, and no less
In that beloved Vale to which, erelong,
I was transplanted. Well I call to mind
('Twas at an early age, ere I had seen
Nine summers) when upon the mountain slope
The frost and breath of frosty wind had snapp'd
The last autumnal crocus, 'twas my joy
To wander half the night among the Cliffs
And the smooth Hollows, where the woodcocks ran
Along the open turf. In thought and wish
That time, my shoulder all with springes hung,
I was a fell destroyer. On the heights
Scudding away from snare to snare, I plied
My anxious visitation, hurrying on,
Still hurrying, hurrying onward; moon and stars
Were shining o'er my head; I was alone,
And seem'd to be a trouble to the peace
That was among them. Sometimes it befel
In these night-wanderings, that a strong desire
O'erpower'd my better reason, and the bird
Which was the captive of another's toils
Became my prey; and, when the deed was done
I heard among the solitary hills
Low breathings coming after me, and sounds

Of undistinguishable motion, steps
Almost as silent as the turf they trod.
Nor less in springtime when on southern banks
The shining sun had from his knot of leaves
Decoy'd the primrose flower, and when the Vales
And woods were warm, was I a plunderer then
In the high places, on the lonesome peaks
Where'er, among the mountains and the winds,
The Mother Bird had built her lodge. Though mean
My object, and inglorious, yet the end
Was not ignoble. Oh! when I have hung
Above the raven's nest, by knots of grass
And half-inch fissures in the slippery rock
But ill sustain'd, and almost, as it seem'd,
Suspended by the blast which blew amain,
Shouldering the naked crag; Oh! at that time,
While on the perilous ridge I hung alone,
With what strange utterance did the loud dry wind
Blow through my ears! the sky seem'd not a sky
Of earth, and with what motion mov'd the clouds!

*

The moon was up, the Lake was shining clear
Among the hoary mountains; from the Shore
I push'd, and struck the oars and struck again
In cadence, and my little Boat mov'd on
Even like a Man who walks with stately step
Though bent on speed. It was an act of stealth
And troubled pleasure; not without the voice
Of mountain-echoes did my Boat move on,
Leaving behind her still on either side
Small circles glittering idly in the moon,
Until they melted all into one track
Of sparkling light. A rocky Steep uprose
Above the Cavern of the Willow tree
And now, as suited one who proudly row'd
With his best skill, I fix'd a steady view
Upon the top of that same craggy ridge,
The bound of the horizon, for behind
Was nothing but the stars and the grey sky.
She was an elfin Pinnace; lustily

Wordsworth

I dipp'd my oars into the silent Lake,
And, as I rose upon the stroke, my Boat
Went heaving through the water, like a Swan;
When from behind that craggy Steep, till then
The bound of the horizon, a huge Cliff,
As if with voluntary power instinct,
Uprear'd its head. I struck, and struck again,
And, growing still in stature, the huge Cliff
Rose up between me and the stars, and still,
With measur'd motion, like a living thing,
Strode after me. With trembling hands I turn'd,
And through the silent water stole my way
Back to the Cavern of the Willow tree.
There, in her mooring-place, I left my Bark,
And, through the meadows homeward went, with grave
And serious thoughts; and after I had seen
That spectacle, for many days, my brain
Work'd with a dim and undetermin'd sense
Of unknown modes of being; in my thoughts
There was a darkness, call it solitude,
Or blank desertion, no familiar shapes
Of hourly objects, images of trees,
Of sea or sky, no colours of green fields;
But huge and mighty Forms that do not live
Like living men mov'd slowly through the mind
By day and were the trouble of my dreams.

Wisdom and Spirit of the universe!
Thou Soul that art the eternity of thought!
That giv'st to forms and images a breath
And everlasting motion! not in vain,
By day or star-light thus from my first dawn
Of Childhood didst Thou intertwine for me
The passions that build up our human Soul,
Not with the mean and vulgar works of Man,
But with high objects, with enduring things,
With life and nature, purifying thus
The elements of feeling and of thought,
And sanctifying, by such discipline,
Both pain and fear, until we recognize
A grandeur in the beatings of the heart.

Nor was this fellowship vouchsaf'd to me
With stinted kindness. In November days,
When vapours, rolling down the valleys, made
A lonely scene more lonesome; among woods
At noon, and 'mid the calm of summer nights,
When, by the margin of the trembling Lake,
Beneath the gloomy hills I homeward went
In solitude, such intercourse was mine;
'Twas mine among the fields both day and night,
And by the waters all the summer long.

And in the frosty season, when the sun
Was set, and visible for many a mile
The cottage windows through the twilight blaz'd,
I heeded not the summons: – happy time
It was, indeed, for all of us; to me
It was a time of rapture: clear and loud
The village clock toll'd six; I wheel'd about,
Proud and exulting, like an untir'd horse,
That cares not for his home. – All shod with steel,
We hiss'd along the polish'd ice, in games
Confederate, imitative of the chace
And woodland pleasures, the resounding horn,
The Pack loud bellowing, and the hunted hare.
So through the darkness and the cold we flew,
And not a voice was idle; with the din,
Meanwhile, the precipices rang aloud,
The leafless trees, and every icy crag
Tinkled like iron, while the distant hills
Into the tumult sent an alien sound
Of melancholy, not unnoticed, while the stars,
Eastward, were sparkling clear, and in the west
The orange sky of evening died away.

Not seldom from the uproar I retired
Into a silent bay, or sportively
Glanced sideway, leaving the tumultuous throng,
To cut across the image of a star
That gleam'd upon the ice: and oftentimes
When we had given our bodies to the wind,
And all the shadowy banks, on either side,
Came sweeping through the darkness, spinning still

The rapid line of motion; then at once
Have I, reclining back upon my heels,
Stopp'd short, yet still the solitary Cliffs
Wheeled by me, even as if the earth had roll'd
With visible motion her diurnal round;
Behind me did they stretch in solemn train
Feebler and feebler, and I stood and watch'd
Till all was tranquil as a dreamless sleep.

['THERE WAS A BOY']

THERE was a Boy, ye knew him well, ye Cliffs
And Islands of Winander! many a time
At evening, when the stars had just begun
To move along the edges of the hills,
Rising or setting, would he stand alone
Beneath the trees, or by the glimmering Lake,
And there, with fingers interwoven, both hands
Press'd closely, palm to palm, and to his mouth
Uplifted, he, as through an instrument,
Blew mimic hootings to the silent owls
That they might answer him. – And they would shout
Across the watery Vale, and shout again,
Responsive to his call, with quivering peals,
And long halloos, and screams, and echoes loud
Redoubled and redoubled; concourse wild
Of mirth and jocund din! And when it chanced
That pauses of deep silence mock'd his skill,
Then sometimes, in that silence, while he hung
Listening, a gentle shock of mild surprize
Has carried far into his heart the voice
Of mountain torrents; or the visible scene
Would enter unawares into his mind
With all its solemn imagery, its rocks,
Its woods, and that uncertain Heaven, receiv'd
Into the bosom of the steady Lake.

CONCLUSION

IT was a Summer's night, a close warm night,
Wan, dull and glaring, with a dripping mist

Low-hung and thick that cover'd all the sky,
Half threatening storm and rain; but on we went
Uncheck'd, being full of heart and having faith
In our tried Pilot. Little could we see
Hemm'd round on every side with fog and damp,
And, after ordinary travellers' chat
With our Conductor, silently we sank
Each into commerce with his private thoughts:
Thus did we breast the ascent, and by myself
Was nothing either seen or heard the while
Which took me from my musings, save that once
The Shepherd's Cur did to his own great joy
Unearth a hedgehog in the mountain crags
Round which he made a barking turbulent.
This small adventure, for even such it seemed
In that wild place and at the dead of night,
Being over and forgotten, on we wound
In silence as before. With forehead bent
Earthward, as if in opposition set
Against an enemy, I panted up
With eager pace, and no less eager thoughts.
Thus might we wear perhaps an hour away,
Ascending at loose distance each from each,
And I, as chanced, the foremost of the Band;
When at my feet the ground appear'd to brighten,
And with a step or two seem'd brighter still;
Nor had I time to ask the cause of this,
For instantly a Light upon the turf
Fell like a flash: I looked about, and lo!
The Moon stood naked in the Heavens, at height
Immense above my head, and on the shore
I found myself of a huge sea of mist,
Which, meek and silent, rested at my feet:
A hundred hills their dusky backs upheaved
All over this still Ocean, and beyond,
Far, far beyond, the vapours shot themselves,
In headlands, tongues, and promontory shapes,
Into the Sea, the real Sea, that seem'd
To dwindle, and give up its majesty,
Usurp'd upon as far as sight could reach.
Meanwhile, the Moon look'd down upon this shew

In single glory, and we stood, the mist
Touching our very feet; and from the shore
At distance not the third part of a mile
Was a blue chasm; a fracture in the vapour,
A deep and gloomy breathing-place through which
Mounted the roar of waters, torrents, streams
Innumerable, roaring with one voice.
The universal spectacle throughout
Was shaped for admiration and delight,
Grand in itself alone, but in that breach
Through which the homeless voice of waters rose,
That dark deep thoroughfare had Nature lodg'd
The Soul, the Imagination of the whole.

ROGERS

CAPTIVITY

Caged in old woods, whose reverend echoes wake
When the hern screams along the distant lake,
Her little heart oft flutters to be free,
Oft sighs to turn the unrelenting key.
In vain! the nurse that rusted relic wears,
Nor mov'd by gold – nor to be mov'd by tears;
And terraced walls their black reflection throw
On the green-mantled moat that sleeps below.

BRYANT

TO A WATERFOWL

Whither, midst falling dew,
While glow the heavens with the last steps of day,
Far, through their rosy depths, dost thou pursue
Thy solitary way?

Vainly the fowler's eye
Might mark thy distant flight to do thee wrong,
As darkly seen against the crimson sky,
Thy figure floats along.

Seek'st thou the plashy brink
Of weedy lake, or marge of river wide,
Or where the rocking billows rise and sink
On the chafed ocean-side?

There is a Power whose care
Teaches thy way along that pathless coast –
The desert and illimitable air –
Lone wandering, but not lost.

All day thy wings have found
At that far height, the cold, thin, atmosphere,
Yet stoop not, weary, to the welcome land,
Though the dark night is near.

And soon that toil shall end;
Soon shalt thou find a summer home, and rest,
And scream among thy fellows; reeds shall bend,
Soon, o'er thy sheltered nest.

Thou'rt gone, the abyss of heaven
Hath swallowed up thy form; yet, on my heart
Deeply has sunk the lesson thou hast given
And shall not soon depart.

He who, from zone to zone,
Guides through the boundless sky thy certain flight,
In the long way that I must tread alone,
Will lead my steps aright.

LANDOR

[THE SEA-NYMPH'S PARTING]

She smil'd, and more of pleasure than disdain
Was in her dimpled chin, and liberal lip,
And eyes that languished, lengthening, – just like love.
She went away; I on the wicker gate
Leant, and could follow with my eyes alone . . .
Restless then ran I to the highest ground
To watch her; she was gone; gone down the tide;
And the long moonbeam on the hard wet sand
Lay like a jasper column half-uprear'd.

IANTHE

WELL I remember how you smiled
To see me write your name upon
The soft sea-sand. . . . '*O! What a child!*
You think you're writing upon stone!'
I have since written what no tide
Shall ever wash away, what men
Unborn shall read o'er ocean wide
And find Ianthe's name agen.

*

PAST ruin'd Ilion Helen lives,
Alcestis rises from the shades;
Verse calls them forth; 'tis verse that gives
Immortal youth to mortal maids.

Soon shall Oblivion's deepening veil
Hide all the peopled hills you see,
The gay, the proud, while lovers hail
These many summers you and me.

The tear for fading beauty check,
For passing glory cease to sigh;
One form shall rise above the wreck,
One name, Ianthe, shall not die.

ROSE AYLMER

O what avails the sceptred race,
Ah what the form divine!
What, every virtue, every grace!
Rose Aylmer, all were thine!

Rose Aylmer, whom these wakeful eyes
May weep but never see,
A night of sorrows and of sighs
I consecrate to thee.

DIRCE

Stand close around, ye Stygian set,
With Dirce, in one boat conveyed!
Or Charon, seeing, may forget
That he is old and she a shade.

[TERNISSA]

Ternissa! you are fled!
I say not to the dead,
But to the happy ones who rest below:
For surely, surely, where
Your voice and graces are,
Nothing of death can any feel or know.
Girls who delight to dwell
Where grows most asphodel,
Gather to their calm breasts each word you speak:
The mild Persephone
Places you on her knee,
And your cool palm smoothes down stern Pluto's cheek.

[ENVOI]

I strove with none, for none was worth my strife,
Nature I loved, and next to Nature, Art;
I warmed both hands before the fire of life,
It sinks, and I am ready to depart.

MOORE

AT THE MID HOUR OF NIGHT

At the mid hour of night, when stars are weeping, I fly
To the lone vale we loved, when life shone warm in thine eye;
And I think that if spirits can steal from the regions of air,
To revisit past scenes of delight, thou wilt come to me there,
And tell me our love is remember'd, even in the sky!

Then I sing the wild song it once was rapture to hear,
When our voices, commingling, breathed, like one, on the ear;
  And, as Echo far off through the vale my sad orison rolls,
  I think, O my love! 'tis thy voice, from the Kingdom of Souls.
Faintly answering still the notes that once were so clear.

BYRON

'SHE WALKS IN BEAUTY'

SHE walks in beauty, like the night
  Of cloudless climes and starry skies;
And all that's best of dark and bright
  Meet in her aspect and her eyes:
Thus mellow'd to that tender light
  Which heaven to gaudy day denies.

One shade the more, one ray the less,
  Had half impair'd the nameless grace
Which waves in every raven tress,
  Or softly lightens o'er her face;
Where thoughts serenely sweet express
  How pure, how dear their dwelling-place.

And on that cheek, and o'er that brow,
  So soft, so calm, yet eloquent,
The smiles that win, the tints that glow,
  But tell of days in goodness spent,
A mind at peace with all below,
  A heart whose love is innocent!

TO IANTHE

NOT in those climes where I have late been straying,
Though Beauty there hath long been matchless deem'd;
Not in those visions to the heart displaying
Forms which it sighs but to have only dream'd,
Hath aught like thee in truth or fancy seem'd:
Nor, having seen thee, shall I vainly seek
To paint those charms which varied as they beam'd –

To such as see thee not my words were weak;
To those who gaze on thee what language could they speak?

Ah! may'st thou ever be what now thou art,
Nor unbeseem the promise of thy spring,
As fair in form, as warm yet pure in heart,
Love's image upon earth without his wing,
And guileless beyond hope's imagining!
And surely she who now so fondly rears
Thy youth, in thee, thus hourly brightening,
Beholds the rainbow of her future years,
Before whose heavenly hues all sorrow disappears.

Young Peri of the West! – 'tis well for me
My years already doubly number thine;
My loveless eye unmoved may gaze on thee,
And safely view thy ripening beauties shine;
Happy, I ne'er shall see them in decline;
Happier, that while all younger hearts shall bleed,
Mine shall escape the doom thine eyes assign
To those whose admiration shall succeed,
But mix'd with pangs to Love's even loveliest hours decreed.

Oh! let that eye, which, wild as the Gazelle's,
Now brightly bold or beautifully shy,
Wins as it wanders, dazzles where it dwells,
Glance o'er this page, nor to my verse deny
That smile for which my breast might vainly sigh
Could I to thee be ever more than friend:
This much, dear maid, accord; nor question why
To one so young my strain I would commend,
But bid me with my wreath one matchless lily blend.

Such is thy name with this my verse entwined;
And long as kinder eyes a look shall cast
On Harold's page, Ianthe's here enshrined
Shall thus be first beheld, forgotten last:
My days once number'd, should this homage past
Attract thy fairy fingers near the lyre
Of him who hail'd thee, loveliest as thou wast,
Such is the most my memory may desire;
Though more than Hope can claim, could Friendship less
require?

[THE EVE OF WATERLOO]

THERE was a sound of revelry by night,
And Belgium's capital had gather'd then
Her Beauty and her Chivalry, and bright
The lamps shone o'er fair women and brave men;
A thousand hearts beat happily; and when
Music arose with its voluptuous swell,
Soft eyes look'd love to eyes which spake again,
And all went merry as a marriage bell;
But hush! hark! a deep sound strikes like a rising knell!

Did ye not hear it? – No; 't was but the wind,
Or the car rattling o'er the stony street;
On with the dance! let joy be unconfined;
No sleep till morn, when Youth and Pleasure meet
To chase the glowing Hours with flying feet –
But hark! – that heavy sound breaks in once more,
As if the clouds its echo would repeat;
And nearer, clearer, deadlier than before!
Arm! Arm! it is – it is – the cannon's opening roar!

Within a window'd niche of that high hall
Sate Brunswick's fated chieftain; he did hear
That sound the first amidst the festival,
And caught its tone with Death's prophetic ear;
And when they smiled because he deem'd it near,
His heart more truly knew that peal too well
Which stretch'd his father on a bloody bier,
And roused the vengeance blood alone could quell;
He rush'd into the field, and, foremost fighting, fell.

Ah! then and there was hurrying to and fro,
And gathering tears, and tremblings of distress,
And cheeks all pale, which but an hour ago
Blush'd at the praise of their own loveliness;
And there were sudden partings, such as press
The life from out young hearts, and choking sighs
Which ne'er might be repeated; who could guess
If evermore should meet those mutual eyes
Since upon night so sweet such awful morn could rise!

And there was mounting in hot haste: the steed,
The mustering squadron, and the clattering car,
Went pouring forward with impetuous speed,
And swiftly forming in the ranks of war;
And the deep thunder peal on peal afar;
And near, the beat of the alarming drum
Roused up the soldier ere the morning star;
While throng'd the citizens with terror dumb,
Or whispering, with white lips – 'The foe! they come! they
come!'

And wild and high the 'Cameron's gathering' rose!
The war-note of Lochiel, when Albyn's hills
Have heard, and heard, too, have her Saxon foes: –
How in the noon of night that pibroch thrills,
Savage and shrill! But with the breath which fills
Their mountain-pipe, so fill the mountaineers
With the fierce native daring which instils
The stirring memory of a thousand years,
And Evan's, Donald's fame rings in each clansman's ears!

And Ardennes waves above them her green leaves,
Dewy with nature's tear-drops as they pass,
Grieving, if aught inanimate e'er grieves,
O'er the returning brave, – alas!
Ere evening to be trodden like the grass
Which now beneath them, but above shall grow
In its next verdure, when this fiery mass
Of living valour, rolling on the foe
And burning with high hope shall moulder cold and low.

Last noon beheld them full of lusty life,
Last eve in Beauty's circle proudly gay,
The midnight brought the signal-sound of strife,
The morn the marshalling in arms, – the day
Battle's magnificently stern array!
The thunder-clouds close o'er it, which when rent
The earth is cover'd thick with other clay,
Which her own clay shall cover, heap'd and pent,
Rider and horse, – friend, foe, – in one red burial blent!

Byron

['MY DAYS OF LOVE ARE OVER']

No more – no more – Oh! never more on me
  The freshness of the heart can fall like dew,
Which out of all the lovely things we see
  Extracts emotions beautiful and new;
Hived in our bosoms like the bag o' the bee.
  Think'st thou the honey with those objects grew?
Alas! 'twas not in them, but in thy power
To double even the sweetness of a flower.

No more – no more – Oh! never more, my heart,
  Canst thou be my sole world, my universe!
Once all in all, but now a thing apart,
  Thou canst not be my blessing or my curse:
The illusion's gone for ever, and thou art
  Insensible, I trust, but none the worse,
And in thy stead I've got a deal of judgment,
Though heaven knows how it ever found a lodgment.

My days of love are over; me no more
  The charms of maid, wife, and still less of widow,
Can make the fool of which they made before, –
  In short, I must not lead the life I did do;
The credulous hope of mutual minds is o'er,
  The copious use of claret is forbid too,
So for a good old-gentlemanly vice,
I think I must take up with avarice.

Ambition was my idol, which was broken
  Before the shrines of Sorrow, and of Pleasure;
And the two last have left me many a token
  O'er which reflection may be made at leisure;
Now, like Friar Bacon's brazen head, I've spoken,
  'Time is, Time was, Time's past:' – a chymic treasure
Is glittering youth, which I have spent betimes –
My heart in passion, and my head on rhymes.

What is the end of fame? 'tis but to fill
  A certain portion of uncertain paper:
Some liken it to climbing up a hill,
  Whose summit, like all hills, is lost in vapour;

For this men write, speak, preach, and heroes kill,
  And bards burn what they call their 'midnight taper,'
To have, when the original is dust,
A name, a wretched picture, and worse bust.

['THE ISLES OF GREECE']

The isles of Greece, the isles of Greece!
  Where burning Sappho loved and sung,
Where grew the arts of war and peace,
  Where Delos rose, and Phœbus sprung!
Eternal summer gilds them yet,
But all, except their sun, is set.

The Scian and the Teian muse,
  The hero's harp, the lover's lute,
Have found the fame your shores refuse:
  Their place of birth alone is mute
To sounds which echo further west
Than your sires' 'Islands of the Blest.'

The mountains look on Marathon –
  And Marathon looks on the sea;
And musing there an hour alone,
  I dream'd that Greece might still be free;
For standing on the Persians' grave,
I could not deem myself a slave.

A king sate on the rocky brow
  Which looks o'er sea-born Salamis;
And ships, by thousands, lay below,
  And men in nations; – all were his!
He counted them at break of day –
And when the sun set where were they?

And where are they? and where art thou,
  My country? On thy voiceless shore
The heroic lay is tuneless now –
  The heroic bosom beats no more!
And must thy lyre, so long divine,
Degenerate into hands like mine?

'Tis something, in the dearth of fame,
Though link'd among a fetter'd race,
To feel at least a patriot's shame,
Even as I sing, suffuse my face;
For what is left the poet here?
For Greeks a blush – for Greece a tear.

Must *we* but weep o'er days more blest?
Must *we* but blush? – Our fathers bled.
Earth! render back from out thy breast
A remnant of our Spartan dead!
Of the three hundred grant but three,
To make a new Thermopylæ!

What, silent still? and silent all?
Ah! no; – the voices of the dead
Sound like a distant torrent's fall,
And answer, 'Let one living head,
But one arise, – we come, we come!'
'Tis but the living who are dumb.

In vain – in vain: strike other chords;
Fill high the cup with Samian wine!
Leave battles to the Turkish hordes,
And shed the blood of Scio's vine!
Hark! rising to the ignoble call –
How answers each bold Bacchanal!

You have the Pyrrhic dance as yet;
Where is the Pyrrhic phalanx gone?
Of two such lessons, why forget
The nobler and the manlier one?
You have the letters Cadmus gave –
Think ye he meant them for a slave?

Fill high the bowl with Samian wine!
We will not think of themes like these!
It made Anacreon's song divine:
He served – but served Polycrates –
A tyrant; but our masters then
Were still, at least, our countrymen.

The tyrant of the Chersonese
  Was freedom's best and bravest friend;
That tyrant was Miltiades!
  Oh! that the present hour would lend
Another despot of the kind!
Such chains as his were sure to bind.

Fill high the bowl with Samian wine!
  On Suli's rock, and Parga's shore,
Exists the remnant of a line
  Such as the Doric mothers bore;
And there, perhaps, some seed is sown,
The Heracleidan blood might own.

Trust not for freedom to the Franks –
  They have a king who buys and sells;
In native swords, and native ranks,
  The only hope of courage dwells:
But Turkish force, and Latin fraud,
Would break your shield, however broad.

Fill high the bowl with Samian wine!
  Our virgins dance beneath the shade –
I see their glorious black eyes shine;
  But gazing on each glowing maid,
My own the burning tear-drop laves,
To think such breasts must suckle slaves.

Place me on Sunium's marbled steep,
  Where nothing, save the waves and I,
May hear our mutual murmurs sweep;
  There, swan-like, let me sing and die:
A land of slaves shall ne'er be mine –
Dash down yon cup of Samian wine!

['SO WE'LL GO NO MORE A ROVING']

So, we'll go no more a roving
  So late into the night,
Though the heart be still as loving,
  And the moon be still as bright.

For the sword outwears its sheath,
   And the soul wears out the breast,
And the heart must pause to breathe,
   And love itself have rest.

Though the night was made for loving,
   And the day returns too soon,
Yet we'll go no more a roving
   By the light of the moon.

SHELLEY

ODE TO THE WEST WIND

O WILD West Wind, thou breath of Autumn's being,
Thou, from whose unseen presence the leaves dead
Are driven, like ghosts from an enchanter fleeing,

Yellow, and black, and pale, and hectic red,
Pestilence-stricken multitudes: O thou,
Who chariotest to their dark wintry bed

The wingèd seeds, where they lie cold and low,
Each like a corpse within its grave, until
Thine azure sister of the Spring shall blow

Her clarion o'er the dreaming earth, and fill
(Driving sweet buds like flocks to feed in air)
With living hues and odours plain and hill:

Wild Spirit, which art moving everywhere;
Destroyer and preserver; hear, oh, hear!

Thou on whose streams, mid the steep sky's commotion,
Loose clouds like earth's decaying leaves are shed,
Shook from the tangled boughs of Heaven and Ocean,

Angels of rain and lightning: there are spread
On the blue surface of thine aëry surge,
Like the bright hair uplifted from the head

Of some fierce Maenad, even from the dim verge
Of the horizon to the zenith's height,
The locks of the approaching storm. Thou dirge

Of the dying year, to which this closing night
Will be the dome of a vast sepulchre,
Vaulted with all thy congregated might

Of vapours, from whose solid atmosphere
Black rain, and fire, and hail will burst: oh, hear!

Thou who didst waken from his summer dreams
The blue Mediterranean, where he lay,
Lulled by the coil of his crystàlline streams,

Beside a pumice isle in Baiae's bay,
And saw in sleep old palaces and towers
Quivering within the wave's intenser day,

All overgrown with azure moss and flowers
So sweet, the sense faints picturing them! Thou
For whose path the Atlantic's level powers

Cleave themselves into chasms, while far below
The sea-blooms and the oozy woods which wear
The sapless foliage of the ocean, know

Thy voice, and suddenly grow gray with fear,
And tremble and despoil themselves: oh, hear!

If I were a dead leaf thou mightest bear;
If I were a swift cloud to fly with thee;
A wave to pant beneath thy power, and share

The impulse of thy strength, only less free
Than thou, O uncontrollable! If even
I were as in my boyhood, and could be

The comrade of thy wanderings over Heaven,
As then, when to outstrip thy skiey speed
Scarce seemed a vision; I would ne'er have striven

As thus with thee in prayer in my sore need.
Oh, lift me as a wave, a leaf, a cloud!
I fall upon the thorns of life! I bleed!

A heavy weight of hours has chained and bowed
One too like thee: tameless, and swift, and proud.

Make me thy lyre, even as the forest is:
What if my leaves are falling like its own!
The tumult of thy mighty harmonies

Will take from both a deep, autumnal tone,
Sweet though in sadness. Be thou, Spirit fierce,
My spirit! Be thou me, impetuous one!

Drive my dead thoughts over the universe
Like withered leaves to quicken a new birth!
And, by the incantation of this verse,

Scatter, as from an unextinguished hearth
Ashes and sparks, my words among mankind!
Be through my lips to unawakened earth

The trumpet of a prophecy! O, Wind,
If Winter comes, can Spring be far behind?

CHORUS *from* HELLAS

The world's great age begins anew,
  The golden years return,
The earth doth like a snake renew
  Her winter weeds outworn:
Heaven smiles, and faiths and empires gleam,
Like wrecks of a dissolving dream.

A brighter Hellas rears its mountains
  From waves serener far;
A new Peneus rolls his fountains
  Against the morning star.
Where fairer Tempes bloom, there sleep
Young Cyclads on a sunnier deep.

A loftier Argo cleaves the main,
  Fraught with a later prize;
Another Orpheus sings again,
  And loves, and weeps, and dies.
A new Ulysses leaves once more
Calypso for his native shore.

Oh, write no more the tale of Troy,
  If earth Death's scroll must be!
Nor mix with Laian rage the joy
  Which dawns upon the free:
Although a subtler Sphinx renew
Riddles of death Thebes never knew.

Another Athens shall arise,
  And to remoter time
Bequeath, like sunset to the skies,
  The splendour of its prime;
And leave, if nought so bright may live,
All earth can take or Heaven can give.

Saturn and Love their long repose
  Shall burst, more bright and good
Than all who fell, than One who rose,
  Than many unsubdued:
Not gold, not blood, their altar dowers,
But votive tears and symbol flowers.

Oh, cease! must hate and death return?
  Cease! must men kill and die?
Cease! drain not to its dregs the urn
  Of bitter prophecy.
The world is weary of the past,
Oh, might it die or rest at last!

from ADONAIS

AN ELEGY ON THE DEATH OF JOHN KEATS

PEACE, peace! he is not dead, he doth not sleep –
He hath awakened from the dream of life –
'Tis we, who lost in stormy visions, keep
With phantoms an unprofitable strife,
And in mad trance, strike with our spirit's knife
Invulnerable nothings. – *We* decay
Like corpses in a charnel; fear and grief
Convulse us and consume us day by day,
And cold hopes swarm like worms within our living clay.

He has outsoared the shadow of our night;
Envy and calumny and hate and pain,
And that unrest which men miscall delight,
Can touch him not and torture not again;
From the contagion of the world's slow stain
He is secure, and now can never mourn
A heart grown cold, a head grown gray in vain;
Nor, when the spirit's self has ceased to burn,
With sparkless ashes load an unlamented urn.

He lives, he wakes – 'tis Death is dead, not he;
Mourn not for Adonais. – Thou young Dawn
Turn all thy dew to splendour, for from thee
The spirit thou lamentest is not gone;
Ye caverns and ye forests, cease to moan!
Cease ye faint flowers and fountains, and thou Air,
Which like a mourning veil thy scarf hadst thrown
O'er the abandoned Earth, now leave it bare
Even to the joyous stars which smile on its despair!

He is made one with Nature: there is heard
His voice in all her music, from the moan
Of thunder, to the song of night's sweet bird;
He is a presence to be felt and known
In darkness and in light, from herb and stone,
Spreading itself where'er that Power may move
Which has withdrawn his being to its own;
Which wields the world with never wearied love,
Sustains it from beneath, and kindles it above.

He is a portion of the loveliness
Which once he made more lovely: he doth bear
His part, while the one Spirit's plastic stress
Sweeps through the dull dense world, compelling there,
All new successions to the forms they wear;
Torturing th' unwilling dross that checks its flight
To its own likeness, as each mass may bear;
And bursting in its beauty and its might
From trees and beasts and men into the Heaven's light.

The splendours of the firmament of time
May be eclipsed, but are extinguished not;
Like stars to their appointed height they climb

And death is a low mist which cannot blot
The brightness it may veil. When lofty thought
Lifts a young heart above its mortal lair,
And love and life contend in it, for what
Shall be its earthly doom, the dead live there
And move like winds of light on dark and stormy air.

*

The One remains, the many change and pass;
Heaven's light forever shines, Earth's shadows fly;
Life, like a dome of many-coloured glass,
Stains the white radiance of Eternity,
Until Death tramples it to fragments. – Die,
If thou wouldst be with that which thou dost seek!
Follow where all is fled! – Rome's azure sky,
Flowers, ruins, statues, music, words, are weak
The glory they transfuse with fitting truth to speak.

Why linger, why turn back, why shrink, my Heart?
Thy hopes are gone before: from all things here
They have departed; thou shouldst now depart!
A light is past from the revolving year,
And man, and woman; and what still is dear
Attracts to crush, repels to make thee wither.
The soft sky smiles, – the low wind whispers near:
'Tis Adonais calls! oh, hasten thither,
No more let Life divide what Death can join together.

That Light whose smile kindles the Universe,
That Beauty in which all things work and move,
That Benediction which the eclipsing Curse
Of birth can quench not, that sustaining Love
Which through the web of being blindly wove
By man and beast and earth and air and sea,
Burns bright or dim, as each are mirrors of
The fire for which all thirst; now beams on me,
Consuming the last clouds of cold mortality.

The breath whose might I have invoked in song
Descends on me; my spirit's bark is driven,
Far from the shore, far from the trembling throng
Whose sails were never to the tempest given;

The massy earth and sphered skies are riven!
I am borne darkly, fearfully, afar;
Whilst burning through the inmost veil of Heaven,
The soul of Adonais, like a star,
Beacons from the abode where the Eternal are.

SONNET

LIFT not the painted veil which those who live
Call Life: though unreal shapes be pictured there,
And it but mimic all we would believe
With colours idly spread, – behind, lurk Fear
And Hope, twin Destinies; who ever weave
Their shadows, o'er the chasm, sightless and drear.
I knew one who lifted it – he sought,
For his lost heart was tender, things to love,
But found them not, alas! nor was there aught
The world contains, the which he could approve.
Through the unheeding many he did move,
A splendour among shadows, a bright blot
Upon this gloomy scene, a Spirit that strove
For truth, and like the Preacher found it not.

OZYMANDIAS

I MET a traveller from an antique land
Who said: Two vast and trunkless legs of stone
Stand in the desert ... Near them, on the sand,
Half sunk, a shattered visage lies, whose frown,
And wrinkled lip, and sneer of cold command,
Tell that its sculptor well those passions read
Which yet survive, stamped on these lifeless things,
The hand that mocked them, and the heart that fed:
And on the pedestal these words appear:
'My name is Ozymandias, king of kings:
Look on my works, ye Mighty, and despair!'
Nothing beside remains. Round the decay
Of that colossal wreck, boundless and bare
The lone and level sands stretch far away.

MUTABILITY

The flower that smiles to-day
 To-morrow dies;
All that we wish to stay
 Tempts and then flies.
What is this world's delight?
Lightning that mocks the night,
 Brief even as bright.

Virtue, how frail it is!
 Friendship how rare!
Love, how it sells poor bliss
 For proud despair!
But we, though soon they fall,
Survive their joy, and all
 Which ours we call.

Whilst skies are blue and bright,
 Whilst flowers are gay,
Whilst eyes that change ere night
 Make glad the day;
Whilst yet the calm hours creep,
Dream thou – and from thy sleep
 Then wake to weep.

TO ——

One word is too often profaned
 For me to profane it,
One feeling too falsely disdained
 For thee to disdain it;
One hope is too like despair
 For prudence to smother,
And pity from thee more dear
 Than that from another.

I can give not what men call love,
 But wilt thou accept not
The worship the heart lifts above
 And the Heavens reject not, –

The desire of the moth for the star,
Of the night for the morrow,
The devotion to something afar
From the sphere of our sorrow?

ON FANNY GODWIN

Her voice did quiver as we parted,
Yet knew I not that heart was broken
From which it came, and I departed
Heeding not the words then spoken.
Misery – O Misery,
This world is all too wide for thee.

A SONG

A widow bird sate mourning for her love
Upon a wintry bough;
The frozen wind crept on above,
The freezing stream below.

There was no leaf upon the forest bare,
No flower upon the ground,
And little motion in the air
Except the mill-wheel's sound.

KEATS

ON FIRST LOOKING INTO CHAPMAN'S *HOMER*

Much have I travell'd in the realms of gold,
And many goodly states and kingdoms seen;
Round many western islands have I been
Which bards in fealty to Apollo hold.
Oft of one wide expanse had I been told
That deep-brow'd Homer ruled as his demesne;
Yet did I never breathe its pure serene
Till I heard Chapman speak out loud and bold:

Then felt I like some watcher of the skies
　When a new planet swims into his ken;
Or like stout Cortez when with eagle eyes
　He star'd at the Pacific – and all his men
Look'd at each other with a wild surmise –
　Silent, upon a peak in Darien.

ODE TO A NIGHTINGALE

My heart aches, and a drowsy numbness pains
　My sense, as though of hemlock I had drunk,
Or emptied some dull opiate to the drains
　One minute past, and Lethe-wards had sunk:
'Tis not through envy of thy happy lot,
　But being too happy in thy happiness, –
　　That thou, light-wingèd Dryad of the trees,
　　　In some melodious plot
　Of beechen green, and shadows numberless,
　　Singest of summer in full-throated ease.

O, for a draught of vintage! that hath been
　Cool'd a long age in the deep-delved earth,
Tasting of Flora and the country green,
　Dance, and Provençal song, and sunburnt mirth!
O for a beaker full of the warm South,
　Full of the true, the blushful Hippocrene,
　　With beaded bubbles winking at the brim,
　　　And purple-stained mouth;
　That I might drink, and leave the world unseen,
　　And with thee fade away into the forest dim:

Fade far away, dissolve, and quite forget
　What thou among the leaves hast never known,
The weariness, the fever, and the fret
　Here, where men sit and hear each other groan;
Where palsy shakes a few, sad, last gray hairs,
　Where youth grows pale, and spectre-thin, and dies;
　　Where but to think is to be full of sorrow
　　　And leaden-eyed despairs;
　Where Beauty cannot keep her lustrous eyes,
　　Or new Love pine at them beyond to-morrow.

Away! away! for I will fly to thee,
Not charioted by Bacchus and his pards,
But on the viewless wings of Poesy,
Though the dull brain perplexes and retards:
Already with thee! tender is the night,
And haply the Queen-Moon is on her throne,
Cluster'd around by all her starry Fays;
But here there is no light,
Save what from heaven is with the breezes blown
Through verdurous glooms and winding mossy ways.

I cannot see what flowers are at my feet,
Nor what soft incense hangs upon the boughs,
But, in embalmed darkness, guess each sweet
Wherewith the seasonable month endows
The grass, the thicket, and the fruit-tree wild;
White hawthorn, and the pastoral eglantine;
Fast fading violets cover'd up in leaves;
And mid-May's eldest child,
The coming musk-rose, full of dewy wine,
The murmurous haunt of flies on summer eves.

Darkling I listen; and for many a time
I have been half in love with easeful Death,
Call'd him soft names in many a mused rhyme,
To take into the air my quiet breath;
Now more than ever seems it rich to die,
To cease upon the midnight with no pain,
While thou art pouring forth thy soul abroad
In such an ecstasy!
Still wouldst thou sing, and I have ears in vain –
To thy high requiem become a sod.

Thou wast not born for death, immortal Bird!
No hungry generations tread thee down;
The voice I hear this passing night was heard
In ancient days by emperor and clown:
Perhaps the self-same song that found a path
Through the sad heart of Ruth, when, sick for home,
She stood in tears amid the alien corn;
The same that oft-times hath
Charm'd magic casements, opening on the foam
Of perilous seas, in faery lands forlorn.

Forlorn! the very word is like a bell
  To toll me back from thee to my sole self!
Adieu! the fancy cannot cheat so well
  As she is fam'd to do, deceiving elf.
Adieu! adieu! thy plaintive anthem fades
  Past the near meadows, over the still stream,
    Up the hill-side; and now 'tis buried deep
      In the next valley-glades:
  Was it a vision, or a waking dream?
    Fled is that music: – Do I wake or sleep?

ODE ON A GRECIAN URN

THOU still unravish'd bride of quietness!
  Thou foster-child of silence and slow time,
Sylvan historian, who canst thus express
  A flowery tale more sweetly than our rhyme:
What leaf-fringed legend haunts about thy shape
  Of deities or mortals, or of both,
    In Tempe or the dales of Arcady?
  What men or gods are these? What maidens loath?
What mad pursuit? What struggle to escape?
    What pipes and timbrels? What wild ecstasy?

Heard melodies are sweet, but those unheard
  Are sweeter; therefore, ye soft pipes, play on;
Not to the sensual ear, but, more endear'd,
  Pipe to the spirit ditties of no tone:
Fair youth, beneath the trees, thou canst not leave
  Thy song, nor ever can those trees be bare;
    Bold Lover, never, never canst thou kiss,
  Though winning near the goal – yet, do not grieve;
She cannot fade, though thou hast not thy bliss,
    For ever wilt thou love, and she be fair!

Ah, happy, happy boughs! that cannot shed
  Your leaves, nor ever bid the Spring adieu;
And, happy melodist, unwearied,
  For ever piping songs for ever new;
More happy love! more happy, happy love!
  For ever warm and still to be enjoy'd,

For ever panting and for ever young;
All breathing human passion far above,
That leaves a heart high-sorrowful and cloy'd,
A burning forehead, and a parching tongue.

Who are these coming to the sacrifice?
To what green altar, O mysterious priest,
Lead'st thou that heifer lowing at the skies,
And all her silken flanks with garlands drest?
What little town by river or sea shore,
Or mountain-built with peaceful citadel,
Is emptied of its folk, this pious morn?
And, little town, thy streets for evermore
Will silent be; and not a soul to tell
Why thou art desolate, can e'er return.

O Attic shape! Fair attitude! with brede
Of marble men and maidens overwrought,
With forest branches and the trodden weed;
Thou, silent form, dost tease us out of thought
As doth eternity: Cold Pastoral!
When old age shall this generation waste,
Thou shalt remain, in midst of other woe
Than ours, a friend to man, to whom thou say'st,
'Beauty is truth, truth beauty,' – that is all
Ye know on earth, and all ye need to know.

TO AUTUMN

SEASON of mists and mellow fruitfulness,
Close bosom-friend of the maturing sun;
Conspiring with him how to load and bless
With fruit the vines that round the thatch-eves run;
To bend with apples the moss'd cottage-trees,
And fill all fruit with ripeness to the core;
To swell the gourd, and plump the hazel shells
With a sweet kernel; to set budding more,
And still more, later flowers for the bees,
Until they think warm days will never cease,
For Summer has o'er-brimm'd their clammy cells.

Who hath not seen thee oft amid thy store?
  Sometimes whoever seeks abroad may find
Thee sitting careless on a granary floor,
  Thy hair soft-lifted by the winnowing wind;
Or on a half-reap'd furrow sound asleep,
  Drowsed with the fumes of poppies, while thy hook
    Spares the next swath and all its twined flowers:
And sometimes like a gleaner thou dost keep
  Steady thy laden head across a brook;
  Or by a cyder-press, with patient look,
    Thou watchest the last oozings hours by hours.

Where are the songs of Spring? Ay, where are they?
  Think not of them, thou hast thy music too, –
While barred clouds bloom the soft-dying day,
  And touch the stubble-plains with rosy hue;
Then in a wailful choir the small gnats mourn
  Among the river sallows, borne aloft
    Or sinking as the light wind lives or dies;
And full-grown lambs loud bleat from hilly bourn;
  Hedge-crickets sing; and now with treble soft
  The red-breast whistles from a garden-croft;
    And gathering swallows twitter in the skies.

ODE ON MELANCHOLY

No, no, go not to Lethe, neither twist
  Wolf's-bane, tight-rooted, for its poisonous wine;
Nor suffer thy pale forehead to be kiss'd
  By nightshade, ruby grape of Proserpine;
Make not your rosary of yew-berries,
  Nor let the beetle, nor the death-moth be
    Your mournful Psyche, nor the downy owl
A partner in your sorrow's mysteries;
  For shade to shade will come too drowsily,
    And drown the wakeful anguish of the soul.

But when the melancholy fit shall fall
  Sudden from heaven like a weeping cloud,
That fosters the droop-headed flowers all,
  And hides the green hill in an April shroud;

Then glut thy sorrow on a morning rose,
Or on the rainbow of the salt sand-wave,
Or on the wealth of globed peonies;
Or if thy mistress some rich anger shows,
Emprison her soft hand, and let her rave,
And feed deep, deep upon her peerless eyes.

She dwells with Beauty – Beauty that must die;
And Joy, whose hand is ever at his lips
Bidding adieu; and aching Pleasure nigh,
Turning to poison while the bee-mouth sips:
Ay, in the very temple of Delight
Veil'd Melancholy has her sovran shrine,
Though seen of none save him whose strenuous tongue
Can burst Joy's grape against his palate fine;
His soul shall taste the sadness of her might,
And be among her cloudy trophies hung.

from HYPERION

DEEP in the shady sadness of a vale
Far sunken from the healthy breath of morn,
Far from the fiery noon, and eve's one star,
Sat gray-hair'd Saturn, quiet as a stone,
Still as the silence round about his lair;
Forest on forest hung about his head
Like cloud on cloud. No stir of air was there,
Not so much life as on a summer's day
Robs not one light seed from the feather'd grass,
But where the dead leaf fell, there did it rest.
A stream went voiceless by, still deadened more
By reason of his fallen divinity
Spreading a shade: the Naiad 'mid her reeds
Press'd her cold finger closer to her lips.

Along the margin-sand large foot-marks went,
No further than to where his feet had stray'd,
And slept there since. Upon the sodden ground
His old right hand lay nerveless, listless, dead,
Unsceptred; and his realmless eyes were closed;
While his bow'd head seem'd list'ning to the Earth,
His ancient mother, for some comfort yet.

It seem'd no force could wake him from his place;
But there came one, who with a kindred hand
Touch'd his wide shoulders, after bending low
With reverence, though to one who knew it not.
She was a Goddess of the infant world;
By her in stature the tall Amazon
Had stood a pigmy's height: she would have ta'en
Achilles by the hair and bent his neck;
Or with a finger stay'd Ixion's wheel.
Her face was large as that of Memphian sphinx,
Pedestal'd haply in a palace court,
When sages look'd to Egypt for their lore.
But oh! how unlike marble was that face:
How beautiful, if sorrow had not made
Sorrow more beautiful than Beauty's self.
There was a listening fear in her regard,
As if calamity had but begun;
As if the vanward clouds of evil days
Had spent their malice, and the sullen rear
Was with its stored thunder labouring up.
One hand she press'd upon that aching spot
Where beats the human heart, as if just there,
Though an immortal, she felt cruel pain:
The other upon Saturn's bended neck
She laid, and to the level of his ear
Leaning with parted lips, some words she spake
In solemn tenour and deep organ tone:
Some mourning words, which in our feeble tongue
Would come in these like accents; O how frail
To that large utterance of the early Gods!
'Saturn, look up! – though wherefore, poor old King?
I have no comfort for thee, no not one:
I cannot say, "O wherefore sleepest thou?"
For heaven is parted from thee, and the earth
Knows thee not, thus afflicted, for a God;
And ocean too, with all its solemn noise,
Has from thy sceptre pass'd; and all the air
Is emptied of thine hoary majesty.
Thy thunder, conscious of the new command,
Rumbles reluctant o'er our fallen house;
And thy sharp lightning in unpractised hands

Scorches and burns our once serene domain.
O aching time! O moments big as years!
All as ye pass swell out the monstrous truth,
And press it so upon our weary griefs
That unbelief has not a space to breathe.
Saturn, sleep on: – O thoughtless, why did I
Thus violate thy slumbrous solitude?
Why should I ope thy melancholy eyes?
Saturn, sleep on! while at thy feet I weep.'

As when, upon a tranced summer-night,
Those green-rob'd senators of mighty woods,
Tall oaks, branch-charmed by the earnest stars,
Dream, and so dream all night without a stir,
Save from one gradual solitary gust
Which comes upon the silence, and dies off,
As if the ebbing air had but one wave;
So came these words and went; the while in tears
She touch'd her fair large forehead to the ground,
Just where her falling hair might be outspread
A soft and silken mat for Saturn's feet.
One moon, with alterations slow, had shed
Her silver seasons four upon the night,
And still these two were postured motionless,
Like natural sculpture in cathedral cavern;
The frozen God still couchant on the earth,
And the sad Goddess weeping at his feet.

[WRITTEN ON A BLANK PAGE IN SHAKESPEARE'S *POEMS*]

Bright star, would I were stedfast as thou art –
  Not in lone splendour hung aloft the night
And watching, with eternal lids apart,
  Like Nature's patient, sleepless Eremite,
The moving waters at their priestlike task
  Of pure ablution round earth's human shores,
Or gazing on the new soft-fallen mask
  Of snow upon the mountains and the moors –
No – yet still stedfast, still unchangeable,

Pillow'd upon my fair love's ripening breast,
To feel for ever its soft fall and swell,
Awake for ever in a sweet unrest,
Still, still to hear her tender-taken breath,
And so live ever – or else swoon to death.

DARLEY

THE MERMAIDENS' VESPER-HYMN

Troop home to silent grots and caves!
Troop home! and mimic as you go
The mournful winding of the waves
Which to their dark abysses flow!

At this sweet hour, all things beside
In amorous pairs to covert creep;
The swans that brush the evening tide
Homeward in snowy couples keep;

In his green den the murmuring seal
Close by his sleek companion lies;
While singly we to bedward steal,
And close in fruitless sleep our eyes.

In bowers of love men take their rest,
In loveless bowers we sigh alone!
With bosom-friends are others blest, –
But we have none! But we have none!

[THE UNICORN]

Lo! in the mute, mid wilderness,
What wondrous Creature? – of no kind! –
His burning lair doth largely press, –
Gaze fixt, and feeding on the wind?
His fell is of the desert dye,
And tissue adust, dun-yellow and dry,
Compact of living sands; his eye
Black luminary, soft and mild,
With its dark lustre cools the wild;

From his stately forehead springs,
Piercing to heaven, a radiant horn, –
Lo! the compeer of lion-kings!
The steed self-armed, the Unicorn!
Ever heard of, never seen,
With a main of sands between
Him and approach; his lonely pride
To course his arid arena wide,
Free as the hurricane, or lie here,
Lord of his couch as his career! –
Wherefore should this foot profane
His sanctuary, still domain?
Let me turn, ere eye so bland
Perchance be fire-shot, like heaven's brand,
To wither my boldness! Northward now,
Behind the white star on his brow
Glittering straight against the sun,
Far athwart his lair I run.

HOOD

THE SEA OF DEATH

A FRAGMENT

METHOUGHT I saw
Life swiftly treading over endless space;
And, at her foot-print, but a bygone pace,
The ocean-past, which, with increasing wave,
Swallow'd her steps like a pursuing grave.
Sad were my thoughts that anchor'd silently
On the dead waters of that passionless sea,
Unstirr'd by any touch of living breath:
Silence hung over it, and drowsy Death,
Like a gorged sea-bird, slept with folded wings
On crowded carcases – sad passive things
That wore the thin grey surface, like a veil
Over the calmness of their features pale.

And there were Spring-faced cherubs that did sleep
Like water-lilies on that motionless deep,

How beautiful! with bright unruffled hair
On sleek unfretted brows, and eyes that were
Buried in marble tombs, a pale eclipse!
And smile-bedimpled cheeks, and pleasant lips,
Meekly apart, as if the soul intense
Spake out in dreams of its own innocence:
And so they lay in loveliness and kept
The birth-night of their peace, that Life e'en wept
With very envy of their happy fronts;
For there were neighbour brows scarr'd by the brunts
Of strife and sorrowing – where Care had set
His crooked autograph, and marr'd the jet
Of glossy locks with hollow eyes forlorn,
And lips that curl'd in bitterness and scorn –
Wretched, – as they had breath'd of this world's pain,
And so bequeath'd it to the world again
Through the beholder's heart with heavy sighs.

So lay they garmented in torpid light,
Under the pall of a transparent night,
Like solemn apparitions lull'd sublime
To everlasting rest, – and with them Time
Slept, as he sleeps upon the silent face
Of a dark dial in a sunless place.

SILENCE

There is a silence where hath been no sound,
    There is a silence where no sound may be,
    In the cold grave – under the deep deep sea,
Or in wide desert where no life is found,
Which hath been mute, and still must sleep profound;
    No voice is hush'd – no life treads silently,
    But clouds and cloudy shadows wander free,
That never spoke, over the idle ground:
But in green ruins, in the desolate walls
    Of antique palaces, where Man hath been,
Though the dun fox, or wild hyaena, calls,
    And owls, that flit continually between,
Shriek to the echo, and the low winds moan,
There the true Silence is, self-conscious and alone.

CLARE

EMMONSAIL'S HEATH IN WINTER

I LOVE to see the old heath's withered brake
Mingle its crimpled leaves with furze and ling,
While the old heron from the lonely lake
Starts slow and flaps his melancholy wing,
And oddling crow in idle motions swing
On the half-rotten ash-tree's topmost twig,
Beside whose trunk the gipsy makes his bed.
Up flies the bouncing woodcock from the brig
Where a black quagmire quakes beneath the tread;
The fieldfares chatter in the whistling thorn
And for the haw round fields and closen rove,
And coy bumbarrels, twenty in a drove,
Flit down the hedgerows in the frozen plain
And hang on little twigs and start again.

MARY

It is the evening hour,
  How silent all doth lie:
The hornèd moon she shows her face
  In the river with the sky.
Prest by the path on which we pass,
The flaggy lake lies still as glass.

Spirit of her I love,
  Whispering to me
Stores of sweet visions as I rove,
  Here stop, and crop with me
Sweet flowers that in the still hour grew –
We'll take them home, nor shake off the bright dew.

Mary, or sweet spirit of thee,
  As the bright sun shines to-morrow
Thy dark eyes these flowers shall see,
  Gathered by me in sorrow,
In the still hour when my mind was free
To walk alone – yet wish I walked with thee.

I AM

I AM: yet what I am none cares or knows,
My friends forsake me like a memory lost;
I am the self-consumer of my woes,
They rise and vanish in oblivious host,
Like shades in love and death's oblivion lost;
And yet I am, and live with shadows tost

Into the nothingness of scorn and noise,
Into the living sea of waking dreams,
Where there is neither sense of life nor joys,
But the vast shipwreck of my life's esteems;
And een the dearest – that I loved the best –
Are strange – nay, rather stranger than the rest.

I long for scenes where man has never trod;
A place where woman never smiled or wept;
There to abide with my Creator, GOD,
And sleep as I in childhood sweetly slept:
Untroubling and untroubled where I lie;
The grass below – above the vaulted sky.

'LOVE LIVES BEYOND THE TOMB'

LOVE lives beyond
The tomb, the earth, which fades like dew!
I love the fond,
The faithful, and the true.

Love lives in sleep,
The happiness of healthy dreams:
Eve's dews may weep,
But love delightful seems.

'Tis seen in flowers,
And in the morning's pearly dew;
In earth's green hours,
And in the heaven's eternal blue.

'Tis heard in Spring
When light and sunbeams, warm and kind,
An angel's wing
Bring love and music to the mind.

And where is voice,
So young, so beautiful, and sweet
As Nature's choice,
Where Spring and lovers meet?

Love lives beyond
The tomb, the earth, the flowers, and dew,
I love the fond,
The faithful, young, and true.

EMERSON

HAMATREYA

MINOTT, Lee, Willard, Hosmer, Meriam, Flint
Possessed the land which rendered to their toil
Hay, corn, roots, hemp, flax, apples, wool, and wood.
Each of these landlords walked amidst his farm,
Saying, ''Tis mine, my children's, and my name's:
How sweet the west wind sounds in my own trees!
How graceful climb those shadows on my hill!
I fancy these pure waters and the flags
Know me, as does my dog: we sympathize;
And, I affirm, my actions smack of the soil.'
Where are these men? Asleep beneath their grounds,
And strangers, fond as they, their furrows plough.
Earth laughs in flowers, to see her boastful boys
Earth-proud, proud of the earth which is not theirs;
Who steer the plough, but cannot steer their feet
Clear of the grave.
They added ridge to valley, brook to pond,
And sighed for all that bounded their domain.
'This suits me for a pasture; that's my park;
We must have clay, lime, gravel, granite-ledge,
And misty lowland, where to go for peat.
The land is well, – lies fairly to the south.
'Tis good, when you have crossed the sea and back,
To find the sitfast acres where you left them.'

Ah! the hot owner sees not Death, who adds
Him to his land, a lump of mould the more.
Hear what the Earth says: –

EARTH-SONG

'Mine and yours;
Mine, not yours.
Earth endures;
Stars abide –
Shine down in the old sea;
Old are the shores;
But where are old men?
I who have seen much,
Such have I never seen.

'The lawyer's deed
Ran sure
In tail,
To them, and to their heirs
Who shall succeed,
Without fail,
For evermore.

'Here is the land,
Shaggy with wood,
With its old valley,
Mound, and flood.
But the heritors?
Fled like the flood's foam, –
The lawyer, and the laws,
And the kingdom,
Clean swept herefrom.

'They called me theirs,
Who so controlled me;
Yet every one
Wished to stay, and is gone.
How am I theirs,
If they cannot hold me,
But I hold them?'

When I heard the Earth-song,
I was no longer brave;
My avarice was cooled
Like lust in the chill of the grave.

'GIVE ALL TO LOVE'

GIVE all to love;
Obey thy heart;
Friends, kindred, days,
Estate, good-fame,
Plans, credit, and the Muse, –
Nothing refuse.

'Tis a brave master;
Let it have scope:
Follow it utterly,
Hope beyond hope:
High and more high
It dives into noon,
With wing unspent,
Untold intent;
But it is a god,
Knows its own path,
And the outlets of the sky.

It was not for the mean;
It requireth courage stout,
Souls above doubt,
Valour unbending;
Such 'twill reward, –
They shall return
More than they were,
And ever ascending.

Leave all for love;
Yet, hear me, yet,
One word more thy heart behoved,
One pulse more of firm endeavour, –
Keep thee to-day,
To-morrow, for ever,
Free as an Arab
Of thy beloved.

Cling with life to the maid;
But when the surprise,
First vague shadow of surmise
Flits across her bosom young
Of a joy apart from thee,
Free be she, fancy-free;
Nor thou detain her vesture's hem,
Nor the palest rose she flung
From her summer diadem.

Though thou loved her as thyself,
As a self of purer clay,
Though her parting dims the day,
Stealing grace from all alive;
Heartily know,
When half-gods go,
The gods arrive.

MEROPS

What care I, so they stand the same, –
Things of the heavenly mind, –
How long the power to give them name
Tarries yet behind?

Thus far to-day your favours reach,
O fair, appeasing presences!
Ye taught my lips a single speech,
And a thousand silences.

Space grants beyond his fated road
No inch to the god of day;
And copious language still bestowed
One word, no more, to say.

HYMN

SUNG AT THE COMPLETION OF THE CONCORD MONUMENT,
APRIL 19TH, 1836

By the rude bridge that arched the flood,
Their flag to April's breeze unfurled,
Here once the embattled farmers stood,
And fired the shot heard round the world.

The foe long since in silence slept;
  Alike the conqueror silent sleeps;
And Time the ruined bridge has swept
  Down the dark stream which seaward creeps.

On this green bank, by this soft stream,
  We set to-day a votive stone;
That memory may their deed redeem,
  When, like our sires, our sons are gone.

Spirit, that made those heroes dare
  To die, and leave their children free,
Bid Time and Nature gently spare
  The shaft we raise to them and thee.

BEDDOES

SONG

BY FEMALE VOICES

We have bathed, where none have seen us,
  In the lake and in the fountain,
    Underneath the charmèd statue
Of the timid, bending Venus,
  When the water-nymphs were counting
In the waves the stars of night,
    And those maidens started at you,
Your limbs shone through so soft and bright.
    But no secrets dare we tell,
      For thy slaves unlace thee,
      And he, who shall embrace thee,
    Waits to try thy beauty's spell.

BY MALE VOICES

We have crowned thee queen of women,
  Since love's love, the rose, hath kept her
    Court within thy lips and blushes,
And thine eye, in beauty swimming,
  Kissing, we rendered up the sceptre,

At whose touch the startled soul
Like an ocean bounds and gushes,
And spirits bend at thy controul.
But no secrets dare we tell,
For thy slaves unlace thee,
And he, who shall embrace thee,
Is at hand, and so farewell.

POE

TO HELEN

Helen, thy beauty is to me
Like those Nicean barks of yore,
That gently o'er a perfumed sea,
The weary, way-worn wanderer bore
To his own native shore.

On desperate seas long wont to roam,
Thy hyacinth hair, thy classic face,
Thy Naiad airs have brought me home
To the glory that was Greece,
And the grandeur that was Rome.

Lo! in yon brilliant window-niche
How statue-like I see thee stand,
The agate lamp within thy hand!
Ah, Psyche, from the regions which
Are Holy-Land!

THE CITY IN THE SEA

Lo! Death has reared himself a throne
In a strange city lying alone
Far down within the dim West,
Where the good and the bad and the worst and the best
Have gone to their eternal rest.

There shrines and palaces and towers
(Time-eaten towers that tremble not!)
Resemble nothing that is ours.
Around, by lifting winds forgot,
Resignedly beneath the sky
The melancholy waters lie.

No rays from the holy heaven come down
On the long night-time of that town;
But light from out the lurid sea
Streams up the turrets silently –
Gleams up the pinnacles far and free –
Up domes – up spires – up kingly halls –
Up fanes – up Babylon-like walls –
Up shadowy long-forgotten bowers
Of sculptured ivy and stone flowers –
Up many and many a marvellous shrine
Whose wreathèd friezes intertwine
The viol, the violet, and the vine.
Resignedly beneath the sky
The melancholy waters lie.
So blend the turrets and shadows there
That all seem pendulous in air,
While from a proud tower in the town
Death looks gigantically down.

There open fanes and gaping graves
Yawn level with the luminous waves;
But not the riches there that lie
In each idol's diamond eye –
Not the gaily-jewelled dead
Tempt the waters from their bed;
For no ripples curl, alas!
Along that wilderness of glass –
No swellings tell that winds may be
Upon some far-off happier sea –
No heavings hint that winds have been
On seas less hideously serene.

But lo, a stir is in the air!
The wave – there is a movement there.
As if the towers had thrust aside,

In slightly sinking, the dull tide –
As if their tops had feebly given
A void within the filmy Heaven.
The waves have now a redder glow –
The hours are breathing faint and low –
And when, amid no earthly moans,
Down, down that town shall settle hence,
Hell, rising from a thousand thrones,
Shall do it reverence.

ROMANCE

Romance, who loves to nod and sing,
With drowsy head and folded wing,
Among the green leaves as they shake
Far down within some shadowy lake,
To me a painted paroquet
Hath been – a most familiar bird –
Taught me my alphabet to say –
To lisp my very earliest word
While in the wild wood I did lie,
A child – with a most knowing eye.

Of late, eternal Condor years
So shake the very Heaven on high
With tumult as they thunder by,
I have no time for idle cares
Through gazing on the unquiet sky.
And when an hour with calmer wings
Its down upon my spirit flings –
That little time with lyre and rhyme
To while away – forbidden things!
My heart would feel to be a crime
Unless it trembled with the strings.

TENNYSON

TITHONUS

THE woods decay, the woods decay and fall,
The vapours weep their burthen to the ground,
Man comes and tills the field and lies beneath,
And after many a summer dies the swan.
Me only cruel immortality
Consumes: I wither slowly in thine arms,
Here at the quiet limit of the world,
A white-hair'd shadow roaming like a dream
The ever silent spaces of the East,
Far-folded mists, and gleaming halls of morn.

Alas! for this grey shadow, once a man –
So glorious in his beauty and thy choice,
Who madest him thy chosen, that he seem'd
To his great heart none other than a God!
I ask'd thee, 'Give me immortality.'
Then didst thou grant mine asking with a smile,
Like wealthy men who care not how they give.
But thy strong Hours indignant work'd their wills,
And beat me down and marr'd and wasted me,
And tho' they could not end me, left me maim'd
To dwell in presence of immortal youth,
Immortal age beside immortal youth,
And all I was, in ashes. Can thy love,
Thy beauty, make amends, tho' even now,
Close over us, the silver star, thy guide,
Shines in those tremulous eyes that fill with tears
To hear me? Let me go: take back thy gift:
Why should a man desire in any way
To vary from the kindly race of men,
Or pass beyond the goal of ordinance
Where all should pause, as is most meet for all?

A soft air fans the cloud apart; there comes
A glimpse of that dark world where I was born.
Once more the old mysterious glimmer steals
From thy pure brows, and from thy shoulders pure,

And bosom beating with a heart renew'd,
Thy cheek begins to redden thro' the gloom,
Thy sweet eyes brighten slowly close to mine,
Ere yet they blind the stars, and the wild team
Which love thee, yearning for thy yoke, arise,
And shake the darkness from their loosen'd manes,
And beat the twilight into flakes of fire.

Lo! ever thus thou growest beautiful
In silence, then before thine answer given
Departest, and thy tears are on my cheek.

Why wilt thou ever scare me with thy tears,
And make me tremble lest a saying learnt
In days far-off, on that dark earth, be true?
'The Gods themselves cannot recall their gifts.'

Ay me! ay me! with what another heart
In days far-off, and with what other eyes
I used to watch – if I be he that watch'd –
The lucid outline forming round thee; saw
The dim curls kindle into sunny rings;
Changed with thy mystic change, and felt my blood
Glow with the glow that slowly crimson'd all
Thy presence and thy portals, while I lay,
Mouth, forehead, eyelids, growing dewy-warm
With kisses balmier than half-opening buds
Of April, and could hear the lips that kiss'd
Whispering I knew not what of wild and sweet,
Like that strange song I heard Apollo sing,
While Ilion like a mist rose into towers.

Yet hold me not for ever in thine East:
How can my nature longer mix with thine?
Coldly thy rosy shadows bathe me, cold
Are all thy lights, and cold my wrinkled feet
Upon thy glimmering thresholds, when the steam
Floats up from those dim fields about the homes
Of happy men that have the power to die,
And grassy barrows of the happier dead.
Release me, and restore me to the ground;
Thou seëst all things, thou wilt see my grave:

Thou wilt renew thy beauty morn by morn!
I earth in earth forget these empty courts,
And thee returning on thy silver wheels.

[THE SLEEPING HOUSE]

I HEARD no sound where I stood
But the rivulet on from the lawn
Running down to my own dark wood;
Or the voice of the long sea-wave as it swell'd
Now and then in the dim-gray dawn;
But I look'd, and round, all round the house I beheld
The death-white curtain drawn;
Felt a horror over me creep,
Prickle my skin and catch my breath,
Knew that the death-white curtain meant but sleep,
Yet I shudder'd and thought like a fool of the sleep of death.

['THERE IS NONE LIKE HER']

THERE is none like her, none.
Nor will be when our summers have deceased.
O, art thou sighing for Lebanon
In the long breeze that streams to thy delicious East,
Sighing for Lebanon,
Dark cedar, tho' thy limbs have here increased,
Upon a pastoral slope as fair,
And looking to the South, and fed
With honey'd rain and delicate air,
And haunted by the starry head
Of her whose gentle will has changed my fate,
And made my life a perfumed altar-flame;
And over whom thy darkness must have spread
With such delight as theirs of old, thy great
Forefathers of the thornless garden, there
Shadowing the snow-limb'd Eve from whom she came.

[I]

COME down, O maid, from yonder mountain height:
What pleasure lives in height (the shepherd sang),
In height and cold, the splendour of the hills?
But cease to move so near the Heavens, and cease
To glide a sunbeam by the blasted Pine,
To sit a star upon the sparkling spire;
And come, for Love is of the valley, come,
For Love is of the valley, come thou down
And find him; by the happy threshold, he,
Or hand in hand with Plenty in the maize,
Or red with spirted purple of the vats,
Or foxlike in the vine; nor cares to walk
With Death and Morning on the silver horns,
Nor wilt thou snare him in the white ravine,
Nor find him dropt upon the firths of ice,
That huddling slant in furrow-cloven falls
To roll the torrent out of dusky doors:
But follow; let the torrent dance thee down
To find him in the valley; let the wild
Lean-headed Eagles yelp alone, and leave
The monstrous ledges there to slope, and spill
Their thousand wreaths of dangling water-smoke,
That like a broken purpose waste in air:
So waste not thou; but come; for all the vales
Await thee; azure pillars of the hearth
Arise to thee; the children call, and I
Thy shepherd pipe, and sweet is every sound,
Sweeter thy voice, but every sound is sweet;
Myriads of rivulets hurrying thro' the lawn,
The moan of doves in immemorial elms,
And murmuring of innumerable bees.

[II]

TEARS, idle tears, I know not what they mean,
Tears from the depth of some divine despair
Rise in the heart, and gather to the eyes,
In looking on the happy Autumn-fields,
And thinking of the days that are no more.

Fresh as the first beam glittering on a sail,
That brings our friends up from the underworld,
Sad as the last which reddens over one
That sinks with all we love below the verge;
So sad, so fresh, the days that are no more.

Ah, sad and strange as in dark summer dawns
The earliest pipe of half-awaken'd birds
To dying ears, when unto dying eyes
The casement slowly grows a glimmering square;
So sad, so strange, the days that are no more.

Dear as remember'd kisses after death,
And sweet as those by hopeless fancy feign'd
On lips that are for others; deep as love,
Deep as first love, and wild with all regret;
O Death in Life, the days that are no more.

[ELAINE'S SONG]

Sweet is true love tho' given in vain, in vain;
And sweet is death who puts an end to pain:
I know not which is sweeter, no, not I.

Love, art thou sweet? then bitter death must be:
Love, thou art bitter; sweet is death to me.
O Love, if death be sweeter, let me die.

Sweet love, that seems not made to fade away,
Sweet death, that seems to make us loveless clay,
I know not which is sweeter, no, not I.

I fain would follow love, if that could be;
I needs must follow death, who calls for me;
Call and I follow, I follow! Let me die.

[VIVIEN'S SONG]

In Love, if Love be Love, if Love be ours,
Faith and unfaith can ne'er be equal powers:
Unfaith in aught is want of faith in all.

It is the little rift within the lute,
That by and by will make the music mute,
And ever widening slowly silence all.

The little rift within the lover's lute,
Or little pitted speck in garner'd fruit,
That rotting inward slowly moulders all.

It is not worth the keeping: let it go:
But shall it? answer, darling, answer, no.
And trust me not at all or all in all.

from MORTE D'ARTHUR

AND slowly answered Arthur from the barge:
'The old order changeth, yielding place to new,
And God fulfils Himself in many ways,
Lest one good custom should corrupt the world.
Comfort thyself: what comfort is in me?
I have lived my life, and that which I have done
May He within himself make pure! but thou –
If thou shouldst never see my face again,
Pray for my soul. More things are wrought by prayer
Than this world dreams of. Wherefore, let thy voice
Rise like a fountain for me night and day.
For what are men better than sheep or goats
That nourish a blind life within the brain,
If, knowing God, they lift not hands of prayer
Both for themselves and those who call them friend?
For so the whole round earth is every way
Bound by gold chains about the feet of God.
But now farewell. I am going a long way
With these thou seëst – if indeed I go –
(For all my mind is clouded with a doubt)
To the island-valley of Avilion;
Where falls not hail, or rain, or any snow,
Nor ever wind blows loudly; but it lies
Deep-meadow'd, happy, fair with orchard-lawns
And bowery hollows crown'd with summer sea,
Where I will heal me of my grievous wound.'

So said he, and the barge with oar and sail
Moved from the brink, like some full-breasted swan
That, fluting a wild carol ere her death,
Ruffles her pure cold plume, and takes the flood
With swarthy webs. Long stood Sir Bedivere
Revolving many memories, till the hull
Look'd one black dot against the verge of dawn,
And on the meer the wailing died away.

from IN MEMORIAM

OLD Yew, which graspest at the stones
That name the under-lying dead,
Thy fibres net the dreamless head;
Thy roots are wrapt about the bones.

The seasons bring the flower again,
And bring the firstling to the flock;
And in the dusk of thee, the clock
Beats out the little lives of men.

O not for thee the glow, the bloom,
Who changest not in any gale!
Nor branding summer suns avail
To touch thy thousand years of gloom.

And gazing on thee, sullen tree,
Sick for thy stubborn hardihood,
I seem to fail from out my blood,
And grow incorporate into thee.

*

Dark house, by which once more I stand
Here in the long unlovely street,
Doors, where my heart was used to beat
So quickly, waiting for a hand,

A hand that can be clasp'd no more –
Behold me, for I cannot sleep,
And like a guilty thing I creep
At earliest morning to the door.

He is not here; but far away
    The noise of life begins again,
    And ghastly thro' the drizzling rain
On the bald street breaks the blank day.

★

Calm is the morn without a sound,
    Calm as to suit a calmer grief,
    And only thro' the faded leaf
The chesnut* pattering to the ground:

Calm and deep peace on this high wold,
    And on these dews that drench the furze,
    And all the silvery gossamers
That twinkle into green and gold:

Calm and still light on yon great plain
    That sweeps with all its autumn bowers,
    And crowded farms and lessening towers,
To mingle with the bounding main:

Calm and deep peace in this wide air,
    These leaves that redden to the fall;
    And in my heart, if calm at all,
If any calm, a calm despair:

Calm on the seas, and silver sleep,
    And waves that sway themselves in rest,
    And dead calm in that noble breast
Which heaves but with the heaving deep.

★

To-night the winds begin to rise
    And roar from yonder dropping day:
    The last red leaf is whirl'd away,
The rooks are blown about the skies;

The forest crack'd, the waters curl'd,
    The cattle huddled on the lea;
    And wildly dash'd on tower and tree
The sunbeam strikes along the world:

★ An alternative form, characteristically used to enhance the onomatopoetic quality of the line.

And but for fancies, which aver
    That all thy motions gently pass
    Athwart a plane of molten glass,
I scarce could brook the strain and stir

That makes the barren branches loud;
    And but for fear it is not so,
    The wild unrest that lives in woe
Would dote and pore on yonder cloud

That rises upward always higher,
    And onward drags a labouring breast,
    And topples round the dreary west,
A looming bastion fringed with fire.

*

I envy not in any moods
    The captive void of noble rage,
    The linnet born within the cage,
That never knew the summer woods:

I envy not the beast that takes
    His license in the field of time,
    Unfetter'd by the sense of crime,
To whom a conscience never wakes;

Nor, what may count itself as blest,
    The heart that never plighted troth
    But stagnates in the weeds of sloth,
Nor any want-begotten rest.

I hold it true, whate'er befall;
    I feel it when I sorrow most;
    'Tis better to have loved and lost
Than never to have loved at all.

*

When rosy plumelets tuft the larch,
    And rarely pipes the mounted thrush;
    Or underneath the barren bush
Flits by the sea-blue bird of March;

Come, wear the form by which I know
    Thy spirit in time among thy peers;
    The hope of unaccomplish'd years
Be large and lucid round thy brow.

When summer's hourly-mellowing change
    May breathe with many roses sweet
    Upon the thousand waves of wheat,
That ripple round the lonely grange;

Come: not in watches of the night,
    But where the sunbeam broodeth warm,
    Come, beauteous in thine after form,
And like a finer light in light.

*

Now fades the last long streak of snow,
    Now burgeons every maze of quick
    About the flowering squares, and thick
By ashen roots the violets blow.

Now rings the woodland loud and long,
    The distance takes a lovelier hue,
    And drown'd in yonder living blue
The lark becomes a sightless song.

Now dance the lights on lawn and lea,
    The flocks are whiter down the vale,
    And milkier every milky sail
On winding stream or distant sea;

Where now the seamew pipes, or dives
    In yonder greening gleam, and fly
    The happy birds, that change their sky
To build and brood; that live their lives

From land to land; and in my breast
    Spring wakens too; and my regret
    Becomes an April violet,
And buds and blossoms like the rest.

'BREAK, BREAK, BREAK'

BREAK, break, break
  On thy cold grey stones, O Sea!
And I would that my tongue could utter
  The thoughts that arise in me.

O well for the fisherman's boy,
  That he shouts with his sister at play!
O well for the sailor lad,
  That he sings in his boat on the bay!

And the stately ships go on
  To their haven under the hill;
But O for the touch of a vanish'd hand,
  And the sound of a voice that is still!

Break, break, break
  At the foot of thy crags, O Sea!
But the tender grace of a day that is dead
  Will never come back to me.

CROSSING THE BAR

SUNSET and evening star,
  And one clear call for me.
And may there be no moaning of the bar,
  When I put out to sea,

But such a tide as moving seems asleep,
  Too full for sound and foam,
When that which drew from out the boundless deep
  Turns again home.

Twilight and evening bell,
  And after that the dark:
And may there be no sadness of farewell,
  When I embark;

For tho' from out our bourne of Time and Place
  The flood may bear me far,
I hope to see my Pilot face to face,
  When I have crost the bar.

LONGFELLOW

from TO A CHILD

By what astrology of fear or hope
Dare I to cast thy horoscope!
Like the new moon thy life appears;
A little strip of silver light,
And widening outward into night
The shadowy disk of future years;
And yet upon its outer rim,
A luminous circle, faint and dim,
And scarcely visible to us here,
Rounds and completes the perfect sphere;
A prophecy and intimation,
A pale and feeble adumbration,
Of the great world of light, that lies
Behind all human destinies.

from EVANGELINE

They were approaching the region where reigns perpetual summer,
Where through the Golden Coast, and groves of orange and citron,
Sweeps with majestic curve the river away to the eastward.
They, too, swerved from their course; and, entering the Bayou of Plaquemine,
Soon were lost in a maze of sluggish and devious waters,
Which, like a network of steel, extended in every direction.
Over their heads the towering and tenebrous boughs of the cypress
Met in a dusky arch, and trailing mosses in mid-air
Waved like banners that hang on the walls of ancient cathedrals.
Deathlike the silence seemed, and unbroken, save by the herons
Home to their roosts in the cedar-trees returning at sunset,
Or by the owl, as he greeted the moon with demoniac laughter.
Lovely the moonlight was as it glanced and gleamed on the water,
Gleamed on the columns of cypress and cedar sustaining the arches,

Down through whose broken vaults it fell as through chinks in a ruin.
Dreamlike, and indistinct, and strange were all things around them;
And o'er their spirits there came a feeling of wonder and sadness, –
Strange forebodings of ill, unseen and that cannot be compassed.
As, at the tramp of a horse's hoof on the turf of the prairies,
Far in advance are closed the leaves of the shrinking mimosa,
So, at the hoof-beats of fate, with sad foreboding of evil,
Shrinks & closes the heart, ere the stroke of doom has attained it.

TO THE DRIVING CLOUD

GLOOMY and dark art thou, O chief of the mighty Omahas;
Gloomy and dark as the driving cloud, whose name thou hast taken!
Wrapped in thy scarlet blanket, I see thee stalk through the city's
Narrow and populous streets, as once by the margin of rivers
Stalked those birds unknown, that have left us only their footprints.
What, in a few short years, will remain of thy race but the footprints?

How canst thou walk these streets, who hast trod the green turf of the prairies?
How canst thou breathe this air, who hast breathed the sweet air of the mountains?
Ah! 'tis in vain that with lordly looks of disdain thou dost challenge
Looks of disdain in return, and question these walls and these pavements,
Claiming the soil for thy hunting-grounds, while down-trodden millions
Starve in the garrets of Europe, and cry from its caverns that they, too,
Have been created heirs of the earth, and claim its division!

Back, then, back to thy woods in the regions west of the
Wabash!
There as a monarch thou reignest. In autumn the leaves of the
maple
Pave the floors of thy palace-halls with gold, and in summer
Pine-trees waft through its chambers the odourous breath of
their branches.
There thou art strong and great, a hero, a tamer of horses!
There thou chasest the stately stag on the banks of the Elkhorn,
Or by the roaring of the Running-Water, or where the Omaha
Calls thee, and leaps through the wild ravine like a brave of the
Blackfeet! [deserts?
Hark! what murmurs arise from the heart of those mountainous
Is it the cry of the Foxes and Crows, or the mighty Behemoth,
Who, unharmed, on his tusks once caught the bolts of the
thunder,
And now lurks in his lair to destroy the race of the red man?
Far more fatal to thee and thy race than the Crows and the
Foxes,
Far more fatal to thee and thy race than the tread of Behemoth,
Lo! the big thunder-canoe, that steadily breasts the Missouri's
Merciless current! and yonder, afar on the prairies, the camp-
fires
Gleam through the night; and the cloud of dust in the gray of
the daybreak [horse-race;
Marks not the buffalo's track, nor the Mandan's dexterous
It is a caravan, whitening the desert where dwell the Camanches!
Ha! how the breath of these Saxons and Celts, like the blast of
the east wind,
Drifts evermore to the west the scanty smokes of the wigwams!

BROWNING

THE LOST MISTRESS

All's over, then – does truth sound bitter
As one at first believes?
Hark, 'tis the sparrows' good-night twitter
About your cottage eaves.

And the leaf-buds on the vine are woolly,
  I noticed that to-day;
One day more bursts them open fully
  – You know the red turns gray.

To-morrow we meet the same then, dearest?
  May I take your hand in mine?
Mere friends are we, – well, friends the merest
  Keep much that I resign:

For each glance of the eye so bright and black,
  Though I keep with heart's endeavour, –
Your voice, when you wish the snowdrops back,
  Though it stay in my soul for ever! –

Yet I will but say what mere friends say,
  Or only a thought stronger;
I will hold your hand but as long as all may,
  Or so very little longer!

MEETING AT NIGHT

THE grey sea and the long black land;
And the yellow half-moon large and low;
And the startled little waves that leap
In fiery ringlets from their sleep,
As I gain the cove with pushing prow,
And quench its speed i' the slushy sand.

Then a mile of warm sea-scented beach;
Three fields to cross till a farm appears;
A tap at the pane, the quick sharp scratch
And blue spurt of a lighted match,
And a voice less loud, thro' its joys and fears,
Than the two hearts beating each to each!

PARTING AT MORNING

ROUND the cape of a sudden came the sea,
And the sun looked over the mountain's rim:
And straight was a path of gold for him,
And the need of a world of men for me.

HOME-THOUGHTS, FROM ABROAD

Oh, to be in England
Now that April's there,
And whoever wakes in England
Sees, some morning, unaware,
That the lowest boughs and the brushwood sheaf
Round the elm-tree bole are in tiny leaf,
While the chaffinch sings on the orchard bough
In England – now!

And after April, when May follows,
And the whitethroat builds, and all the swallows –
Hark! where my blossomed pear-tree in the hedge
Leans to the field and scatters on the clover
Blossoms and dewdrops – at the bent spray's edge –
That's the wise thrush; he sings each song twice over,
Lest you should think he never could recapture
The first fine careless rapture!
And though the fields look rough with hoary dew,
All will be gay when noontide wakes anew
The buttercups, the little children's dower,
– Far brighter than this gaudy melon-flower!

ANY WIFE TO ANY HUSBAND

My love, this is the bitterest, that thou
Who art all truth and who dost love me now
  As thine eyes say, as thy voice breaks to say –
Should'st love so truly, and could'st love me still
A whole long life through, had but love its will,
  Would death that leads me from thee brook delay!

I have but to be by thee, and thy hand
Will never let mine go, nor heart withstand
  The beating of my heart to reach its place.
When shall I look for thee and feel thee gone?
When cry for the old comfort and find none?
  Never, I know! Thy soul is in thy face.

Browning

Oh, I should fade – 'tis willed so! Might I save,
Gladly I would, whatever beauty gave
  Joy to thy sense, for that was precious too.
It is not to be granted. But the soul
Whence the love comes, all ravage leaves that whole;
  Vainly the flesh fades; soul makes all things new.

It would not be because my eye grew dim
Thou couldst not find the love there, thanks to Him
  Who never is dishonoured in the spark
He gave us from his fire of fires, and bade
Remember whence it sprang, nor be afraid
  While that burns on, though all the rest grow dark.

So, how thou would'st be perfect, white and clean
Outside as inside, soul and soul's demesne
  Alike, this body given to show it by!
Oh, three-parts through the worst of life's abyss,
What plaudits from the next world after this,
  Could'st thou repeat a stroke and gain the sky!

And is it not the bitterer to think
That, disengage our hands and thou wilt sink
  Although thy love was love in very deed?
I know that nature! Pass a festive day,
Thou dost not throw its relic-flower away
  Nor bid its music's loitering echo speed.

Thou let'st the stranger's glove lie where it fell;
If old things remain old things all is well,
  For thou art grateful as becomes man best:
And hadst thou only heard me play one tune,
Or viewed me from a window, not so soon
  With thee would such things fade as with the rest.

I seem to see! We meet and part: 'tis brief:
The book I opened keeps a folded leaf,
  The very chair I sat on, breaks the rank;
That is a portrait of me on the wall –
Three lines, my face comes at so slight a call;
  And for all this, one little hour to thank.

But now, because the hour through years was fixed,
Because our inmost beings met and mixed,
  Because thou once hast loved me – wilt thou dare
Say to thy soul and Who may list beside,
'Therefore she is immortally my bride,
  Chance cannot change my love, nor time impair.

'So, what if in the dusk of life that's left,
I, a tired traveller of my sun bereft,
  Look from my path when, mimicking the same,
The fire-fly glimpses past me, come and gone?
– Where was it till the sunset? where anon
  It will be at the sunrise! What's to blame?'

Is it so helpful to thee? canst thou take
The mimic up, nor, for the true thing's sake,
  Put gently by such efforts at a beam?
Is the remainder of the way so long
Thou need'st the little solace, thou the strong?
  Watch out thy watch, let weak ones doze and dream!

– Ah, but the fresher faces! 'Is it true,'
Thou'lt ask, 'some eyes are beautiful and new?
  Some hair, – how can one choose but grasp such wealth?
And if a man would press his lips to lips
Fresh as the wilding hedge-rose-cup there slips
  The dew-drop out of, must it be by stealth?

'It cannot change the love kept still for Her,
More than if such a picture I prefer
  Passing a day with, to a room's bare side:
The painted form takes nothing she possessed,
Yet, while the Titian's Venus lies at rest,
  A man looks. Once more, what is there to chide?'

So must I see, from where I sit and watch,
My own self sell myself, my hand attach
  Its warrant to the very thefts from me –
Thy singleness of soul that made me proud,
Thy purity of heart I loved aloud,
  Thy man's truth I was bold to bid God see!

Love so, then, if thou wilt! Give all thou canst
Away to the new faces – disentranced,
  (Say it and think it) obdurate no more:
Re-issue looks and words from the old mint –
Pass them afresh, no matter whose the print
  Image and superscription once they bore!

Re-coin thyself and give it them to spend, –
It all comes to the same thing at the end,
  Since mine thou wast, mine art and mine shalt be,
Faithful or faithless, sealing up the sum
Or lavish of my treasure, thou must come
  Back to the heart's place here I keep for thee!

Only, why should it be with stain at all?
Why must I, 'twixt the leaves of coronal,
  Put any kiss of pardon on thy brow?
Why need the other women know so much,
And talk together, 'Such the look and such
  The smile he used to love with, then as now!'

Might I die last and shew thee! Should I find
Such hardship in the few years left behind,
  If free to take and light my lamp, and go
Into thy tomb, and shut the door and sit,
Seeing thy face on those four sides of it
  The better that they are so blank, I know!

Why, time was what I wanted, to turn o'er
Within my mind each look, get more and more
  By heart each word, too much to learn at first;
And join thee all the fitter for the pause
'Neath the low door-way's lintel. That were cause
  For lingering, though thou calledst, if I durst!

And yet thou art the nobler of us two.
What dare I dream of, that thou canst not do,
  Outstripping my ten small steps with one stride?
I'll say then, here's a trial and a task –
Is it to bear? – if easy, I'll not ask –
  Though love fail, I can trust on in thy pride.

Pride? – when those eyes forestal the life behind
The death I have to go through! – when I find,
  Now that I want thy help most, all of thee!
What did I fear? Thy love shall hold me fast
Until the little minute's sleep is past
  And I wake saved. – And yet it will not be!

TWO IN THE CAMPAGNA

I WONDER do you feel to-day
  As I have felt, since, hand in hand,
We sat down on the grass, to stray
  In spirit better through the land,
This morn of Rome and May?

For me, I touched a thought, I know,
  Has tantalised me many times,
(Like turns of thread the spiders throw
  Mocking across our path) for rhymes
To catch at and let go.

Help me to hold it: first it left
  The yellowing fennel, run to seed
There, branching from the brickwork's cleft,
  Some old tomb's ruin: yonder weed
Took up the floating weft,

Where one small orange cup amassed
  Five beetles, – blind and green they grope
Among the honey-meal, – and last,
  Everywhere on the grassy slope
I traced it. Hold it fast!

The champaign with its endless fleece
  Of feathery grasses everywhere!
Silence and passion, joy and peace,
  An everlasting wash of air –
Rome's ghost since her decease.

Such life here, through such lengths of hours,
  Such miracles performed in play,
Such primal naked forms of flowers,
  Such letting Nature have her way
While Heaven looks from its towers.

How say you? Let us, O my dove,
  Let us be unashamed of soul,
As earth lies bare to heaven above.
  How is it under our control
To love or not to love?

I would that you were all to me,
  You that are just so much, no more –
Nor yours nor mine, – nor slave nor free!
  Where does the fault lie? what the core
Of the wound, since wound must be?

I would I could adopt your will,
  See with your eyes, and set my heart
Beating by yours, and drink my fill
  At your soul's springs, – your part, my part
In life, for good and ill.

No. I yearn upward – touch you close,
  Then stand away. I kiss your cheek,
Catch your soul's warmth, – I pluck the rose
  And love it more than tongue can speak –
Then the good minute goes.

Already how am I so far
  Out of that minute? Must I go
Still like the thistle-ball, no bar,
  Onward, whenever light winds blow,
Fixed by no friendly star?

Just when I seemed about to learn!
  Where is the thread now? Off again!
The old trick! Only I discern –
  Infinite passion and the pain
Of finite hearts that yearn.

MEMORABILIA

Ah, did you once see Shelley plain,
  And did he stop and speak to you?
And did you speak to him again?
  How strange it seems, and new!

But you were living before that,
   And also you are living after;
And the memory I started at –
   My starting moves your laughter.

I crossed a moor, with a name of its own
   And a certain use in the world no doubt,
Yet a hand's-breadth of it shines alone
   'Mid the blank miles round about –

For there I picked up on the heather
   And there I put inside my breast
A moulted feather, an eagle-feather –
   Well, I forget the rest.

MY LAST DUCHESS

FERRARA

THAT'S my last Duchess painted on the wall,
Looking as if she were alive. I call
That piece a wonder, now: Frà Pandolf's hands
Worked busily a day, and there she stands.
Will't please you sit and look at her? I said
'Frà Pandolf' by design, for never read
Strangers like you that pictured countenance,
The depth and passion of its earnest glance,
But to myself they turned (since none puts by
The curtain I have drawn for you, but I)
And seemed as they would ask me, if they durst,
How such a glance came there; so, not the first
Are you to turn and ask thus. Sir, 'twas not
Her husband's presence only, called that spot
Of joy into the Duchess' cheek: perhaps
Frà Pandolf chanced to say 'Her mantle laps
Over my lady's wrist too much,' or 'Paint
Must never hope to reproduce the faint
Half-flush that dies along her throat:' such stuff
Was courtesy, she thought, and cause enough
For calling up that spot of joy. She had
A heart – how shall I say? – too soon made glad,
Too easily impressed; she liked whate'er

She looked on, and her looks went everywhere.
Sir, 'twas all one! My favour at her breast,
The dropping of the daylight in the West,
The bough of cherries some officious fool
Broke in the orchard for her, the white mule
She rode with round the terrace – all and each
Would draw from her alike the approving speech,
Or blush, at least. She thanked men, – good! but thanked
Somehow – I know not how – as if she ranked
My gift of a nine-hundred-years-old name
With anybody's gift. Who'd stoop to blame
This sort of trifling? Even had you skill
In speech – (which I have not) – to make your will
Quite clear to such an one, and say, 'Just this
Or that in you disgusts me; here you miss,
Or there exceed the mark' – and if she let
Herself be lessoned so, nor plainly set
Her wits to yours, forsooth, and made excuse,
– E'en then would be some stooping; and I choose
Never to stoop. Oh sir, she smiled, no doubt,
Whene'er I passed her; but who passed without
Much the same smile? This grew; I gave commands;
Then all smiles stopped together. There she stands
As if alive. Will't please you rise? We'll meet
The company below, then. I repeat,
The Count your master's known munificence
Is ample warrant that no just pretence
Of mine for dowry will be disallowed;
Though his fair daughter's self, as I avowed
At starting, is my object. Nay, we'll go
Together down, sir. Notice Neptune, though,
Taming a sea-horse, thought a rarity,
Which Claus of Innsbruck cast in bronze for me!

PROSPICE

Fear death? – to feel the fog in my throat,
        The mist in my face,
When the snows begin, and the blasts denote
        I am nearing the place,

The power of the night, the press of the storm,
    The post of the foe;
Where he stands, the Arch Fear in a visible form,
    Yet the strong man must go:
For the journey is done and the summit attained,
    And the barriers fall,
Though a battle's to fight ere the guerdon be gained,
    The reward of it all.
I was ever a fighter, so – one fight more,
    The best and the last!
I would hate that death bandaged my eyes, and forbore,
    And bade me creep past.
No! let me taste the whole of it, fare like my peers
    The heroes of old,
Bear the brunt, in a minute pay glad life's arrears
    Of pain, darkness and cold.
For sudden the worst turns the best to the brave,
    The black minute's at end,
And the elements' rage, the fiend-voices that rave,
    Shall dwindle, shall blend,
Shall change, shall become first a peace out of pain,
    Then a light, then thy breast,
O thou soul of my soul! I shall clasp thee again,
    And with God be the rest!

EPILOGUE TO *ASOLANDO*

At the midnight in the silence of the sleep-time,
  When you set your fancies free,
Will they pass to where – by death, fools think, imprisoned –
Low he lies who once so loved you, whom you loved so,
      – Pity me?

Oh to love so, be so loved, yet so mistaken!
  What had I on earth to do
With the slothful, with the mawkish, the unmanly?
Like the aimless, helpless, hopeless, did I drivel
      – Being – who?

One who never turned his back but marched breast forward,
  Never doubted clouds would break,

Never dreamed, though right were worsted, wrong would
 triumph,
Held we fall to rise, are baffled to fight better,
 Sleep to wake.

No, at noonday in the bustle of man's work-time
 Greet the unseen with a cheer!
Bid him forward, breast and back as either should be,
'Strive and thrive!' cry 'Speed, – fight on, fare ever
 There as here!'

EMILY BRONTË

REMEMBRANCE*

COLD in the earth – and the deep snow piled above thee,
Far, far, removed, cold in the dreary grave!
Have I forgot, my only Love, to love thee,
Severed at last by Time's all-severing wave?

Now, when alone, do my thoughts no longer hover
Over the mountains, on that northern shore,
Resting their wings where heath and fern-leaves cover
That noble heart for ever, ever more?

Cold in the earth, and fifteen wild Decembers
From those brown hills have melted into spring:
Faithful, indeed, is the spirit that remembers
After such years of change and suffering!

Sweet Love of youth, forgive, if I forget thee,
While the world's tide is bearing me along;
Other desires and other hopes beset me,
Hopes which obscure, but cannot do thee wrong!

No later light has lightened up my heaven,
No second morn has ever shone for me;
All my life's bliss from thy dear life was given,
All my life's bliss is in the grave with thee.

* Originally a lament of Rosina Alcona for the death of Julius Brenzaida, from the Gondal saga, this poem was slightly altered (probably by Charlotte Brontë), in order to give it a more general application, when it was printed in *Poems*, 1846, the text followed here.

But, when the days of golden dreams had perished,
And even Despair was powerless to destroy;
Then did I learn how existence could be cherished,
Strengthened, and fed without the aid of joy.

Emily Brontë

Then did I check the tears of useless passion –
Weaned my young soul from yearning after thine;
Sternly denied its burning wish to hasten
Down to that tomb already more than mine.

And, even yet, I dare not let it languish,
Dare not indulge in memory's rapturous pain;
Once drinking deep of that divinest anguish,
How could I seek the empty world again?

['NO COWARD SOUL IS MINE']

JAN. 2, 1846

No coward soul is mine
No trembler in the world's storm-troubled sphere,
I see Heaven's glories shine
And Faith shines equal arming me from Fear.

O God within my breast
Almighty ever-present Deity,
Life – that in me has rest,
As I Undying Life, have power in Thee.

Vain are the thousand creeds
That move men's hearts, unutterably vain,
Worthless as withered weeds
Or idlest froth amid the boundless main,

To waken doubt in one
Holding so fast by thy infinity
So surely anchored on
The steadfast rock of Immortality.

With wide-embracing love
Thy spirit animates eternal years
Pervades and broods above,
Changes, sustains, dissolves, creates and rears.

Though earth and man were gone,
And suns and universes ceased to be
And Thou wert left alone
Every Existence would exist in thee.

There is not room for Death
Nor atom that his might could render void,
Thou – Thou art Being and Breath,
And what Thou art may never be destroyed.

STANZAS*

Often rebuked, yet always back returning
To those first feelings that were born with me,
And leaving busy chase of wealth and learning
For idle dreams of things that cannot be:

To-day, I will seek not the shadowy region;
Its unsustaining vastness waxes drear;
And visions rising, legion after legion,
Bring the unreal world too strangely near.

I'll walk, but not in old heroic traces,
And not in paths of high morality,
And not among the half-distinguished faces,
The clouded forms of long-past history.

I'll walk where my own nature would be leading:
It vexes me to choose another guide:
Where the gray flocks in ferny glens are feeding;
Where the wild wind blows on the mountain side.

What have those lonely mountains worth revealing?
More glory and more grief than I can tell:
The earth that wakes *one* human heart to feeling
Can centre both the worlds of Heaven and Hell.

* The authorship of this poem is doubtful. It should probably be ascribed to Charlotte Brontë and not to her sister, Emily.

ARNOLD

TO MARGUERITE

Yes: in the sea of life enisl'd,
With echoing straits between us thrown,
Dotting the shoreless watery wild,
We mortal millions live *alone*.
The islands feel the enclasping flow,
And then their endless bounds they know.

But when the moon their hollows lights
And they are swept by balms of spring,
And in their glens, on starry nights,
The nightingales divinely sing;
And lovely notes, from shore to shore,
Across the sounds and channels pour;

Oh then a longing like despair
Is to their farthest caverns sent;
For surely once, they feel, we were
Parts of a single continent.
Now round us spreads the watery plain –
Oh might our marges meet again!

Who order'd, that their longing's fire
Should be, as soon as kindled, cool'd?
Who renders vain their deep desire? –
A God, a God their severance ruled;
And bade betwixt their shores to be
The unplumb'd, salt, estranging sea.

DOVER BEACH

The sea is calm to-night.
The tide is full, the moon lies fair
Upon the Straits; – on the French coast, the light
Gleams, and is gone; the cliffs of England stand,
Glimmering and vast, out in the tranquil bay.
Come to the window, sweet is the night air!
Only, from the long line of spray

THOREAU

['I AM A PARCEL OF VAIN STRIVINGS']

I am a parcel of vain strivings tied
By a chance bond together,
Dangling this way and that, their links
Were made so loose and wide,
Methinks,
For milder weather.

A bunch of violets without their roots,
And sorrel intermixed,
Encircled by a wisp of straw
Once coiled about their shoots,
The law
By which I'm fixed.

A nosegay which Time clutched from out
Those fair Elysian fields,
With weeds and broken stems, in haste,
Doth make the rabble rout
That waste
The day he yields.

And here I bloom for a short hour unseen,
Drinking my juices up,
With no root in the land
To keep my branches green,
But stand
In a bare cup.

Some tender buds were left upon my stem
In mimicry of life,
But ah! the children will not know,
Till time has withered them,
The woe
With which they're rife.

But now I see I was not plucked for naught,
And after in life's vase
Of glass set while I might survive,
But by a kind hand brought
Alive
To a strange place.

That stock thus thinned will soon redeem its hours,
And by another year,
Such as God knows, with freer air,
More fruits and fairer flowers
Will bear,
While I droop here.

['THE MOON NOW RISES']

THE moon now rises to her absolute rule,
And the husbandman and hunter
Acknowledge her for their mistress.
Asters and golden reign in the fields
And the life everlasting withers not.
The fields are reaped and shorn of their pride
But an inward verdure still crowns them
The thistle scatters its down on the pool
And yellow leaves clothe the river –
And nought disturbs the serious life of men.
But behind the sheaves and under the sod
There lurks a ripe fruit which the reapers have not gathered
The true harvest of the year – the boreal fruit
Which it bears forever.
With fondness annually watering and maturing it.
But man never severs the stalk
Which bears this palatable fruit.

['FOR THOUGH THE CAVES WERE RABITTED']

FOR though the caves were rabitted,
And the well sweeps were slanted,
Each house seemed not inhabited
But haunted.

The pensive traveller held his way,
Silent & melancholy,
For every man an ideot was,
And every house a folly.

['I WAS MADE

I WA
A

St
To t
Where
If age ch
If age choo
Take the sap

CLOUGH

SAY not, the struggle nought av
The labour and the wounds are
The enemy faints not, nor faileth,
And as things have been they remai

If hopes were dupes, fears may be liars;
It may be, in yon smoke concealed,
Your comrades chase e'en now the fliers,
And, but for you, possess the field.

For while the tired waves, vainly breaking,
Seem here no painful inch to gain,
Far back, through creeks and inlets making,
Comes silent, flooding in, the main.

And not by eastern windows only,
When daylight comes, comes in the light,
In front, the sun climbs slow, how slowly,
But westward, look, the land is bright.

Where the ebb meets the moon-blanch'd sand,
Listen! you hear the grating roar
Of pebbles which the waves suck back, and fling,
At their return, up the high strand,
Begin, and cease, and then again begin,
With tremulous cadence slow, and bring
The eternal note of sadness in.

Sophocles long ago
Heard it on the Ægæan, and it brought
Into his mind the turbid ebb and flow
Of human misery; we
Find also in the sound a thought,
Hearing it by this distant northern sea.

The sea of faith
Was once, too, at the full, and round earth's shore
Lay like the folds of a bright girdle furl'd;
But now I only hear
Its melancholy, long, withdrawing roar,
Retreating to the breath
Of the night-wind down the vast edges drear
And naked shingles of the world.

Ah, love, let us be true
To one another! for the world, which seems
To lie before us like a land of dreams,
So various, so beautiful, so new,
Hath really neither joy, nor love, nor light,
Nor certitude, nor peace, nor help for pain;
And we are here as on a darkling plain
Swept with confused alarms of struggle and flight,
Where ignorant armies clash by night.

PALLADIUM

SET where the upper streams of Simois flow
Was the Palladium, high 'mid rock and wood;
And Hector was in Ilium, far below,
And fought, and saw it not, but there it stood.

It stood; and sun and moonshine rain'd their light
On the pure columns of its glen-built hall.
Backward and forward roll'd the waves of fight
Round Troy; but while this stood, Troy could not fall.

So, in its lovely moonlight, lives the soul.
Mountains surround it, and sweet virgin air;
Cold plashing, past it, crystal waters roll;
We visit it by moments, ah! too rare.

Men will renew the battle in the plain
To-morrow; red with blood will Xanthus be;
Hector and Ajax will be there again;
Helen will come upon the wall to see.

Then we shall rust in shade, or shine in strife,
And fluctuate 'twixt blind hopes and blind despairs,
And fancy that we put forth all our life,
And never know how with the soul it fares.

Still doth the soul, from its lone fastness high,
Upon our life a ruling effluence send;
And when it fails, fight as we will, we die,
And while it lasts, we cannot wholly end.

THE SCHOLAR GIPSY

Go, for they call you, Shepherd, from the hill;
Go, Shepherd, and untie the wattled cotes:
No longer leave thy wistful flock unfed,
Nor let thy bawling fellows rack their throats,
Nor the cropp'd herbage shoot another head.
But when the fields are still,
And the tired men and dogs all gone to rest,
And only the white sheep are sometimes seen
Cross and recross the strips of moon-blanch'd green;
Come, Shepherd, and again renew the quest.

Here, where the reaper was at work of late,
In this high field's dark corner, where he leaves
His coat, his basket, and his earthen cruise,
And in the sun all morning binds the sheaves,

Then here, at noon, comes back his stores to use;
Here will I sit and wait,
While to my ear from uplands far away
The bleating of the folded flocks is borne;
With distant cries of reapers in the corn –
All the live murmur of a summer's day.

Screen'd is this nook o'er the high, half-reap'd field,
And here till sun-down, Shepherd, will I be.
Through the thick corn the scarlet poppies peep
And round green roots and yellowing stalks I see
Pale pink convolvulus in tendrils creep:
And air-swept lindens yield
Their scent, and rustle down their perfum'd showers
Of bloom on the bent grass where I am laid,
And bower me from the August sun with shade;
And the eye travels down to Oxford's towers:

And near me on the grass lies Glanvil's book –
Come, let me read the oft-read tale again,
The story of that Oxford scholar poor,
Of pregnant parts and quick inventive brain,
Who, tir'd of knocking at Preferment's door,
One summer morn forsook
His friends, and went to learn the Gipsy lore,
And roam'd the world with that wild brotherhood,
And came, as most men deem'd, to little good,
But came to Oxford and his friends no more.

But once, years after, in the country lanes,
Two scholars, whom at college erst he knew,
Met him, and of his way of life enquir'd.
Whereat he answer'd, that the Gipsy crew,
His mates, had arts to rule as they desir'd
The workings of men's brains;
And they can bind them to what thoughts they will:
'And I,' he said, 'the secret of their art,
When fully learn'd, will to the world impart:
But it needs happy moments for this skill.'

This said, he left them, and return'd no more. –
But rumours hung about the country-side,
That the lost Scholar long was seen to stray,

Seen by rare glimpses, pensive and tongue-tied,
In hat of antique shape, and cloak of grey,
The same the Gipsies wore.
Shepherds had met him on the Hurst in spring:
At some lone alehouse in the Berkshire moors,
On the warm ingle bench, the smock-frock'd boors
Had found him seated at their entering,

But, 'mid their drink and clatter, he would fly:
And I myself seem half to know thy looks,
And put the shepherds, Wanderer, on thy trace;
And boys who in lone wheatfields scare the rooks
I ask if thou hast pass'd their quiet place;
Or in my boat I lie
Moor'd to the cool bank in the summer heats,
Mid wide grass meadows which the sunshine fills,
And watch the warm, green-muffled Cumner hills,
And wonder if thou haunt'st their shy retreats.

For most, I know, thou lov'st retired ground.
Thee, at the ferry, Oxford riders blithe,
Returning home on summer nights, have met
Crossing the stripling Thames at Bab-lock-hithe,
Trailing in the cool stream thy fingers wet,
As the slow punt swings round:
And leaning backward in a pensive dream,
And fostering in thy lap a heap of flowers
Pluck'd in shy fields and distant Wychwood bowers,
And thine eyes resting on the moonlit stream.

And then they land, and thou art seen no more.
Maidens who from the distant hamlets come
To dance around the Fyfield elm in May,
Oft through the darkening fields have seen thee roam,
Or cross a stile into the public way.
Oft thou hast given them store
Of flowers – the frail-leaf'd, white anemone –
Dark bluebells drench'd with dews of summer eves –
And purple orchises with spotted leaves –
But none has words she can report of thee.

And, above Godstow Bridge, when hay-time's here
In June, and many a scythe in sunshine flames,

Men who through those wide fields of breezy grass
Where black-wing'd swallows haunt the glittering Thames,
To bathe in the abandon'd lasher pass,
Have often pass'd thee near
Sitting upon the river bank o'ergrown:
Mark'd thine outlandish garb, thy figure spare,
Thy dark vague eyes, and soft abstracted air;
But, when they came from bathing, thou wert gone.

At some lone homestead in the Cumner hills,
Where at her open door the housewife darns,
Thou hast been seen, or hanging on a gate
To watch the threshers in the mossy barns.
Children, who early range these slopes and late
For cresses from the rills,
Have known thee watching, all an April day,
The springing pastures and the feeding kine;
And mark'd thee, when the stars come out and shine,
Through the long dewy grass move slow away.

In autumn, on the skirts of Bagley Wood,
Where most the Gipsies by the turf-edg'd way
Pitch their smok'd tents, and every bush you see
With scarlet patches tagg'd and shreds of grey,
Above the forest ground called Thessaly –
The blackbird picking food
Sees thee, nor stops his meal, nor fears at all;
So often has he known thee past him stray,
Rapt, twirling in thy hand a wither'd spray,
And waiting for the spark from Heaven to fall.

And once, in winter, on the causeway chill
Where home through flooded fields foot-
Have I not pass'd thee on the wooden
Wrapt in thy cloak and battling with the
Thy face towards Hinksey and its w
And thou hast climb'd the hill,
And gain'd the white brow of the C
Turn'd once to watch, while thi
The line of festal light in Christ
Then sought thy straw in some se

But what – I dream! Two hundred years are flown
Since first thy story ran through Oxford halls,
And the grave Glanvil did the tale inscribe
That thou wert wander'd from the studious walls
To learn strange arts, and join a Gipsy tribe:
And thou from earth art gone
Long since, and in some quiet churchyard laid;
Some country nook, where o'er thy unknown grave
Tall grasses and white flowering nettles wave –
Under a dark red-fruited yew-tree's shade.

– No, no, thou hast not felt the lapse of hours.
For what wears out the life of mortal men?
'Tis that from change to change their being rolls;
'Tis that repeated shocks, again, again,
Exhaust the energy of strongest souls,
And numb the elastic powers.
Till having us'd our nerves with bliss and teen,
And tired upon a thousand schemes our wit,
To the just-pausing Genius we remit
Our worn-out life, and are – what we have been.

Thou hast not lived, why should'st thou perish, so?
Thou hadst *one* aim, *one* business, *one* desire:
Else wert thou long since number'd with the dead –
Else hadst thou spent, like other men, thy fire.
The generations of thy peers are fled,
And we ourselves shall go;
But thou possessest an immortal lot,
And we imagine thee exempt from age
And living as thou liv'st on Glanvil's page,
Because thou hadst – what we, alas, have not!

For early didst thou leave the world, with powers
Fresh, undiverted to the world without,
Firm to their mark, not spent on other things;
Free from the sick fatigue, the languid doubt,
Which much to have tried, in much been baffled, brings.
O life unlike to ours!
Who fluctuate idly without term or scope,
Of whom each strives, nor knows for what he strives,
And each half lives a hundred different lives;
Who wait like thee, but not, like thee, in hope.

Thou waitest for the spark from Heaven: and we,
Light half-believers of our casual creeds,
Who never deeply felt, nor clearly will'd,
Whose insight never has borne fruit in deeds,
Whose vague resolves never have been fulfill'd:
For whom each year we see
Breeds new beginnings, disappointments new;
Who hesitate and falter life away,
And lose to-morrow the ground won to-day –
Ah! do not we, Wanderer! await it too?

Yes, we await it, but it still delays,
And then we suffer; and amongst us One,
Who most has suffer'd, takes dejectedly
His seat upon the intellectual throne;
And all his store of sad experience he
Lays bare of wretched days;
Tells us his misery's birth and growth and signs,
And how the dying spark of hope was fed,
And how the breast was sooth'd, and how the head,
And all his hourly varied anodynes.

This for our wisest: and we others pine,
And wish the long unhappy dream would end,
And waive all claim to bliss, and try to bear
With close-lipp'd Patience for our only friend,
Sad Patience, too near neighbour to Despair:
But none has hope like thine.
Thou through the fields and through the woods dost stray,
Roaming the country side, a truant boy,
Nursing thy project in unclouded joy,
And every doubt long blown by time away.

O born in days when wits were fresh and clear,
And life ran gaily as the sparkling Thames;
Before this strange disease of modern life,
With its sick hurry, its divided aims,
Its heads o'ertax'd, its palsied hearts, was rife –
Fly hence, our contact fear!
Still fly, plunge deeper in the bowering wood!
Averse, as Dido did with gesture stern
From her false friend's approach in Hades turn,
Wave us away, and keep thy solitude!

Still nursing the unconquerable hope,
Still clutching the inviolable shade,
With a free, onward impulse brushing through,
By night, the silver'd branches of the glade –
Far on the forest skirts, where none pursue,
On some mild pastoral slope
Emerge, and resting on the moonlit pales,
Freshen thy flowers, as in former years,
With dew, or listen with enchanted ears,
From the dark dingles, to the nightingales.

But fly our paths, our feverish contact fly!
For strong the infection of our mental strife,
Which, though it gives no bliss, yet spoils for rest;
And we should win thee from thy own fair life,
Like us distracted, and like us unblest.
Soon, soon thy cheer would die,
Thy hopes grow timorous, and unfix'd thy powers,
And thy clear aims be cross and shifting made:
And then thy glad perennial youth would fade,
Fade, and grow old at last and die like ours.

Then fly our greetings, fly our speech and smiles!
– As some grave Tyrian trader, from the sea,
Descried at sunrise an emerging prow
Lifting the cool-hair'd creepers stealthily,
The fringes of a southward-facing brow
Among the Ægæan isles;
And saw the merry Grecian coaster come,
Freighted with amber grapes, and Chian wine,
Green bursting figs, and tunnies steep'd in brine;
And knew the intruders on his ancient home,

The young light-hearted Masters of the waves;
And snatch'd his rudder, and shook out more sail,
And day and night held on indignantly
O'er the blue Midland waters with the gale,
Betwixt the Syrtes and soft Sicily,
To where the Atlantic raves
Outside the Western Straits; and unbent sails
There, where down cloudy cliffs, through sheets of foam,
Shy traffickers, the dark Iberians come;
And on the beach undid his corded bales.

Creep into thy narrow bed,
Creep, and let no more be said!
Vain thy onset! all stands fast;
Thou thyself must break at last.

Let the long contention cease!
Geese are swans, and swans are geese.
Let them have it how they will!
Thou art tired; best be still!

They out-talk'd thee, hiss'd thee, tore thee.
Better men fared thus before thee;
Fired their ringing shot and pass'd,
Hotly charged – and broke at last.

Charge once more, then, and be dumb!
Let the victors, when they come,
When the forts of folly fall,
Find thy body by the wall.

WHITMAN

THE DALLIANCE OF THE EAGLES

Skirting the river road, (my forenoon walk, my rest,)
Skyward in air a sudden muffled sound, the dalliance of the eagles,
The rushing amorous contact high in space together,
The clinching interlocking claws, a living, fierce, gyrating wheel,
Four beating wings, two beaks, a swirling mass tight grappling,
In tumbling turning clustering loops, straight downward falling,
Till o'er the river pois'd, the twain yet one, a moment's lull,
A motionless still balance in the air, then parting, talons loosing,
Upward again on slow-firm pinions slanting, their separate diverse flight,
She hers, he his, pursuing.

'WHEN LILACS LAST IN THE DOORYARD BLOOM'D'

WHEN lilacs last in the dooryard bloom'd,
And the great star early droop'd in the western sky in the night,
I mourn'd, and yet shall mourn with ever-returning spring.

Ever-returning spring, trinity sure to me you bring,
Lilac blooming perennial and drooping star in the west,
And thought of him I love.*

O powerful western fallen star!
O shades of night – O moody, tearful night!
O great star disappear'd – O the black murk that hides the star!
O cruel hands that hold me powerless – O helpless soul of me!
O harsh surrounding cloud that will not free my soul.

In the dooryard fronting an old farm-house near the white-wash'd palings,
Stands the lilac-bush tall-growing with heart-shaped leaves of rich green,
With many a pointed blossom rising delicate, with the perfume strong I love,
With every leaf a miracle – and from this bush in the dooryard,
With delicate-color'd blossoms and heart-shaped leaves of rich green,
A sprig with its flower I break.

In the swamp in secluded recesses,
A shy and hidden bird is warbling a song.

Solitary the thrush,
The hermit withdrawn to himself, avoiding the settlements,
Sings by himself a song.

Song of the bleeding throat,
Death's outlet song of life, (for well dear brother I know,
If thou wast not granted to sing thou would'st surely die.)

Over the breast of the spring, the land, amid cities,
Amid lanes and through old woods, where lately the violets peep'd from the ground, spotting the gray debris,

* President Lincoln

Amid the grass in the fields each side of the lanes, passing the endless grass,
Passing the yellow-spear'd wheat, every grain from its shroud in the dark-brown fields uprisen,
Passing the apple-tree blows of white and pink in the orchards,
Carrying a corpse to where it shall rest in the grave,
Night and day journeys a coffin.

Coffin that passes through lanes and streets,
Through day and night with the great cloud darkening the land,
With the pomp of the inloop'd flags with the cities draped in black,
With the show of the States themselves as of crape-veil'd women standing,
With processions long and winding and the flambeaus of the night,
With the countless torches lit, with the silent sea of faces and the unbared heads,
With the waiting depot, the arriving coffin, and the sombre faces,
With dirges through the night, with the thousand voices rising strong and solemn,
With all the mournful voices of the dirges pour'd around the coffin,
The dim-lit churches and the shuddering organs – where amid these you journey,
With the tolling tolling bells' perpetual clang,
Here, coffin that slowly passes,
I give you my sprig of lilac.

(Nor for you, for one alone,
Blossoms and branches green to coffins all I bring,
For fresh as the morning, thus would I chant a song for you O sane and sacred death.

All over bouquets of roses,
O death, I cover you over with roses and early lilies,
But mostly and now the lilac that blooms the first,
Copious I break, I break the sprigs from the bushes,
With loaded arms I come, pouring for you,
For you and the coffins all of you O death.)

Whitman O western orb sailing the heaven,
Now I know what you must have meant as a month since I walk'd,
As I walk'd in silence the transparent shadowy night,
As I saw you had something to tell as you bent to me night after night,
As you droop'd from the sky low down as if to my side, (while the other stars all look'd on,)
As we wander'd together the solemn night, (for something I know not what kept me from sleep,)
As the night advanced, and I saw on the rim of the west how full you were of woe,
As I stood on the rising ground in the breeze in the cool transparent night,
As I watch'd where you pass'd and was lost in the netherward black of the night,
As my soul in its trouble dissatisfied sank, as where you sad orb,
Concluded, dropt in the night, and was gone.

Sing on there in the swamp,
O singer bashful and tender, I hear your notes, I hear your call,
I hear, I come presently, I understand you,
But a moment I linger, for the lustrous star has detain'd me,
The star my departing comrade holds and detains me.

O how shall I warble myself for the dead one there I loved?
And how shall I deck my song for the large sweet soul that has gone?
And what shall my perfume be for the grave of him I love?

Sea-winds blown from east and west,
Blown from the Eastern sea and blown from the Western sea, till there on the prairies meeting,
These and with these and the breath of my chant,
I'll perfume the grave of him I love.

O what shall I hang on the chamber walls?
And what shall the pictures be that I hang on the walls,
To adorn the burial-house of him I love?

Pictures of growing spring and farms and homes,
With the Fourth-month eve at sundown, and the gray smoke lucid and bright,

With floods of the yellow gold of the gorgeous, indolent sinking sun, burning, expanding the air,
With the fresh sweet herbage under foot, and the pale green leaves of the trees prolific,
In the distance the flowing glaze, the breast of the river, with a wind-dapple here and there,
With ranging hills on the banks, with many a line against the sky, and shadows,
And the city at hand with dwellings so dense, and stacks of chimneys,
And all the scenes of life and the workshops, and the workmen homeward returning.

Lo, body and soul – this land,
My own Manhattan with spires, and the sparkling and hurrying tides, and the ships,
The varied and ample land, the South and the North in the light, Ohio's shores and flashing Missouri,
And ever the far-spreading prairies cover'd with grass and corn.

Lo, the most excellent sun so calm and haughty,
The violet and purple morn with just-felt breezes,
The gentle soft-born measureless light,
The miracle spreading bathing all, the fulfill'd noon,
The coming eve delicious, the welcome night and the stars,
Over my cities shining all, enveloping man and land.

Sing on, sing on you gray-brown bird,
Sing from the swamps, the recesses, pour your chant from the bushes,
Limitless out of the dusk, out of the cedars and pines.

Sing on dearest brother, warble your reedy song,
Loud human song, with voice of uttermost woe.

O liquid and free and tender!
O wild and loose to my soul – O wondrous singer!
You only I hear – yet the star holds me, (but will soon depart,)
Yet the lilac with mastering odor holds me.

Now while I sat in the day and look'd forth,
In the close of the day with its light and the fields of spring, and the farmers preparing their crops,

Whitman In the large unconscious scenery of my land with its lakes and forests,
In the heavenly aerial beauty, (after the perturb'd winds and the storms,)
Under the arching heavens of the afternoon swift passing, and the voices of children and women,
The many-moving sea-tides, and I saw the ships how they sail'd,
And the summer approaching with richness, and the fields all busy with labor,
And the infinite separate houses, how they all went on, each with its meals and minutiæ of daily usages,
And the streets how their throbbings throbb'd, and the cities pent – lo, then and there,
Falling upon them all and among them all, enveloping me with the rest,
Appear'd the cloud, appear'd the long black trail,
And I knew death, its thought, and the sacred knowledge of death.

Then with the knowledge of death as walking one side of me,
And the thought of death close-walking the other side of me,
And I in the middle as with companions, and as holding the hands of companions,
I fled forth to the hiding receiving night that talks not,
Down to the shores of the water, the path by the swamp in the dimness,
To the solemn shadowy cedars and ghostly pines so still.

And the singer so shy to the rest receiv'd me,
The gray-brown bird I know receiv'd us comrades three,
And he sang the carol of death, and a verse for him I love.

From deep secluded recesses,
From the fragrant cedars and the ghostly pines so still,
Came the carol of the bird.

And the charm of the carol rapt me,
As I held as if by their hands my comrades in the night,
And the voice of my spirit tallied the song of the bird.

[*The Song of the Bird omitted*]

To the tally of my soul,
Loud and strong kept up the gray-brown bird,
With pure deliberate notes spreading filling the night.
Loud in the pines and cedars dim,
Clear in the freshness moist and the swamp-perfume,
And I with my comrades there in the night.

While my sight that was bound in my eyes unclosed,
As to long panoramas of visions.

And I saw askant the armies,
I saw as in noiseless dreams hundreds of battle-flags,
Borne through the smoke of the battles and pierc'd with missiles I saw them,
And carried hither and yon through the smoke, and torn and bloody,
And at last but a few shreds left on the staffs, (and all in silence,)
And the staffs all splinter'd and broken.

I saw battle-corpses, myriads of them,
And the white skeletons of young men, I saw them,
I saw the debris and debris of all the slain soldiers of the war,
But I saw they were not as was thought,
They themselves were fully at rest, they suffer'd not,
The living remain'd and suffer'd, the mother suffer'd,
And the wife and the child and the musing comrade suffer'd,
And the armies that remain'd suffer'd.

Passing the visions, passing the night,
Passing, unloosing the hold of my comrades' hands,
Passing the song of the hermit bird and the tallying song of my soul,
Victorious song, death's outlet song, yet varying ever-altering song,
As low and wailing, yet clear the notes, rising and falling, flooding the night,
Sadly sinking and fainting, as warning and warning, and yet again bursting with joy,
Covering the earth and filling the spread of the heaven,
As that powerful psalm in the night I heard from recesses,
Passing, I leave thee lilac with heart-shaped leaves,
I leave thee there in the door-yard, blooming, returning with spring.

I cease from my song for thee,
From my gaze on thee in the west, fronting the west, communing with thee,
O comrade lustrous with silver face in the night.

Yet each to keep and all, retrievements out of the night,
The song, the wondrous chant of the gray-brown bird,
And the tallying chant, the echo arous'd in my soul,
With the lustrous and drooping star with the countenance full of woe,
With the holders holding my hand nearing the call of the bird,
Comrades mine and I in the midst, and their memory ever to keep, for the dead I loved so well,
For the sweetest, wisest soul of all my days and lands – and this for his dear sake,
Lilac and star and bird twined with the chant of my soul,
There in the fragrant pines and the cedars dusk and dim.

SPARKLES FROM THE WHEEL

WHERE the city's ceaseless crowd moves on the livelong day,
Withdrawn I join a group of children watching, I pause aside with them.

By the curb toward the edge of the flagging,
A knife-grinder works at his wheel sharpening a great knife,
Bending over he carefully holds it to the stone, by foot and knee,
With measur'd tread he turns rapidly, as he presses with light but firm hand,
Forth issue then in copious golden jets,
Sparkles from the wheel.

The scene and all its belongings, how they seize and affect me,
The sad sharp-chinn'd old man with worn clothes and broad shoulder-band of leather,
Myself effusing and fluid, a phantom curiously floating, now here absorb'd and arrested,
The group, (an unminded point set in a vast surrounding,)
The attentive, quiet children, the loud, proud, restive base of the streets,

The low hoarse purr of the whirling stone, the light-press'd blade,
Diffusing, dropping, sideways-darting, in tiny showers of gold,
Sparkles from the wheel.

RECONCILIATION

Word over all, beautiful as the sky,
Beautiful that war and all its deeds of carnage must in time be utterly lost,
That the hands of the sisters Death and Night incessantly softly wash again, and ever again, this soil'd world;
For my enemy is dead, a man divine as myself is dead,
I look where he lies white-faced and still in the coffin – I draw near,
Bend down and touch lightly with my lips the white face in the coffin.

ROSSETTI

from THE HOUSE OF LIFE

LOVESIGHT

When do I see thee most, beloved one?
When in the light the spirits of mine eyes
Before thy face, their altar, solemnize
The worship of that Love through thee made known?
Or when in the dusk hours, (we two alone,)
Close-kissed and eloquent of still replies
Thy twilight-hidden glimmering visage lies,
And my soul only sees thy soul its own?

O love, my love! if I no more should see
Thyself, nor on the earth the shadow of thee,
Nor image of thine eyes in any spring, –
How then should sound upon Life's darkening slope
The ground-whirl of the perished leaves of Hope,
The wind of Death's imperishable wing?

PRIDE OF YOUTH

EVEN as a child, of sorrow that we give
  The dead, but little in his heart can find,
  Since without need of thought to his clear mind
Their turn it is to die and his to live: –
Even so the winged New Love smiles to receive
  Along his eddying plumes the auroral wind,
  Nor, forward glorying, casts one look behind
Where night-rack shrouds the Old Love fugitive.

There is a change in every hour's recall,
  And the last cowslip in the fields we see
  On the same day with the first corn-poppy.
Alas for hourly change! Alas for all
The loves that from his hand proud Youth lets fall,
  Even as the beads of a told rosary!

BARREN SPRING

ONCE more the changed year's turning wheel returns:
  And as a girl sails balanced in the wind,
  And now before and now again behind
Stoops as it swoops, with cheek that laughs and burns, –
So Spring comes merry towards me here, but earns
  No answering smile from me, whose life is twin'd
  With the dead boughs that winter still must bind,
And whom today the Spring no more concerns.

Behold, this crocus is a withering flame;
  This snowdrop, snow; this apple-blossom's part
  To breed the fruit that breeds the serpent's art.
Nay, for these Spring-flowers, turn thy face from them,
Nor stay till on the year's last lily-stem
  The white cup shrivels round the golden heart.

A SUPERSCRIPTION

LOOK in my face; my name is Might-have-been;
  I am also called No-more, Too-late, Farewell;
  Unto thine ear I hold the dead-sea shell

Cast up thy Life's foam-fretted feet between;
Unto thine eyes the glass where that is seen
  Which had Life's form and Love's, but by my spell
  Is now a shaken shadow intolerable,
Of ultimate things unuttered the frail screen.

Mark me, how still I am! But should there dart
  One moment through thy soul the soft surprise
  Of that winged Peace which lulls the breath of sighs, –
Then shalt thou see me smile, and turn apart
Thy visage to mine ambush at thy heart
  Sleepless with cold commemorative eyes.

SUDDEN LIGHT

I HAVE been here before,
  But when or how I cannot tell:
I know the grass beyond the door,
  The sweet keen smell,
The sighing sound, the lights around the shore.

You have been mine before, –
  How long ago I may not know:
But just when at that swallow's soar
  Your neck turned so,
Some veil did fall, – I knew it all of yore.

Has this been thus before?
  And shall not thus time's eddying flight
Still with our lives our love restore
  In death's despite,
And day and night yield one delight once more?

THE WOODSPURGE

THE wind flapped loose, the wind was still,
Shaken out dead from tree and hill:
I had walked on at the wind's will, –
I sat now, for the wind was still.

Between my knees my forehead was, –
My lips, drawn in, said not Alas!
My hair was over in the grass,
My naked ears heard the day pass.

My eyes, wide open, had the run
Of some ten weeds to fix upon;
Among those few, out of the sun,
The woodspurge flowered, three cups in one.

From perfect grief there need not be
Wisdom or even memory:
One thing then learnt remains to me, –
The woodspurge has a cup of three.

CHRISTINA ROSSETTI

REMEMBER

REMEMBER me when I am gone away,
  Gone far away into the silent land;
  When you can no more hold me by the hand,
Nor I half turn to go yet turning stay.
Remember me when no more day by day
  You tell me of our future that you planned.
  Only remember me; you understand
It will be late to counsel then or pray.
Yet if you should forget me for a while
  And afterwards remember, do not grieve:
  For if the darkness and corruption leave
  A vestige of the thoughts that once I had,
Better by far you should forget and smile
  Than that you should remember and be sad.

THE BOURNE

UNDERNEATH the growing grass,
  Underneath the living flowers,
  Deeper than the sound of showers:
  There we shall not count the hours
By the shadows as they pass.

Youth and health will be but vain,
  Beauty reckoned of no worth:
  There a very little girth
  Can hold round what once the earth
Seemed too narrow to contain.

A PAUSE OF THOUGHT

I LOOKED for that which is not, nor can be,
  And hope deferred made my heart sick in truth:
  But years must pass before a hope of youth
    Is resigned utterly.

I watched and waited with a steadfast will:
  And though the object seemed to flee away
  That I so longed for, ever day by day
    I watched and waited still.

Sometimes I said: This thing shall be no more;
  My expectation wearies and shall cease;
  I will resign it now and be at peace:
    Yet never gave it o'er.

Sometimes I said: It is an empty name
  I long for; to a name why should I give
  The peace of all the days I have to live? –
    Yet gave it all the same.

Alas, thou foolish one! alike unfit
  For healthy joy and salutary pain:
  Thou knowest the chase useless, and again
    Turnest to follow it.

PASSING AND GLASSING

ALL things that pass
Are woman's looking-glass;
They show her how her bloom must fade,
And she herself be laid
With withered roses in the shade;
  With withered roses and the fallen peach,
  Unlovely, out of reach
    Of summer joy that was.

All things that pass
Are woman's tiring-glass;
The faded lavender is sweet,
Sweet the dead violet
Culled and laid by and cared for yet;
The dried-up violets and dried lavender
Still sweet, may comfort her,
Nor need she cry Alas!

All things that pass
Are wisdom's looking-glass;
Being full of hope and fear, and still
Brimful of good or ill,
According to our work and will;
For there is nothing new beneath the sun;
Our doings have been done,
And that which shall be was.

THE THREAD OF LIFE

THE irresponsive silence of the land,
The irresponsive sounding of the sea,
Speak both one message of one sense to me; –
Aloof, aloof, we stand aloof, so stand
Thou too aloof bound with the flawless band
Of inner solitude; we bind not thee;
But who from thy self-chain shall set thee free?
What heart shall touch thy heart? what hand thy hand? –
And I am sometimes proud and sometimes meek,
And sometimes I remember days of old
When fellowship seemed not so far to seek
And all the world and I seemed much less cold,
And at the rainbow's foot lay surely gold,
And hope felt strong and life itself not weak.

EMILY DICKINSON

There came a wind like a bugle;
It quivered through the grass,
And a green chill upon the heat
So ominous did pass
We barred the windows and the doors
As from an emerald ghost;
The doom's electric moccasin
That very instant passed.
On a strange mob of panting trees,
And fences fled away,
And rivers where the houses ran
The living looked that day.
The bell within the steeple wild
The flying tidings whirled.
How much can come
And much can go,
And yet abide the world!

My life closed twice before its close;
It yet remains to see
If Immortality unveil
A third event to me,
So huge, so hopeless to conceive,
As these that twice befell.
Parting is all we know of heaven,
And all we need of hell.

Presentiment is that long shadow on the lawn
Indicative that suns go down;
The notice to the startled grass
That darkness is about to pass.

Elysium is as far as to
The very nearest room,
If in that room a friend await
Felicity or doom.

What fortitude the soul contains,
That it can so endure
The accent of a coming foot,
The opening of a door!

She rose to his requirement, dropped
The playthings of her life
To take the honorable work
Of woman and of wife.

If aught she missed in her new day
Of amplitude, or awe,
Or first prospective, or the gold
In using wore away,

It lay unmentioned, as the sea
Develops pearl and weed,
But only to himself is known
The fathoms they abide.

After a hundred years
Nobody knows the place, –
Agony, that enacted there,
Motionless as peace.

Weeds triumphant ranged,
Strangers strolled and spelled
At the lone orthography
Of the elder dead.

Winds of summer fields
Recollect the way, –
Instinct picking up the key
Dropped by memory.

The sky is low, the clouds are mean,
A traveling flake of snow
Across a barn or through a rut
Debates if it will go.

A narrow wind complains all day
How someone treated him;
Nature, like us, is sometimes caught
Without her diadem.

As imperceptibly as grief
The summer lapsed away, –
Too imperceptible, at last,
To seem like perfidy.

A quietness distilled,
As twilight long began,
Or Nature, spending with herself
Sequestered afternoon.

The dusk drew earlier in,
The morning foreign shone, –
A courteous, yet harrowing grace,
As guest who would be gone.

And thus, without a wing,
Or service of a keel,
Our summer made her light escape
Into the beautiful.

MORRIS

PROLOGUE TO *THE EARTHLY PARADISE*

Of Heaven or Hell I have no power to sing,
I cannot ease the burden of your fears,
Or make quick-coming death a little thing,
Or bring again the pleasure of past years,
Nor for my words shall ye forget your tears,
Or hope again for aught that I can say,
The idle singer of an empty day.

But rather, when aweary of your mirth,
From full hearts still unsatisfied ye sigh,
And, feeling kindly unto all the earth,
Grudge every minute as it passes by,
Made the more mindful that the sweet days die –
– Remember me a little then I pray,
The idle singer of an empty day.

The heavy trouble, the bewildering care
That weighs us down who live and earn our bread,
These idle verses have no power to bear;
So let me sing of names remembered,
Because they, living not, can ne'er be dead,
Or long time take their memory quite away
From us poor singers of an empty day.

Dreamer of dreams, born out of my due time,
Why should I strive to set the crooked straight?
Let it suffice me that my murmuring rhyme
Beats with light wing against the ivory gate,
Telling a tale not too importunate
To those who in the sleepy region stay,
Lulled by the singer of an empty day.

Folk say, a wizard to a northern king
At Christmas-tide such wondrous things did show,
That through one window men beheld the spring,
And through another saw the summer glow,
And through a third the fruited vines a-row
While still, unheard, but in its wonted way,
Piped the drear wind of that December day.

So with this Earthly Paradise it is,
If ye will read aright, and pardon me,
Who strive to build a shadowy isle of bliss
Midmost the beating of the steely sea,
Where tossed about all hearts of men must be;
Whose ravening monsters mighty men shall slay,
Not the poor singer of an empty day.

from OCTOBER

O LOVE, turn from the unchanging sea, and gaze
Down these grey slopes upon the year grown old,
A-dying mid the autumn-scented haze,
That hangeth o'er the hollow in the wold,
Where the wind-bitten ancient elms enfold
Grey church, long barn, orchard, and red-roofed stead,
Wrought in dead days for men a long while dead.

Come down, O love; may not our hands still meet,
Since still we live to-day, forgetting June,
Forgetting May, deeming October sweet –
– O hearken, hearken! through the afternoon,
The grey tower sings a strange old tinkling tune!
Sweet, sweet, and sad, the toiling year's last breath,
Too satiate of life to strive with death.

And we too – will it not be soft and kind,
That rest from life, from patience and from pain;
That rest from bliss we know not when we find;
That rest from Love which ne'er the end can gain? –
Hark, how the tune swells, that erewhile did wane!
Look up, love! – ah, cling close and never move!
How can I ever have enough of life and love?

SUMMER DAWN

PRAY but one prayer for me 'twixt thy closed lips,
  Think but one thought of me up in the stars.
The summer night waneth, the morning light slips,
  Faint and grey 'twixt the leaves of the aspen, betwixt
    the cloud bars,
That are patiently waiting there for the dawn:
  Patient and colourless, though Heaven's gold
Waits to float through them along with the sun.
Far out in the meadows, above the young corn,
  The heavy elms wait, and restless and cold
The uneasy wind rises; the roses are dun;
Through the long twilight they pray for the dawn,
Round the lone house in the midst of the corn.
  Speak but one word to me over the corn,
  Over the tender, bow'd locks of the corn.

SWINBURNE

A LEAVE-TAKING

Let us go hence, my songs; she will not hear.
Let us go hence together without fear;
Keep silence now, for singing-time is over,
And over all old things and all things dear.
She loves not you nor me as all we love her.
Yea, though we sang as angels in her ear,
She would not hear.

Let us rise up and part; she will not know.
Let us go seaward as the great winds go,
Full of blown sand and foam; what help is here?
There is no help, for all these things are so,
And all the world is bitter as a tear.
And how these things are, though ye strove to show,
She would not know.

Let us go home and hence; she will not weep.
We gave love many dreams and days to keep,
Flowers without scent, and fruits that would not grow,
Saying 'If thou wilt, thrust in thy sickle and reap.'
All is reaped now; no grass is left to mow;
And we that sowed, though all we fell on sleep,
She would not weep.

Let us go hence and rest; she will not love.
She shall not hear us if we sing hereof,
Nor see love's ways, how sore they are and steep.
Come hence, let be, lie still; it is enough.
Love is a barren sea, bitter and deep;
And though she saw all heaven in flower above,
She would not love.

Let us give up, go down; she will not care.
Though all the stars made gold of all the air,
And the sea moving saw before it move
One moon-flower making all the foam-flowers fair;
Though all those waves went over us, and drove
Deep down the stifling lips and drowning hair,
She would not care.

Let us go hence, go hence; she will not see.
Sing all once more together; surely she,
She too, remembering days and words that were,
Will turn a little towards us, sighing; but we,
We are hence, we are gone, as though we had not been there.
Nay, and though all men seeing had pity on me,
She would not see.

from THE GARDEN OF PROSERPINE

PALE, beyond porch and portal,
Crowned with calm leaves, she stands
Who gathers all things mortal
With cold immortal hands;
Her languid lips are sweeter
Than love's who fears to greet her
To men that mix and meet her
From many times and lands.

She waits for each and other,
She waits for all men born;
Forgets the earth her mother,
The life of fruits and corn;
And spring and seed and swallow
Take wing for her and follow
Where summer song rings hollow
And flowers are put to scorn.

There go the loves that wither,
The old loves with wearier wings;
And all dead years draw thither,
And all disastrous things;
Dead dreams of days forsaken,
Blind buds that snows have shaken,
Wild leaves that winds have taken,
Red strays of ruined springs.

We are not sure of sorrow,
And joy was never sure;
To-day will die to-morrow;
Time stoops to no man's lure;

And love, grown faint and fretful,
With lips but half regretful
Sighs, and with eyes forgetful
  Weeps that no loves endure.

From too much love of living,
  From hope and fear set free,
We thank with brief thanksgiving
  Whatever gods may be
That no life lives for ever;
That dead men rise up never;
That even the weariest river
  Winds somewhere safe to sea.

Then star nor sun shall waken,
  Nor any change of light:
Nor sound of waters shaken,
  Nor any sound or sight:
Nor wintry leaves nor vernal,
Nor days nor things diurnal;
Only the sleep eternal
  In an eternal night.

A FORSAKEN GARDEN

In a coign of the cliff between lowland and highland,
  At the sea-down's edge between windward and lee,
Walled round with rocks as an inland island,
  The ghost of a garden fronts the sea.
A girdle of brushwood and thorn encloses
  The steep square slope of the blossomless bed
Where the weeds that grew green from the graves of its roses
      Now lie dead.

The fields fall southward, abrupt and broken,
  To the low last edge of the long lone land.
If a step should sound or a word be spoken,
  Would a ghost not rise at the strange guest's hand?
So long have the grey bare walks lain guestless,
  Through branches and briars if a man make way,
He shall find no life but the sea-wind's, restless
      Night and day.

The dense hard passage is blind and stifled
  That crawls by a track none turn to climb
To the strait waste place that the years have rifled
  Of all but the thorns that are touched not of time.
The thorns he spares when the rose is taken;
  The rocks are left when he wastes the plain.
The wind that wanders, the weeds wind-shaken,
      These remain.

Not a flower to be pressed of the foot that falls not;
  As the heart of a dead man the seed-plots are dry;
From the thicket of thorns whence the nightingale calls not,
  Could she call, there were never a rose to reply.
Over the meadows that blossom and wither
  Rings but the note of a sea-bird's song;
Only the sun and the rain come hither
      All year long.

The sun burns sere and the rain dishevels
  One gaunt bleak blossom of scentless breath.
Only the wind here hovers and revels
  In a round where life seems barren as death.
Here there was laughing of old, there was weeping,
  Haply, of lovers none ever will know,
Whose eyes went seaward a hundred sleeping
      Years ago.

Heart handfast in heart as they stood, 'Look thither,'
  Did he whisper? 'look forth from the flowers to the sea;
For the foam-flowers endure when the rose-blossoms wither,
  And men that love lightly may die – but we?'
And the same wind sang and the same waves whitened,
  And or ever the garden's last petals were shed,
In the lips that had whispered, the eyes that had lightened,
      Love was dead.

Or they loved their life through, and then went whither?
  And were one to the end – but what end who knows?
Love deep as the sea as a rose must wither,
  As the rose-red seaweed that mocks the rose.
Shall the dead take thought for the dead to love them?
  What love was ever as deep as a grave?
They are loveless now as the grass above them
      Or the wave.

All are at one now, roses and lovers,
  Not known of the cliffs and the fields and the sea.
Not a breath of the time that has been hovers
  In the air now soft with a summer to be.
Not a breath shall there sweeten the seasons hereafter
  Of the flowers or the lovers that laugh now or weep,
When as they that are free now of weeping and laughter
    We shall sleep.

Here death may deal not again for ever;
  Here change may come not till all change end.
From the graves they have made they shall rise up never,
  Who have left nought living to ravage and rend.
Earth, stones, and thorns of the wild ground growing,
  While the sun and the rain live, these shall be;
Till a last wind's breath upon all these blowing
    Roll the sea.

Till the slow sea rise and the sheer cliff crumble,
  Till terrace and meadow the deep gulfs drink,
Till the strength of the waves of the high tides humble
  The fields that lessen, the rocks that shrink.
Here now in his triumph where all things falter,
  Stretched out on the spoils that his own hand spread,
As a god self-slain on his own strange altar,
    Death lies dead.

CHORUS *from ATALANTA IN CALYDON*

When the hounds of spring are on winter's traces,
  The mother of months in meadow or plain
Fills the shadows and windy places
  With lisp of leaves and ripple of rain;
And the brown bright nightingale amorous
Is half assuaged for Itylus,
For the Thracian ships and the foreign faces,
  The tongueless vigil, and all the pain.

Come with bows bent and with emptying of quivers,
  Maiden most perfect, lady of light,
With a noise of winds and many rivers,
  With a clamour of waters, and with might;

Bind on thy sandals, O thou most fleet,
Over the splendour and speed of thy feet;
For the faint east quickens, the wan west shivers,
  Round the feet of the day and the feet of the night.

Where shall we find her, how shall we sing to her,
  Fold our hands round her knees, and cling?
O that man's heart were as fire and could spring to her,
  Fire, or the strength of the streams that spring!
For the stars and the winds are unto her
As raiment, as songs of the harp-player;
For the risen stars and the fallen cling to her,
  And the southwest-wind and the west-wind sing.

For winter's rains and ruins are over,
  And all the season of snows and sins;
The days dividing lover and lover,
  The light that loses, the night that wins;
And time remembered is grief forgotten,
And frosts are slain and flowers begotten,
And in green underwood and cover
  Blossom by blossom the spring begins.

The full streams feed on flower of rushes,
  Ripe grasses trammel a travelling foot,
The faint fresh flame of the young year flushes
  From leaf to flower and flower to fruit;
And fruit and leaf are as gold and fire,
And the oat is heard above the lyre,
And the hoofèd heel of a satyr crushes
  The chestnut-husk at the chestnut-root.

And Pan by noon and Bacchus by night,
  Fleeter of foot than the fleet-foot kid,
Follows with dancing and fills with delight
  The Mænad and the Bassarid;
And soft as lips that laugh and hide
The laughing leaves of the trees divide,
And screen from seeing and leave in sight
  The god pursuing, the maiden hid.

The ivy falls with the Bacchanal's hair
  Over her eyebrows hiding her eyes;

The wild vine slipping down leaves bare
  Her bright breast shortening into sighs;
The wild vine slips with the weight of its leaves,
But the berried ivy catches and cleaves
To the limbs that glitter, the feet that scare
  The wolf that follows, the fawn that flies.

THOMSON (B. V.)

from THE CITY OF DREADFUL NIGHT

ANEAR the centre of that northern crest
  Stands out a level upland bleak and bare,
From which the city east and south and west
  Sinks gently in long waves; and thronèd there
An Image sits, stupendous, superhuman,
The bronze colossus of a wingèd Woman,
  Upon a graded granite base foursquare.

Low-seated she leans forward massively,
  With cheek on clenched left hand, the forearm's might
Erect, its elbow on her rounded knee;
  Across a clasped book in her lap the right
Upholds a pair of compasses; she gazes
With full set eyes, but wandering in thick mazes
  Of sombre thought beholds no outward sight.

Words cannot picture her; but all men know
  That solemn sketch the pure sad artist wrought
Three centuries and threescore years ago,
  With phantasies of his peculiar thought:
The instruments of carpentry and science
Scattered about her feet, in strange alliance
  With the keen wolf-hound sleeping undistraught;

Scales, hour-glass, bell, and magic-square above;
  The grave and solid infant perched beside,
With open winglets that might bear a dove,
  Intent upon its tablets, heavy-eyed;

Her folded wings as of a mighty eagle,
But all too impotent to lift the regal
  Robustness of her earth-born strength and pride;

And with those wings, and that light wreath which seems
  To mock her grand head and the knotted frown
Of forehead charged with baleful thoughts and dreams,
  The household bunch of keys, the housewife's gown
Voluminous, indented, and yet rigid
As if a shell of burnished metal frigid,
  The feet thick-shod to tread all weakness down;

The comet hanging o'er the waste dark seas,
  The massy rainbow curved in front of it
Beyond the village with the masts and trees;
  The snaky imp, dog-headed, from the Pit,
Bearing upon its batlike leathern pinions
Her name unfolded in the sun's dominions,
  The 'MELENCOLIA' that transcends all wit.

Thus has the artist copied her, and thus
  Surrounded to expound her form sublime,
Her fate heroic and calamitous;
  Fronting the dreadful mysteries of Time,
Unvanquished in defeat and desolation,
Undaunted in the hopeless conflagration
  Of the day setting on her baffled prime.

Baffled and beaten back she works on still,
  Weary and sick of soul she works the more,
Sustained by her indomitable will:
  The hands shall fashion and the brain shall pore,
And all her sorrow shall be turned to labour,
Till Death the friend-foe piercing with his sabre
  That mighty heart of hearts ends bitter war.

But as if blacker night could dawn on night,
  With tenfold gloom on moonless night unstarred,
A sense more tragic than defeat and blight,
  More desperate than strife with hope debarred,
More fatal than the adamantine Never
Encompassing her passionate endeavour,
  Dawns glooming in her tenebrous regard:

The sense that every struggle brings defeat
  Because Fate holds no prize to crown success;
That all the oracles are dumb or cheat
  Because they have no secret to express;
That none can pierce the vast black veil uncertain
Because there is no light beyond the curtain;
  That all is vanity and nothingness.

Titanic from her high throne in the north,
  That City's sombre Patroness and Queen,
In bronze sublimity she gazes forth
  Over her Capital of teen and threne,
Over the river with its isles and bridges,
The marsh and moorland, to the stern rock-ridges,
  Confronting them with a coëval mien.

The moving moon and stars from east to west
  Circle before her in the sea of air;
Shadows and gleams glide round her solemn rest.
  Her subjects often gaze up to her there:
The strong to drink new strength of iron endurance,
The weak new terrors; all, renewed assurance
  And confirmation of the old despair.

LANIER

from SUNRISE

THE tide's at full: the marsh with flooded streams
Glimmers, a limpid labyrinth of dreams.
Each winding creek in grave entrancement lies
A rhapsody of morning stars. The skies
Shine scant with one forked galaxy, –
The marsh brags ten: looped on his breast they lie.

Oh, what if a sound should be made!
Oh, what if a bound should be laid
To this bow-and-string tension of beauty and silence a-spring, –
To the bend of beauty the bow, or the hold of silence the string!

I fear me, I fear me yon dome of diaphanous gleam
Will break as a bubble o'er-blown in a dream, –
Yon dome of too-tenuous tissues of space and of night,
Over-weighted with stars, over-freighted with light,
Over-sated with beauty and silence, will seem
  But a bubble that broke in a dream,
If a bound of degree to this grace be laid,
  Or a sound or a motion made.

But no: it is made: list! somewhere, – mystery, where?
          In the leaves? in the air?
In my heart? is a motion made:
'Tis a motion of dawn, like a flicker of shade on shade.
In the leaves 'tis palpable: low multitudinous stirring
Upwinds through the woods; the little ones, softly conferring,
Have settled my lord's to be looked for; so; they are still;
But the air and my heart and the earth are a-thrill, –
And look where the wild duck sails round the bend of the river, –
  And look where a passionate shiver
  Expectant is bending the blades
Of the marsh-grass in serial shimmers and shades, –
And invisible wings, fast fleeting, fast fleeting,
          Are beating
The dark overhead as my heart beats, – and steady and free
Is the ebb-tide flowing from marsh to sea –
    (Run home, little streams,
    With your lapfulls of stars and dreams), –
And a sailor unseen is hoisting a-peak,
For list, down the inshore curve of the creek
    How merrily flutters the sail, –
And lo, in the East! Will the East unveil?
The East is unveiled, the East hath confessed
A flush: 'tis dead; 'tis alive: 'tis dead, ere the West
Was aware of it: nay, 'tis abiding, 'tis unwithdrawn:
  Have a care, sweet Heaven! 'Tis Dawn.

PATMORE

A FAREWELL

WITH all my will, but much against my heart,
We two now part.
My Very Dear,
Our solace is, the sad road lies so clear.
It needs no art,
With faint, averted feet
And many a tear,
In our opposed paths to persevere.
Go thou to East, I West.
We will not say
There's any hope, it is so far away.
But, O, my Best,
When the one darling of our widowhead,
The nursling Grief,
Is dead,
And no dews blur our eyes
To see the peach-bloom come in evening skies,
Perchance we may,
Where now this night is day,
And even through faith of still averted feet,
Making full circle of our banishment,
Amazed meet;
The bitter journey to the bourne so sweet
Seasoning the termless feast of our content
With tears of recognition never dry.

SAINT VALENTINE'S DAY

WELL dost thou, Love, thy solemn Feast to hold
In vestal February;
Not rather choosing out some rosy day
From the rich coronet of the coming May,
When all things meet to marry!
  O, quick prævernal Power
That signall'st punctual through the sleepy mould
The Snowdrop's time to flower,

Fair as the rash oath of virginity
Which is first-love's first cry;
O, Baby Spring,
That flutter'st sudden 'neath the breast of Earth
A month before the birth;
Whence is the peaceful poignancy,
The joy contrite,
Sadder than sorrow, sweeter than delight,
That burthens now the breath of everything,
Though each one sighs as if to each alone
The cherish'd pang were known?
At dusk of dawn, on his dark spray apart,
With it the Blackbird breaks the young Day's heart;
  In evening's hush
About it talks the heavenly-minded Thrush;
The hill with like remorse
Smiles to the Sun's smile in his westering course;
The fisher's drooping skiff
In yonder sheltering bay;
The choughs that call about the shining cliff;
The children, noisy in the setting ray;
Own the sweet season, each thing as it may;
Thoughts of strange kindness and forgotten peace
In me increase;
And tears arise
Within my happy, happy Mistress' eyes,
And, lo, her lips, averted from my kiss,
Ask from Love's bounty, ah, much more than bliss!
  Is't the sequester'd and exceeding sweet
Of dear Desire electing his defeat?
Is't the waked Earth now to yon purpling cope
Uttering first-love's first cry,
Vainly renouncing, with a Seraph's sigh,
Love's natural hope?
Fair-meaning Earth, foredoom'd to perjury!
Behold, all amorous May,
With roses heap'd upon her laughing brows,
Avoids thee of thy vows!
Were it for thee, with her warm bosom near,
To abide the sharpness of the Seraph's sphere?
Forget thy foolish words;

Go to her summons gay,
Thy heart with dead, wing'd Innocencies fill'd,
Ev'n as a nest with birds
After the old ones by the hawk are kill'd.
  Well dost thou, Love, to celebrate
The noon of thy soft ecstasy,
Or e'er it be too late,
Or e'er the Snowdrop die!

MEREDITH

from THE THRUSH IN FEBRUARY

LOVE born of knowledge, love that gains
Vitality as Earth it mates,
The meaning of the Pleasures, Pains,
The Life, the Death, illuminates.

For love we Earth, then serve we all;
Her mystic secret then is ours:
We fall, or view our treasures fall,
Unclouded, as beholds her flowers

Earth, from a night of frosty wreck,
Enrobed in morning's mounted fire,
When lowly, with a broken neck,
The crocus lays her cheek to mire.

from MODERN LOVE

'I PLAY for Seasons; not Eternities!'
Says Nature, laughing on her way. 'So must
All those whose stake is nothing more than dust!'
And lo, she wins, and of her harmonies
She is full sure! Upon her dying rose
She drops a look of fondness, and goes by,
Scarce any retrospection in her eye;
For she the laws of growth most deeply knows,

Whose hands bear, here, a seed-bag; there, an urn.
Pledged she herself to aught, 'twould mark her end!
This lesson of our only visible friend,
Can we not teach our foolish hearts to learn?
Yes! yes! – but oh, our human rose is fair
Surpassingly! Lose calmly Love's great bliss,
When the renew'd forever of a kiss
Whirls life within the shower of loosened hair!

*

Mark where the pressing wind shoots javelin-like
Its skeleton shadow on the broad-back'd wave!
Here is a fitting spot to dig Love's grave;
Here where the ponderous breakers plunge and strike,
And dart their hissing tongues high up the sand:
In hearing of the ocean, and in sight
Of those ribb'd wind-streaks running into white.
If I the death of Love had deeply plann'd,
I never could have made it half so sure,
As by the unbless'd kisses which upbraid
The full-waked sense; or, failing that, degrade!
'Tis morning: but no morning can restore
What we have forefeited. I see no sin:
The wrong is mix'd. In tragic life, God wot,
No villain need be! Passions spin the plot:
We are betray'd by what is false within.

*

We saw the swallows gathering in the sky,
And in the osier-isle we heard them noise.
We had not to look back on summer joys,
Or forward to a summer of bright dye.
But in the largeness of the evening earth
Our spirits grew as we went side by side.
The hour became her husband and my bride.
Love that had robbed us so, thus blessed our dearth!
The pilgrims of the year wax'd very loud
In multitudinous chatterings, as the flood
Full brown came from the West, and like pale blood
Expanded to the upper crimson cloud.

Love that had robbed us of immortal things,
This little moment mercifully gave,
Where I have seen across the twilight wave
The swan sail with her young beneath her wings.

*

Thus piteously Love closed what he begat:
The union of this ever-diverse pair!
These two were rapid falcons in a snare,
Condemn'd to do the flitting of a bat.
Lovers beneath the singing sky of May,
They wander'd once; clear as the dew on flowers:
But they fed not on the advancing hours:
Their hearts held cravings for the buried day.
Then each applied to each that fatal knife,
Deep questioning, which probes to endless dole.
Ah, what a dusty answer gets the soul
When hot for certainties in this our life! –
In tragic hints here see what evermore
Moves dark as yonder midnight ocean's force,
Thundering like ramping hosts of warrior horse,
To throw that faint thin line upon the shore!

HOPKINS

HEAVEN-HAVEN

A NUN TAKES THE VEIL

I HAVE desired to go
  Where springs not fail,
To fields where flies no sharp and sided hail
  And a few lilies blow.

And I have asked to be
  Where no storms come,
Where the green swell is in the havens dumb,
  And out of the swing of the sea.

SPRING

NOTHING is so beautiful as spring –
When weeds, in wheels, shoot long and lovely and lush;
Thrush's eggs look little low heavens, and thrush
Through the echoing timber does so rinse and wring
The ear, it strikes like lightnings to hear him sing;
The glassy peartree leaves and blooms, they brush
The descending blue; that blue is all in a rush
With richness; the racing lambs too have fair their fling.

What is all this juice and all this joy?
A strain of the earth's sweet being in the beginning
In Eden garden. – Have, get, before it cloy,
Before it cloud, Christ, lord, and sour with sinning,
Innocent mind and Mayday in girl and boy,
Most, O maid's child, thy choice and worthy the winning.

THE WINDHOVER

TO CHRIST OUR LORD

I CAUGHT this morning morning's minion, king-
dom of daylight's dauphin, dapple-dawn-drawn Falcon, in
his riding
Of the rolling level underneath him steady air, and striding
High there, how he rung upon the rein of a wimpling wing
In his ecstacy! then off, off forth on swing,
As a skate's heel sweeps smooth on a bow-bend: the hurl
and gliding
Rebuffed the big wind. My heart in hiding
Stirred for a bird, – the achieve of, the mastery of the thing!

Brute beauty and valour and act, oh, air, pride, plume, here
Buckle! AND the fire that breaks from thee then, a billion
Times told lovelier, more dangerous, O my chevalier!

No wonder of it: shéer plód makes plough down sillion
Shine, and blue-bleak embers, ah my dear,
Fall, gall themselves, and gash gold-vermilion.

PIED BEAUTY

Glory be to God for dappled things –
For skies of couple-colour as a brinded cow;
For rose-moles all in stipple upon trout that swim;
Fresh-firecoal chestnut-falls; finches' wings;
Landscape plotted and pieced – fold, fallow, and plough;
And áll trádes, their gear and tackle and trim.

All things counter, original, spare, strange;
Whatever is fickle, freckles (who knows how?)
With swift, slow; sweet, sour; adazzle, dim;
He fathers-forth whose beauty is past change:
Praise him.

FELIX RANDAL

Felix Randal the farrier, O he is dead then? my duty all ended,
Who have watched his mould of man, big-boned and hardy-handsome
Pining, pining, till time when reason rambled in it and some
Fatal four disorders, fleshed there, all contended?

Sickness broke him. Impatient he cursed at first, but mended
Being anointed and all; though a heavenlier heart began some
Months earlier, since I had our sweet reprieve and ransom
Tendered to him. Ah well, God rest him all road ever he offended!

This seeing the sick endears them to us, us too it endears.
My tongue had taught thee comfort, touch had quenched thy tears,
Thy tears that touched my heart, child, Felix, poor Felix Randal;

How far from then forethought of, all thy more boisterous years,
When thou at the random grim forge, powerful amidst peers,
Didst fettle for the great grey drayhorse his bright and battering sandal!

NOT, I'll not, carrion comfort, Despair, not feast on thee;
Not untwist – slack they may be – these last strands of man
In me ór, most weary, cry *I can no more*. I can;
Can something, hope, wish day come, not choose not to be.
But ah, but O thou terrible, why wouldst thou rude on me
Thy wring-world right foot rock? lay a lionlimb against me? scan
With darksome devouring eyes my bruisèd bones? and fan,
O in turns of tempest, me heaped there; me frantic to avoid thee and flee?

Why? That my chaff might fly; my grain lie, sheer and clear.
Nay in all that toil, that coil, since (seems) I kissed the rod,
Hand rather, my heart lo! lapped strength, stole joy, would laugh, chéer.
Cheer whom though? the hero whose heaven-handling flung me, fóot tród
Me? or me that fought him? O which one? is it each one? That night, that year
Of now done darkness I wretch lay wrestling with (my God!) my God.

NO worst, there is none. Pitched past pitch of grief,
More pangs will, schooled at forepangs, wilder wring.
Comforter, where, where is your comforting?
Mary, mother of us, where is your relief?
My cries heave, herds-long; huddle in a main, a chief
Woe, wórld-sorrow; on an age-old anvil wince and sing –
Then lull, then leave off. Fury had shrieked 'No ling-
ering! Let me be fell: force I must be brief'.

O the mind, mind has mountains; cliffs of fall
Frightful, sheer, no-man-fathomed. Hold them cheap
May who ne'er hung there. Nor does long our small
Durance deal with that steep or deep. Here! creep,
Wretch, under a comfort serves in a whirlwind: all
Life death does end and each day dies with sleep.

PATIENCE, hard thing! the hard thing but to pray,
But bid for, Patience is! Patience who asks
Wants war, wants wounds; weary his times, his tasks;
To do without, take tosses, and obey.
  Rare patience roots in these, and, these away,
Nowhere. Natural heart's ivy, Patience masks
Our ruins of wrecked past purpose. There she basks
Purple eyes and seas of liquid leaves all day.

  We hear our hearts grate on themselves: it kills
To bruise them dearer. Yet the rebellious wills
Of us we do bid God bend to him even so.
  And where is he who more and more distils
Delicious kindness? – He is patient. Patience fills
His crisp combs, and that comes those ways we know.

STEVENSON

TO S. R. CROCKETT

BLOWS the wind today, and the sun and the rain are flying,
  Blows the wind on the moors today and now,
Where about the graves of the martyrs the whaups are crying,
  My heart remembers how!

Grey recumbent tombs of the dead in desert places,
  Standing-stones on the vacant wine-red moor,
Hills of sheep, and the howes of the silent vanished races,
  And winds, austere and pure.

Be it granted me to behold you again in dying,
  Hills of home! and to hear again the call;
Hear about the graves of the martyrs the peewees crying,
  And hear no more at all.

BRIDGES

NIGHTINGALES

Beautiful must be the mountains whence ye come,
And bright in the fruitful valleys the streams, wherefrom
Ye learn your song:
Where are those starry woods? O might I wander there,
Among the flowers, which in that heavenly air
Bloom the year long!

Nay, barren are those mountains and spent the streams:
Our song is the voice of desire, that haunts our dreams,
A throe of the heart,
Whose pining visions dim, forbidden hopes profound,
No dying cadence nor long sigh can sound,
For all our art.

Alone, aloud in the raptured ear of men
We pour our dark nocturnal secret; and then,
As night is withdrawn
From these sweet-springing meads and bursting boughs of May,
Dream, while the innumerable choir of day
Welcome the dawn.

HARDY

THE SELF-UNSEEING

Here is the ancient floor,
Footworn and hollowed and thin,
Here was the former door
Where the dead feet walked in.

She sat here in her chair,
Smiling into the fire;
He who played stood there,
Bowing it higher and higher.

Childlike, I danced in a dream;
Blessings emblazoned that day;
Everything glowed with a gleam;
Yet we were looking away!

IN TENEBRIS

WINTERTIME nighs;
But my bereavement-pain
It cannot bring again:
Twice no one dies.

Flower-petals flee;
But, since it once hath been,
No more that severing scene
Can harrow me.

Birds faint in dread:
I shall not lose old strength
In the lone frost's black length:
Strength long since fled!

Leaves freeze to dun;
But friends can not turn cold
This season as of old
For him with none.

Tempests may scath;
But love can not make smart
Again this year his heart
Who no heart hath.

Black is night's cope;
But death will not appal
One who, past doubtings all,
Waits in unhope.

AT CASTERBRIDGE FAIR

FORMER BEAUTIES

THESE market-dames, mid-aged, with lips thin-drawn,
And tissues sere,
Are they the ones we loved in years agone,
And courted here?

Are these the muslined pink young things to whom
We vowed and swore
In nooks on summer Sundays by the Froom,
Or Budmouth shore?

Do they remember those gay tunes we trod
Clasped on the green;
Aye; trod till moonlight set on the beaten sod
A satin sheen?

They must forget, forget! They cannot know
What once they were,
Or memory would transfigure them, and show
Them always fair.

AFTER THE VISIT

COME again to the place
Where your presence was as a leaf that skims
Down a drouthy way whose ascent bedims
The bloom on the farer's face.

Come again, with the feet
That were light on the green as a thistledown ball,
And those mute ministrations to one and to all
Beyond a man's saying sweet.

Until then the faint scent
Of the bordering flowers swam unheeded away,
And I marked not the charm in the changes of day
As the cloud-colours came and went.

Through the dark corridors
Your walk was so soundless I did not know
Your form from a phantom's of long ago
Said to pass on the ancient floors,

Till you drew from the shade,
And I saw the large luminous living eyes
Regard me in fixed inquiring-wise
As those of a soul that weighed,

Scarce consciously,
The eternal question of what Life was,
And why we were there, and by whose strange laws
That which mattered most could not be.

WESSEX HEIGHTS

There are some heights in Wessex, shaped as if by a kindly hand
For thinking, dreaming, dying on, and at crises when I stand,
Say, on Ingpen Beacon eastward, or on Wylls-Neck westwardly,
I seem where I was before my birth, and after death may be.

In the lowlands I have no comrade, not even the lone man's friend –
Her who suffereth long and is kind; accepts what he is too weak to mend:
Down there they are dubious and askance; there nobody thinks as I,
But mind-chains do not clank where one's next neighbour is the sky.

In the towns I am tracked by phantoms having weird detective ways –
Shadows of beings who fellowed with myself of earlier days:
They hang about at places, and they say harsh heavy things –
Men with a frigid sneer, and women with tart disparagings.

Down there I seem to be false to myself, my simple self that was,
And is not now, and I see him watching, wondering what crass cause
Can have merged him into such a strange continuator as this,
Who yet has something in common with himself, my chrysalis.

I cannot go to the great grey Plain; there's a figure against the moon,
Nobody sees it but I, and it makes my breast beat out of tune;
I cannot go to the tall-spired town, being barred by the forms now passed
For everybody but me, in whose long vision they stand there fast.

There's a ghost at Yell'ham Bottom chiding loud at the fall of the night,
There's a ghost in Froom-side Vale, thin lipped and vague, in a shroud of white,

There is one in the railway-train whenever I do not want it
near,
I see its profile against the pane, saying what I would not hear.

As for one rare fair woman, I am now but a thought of hers,
I enter her mind and another thought succeeds me that she
prefers;
Yet my love for her in its fulness she herself even did not know;
Well, time cures hearts of tenderness, and now I can let her go.

So I am found on Ingpen Beacon, or on Wylls-Neck to the
west,
Or else on homely Bulbarrow, or little Pilsdon Crest,
Where men have never cared to haunt, nor women have walked
with me,
And ghosts then keep their distance; and I know some liberty.

THE VOICE

Woman much missed, how you call to me, call to me,
Saying that now you are not as you were
When you had changed from the one who was all to me,
But as at first, when our day was fair.

Can it be you that I hear? Let me view you, then,
Standing as when I drew near to the town
Where you would wait for me: yes, as I knew you then,
Even to the original air-blue gown!

Or is it only the breeze, in its listlessness
Travelling across the wet mead to me here,
You being ever dissolved to wan wistlessness,
Heard no more again far or near?

Thus I; faltering forward,
Leaves around me falling,
Wind oozing thin through the thorn from norward,
And the woman calling.

AFTER A JOURNEY

HERETO I come to view a voiceless ghost;
  Whither, O whither will its whim now draw me?
Up the cliff, down, till I'm lonely, lost,
  And the unseen waters' ejaculations awe me.
Where you will next be there's no knowing,
  Facing round about me everywhere,
    With your nut-coloured hair,
And gray eyes, and rose-flush coming and going.

Yes: I have re-entered your olden haunts at last;
  Through the years, through the dead scenes I have tracked you;
What have you now found to say of our past –
  Scanned across the dark space wherein I have lacked you?
Summer gave us sweets, but autumn wrought division?
  Things were not lastly as firstly well
    With us twain, you tell?
But all's closed now, despite Time's derision.

I see what you are doing: you are leading me on
  To the spots we knew when we haunted here together,
The waterfall, above which the mist-bow shone
  At the then fair hour in the then fair weather,
And the cave just under, with a voice still so hollow
  That it seems to call out to me from forty years ago,
    When you were all aglow,
And not the thin ghost that I now frailly follow!

Ignorant of what there is flitting here to see,
  The waked birds preen and the seals flop lazily,
Soon you will have, Dear, to vanish from me,
  For the stars close their shutters and the dawn whitens
      hazily.
Trust me, I mind not, though Life lours,
  The bringing me here; nay, bring me here again!
    I am just the same as when
Our days were a joy, and our paths through flowers.

As I drive to the junction of lane and highway,
  And the drizzle bedrenches the waggonette,
I look behind at the fading byway,
  And see on its slope, now glistening wet,
    Distinctly yet

Myself and a girlish form benighted
  In dry March weather. We climb the road
Beside a chaise. We had just alighted
  To ease the sturdy pony's load,
    When he sighed and slowed.

What we did as we climbed, and what we talked of
  Matters not much, nor to what it led, –
Something that life will not be balked of
  Without rude reason till hope is dead,
    And feeling fled.

It filled but a minute. But was there ever
  A time of such quality, since or before,
In that hill's story? To one mind never,
  Though it has been climbed, foot-swift, foot-sore,
    By thousands more.

Primaeval rocks form the road's steep border,
  And much have they faced there, first and last,
Of the transitory in Earth's long order;
  But what they record in colour and cast
    Is – that we two passed.

And to me, though Time's unflinching rigour,
  In mindless rote, has ruled from sight
The substance now, one phantom figure
  Remains on the slope, as when that night
    Saw us alight.

I look back and see it there, shrinking, shrinking,
  I look back at it amid the rain
For the very last time; for my sand is sinking,
  And I shall traverse old love's domain
    Never again.

AFTERWARDS

WHEN the Present has latched its postern behind my tremulous stay,
And the May month flaps its glad green leaves like wings,
Delicate-filmed as new-spun silk, will the neighbours say,
'He was a man who used to notice such things'?

If it be in the dusk when, like an eyelid's soundless blink,
The dewfall-hawk comes crossing the shades to alight
Upon the wind-warped upland thorn, a gazer may think,
'To him this must have been a familiar sight.'

If I pass during some nocturnal blackness, mothy and warm,
When the hedgehog travels furtively over the lawn,
One may say, 'He strove that such innocent creatures should come to no harm,
But he could do little for them; and now he is gone.'

If, when hearing that I have been stilled at last, they stand at the door,
Watching the full-starred heavens that winter sees,
Will this thought rise on those who will meet my face no more,
'He was one who had an eye for such mysteries'?

And will any say when my bell of quittance is heard in the gloom,
And a crossing breeze cuts a pause in its outrollings,
Till they rise again, as they were a new bell's boom,
'He hears it not now, but used to notice such things?'

HOUSMAN

TELL me not here, it needs not saying,
What tune the enchantress plays
In aftermaths of soft September
Or under blanching mays,
For she and I were long acquainted
And I knew all her ways.

On russet floors, by waters idle,
  The pine lets fall its cone;
The cuckoo shouts all day at nothing
  In leafy dells alone;
And traveller's joy beguiles in autumn
  Hearts that have lost their own.

On acres of the seeded grasses
  The changing burnish heaves;
Or marshalled under moons of harvest
  Stand still all night the sheaves;
Or beeches strip in storms for winter
  And stain the wind with leaves.

Possess, as I possessed a season,
  The countries I resign,
Where over elmy plains the highway
  Would mount the hills and shine,
And full of shade the pillared forest
  Would murmur and be mine.

For nature, heartless, witless nature,
  Will neither care nor know
What stranger's feet may find the meadow
  And trespass there and go,
Nor ask amid the dews of morning
  If they are mine or no.

THOMPSON

from CONTEMPLATION

The river has not any care
Its passionless water to the sea to bear;
The leaves have brown content;
The wall to me has freshness like a scent,
And takes half-animate the air,
Making one life with its green moss and stain;
And life with all things seems too perfect blent
For anything of life to be aware.

The very shades on hill, and tree, and plain,
Where they have fallen doze, and where they doze remain.

No hill can idler be than I;
No stone its inter-particled vibration
Investeth with a stiller lie;
No heaven with a more urgent rest betrays
The eyes that on it gaze.
We are too near akin that thou shouldst cheat
Me, Nature, with thy fair deceit.
In poets floating like a water-flower
Upon the bosom of the glassy hour,
In skies that no man sees to move,
Lurk untumultuous vortices of power,
For joy too native, and for agitation
Too instant, too entire for sense thereof,
Motion like gnats when autumn suns are low,
Perpetual as the prisoned feet of love
On the heart's floors with painèd pace that go.
From stones and poets you may know,
Nothing so active is, as that which least seems so.

JOHNSON

from IN MEMORY

Ah! fair face gone from sight,
  with all its light
of eyes, that pierced the deep
  of human night!
Ah! fair face calm in sleep.

Ah! fair lips hushed in death!
  Now their glad breath
Breathes not upon our air
  Music, that saith
Love only, and things fair.

Ah! lost brother! Ah! sweet
still hands and feet!
May those feet haste to reach,
Those hands to greet,
Us, where love needs no speech.

DEAD

In Merioneth, over the sad moor
Drives the rain, the cold wind blows:
Past the ruinous church door,
The poor procession without music goes.

Lonely she wandered out her hour, and died.
Now the mournful curlew cries
Over her, laid down beside
Death's lonely people: lightly down she lies.

In Merioneth, the wind lives and wails,
On from hill to lonely hill:
Down the loud, triumphant gales,
A spirit cries *Be strong!* and cries *Be still!*

DOWSON

THE GARDEN OF SHADOW

Love heeds no more the sighing of the wind
Against the perfect flowers: thy garden's close
Is grown a wilderness, where none shall find
One strayed, last petal of one last year's rose.

O bright, bright hair! O mouth like a ripe fruit!
Can famine be so nigh to harvesting?
Love, that was songful, with a broken lute
In grass of graveyards goeth murmuring.

Let the wind blow against the perfect flowers,
And all thy garden change and glow with spring:
Love is grown blind with no more count of hours
Nor part in seed-time nor in harvesting.

KIPLING

'CITIES AND THRONES AND POWERS'

CITIES and Thrones and Powers
  Stand in Time's eye,
Almost as long as flowers,
  Which daily die:
But, as new buds put forth
  To glad new men,
Out of the spent and unconsidered Earth
  The Cities rise again.

This season's Daffodil,
  She never hears
What change, what chance, what chill,
  Cut down last year's;
But with bold countenance,
  And knowledge small,
Esteems her seven days' continuance
  To be perpetual.

So Time that is o'er-kind
  To all that be,
Ordains us e'en as blind,
  As bold as she:
That in our very death,
  And burial sure,
Shadow to shadow, well persuaded, saith,
  'See how our works endure!'

HARP SONG OF THE DANE WOMEN

WHAT is a woman that you forsake her,
And the hearth-fire and the home-acre,
To go with the old grey Widow-maker?

She has no house to lay a guest in –
But one chill bed for all to rest in,
That the pale suns and the stray bergs nest in.

She has no strong white arms to fold you,
But the ten-times-fingering weed to hold you –
Out on the rocks where the tide has rolled you.

Yet, when the signs of summer thicken,
And the ice breaks, and the birch-buds quicken,
Yearly you turn from our side, and sicken –

Sicken again for the shouts and the slaughters.
You steal away to the lapping waters,
And look at your ship in her winter-quarters.

You forget our mirth, and talk at the tables,
The kine in the shed and the horse in the stables –
To pitch her sides and go over her cables.

Then you drive out where the storm-clouds swallow,
And the sound of your oar-blades, falling hollow,
Is all we have left through the months to follow.

Ah, what is Woman that you forsake her,
And the hearth-fire and the home-acre,
To go with the old grey Widow-maker?

GERTRUDE'S PRAYER

THAT which is marred at birth Time shall not mend,
 Nor water out of bitter well make clean;
All evil thing returneth at the end,
 Or elseway walketh in our blood unseen.
Whereby the more is sorrow in certaine –
Dayspring mishandled cometh not againe.

To-bruizèd be that slender, sterting spray
 Out of the oake's rind that should betide
A branch of girt and goodliness, straightway
 Her spring is turnèd on herself, and wried
And knotted like some gall or veiney wen. –
Dayspring mishandled cometh not agen.

Noontide repayeth never morning-bliss –
 Sith noon to morn is incomparable;

And, so it be our dawning goth amiss,
    None other after-hour serveth well.
Ah! Jesu-Moder, pitie my oe paine –
Dayspring mishandled cometh not againe!

ROBINSON

FOR A DEAD LADY

No more with overflowing light
Shall fill the eyes that now are faded,
Nor shall another's fringe with night
Their woman-hidden world as they did.
No more shall quiver down the days
The flowing wonder of her ways,
Whereof no language may requite
The shifting and the many-shaded.

The grace, divine, definitive,
Clings only as a faint forestalling;
The laugh that love could not forgive
Is hushed, and answers to no calling;
The forehead and the little ears
Have gone where Saturn keeps the years;
The breast where roses could not live
Has done with rising and with falling.

The beauty, shattered by the laws
That have creation in their keeping,
No longer trembles at applause,
Or over children that are sleeping;
And we who delve in beauty's lore
Know all that we have known before
Of what inexorable cause
Makes Time so vicious in his reaping.

No sound of any storm that shakes
Old island walls with older seas
Comes here where now September makes
An island in a sea of trees.

Between the sunlight and the shade
A man may learn till he forgets
The roaring of a world remade,
And all his ruins and regrets;

And if he still remembers here
Poor fights he may have won or lost, –
If he be ridden with the fear
Of what some other fight may cost, –

If, eager to confuse too soon,
What he has known with what may be,
He reads a planet out of tune
For cause of his jarred harmony, –

If here he ventures to unroll
His index of adagios,
And he be given to console
Humanity with what he knows, –

He may by contemplation learn
A little more than what he knew,
And even see great oaks return
To acorns out of which they grew.

He may, if he but listen well,
Through twilight and the silence here
Be told what there are none may tell
To vanity's impatient ear;

And he may never dare again
Say what awaits him, or be sure
What sunlit labyrinth of pain
He may not enter and endure.

Who knows to-day from yesterday
May learn to count no thing too strange.
Love builds of what Time takes away,
Till Death itself is less than Change.

Who sees enough in his duress
May go as far as dreams have gone;
Who sees a little may do less
Than many who are blind have done;

Who sees unchastened here the soul
Triumphant has no other sight
Than has a child who sees the whole
World radiant with his own delight.

Far journeys and hard wandering
Await him in whose crude surmise
Peace, like a mask, hides everything
That is and has been from his eyes;

And all his wisdom is unfound,
Or like a web that error weaves
On airy looms that have a sound
No louder now than falling leaves.

NEW ENGLAND

HERE where the wind is always north-north-east
And children learn to walk on frozen toes,
Wonder begets an envy of all those
Who boil elsewhere with such a lyric yeast
Of love that you will hear them at a feast
Where demons would appeal for some repose,
Still clamouring where the chalice overflows
And crying wildest who have drunk the least.

Passion is here a soilure of the wits,
We're told, and Love a cross for them to bear;
Joy shivers in the corner where she knits
And Conscience always has the rocking-chair,
Cheerful as when she tortured into fits
The first cat that was ever killed by Care.

YEATS

THE ROSE OF THE WORLD

WHO dreamed that beauty passes like a dream?
For these red lips, with all their mournful pride,
Mournful that no new wonder may betide,
Troy passed away in one high funeral gleam,
And Usna's children died.

We and the labouring world are passing by:
Amid men's souls, that waver and give place
Like the pale waters in their wintry race,
Under the passing stars, foam of the sky,
Lives on this lonely face.

Bow down, archangels, in your dim abode:
Before you were, or any hearts to beat,
Weary and kind one lingered by His seat;
He made the world to be a grassy road
Before her wandering feet.

THE SECOND COMING

TURNING and turning in the widening gyre
The falcon cannot hear the falconer;
Things fall apart; the centre cannot hold;
Mere anarchy is loosed upon the world,
The blood-dimmed tide is loosed, and everywhere
The ceremony of innocence is drowned;
The best lack all conviction, while the worst
Are full of passionate intensity.

Surely some revelation is at hand;
Surely the Second Coming is at hand.
The Second Coming! Hardly are those words out
When a vast image out of *Spiritus Mundi*
Troubles my sight: somewhere in the sands of the desert
A shape with lion body and the head of a man,
A gaze blank and pitiless as the sun,
Is moving its slow thighs, while all about it

Reel shadows of the indignant desert birds.
The darkness drops again; but now I know
That twenty centuries of stony sleep
Were vexed to nightmare by a rocking cradle,
And what rough beast, its hour come round at last,
Slouches towards Bethlehem to be born?

SAILING TO BYZANTIUM

THAT is no country for old men. The young
In one another's arms, birds in the trees
– Those dying generations – at their song,
The salmon-falls, the mackerel-crowded seas,
Fish, flesh, or fowl, commend all summer long
Whatever is begotten, born and dies.
Caught in that sensual music all neglect
Monuments of unageing intellect.

An aged man is but a paltry thing,
A tattered coat upon a stick, unless
Soul clap its hands and sing, and louder sing
For every tatter in its mortal dress,
Nor is there singing school but studying
Monuments of its own magnificence;
And therefore have I sailed the seas and come
To the holy city of Byzantium.

O sages standing in God's holy fire
As in the gold mosaic of a wall,
Come from the holy fire, perne in a gyre,
And be the singing-masters of my soul.
Consume my heart away; sick with desire
And fastened to a dying animal
It knows not what it is; and gather me
Into the artifice of eternity.

Once out of nature I shall never take
My bodily form from any natural thing,
But such a form as Grecian goldsmiths make
Of hammered gold and gold enamelling
To keep a drowsy Emperor awake;

Or set upon a golden bough to sing
To lords and ladies of Byzantium
Of what is past, or passing, or to come.

LEDA AND THE SWAN

A SUDDEN blow: the great wings beating still
Above the staggering girl, her thighs caressed
By the dark webs, her nape caught in his bill,
He holds her helpless breast upon his breast.

How can those terrified vague fingers push
The feathered glory from her loosening thighs?
And how can body, laid in that white rush,
But feel the strange heart beating where it lies?

A shudder in the loins engenders there
The broken wall, the burning roof and tower
And Agamemnon dead.
Being so caught up,
So mastered by the brute blood of the air,
Did she put on his knowledge with his power
Before the indifferent beak could let her drop?

AMONG SCHOOL CHILDREN

I WALK through the long schoolroom questioning;
A kind old nun in a white hood replies;
The children learn to cipher and to sing,
To study reading-books and histories,
To cut and sew, be neat in everything
In the best modern way – the children's eyes
In momentary wonder stare upon
A sixty-year-old smiling public man.

I dream of a Ledaean body, bent
Above a sinking fire, a tale that she
Told of a harsh reproof, or trivial event
That changed some childish day to tragedy –
Told, and it seemed that our two natures blent

Into a sphere from youthful sympathy,
Or else, to alter Plato's parable,
Into the yolk and white of the one shell.

And thinking of that fit of grief or rage
I look upon one child or t'other there
And wonder if she stood so at that age –
For even daughters of the swan can share
Something of every paddler's heritage –
And had that colour upon cheek or hair,
And thereupon my heart is driven wild:
She stands before me as a living child.

Her present image floats into the mind –
Did Quattrocento finger fashion it
Hollow of cheek as though it drank the wind
And took a mess of shadows for its meat?
And I though never of Ledaean kind
Had pretty plumage once – enough of that,
Better to smile on all that smile, and show
There is a comfortable kind of old scarecrow.

What youthful mother, a shape upon her lap
Honey of generation had betrayed,
And that must sleep, shriek, struggle to escape
As recollection or the drug decide,
Would think her son, did she but see that shape
With sixty or more winters on its head,
A compensation for the pangs of his birth,
Or the uncertainty of his setting forth?

Plato thought nature but a spume that plays
Upon a ghostly paradigm of things;
Solider Aristotle played the taws
Upon the bottom of a king of kings;
World-famous golden-thighed Pythagoras
Fingered upon a fiddle-stick or strings
What a star sang and careless Muses heard:
Old clothes upon old sticks to scare a bird.

Both nuns and mothers worship images,
But those the candles light are not as those
That animate a mother's reveries,
But keep a marble or a bronze repose.

And yet they too break hearts – O Presences
That passion, piety or affection knows,
And that all heavenly glory symbolise –
O self-born mockers of man's enterprise;

Labour is blossoming or dancing where
The body is not bruised to pleasure soul,
Nor beauty born out of its own despair,
Nor blear-eyed wisdom out of midnight oil.
O chestnut-tree, great-rooted blossomer,
Are you the leaf, the blossom or the bole?
O body swayed to music, O brightening glance,
How can we know the dancer from the dance?

BYZANTIUM

THE unpurged images of day recede;
The Emperor's drunken soldiery are abed;
Night resonance recedes, night-walkers' song
After great cathedral gong;
A starlit or a moonlit dome disdains
All that man is,
All mere complexities,
The fury and the mire of human veins

Before me floats an image, man or shade,
Shade more than man, more image than a shade;
For Hades' bobbin bound in mummy-cloth
May unwind the winding path;
A mouth that has no moisture and no breath
Breathless mouths may summon;
I hail the superhuman;
I call it death-in-life and life-in-death.

Miracle, bird or golden handiwork,
More miracle than bird or handiwork,
Planted on the star-lit golden bough,
Can like the cocks of Hades crow,
Or, by the moon embittered, scorn aloud
In glory of changeless metal
Common bird or petal
And all complexities of mire or blood.

At midnight on the Emperor's pavement flit
Flames that no faggot feeds, nor steel has lit,
Nor storm disturbs, flames begotten of flame,
Where blood-begotten spirits come
And all complexities of fury leave,
Dying into a dance,
An agony of trance,
An agony of flame that cannot singe a sleeve.

Astraddle on the dolphin's mire and blood,
Spirit after spirit! The smithies break the flood,
The golden smithies of the Emperor!
Marbles of the dancing floor
Break bitter furies of complexity,
Those images that yet
Fresh images beget,
That dolphin-torn, that gong-tormented sea.

THREE THINGS

'O CRUEL Death, give three things back,'
Sang a bone upon the shore;
'A child found all a child can lack,
Whether of pleasure or of rest,
Upon the abundance of my breast':
A bone wave-whitened and dried in the wind.

'Three dear things that women know,'
Sang a bone upon the shore;
'A man if I but held him so
When my body was alive
Found all the pleasure that life gave':
A bone wave-whitened and dried in the wind.

'The third thing that I think of yet,'
Sang a bone upon the shore,
'Is that morning when I met
Face to face my rightful man
And did after stretch and yawn':
A bone wave-whitened and dried in the wind.

THAT civilisation may not sink,
Its great battle lost,
Quiet the dog, tether the pony
To a distant post;
Our master Caesar is in the tent
Where the maps are spread,
His eyes fixed upon nothing,
A hand under his head.
Like a long-legged fly upon the stream
His mind moves upon silence.

That the topless towers be burnt
And men recall that face,
Move most gently if move you must
In this lonely place.
She thinks, part woman, three parts a child,
That nobody looks; her feet
Practise a tinker shuffle
Picked up on a street.
Like a long-legged fly upon the stream
Her mind moves upon silence.

That girls at puberty may find
The first Adam in their thought,
Shut the door of the Pope's chapel,
Keep those children out.
There on that scaffolding reclines
Michael Angelo.
With no more sound than the mice make
His hand moves to and fro.
Like a long-legged fly upon the stream
His mind moves upon silence.

DE LA MARE

THE MOTH

ISLED in the midnight air,
Musked with the dark's faint bloom,
Out into glooming and secret haunts
    The flame cries, 'Come!'

Lovely in dye and fan,
A-tremble in shimmering grace,
A moth from her winter swoon
    Uplifts her face:

Stares from her glamorous eyes;
Wafts her on plumes like mist;
In ecstasy swirls and sways
    To her strange tryst.

ESTRANGED

NO one was with me there –
Happy I was – alone;
Yet from the sunshine suddenly
    A joy was gone.

A bird in an empty house
Sad echoes makes to ring,
Flitting from room to room
    On restless wing:

Till from its shades he flies,
And leaves forlorn and dim
The narrow solitudes
    So strange to him.

So, when with fickle heart
I joyed in the passing day,
A presence my mood estranged
    Went grieved away.

GOOD-BYE

THE last of last words spoken is, Good-bye –
The last dismantled flower in the weed-grown hedge,
The last thin rumour of a feeble bell far ringing,
The last blind rat to spurn the mildewed rye.

A hardening darkness glasses the haunted eye,
Shines into nothing the watcher's burnt-out candle,
Wreathes into scentless nothing the wasting incense,
Faints in the outer silence the hunting-cry.

Love of its muted music breathes no sigh,
Thought in her ivory tower gropes in her spinning,
Toss on in vain the whispering trees of Eden,
Last of all last words spoken is, Good-bye.

SOLITUDE

GHOSTS there must be with me in this old house,
Deepening its midnight as the clock beats on.
Whence else upwelled – strange, sweet, yet ominous –
That moment of happiness, and then was gone?

Nimbler than air-borne music, heart may call
A speechless message to the inward ear,
As secret even as that which then befell,
Yet nought that listening could make more clear.

Delicate, subtle senses, instant, fleet! –
But oh, how near the verge at which they fail!
In vain, self hearkens for the fall of feet
Soft as its own may be, beyond the pale.

FROST

TREE AT MY WINDOW

TREE at my window, window tree,
My sash is lowered when night comes on;
But let there never be curtain drawn
Between you and me.

Vague dream-head lifted out of the ground,
And thing next most diffuse to cloud,
Not all your light tongues talking aloud
Could be profound.

But tree, I have seen you taken and tossed,
And if you have seen me when I slept,
You have seen me when I was taken and swept
And all but lost.

That day she put our heads together,
Fate had her imagination about her,
Your head so much concerned with outer,
Mine with inner, weather.

from THE HILL WIFE

LONELINESS

(*Her Word*)

ONE ought not to have to care
So much as you and I
Care when the birds come round the house
To seem to say good-bye;

Or care so much when they come back
With whatever it is they sing;
The truth being we are as much
Too glad for the one thing

As we are too sad for the other here –
With birds that fill their breasts
But with each other and themselves
And their built or driven nests.

PUTTING IN THE SEED

YOU come to fetch me from my work to-night
When supper's on the table, and we'll see
If I can leave off burying the white
Soft petals fallen from the apple tree
(Soft petals, yes, but not so barren quite,

Mingled with these, smooth bean and wrinkled pea);
And go along with you ere you lose sight
Of what you came for and become like me,
Slave to a springtime passion for the earth.
How Love burns through the Putting in the Seed
On through the watching for that early birth
When, just as the soil tarnishes with weed,
The sturdy seedling with arched body comes
Shouldering its way and shedding the earth crumbs.

THE NEED OF BEING VERSED IN COUNTRY THINGS

The house had gone to bring again
To the midnight sky a sunset glow.
Now the chimney was all of the house that stood,
Like a pistil after the petals go.

The barn opposed across the way,
That would have joined the house in flame
Had it been the will of the wind, was left
To bear forsaken the place's name.

No more it opened with all one end
For teams that came by the stony road
To drum on the floor with scurrying hoofs
And brush the mow with the summer load.

The birds that came to it through the air
At broken windows flew out and in,
Their murmur more like the sigh we sigh
From too much dwelling on what has been.

Yet for them the lilac renewed its leaf,
And the aged elm, though touched with fire;
And the dry pump flung up an awkward arm;
And the fence post carried a strand of wire.

For them there was really nothing sad.
But though they rejoiced in the nest they kept,
One had to be versed in country things
Not to believe the phoebes wept.

THE GIFT OUTRIGHT

The land was ours before we were the land's.
She was our land more than a hundred years
Before we were her people. She was ours
In Massachusetts, in Virginia,
But we were England's, still colonials,
Possessing what we still were unpossessed by,
Possessed by what we now no more possessed.
Something we were withholding made us weak
Until we found out that it was ourselves
We were withholding from our land of living,
And forthwith found salvation in surrender.
Such as we were we gave ourselves outright
(The deed of gift was many deeds of war)
To the land vaguely realizing westward,
But still unstoried, artless, unenhanced,
Such as she was, such as she would become.

MASEFIELD

'UP ON THE DOWNS'

Up on the downs the red-eyed kestrels hover,
Eyeing the grass.
The field-mouse flits like a shadow into cover
As their shadows pass.

Men are burning the gorse on the down's shoulder;
A drift of smoke
Glitters with fire and hangs, and the skies smoulder,
And the lungs choke.

Once the tribe did thus on the downs, on these downs burning
Men in the frame,
Crying to the gods of the downs till their brains were turning
And the gods came.

And to-day on the downs, in the wind, the hawks, the grasses,
In blood and air,
Something passes me and cries as it passes,
On the chalk downland bare.

THE UNKNOWN BIRD

THREE lovely notes he whistled, too soft to be heard
If others sang; but others never sang
In the great beech-wood all that May and June.
No one saw him: I alone could hear him
Though many listened. Was it but four years
Ago? or five? He never came again.

Oftenest when I heard him I was alone,
Nor could I ever make another hear.
La-la-la! he called seeming far-off –
As if a cock crowed past the edge of the world,
As if the bird or I were in a dream.
Yet that he travelled through the trees and sometimes
Neared me, was plain, though somehow distant still
He sounded. All the proof is – I told men
What I had heard.

I never knew a voice,
Man, beast, or bird, better than this. I told
The naturalists; but neither had they heard
Anything like the notes that did so haunt me,
I had them clear by heart and have them still.
Four years, or five, have made no difference. Then
As now that La-la-la! was bodiless sweet:
Sad more than joyful it was, if I must say
That it was one or other, but if sad
'Twas sad only with joy too, too far off
For me to taste it. But I cannot tell
If truly never anything but fair
The days were when he sang, as now they seem.
This surely I know, that I who listened then,
Happy sometimes, sometimes suffering
A heavy body and a heavy heart,
Now straightway, if I think of it, become
Light as that bird wandering beyond my shore.

'OUT IN THE DARK'

OUT in the dark over the snow
The fallow fawns invisible go
With the fallow doe;
And the winds blow
Fast as the stars are slow.

Stealthily the dark haunts round
And, when the lamp goes, without sound
At a swifter bound
Than the swiftest hound,
Arrives, and all else is drowned;

And I and star and wind and deer,
Are in the dark together, – near,
Yet far, – and fear
Drums on my ear
In that sage company drear.

How weak and little is the light,
All the universe of sight,
Love and delight,
Before the might,
If you love it not, of night.

BROOKE

THE SOLDIER

IF I should die, think only this of me:
  That there's some corner of a foreign field
That is for ever England. There shall be
  In that rich earth a richer dust concealed;
A dust whom England bore, shaped, made aware,
  Gave, once, her flowers to love, her ways to roam,
A body of England's, breathing English air,
  Washed by the rivers, blest by suns of home.

And think, this heart, all evil shed away,
  A pulse in the eternal mind, no less
    Gives somewhere back the thoughts by England given;
Her sights and sounds; dreams happy as her day;
  And laughter, learnt of friends; and gentleness,
    In hearts at peace, under an English heaven.

ROSENBERG

WEDDED

THEY leave their love-lorn haunts,
Their sigh-warm floating Eden;
And they are mute at once,
Mortals by God unheeden,
By their past kisses chidden.

But they have kist and known
Clear things we dim by guesses –
Spirit to spirit grown:
Heaven, born in hand-caresses.
Love, fall from sheltering tresses.

And they are dumb and strange:
Bared trees boughed from each other.
Their last green interchange
What lost dreams shall discover?
Dead, strayed, to love-strange lover.

OWEN

STRANGE MEETING

IT seemed that out of battle I escaped
Down some profound dull tunnel, long since scooped
Through granites which titanic wars had groined.
Yet also there encumbered sleepers groaned,

Too fast in thought or death to be bestirred.
Then, as I probed them, one sprang up, and stared
With piteous recognition in fixed eyes,
Lifting distressful hands as if to bless.
And by his smile, I knew that sullen hall,
By his dead smile I knew we stood in Hell.
With a thousand pains that vision's face was grained;
Yet no blood reached there from the upper ground,
And no guns thumped, or down the flues made moan.
'Strange friend,' I said, 'here is no cause to mourn.'
'None,' said the other, 'save the undone years,
The hopelessness. Whatever hope is yours,
Was my life also; I went hunting wild
After the wildest beauty in the world,
Which lies not calm in eyes, or braided hair,
But mocks the steady running of the hour,
And if it grieves, grieves richlier than here.
For by my glee might many men have laughed,
And of my weeping something had been left,
Which must die now. I mean the truth untold,
The pity of war, the pity war distilled.
Now men will go content with what we spoiled.
Or, discontent, boil bloody, and be spilled.
They will be swift with swiftness of the tigress,
None will break ranks, though nations trek from progress.
Courage was mine, and I had mystery,
Wisdom was mine, and I had mastery;
To miss the march of this retreating world
Into vain citadels that are not walled.
Then, when much blood had clogged their chariot-wheels
I would go up and wash them from sweet wells,
Even with truths that lie too deep for taint.
I would have poured my spirit without stint
But not through wounds; not on the cess of war.
Foreheads of men have bled where no wounds were.
I am the enemy you killed, my friend.
I knew you in this dark; for so you frowned
Yesterday through me as you jabbed and killed.
I parried; but my hands were loath and cold.
Let us sleep now. . . .'

SUNDAY MORNING

Complacencies of the peignoir, and late
Coffee and oranges in a sunny chair,
And the green freedom of a cockatoo
Upon a rug mingle to dissipate
The holy hush of ancient sacrifice.
She dreams a little, and she feels the dark
Encroachment of that old catastrophe,
As a calm darkens among water-lights.
The pungent oranges and bright, green wings
Seem things in some procession of the dead,
Winding across wide water, without sound.
The day is like wide water, without sound,
Stilled for the passing of her dreaming feet
Over the seas, to silent Palestine,
Dominion of the blood and sepulchre.

Why should she give her bounty to the dead?
What is divinity if it can come
Only in silent shadows and in dreams?
Shall she not find in comforts of the sun,
In pungent fruit and bright, green wings, or else
In any balm or beauty of the earth,
Things to be cherished like the thought of heaven?
Divinity must live within herself:
Passions of rain, or moods in falling snow;
Grievings in loneliness, or unsubdued
Elations when the forest blooms; gusty
Emotions on wet roads on autumn nights;
All pleasures and all pains, remembering
The bough of summer and the winter branch.
These are the measures destined for her soul.

Jove in the clouds had his inhuman birth.
No mother suckled him, no sweet land gave
Large-mannered motions to his mythy mind.
He moved among us, as a muttering king,
Magnificent, would move among his hinds,
Until our blood, commingling, virginal,

With heaven, brought such requital to desire
The very hinds discerned it, in a star.
Shall our blood fail? Or shall it come to be
The blood of paradise? And shall the earth
Seem all of paradise that we shall know?
The sky will be much friendlier then than now,
A part of labour and a part of pain,
And next in glory to enduring love,
Not this dividing and indifferent blue.

She says, 'I am content when wakened birds,
Before they fly, test the reality
Of misty fields, by their sweet questionings;
But when the birds are gone, and their warm fields
Return no more, where, then, is paradise?'
There is not any haunt of prophecy,
Nor any old chimera of the grave,
Neither the golden underground, nor isle
Melodious, where spirits gat them home,
Nor visionary south, nor cloudy palm
Remote on heaven's hill, that has endured
As April's green endures; or will endure
Like her remembrance of awakened birds,
Or her desire for June and evening, tipped
By the consummation of the swallow's wings.

She says, 'But in contentment I still feel
The need of some imperishable bliss.'
Death is the mother of beauty; hence from her,
Alone, shall come fulfilment to our dreams
And our desires. Although she strews the leaves
Of sure obliteration on our paths,
The path sick sorrow took, the many paths
Where triumph rang its brassy phrase, or love
Whispered a little out of tenderness,
She makes the willow shiver in the sun
For maidens who were wont to sit and gaze
Upon the grass, relinquished to their feet.
She causes boys to pile new plums and pears
On disregarded plate. The maidens taste
And stray impassioned in the littering leaves.

Is there no change of death in paradise?
Does ripe fruit never fall? Or do the boughs
Hang always heavy in that perfect sky,
Unchanging, yet so like our perishing earth,
With rivers like our own that seek for seas
They never find, the same receding shores
That never touch with inarticulate pang?
Why set the pear upon those river-banks
Or spice the shores with odors of the plum?
Alas, that they should wear our colors there,
The silken weavings of our afternoons,
And pick the strings of our insipid lutes!
Death is the mother of beauty, mystical,
Within whose burning bosom we devise
Our earthly mothers waiting, sleeplessly.

Supple and turbulent, a ring of men
Shall chant in orgy on a summer morn
Their boisterous devotion to the sun,
Not as a god, but as a god might be,
Naked among them, like a savage source.
Their chant shall be a chant of paradise,
Out of their blood, returning to the sky;
And in their chant shall enter, voice by voice,
The windy lake wherein their lord delights,
The trees, like serafin, and echoing hills,
That choir among themselves long afterward.
They shall know well the heavenly fellowship
Of men that perish and of summer morn.
And whence they came and whither they shall go
The dew upon their feet shall manifest.

She hears, upon that water without sound,
A voice that cries, 'The tomb in Palestine
Is not the porch of spirits lingering.
It is the grave of Jesus, where he lay.'
We live in an old chaos of the sun,
Or old dependency of day and night,
Or island solitude, unsponsored, free,
Of that wide water, inescapable.
Deer walk upon our mountains, and the quail
Whistle about us their spontaneous cries;

Sweet berries ripen in the wilderness;
And, in the isolation of the sky,
At evening, casual flocks of pigeons make
Ambiguous undulations as they sink,
Downward to darkness, on extended wings.

WILLIAMS

GULLS

My townspeople, beyond in the great world,
are many people with whom it were far more
profitable for me to live than here with you.
These whirr about me calling, calling!
and for my own part I answer them, loud as I can,
but they, being free, pass!
I remain! Therefore, listen!
For you will not soon have another singer.

First I say this: you have seen
the strange birds, have you not, that sometimes
rest upon our river in winter?
Let them cause you to think well then of the storms
that drive many to shelter. These things
do not happen without reason.

And the next thing I say is this:
I saw an eagle once circling against the clouds
over one of our principal churches –
Easter, it was – a beautiful day! –:
three gulls came from above the river
and crossed slowly seaward!
Oh, I know you have your own hymns, I have heard them –
and because I knew they invoked some great protector
I could not be angry with you, no matter
how much they outraged true music –

You see, it is not necessary for us to leap at each other,
and, as I told you, in the end
the gulls moved seaward very quietly.

MARIANNE MOORE

A GRAVE

MAN looking into the sea,
taking the view from those who have as much right to it as you
have to it yourself,
it is human nature to stand in the middle of a thing,
but you cannot stand in the middle of this;
the sea has nothing to give but a well excavated grave.
The first stand in a procession, each with an emerald turkey-
foot at the top,
reserved as their contours, saying nothing;
repression, however, is not the most obvious characteristic of
the sea;
the sea is a collector, quick to return a rapacious look.
There are others besides you who have worn that look –
whose expression is no longer a protest; the fish no longer
investigate them
for their bones have not lasted:
men lower nets, unconscious of the fact that they are desecrat-
ing a grave,
and row quickly away – the blades of the oars
moving together like the feet of water-spiders as if there were
no such thing as death.
The wrinkles progress upon themselves in a phalanx – beautiful
under networks of foam,
and fade breathlessly while the sea rustles in and out of the sea-
weed;
the birds swim through the air at top speed, emitting cat-calls
as heretofore –
the tortoise-shell scourges about the feet of the cliffs, in motion
beneath them;
and the ocean, under the pulsation of lighthouses and noise of
bell-buoys,
advances as usual, looking as if it were not that ocean in which
dropped things are bound to sink –
in which if they turn and twist, it is neither with volition nor
consciousness.

SILENCE

My father used to say,
'Superior people never make long visits,
have to be shown Longfellow's grave
or the glass flowers at Harvard.
Self-reliant like the cat –
that takes its prey to privacy,
the mouse's limp tail hanging like a shoelace from its mouth –
they sometimes enjoy solitude,
and can be robbed of speech
by speech which has delighted them.
The deepest feeling always shows itself in silence;
not in silence, but restraint'.
Nor was he insincere in saying, 'Make my house your inn'.
Inns are not residences.

JEFFERS

THE EYE

The Atlantic is a stormy moat; and the Mediterranean
The blue pool in the old garden,
More than five thousand years has drunk sacrifice
Of ships and blood, and shines in the sun; but here the Pacific –
Our ships, planes, wars are perfectly irrelevant.
Neither our present blood-feud with the brave dwarfs
Nor any future world-quarrel of westering
And eastering man, the bloody migrations, greed of power,
  clash of faiths –
Is a speck of dust on the great scale-pan.
Here from this mountain shore, headland beyond stormy
  headland
          plunging like dolphins through the blue sea-smoke
Into pale sea – look west at the hill of water: it is half the
          planet: this dome, this half-globe, this bulging
Eyeball of water, arched over to Asia,
Australia and white Antarctica: those are the eyelids that
          never close; this is the staring unsleeping
Eye of the earth; and what it watches is not our wars.

RANSOM

ANTIQUE HARVESTERS

(Scene: Of the Mississippi the bank sinister, and of the Ohio the bank sinister.)

Tawny are the leaves turned but they still hold,
And it is harvest; what shall this land produce?
A meagre hill of kernels, a runnel of juice;
Declension looks from our land, it is old.
Therefore let us assemble, dry, grey, spare,
And mild as yellow air.

'I hear the croak of a raven's funeral wing.'
The young men would be joying in the song
Of passionate birds; their memories are not long.
What is it thus rehearsed in sable? 'Nothing.'
Trust not but the old endure, and shall be older
Than the scornful beholder.

We pluck the spindling ears and gather the corn.
One spot has special yield? 'On this spot stood
Heroes and drenched it with their only blood.'
And talk meets talk, as echoes from the horn
Of the hunter – echoes are the old men's arts,
Ample are the chambers of their hearts.

Here come the hunters, keepers of a rite;
The horn, the hounds, the lank mares coursing by
Straddled with archetypes of chivalry;
And the fox, lovely ritualist, in flight
Offering his unearthly ghost to quarry;
And the fields, themselves to harry.

Resume, harvesters. The treasure is full bronze
Which you will garner for the Lady, and the morn
Could tinge it no yellower than does this noon;
But grey will quench it shortly – the field, men, stones.
Pluck fast, dreamers; prove as you amble slowly
Not less than men, not wholly.

Bare the arm, dainty youths, bend the knees
Under bronze burdens. And by an autumn tone

As by a grey, as by a green, you will have known
Your famous Lady's image; for so have these;
And if one say that easily will your hands
More prosper in other lands,

Angry as a wasp-music be your cry then:
'Forsake the Proud Lady, of the heart of fire,
The look of snow, to the praise of a dwindled choir,
Song of degenerate spectres that were men?
The sons of the fathers shall keep her, worthy of
What these have done in love.'

True, it is said of our Lady, she ageth.
But see, if you peep shrewdly, she hath not stooped;
Take no thought of her servitors that have drooped,
For we are nothing; and if one talk of death –
Why, the ribs of the earth subsist frail as a breath
If but God wearieth.

POUND

THE RETURN

SEE, they return; ah, see the tentative
Movements, and the slow feet,
The trouble in the pace and the uncertain
Wavering!

See, they return, one, and by one,
With fear, as half-awakened;
As if the snow should hesitate
And murmur in the wind,
        and half turned back;
These were the 'Wing'd-with-Awe',
        Inviolable.

Gods of the wingèd shoe!
With them the silver hounds,
        sniffing the trace of air!

Haie! Haie!
        These were the swift to harry;
These the keen-scented;
These were the souls of blood.

Slow on the leash,
        pallid the leash-men!

E. P. ODE POUR L'ÉLECTION DE SON SÉPULCRE

For three years, out of key with his time,
He strove to resuscitate the dead art
Of poetry; to maintain 'the sublime'
In the old sense. Wrong from the start –

No, hardly, but seeing he had been born
In a half-savage country, out of date;
Bent resolutely on wringing lilies from the acorn;
Capaneus; trout for factitious bait;

Ἴδμεν γάρ τοι πάνθ', ὅσ' ἐνὶ Τροίῃ
Caught in the unstopped ear;
Giving the rocks small lee-way
The chopped seas held him, therefore, that year.

His true Penelope was Flaubert,
He fished by obstinate isles;
Observed the elegance of Circe's hair
Rather than the mottoes on sundials.

Unaffected by 'the march of events',
He passed from men's memory in *l'an trentiesme*
De son eage; the case presents
No adjunct to the Muses' diadem.

from THE PISAN CANTOS

The ant's a centaur in his dragon world.
Pull down thy vanity, it is not man
Made courage, or made order, or made grace,
    Pull down thy vanity, I say pull down.

Learn of the green world what can be thy place
In scaled invention or true artistry,
Pull down thy vanity,
Paquin pull down!
The green casque has outdone your elegance.

'Master thyself, then others shall thee beare'
Pull down thy vanity
Thou art a beaten dog beneath the hail,
A swollen magpie in a fitful sun,
Half black half white
Nor knowst'ou wing from tail
Pull down thy vanity
How mean thy hates
Fostered in falsity,
Pull down thy vanity,
Rathe to destroy, niggard in charity,
Pull down thy vanity,
I say pull down.

But to have done instead of not doing
this is not vanity
To have, with decency, knocked
That a Blunt should open
To have gathered from the air a live tradition
or from a fine old eye the unconquered flame
This is not vanity.
Here error is all in the not done,
all in the diffidence that faltered.

ELIOT

GERONTION

Thou hast nor youth nor age
But as it were an after dinner sleep
Dreaming of both.

HERE I am, an old man in a dry month,
Being read to by a boy, waiting for rain.
I was neither at the hot gates
Nor fought in the warm rain

Nor knee deep in the salt marsh, heaving a cutlass,
Bitten by flies, fought.
My house is a decayed house,
And the jew squats on the window sill, the owner,
Spawned in some estaminet of Antwerp,
Blistered in Brussels, patched and peeled in London.
The goat coughs at night in the field overhead;
Rocks, moss, stonecrop, iron, merds.
The woman keeps the kitchen, makes tea,
Sneezes at evening, poking the peevish gutter.

I an old man,
A dull head among windy spaces.

Signs are taken for wonders, 'We would see a sign!'
The word within a word, unable to speak a word,
Swaddled with darkness. In the juvescence of the year
Came Christ the tiger

In depraved May, dogwood and chestnut, flowering judas,
To be eaten, to be divided, to be drunk
Among whispers; by Mr Silvero
With caressing hands, at Limoges
Who walked all night in the next room;
By Hakagawa, bowing among the Titians;
By Madame de Tornquist, in the dark room
Shifting the candles; Fräulein von Kulp
Who turned in the hall, one hand on the door. Vacant shuttles
Weave the wind. I have no ghosts,
An old man in a draughty house
Under a windy knob.

After such knowledge, what forgiveness? Think now
History has many cunning passages, contrived corridors
And issues; deceives with whispering ambitions,
Guides us by vanities. Think now
She gives when our attention is distracted,
And what she gives, gives with such supple confusions
That the giving famishes the craving. Gives too late
What's not believed in, or if still believed,
In memory only, reconsidered passion. Gives too soon
Into weak hands what's thought can be dispensed with
Till the refusal propagates a fear. Think

Neither fear nor courage saves us. Unnatural vices
Are fathered by our heroism. Virtues
Are forced upon us by our impudent crimes.

These tears are shaken from the wrath-bearing tree.

The tiger springs in the new year. Us he devours. Think at last
We have not reached conclusion, when I
Stiffen in a rented house. Think at last
I have not made this show purposelessly
And it is not by any concitation
Of the backward devils.

I would meet you upon this honestly.
I that was near your heart was removed therefrom
To lose beauty in terror, terror in inquisition.
I have lost my passion: why should I need to keep it
Since what is kept must be adulterated?
I have lost my sight, smell, hearing, taste and touch:
How should I use them for your closer contact?

These with a thousand small deliberations
Protract the profit of their chilled delirium,
Excite the membrane, when the sense has cooled,
With pungent sauces, multiply variety
In a wilderness of mirrors. What will the spider do,
Suspend its operations, will the weevil
Delay? De Bailhache, Fresca, Mrs Cammel, whirled
Beyond the circuit of the shuddering Bear
In fractured atoms. Gull against the wind, in the windy straits
Of Belle Isle, or running on the Horn,
White feathers in the snow, the Gulf claims,
And an old man driven by the Trades
To a sleepy corner.
                                        Tenants of the house,
Thoughts of a dry brain in a dry season.

ASH WEDNESDAY. VI

ALTHOUGH I do not hope to turn again
Although I do not hope
Although I do not hope to turn

Wavering between the profit and the loss
In this brief transit where the dreams cross
The dreamcrossed twilight between birth and dying
(Bless me father) though I do not wish to wish these things
From the wide window towards the granite shore
The white sails still fly seaward, seaward flying
Unbroken wings

And the lost heart stiffens and rejoices
In the lost lilac and the lost sea voices
And the weak spirit quickens to rebel
For the bent golden-rod and the lost sea smell
Quickens to recover
The cry of quail and the whirling plover
And the blind eye creates
The empty forms between the ivory gates
And smell renews the salt savour of the sandy earth

This is the time of tension between dying and birth
The place of solitude where three dreams cross
Between blue rocks
But when the voices shaken from the yew-tree drift away
Let the other yew be shaken and reply.

Blessèd sister, holy mother, spirit of the fountain, spirit of the garden,
Suffer us not to mock ourselves with falsehood
Teach us to care and not to care
Teach us to sit still
Even among these rocks,
Our peace in His will
And even among these rocks
Sister, mother
And spirit of the river, spirit of the sea,
Suffer me not to be separated

And let my cry come unto Thee.

RANNOCH BY GLENCOE

HERE the crow starves, here the patient stag
Breeds for the rifle. Between the soft moor
And the soft sky, scarcely room
To leap or soar. Substance crumbles, in the thin air

Moon cold or moon hot. The road winds in
Listlessness of ancient war,
Languor of broken steel,
Clamour of confused wrong, apt
In silence. Memory is strong
Beyond the bone. Pride snapped,
Shadow of pride is long, in the long pass
No concurrence of bone.

LITTLE GIDDING

I

MIDWINTER spring is its own season
Sempiternal though sodden towards sundown,
Suspended in time, between pole and tropic.
When the short day is brightest, with frost and fire,
The brief sun flames the ice, on pond and ditches,
In windless cold that is the heart's heat,
Reflecting in a watery mirror
A glare that is blindness in the early afternoon.
And glow more intense than blaze of branch, or brazier,
Stirs the dumb spirit: no wind, but pentecostal fire
In the dark time of the year. Between melting and freezing
The soul's sap quivers. There is no earth smell
Or smell of living thing. This is the spring time
But not in time's covenant. Now the hedgerow
Is blanched for an hour with transitory blossom
Of snow, a bloom more sudden
Than that of summer, neither budding nor fading,
Not in the scheme of generation.
Where is the summer, the unimaginable
Zero summer?

If you came this way,
Taking the route you would be likely to take
From the place you would be likely to come from,
If you came this way in may time, you would find the hedges
White again, in May, with voluptuary sweetness.
It would be the same at the end of the journey,
If you came at night like a broken king,

If you came by day not knowing what you came for,
It would be the same, when you leave the rough road
And turn behind the pig-sty to the dull façade
And the tombstone. And what you thought you came for
Is only a shell, a husk of meaning
From which the purpose breaks only when it is fulfilled
If at all. Either you had no purpose
Or the purpose is beyond the end you figured
And is altered in fulfilment. There are other places
Which also are the world's end, some at the sea jaws,
Or over a dark lake, in a desert or a city –
But this is the nearest, in place and time,
Now and in England.

If you came this way,
Taking any route, starting from anywhere,
At any time or at any season,
It would always be the same: you would have to put off
Sense and notion. You are not here to verify,
Instruct yourself, or inform curiosity
Or carry report. You are here to kneel
Where prayer has been valid. And prayer is more
Than an order of words, the conscious occupation
Of the praying mind, or the sound of the voice praying.
And what the dead had no speech for, when living,
They can tell you, being dead: the communication
Of the dead is tongued with fire beyond the language of the living.
Here, the intersection of the timeless moment
Is England and nowhere. Never and always.

II

Ash on an old man's sleeve
Is all the ash the burnt roses leave.
Dust in the air suspended
Marks the place where a story ended.
Dust inbreathed was a house –
The wall, the wainscot and the mouse.
The death of hope and despair,
This is the death of air.

There are flood and drouth
Over the eyes and in the mouth,
Dead water and dead sand
Contending for the upper hand.
The parched eviscerate soil
Gapes at the vanity of toil,
Laughs without mirth.
        This is the death of earth.

Water and fire succeed
The town, the pasture and the weed.
Water and fire deride
The sacrifice that we denied.
Water and fire shall rot
The marred foundations we forgot,
Of sanctuary and choir.
        This is the death of water and fire.

In the uncertain hour before the morning
  Near the ending of interminable night
  At the recurrent end of the unending
After the dark dove with the flickering tongue
  Had passed below the horizon of his homing
  While the dead leaves still rattled on like tin
Over the asphalt where no other sound was
  Between three districts whence the smoke arose
  I met one walking, loitering and hurried
As if blown towards me like the metal leaves
  Before the urban dawn wind unresisting.
  And as I fixed upon the down-turned face
That pointed scrutiny with which we challenge
  The first-met stranger in the waning dusk
  I caught the sudden look of some dead master
Whom I had known, forgotten, half recalled
  Both one and many; in the brown baked features
  The eyes of a familiar compound ghost
Both intimate and unidentifiable.
  So I assumed a double part, and cried
  And heard another's voice cry: 'What! are *you* here?'
Although we were not. I was still the same,
  Knowing myself yet being someone other –
  And he a face still forming; yet the words sufficed

To compel the recognition they preceded.
And so, compliant to the common wind,
Too strange to each other for misunderstanding,
In concord at this intersection time
Of meeting nowhere, no before and after,
We trod the pavement in a dead patrol.
I said: 'The wonder that I feel is easy,
Yet ease is cause of wonder. Therefore speak:
I may not comprehend, may not remember.'
And he: 'I am not eager to rehearse
My thought and theory which you have forgotten.
These things have served their purpose: let them be.
So with your own, and pray they be forgiven
By others, as I pray you to forgive
Both bad and good. Last season's fruit is eaten
And the fullfed beast shall kick the empty pail.
For last year's words belong to last year's language
And next year's words await another voice.
But, as the passage now presents no hindrance
To the spirit unappeased and peregrine
Between two worlds become much like each other,
So I find words I never thought to speak
In streets I never thought I should revisit
When I left my body on a distant shore.
Since our concern was speech, and speech impelled us
To purify the dialect of the tribe
And urge the mind to aftersight and foresight,
Let me disclose the gifts reserved for age
To set a crown upon your lifetime's effort.
First, the cold friction of expiring sense
Without enchantment, offering no promise
But bitter tastelessness of shadow fruit
As body and soul begin to fall asunder.
Second, the conscious impotence of rage
At human folly, and the laceration
Of laughter at what ceases to amuse.
And last, the rending pain of re-enactment
Of all that you have done, and been; the shame
Of motives late revealed, and the awareness
Of things ill done and done to others' harm
Which once you took for exercise of virtue.

Then fools' approval stings, and honour stains.
From wrong to wrong the exasperated spirit
  Proceeds, unless restored by that refining fire
  Where you must move in measure, like a dancer.'
The day was breaking. In the disfigured street
  He left me, with a kind of valediction,
  And faded on the blowing of the horn.

III

There are three conditions which often look alike
Yet differ completely, flourish in the same hedgerow:
Attachment to self and to things and to persons, detachment
From self and from things and from persons; and, growing
    between them, indifference
Which resembles the others as death resembles life,
Being between two lives – unflowering, between
The live and the dead nettle. This is the use of memory:
For liberation – not less of love but expanding
Of love beyond desire, and so liberation
From the future as well as the past. Thus, love of a country
Begins as attachment to our own field of action
And comes to find that action of little importance
Though never indifferent. History may be servitude,
History may be freedom. See, now they vanish,
The faces and places, with the self which, as it could, loved them,
To become renewed, transfigured, in another pattern.

Sin is Behovely, but
All shall be well, and
All manner of thing shall be well.
If I think, again, of this place,
And of people, not wholly commendable,
Of no immediate kin or kindness,
But some of peculiar genius,
All touched by a common genius,
United in the strife which divided them;
If I think of a king at nightfall,
Of three men, and more, on the scaffold
And a few who died forgotten
In other places, here and abroad,
And of one who died blind and quiet,

Why should we celebrate
These dead men more than the dying?
It is not to ring the bell backward
Nor is it an incantation
To summon the spectre of a Rose.
We cannot revive old factions
We cannot restore old policies
Or follow an antique drum.
These men, and those who opposed them
And those whom they opposed
Accept the constitution of silence
And are folded in a single party.
Whatever we inherit from the fortunate
We have taken from the defeated
What they had to leave us – a symbol:
A symbol perfected in death.
And all shall be well and
All manner of thing shall be well
By the purification of the motive
In the ground of our beseeching.

IV

The dove descending breaks the air
With flame of incandescent terror
Of which the tongues declare
The one discharge from sin and error.
The only hope, or else despair
  Lies in the choice of pyre or pyre –
  To be redeemed from fire by fire.

Who then devised the torment? Love.
Love is the unfamiliar Name
Behind the hands that wove
The intolerable shirt of flame
Which human power cannot remove.
  We only live, only suspire
  Consumed by either fire or fire.

V

What we call the beginning is often the end
And to make an end is to make a beginning.

d is where we start from. And every phrase
sentence that is right (where every word is at home,
king its place to support the others,
The word neither diffident nor ostentatious,
An easy commerce of the old and the new,
The common word exact without vulgarity,
The formal word precise but not pedantic,
The complete consort dancing together)
Every phrase and every sentence is an end and a beginning,
Every poem an epitaph. And any action
Is a step to the block, to the fire, down the sea's throat
Or to an illegible stone: and that is where we start.
We die with the dying:
See, they depart, and we go with them.
We are born with the dead:
See, they return, and bring us with them.
The moment of the rose and the moment of the yew-tree
Are of equal duration. A people without history
Is not redeemed from time, for history is a pattern
Of timeless moments. So, while the light fails
On a winter's afternoon, in a secluded chapel
History is now and England.

With the drawing of this Love and the voice of this Calling

We shall not cease from exploration
And the end of all our exploring
Will be to arrive where we started
And know the place for the first time.
Through the unknown, remembered gate
When the last of earth left to discover
Is that which was the beginning;
At the source of the longest river
The voice of the hidden waterfall
And the children in the apple-tree
Not known, because not looked for
But heard, half-heard, in the stillness
Between two waves of the sea.
Quick now, here, now, always –
A condition of complete simplicity
(Costing not less than everything)
And all shall be well and

All manner of thing shall be well
When the tongues of flame are in-folded
Into the crowned knot of fire
And the fire and the rose are one.

MUIR

THE ROAD

THERE is a road that turning always
  Cuts off the country of Again.
Archers stand there on every side
  And as it runs time's deer is slain,
  And lies where it has lain.

That busy clock shows never an hour.
  All flies and all in flight must tarry.
The hunter shoots the empty air
  Far on before the quarry,
  Which falls though nothing's there to parry.

The lion couching in the centre
  With mountain head and sunset brow
Rolls down the everlasting slope
  Bones picked an age ago,
  And the bones rise up and go.

There the beginning finds the end
  Before beginning ever can be,
And the great runner never leaves
  The starting and the finishing tree,
  The budding and the fading tree.

There the ship sailing safe in harbour
  Long since in many a sea was drowned.
The treasure burning in her hold
  So near will never be found,
  Sunk past all sound.

There a man on a summer evening
  Reclines at ease upon his tomb
And is his mortal effigy
  And there within the womb,
  The cell of doom,

The ancestral deed is thought and done,
  And in a million Edens fall
A million Adams drowned in darkness,
  For small is great and great is small.
  And a blind seed all.

THE TRANSMUTATION

THAT all should change to ghost and glance and gleam,
And so transmuted stand beyond all change,
And we be poised between the unmoving dream
And the sole moving moment – this is strange

Past all contrivance, word, or image, or sound,
Or silence, to express, that we who fall
Through time's long ruin should weave this phantom ground
And in its ghostly borders gather all.

There incorruptible the child plays still,
The lover waits beside the trysting tree,
The good hour spans its heaven, and the ill,
Rapt in their silent immortality,

As in commemoration of a day
That having been can never pass away.

EDITH SITWELL

STILL FALLS THE RAIN

The raids, 1940. Night and Dawn

STILL falls the Rain –
Dark as the world of man, black as our loss –
Blind as the nineteen hundred and forty nails
Upon the Cross.

Still falls the Rain
With a sound like the pulse of the heart that is changed to the
hammer-beat
In the Potter's Field, and the sound of the impious feet

On the Tomb:
Still falls the Rain
In the Field of Blood where the small hopes breed and the human
brain
Nurtures its greed, that worm with the brow of Cain.

Still falls the Rain
At the feet of the Starved Man hung upon the Cross.
Christ that each day, each night, nails there, have mercy on us –
On Dives and on Lazarus:
Under the Rain the sore and the gold are as one.

Still falls the Rain –
Still falls the Blood from the Starved Man's wounded Side:
He bears in His Heart all wounds, – those of the light that died,

The last faint spark
In the self-murdered heart, the wounds of the sad uncompre-
hending dark,
The wounds of the baited bear, –
The blind and weeping bear whom the keepers beat
On his helpless flesh . . . the tears of the hunted hare.

Still falls the Rain –
Then – O Ile leape up to my God: who pulles me doune –
See, see where Christ's blood streames in the firmament:
It flows from the Brow we nailed upon the tree
Deep to the dying, to the thirsting heart
That holds the fires of the world, – dark-smirched with pain
As Caesar's laurel crown.

Then sounds the voice of One who like the heart of man
Was once a child who among beasts has lain –
'Still do I love, still shed my innocent light, my Blood, for thee.'

Edith Sitwell

CRANE

VOYAGES. II

AND yet this great wink of eternity,
Of rimless floods, unfettered leewardings,
Samite sheeted and processioned where
Her undinal vast belly moonward bends,
Laughing the wrapped inflections of our love;

Take this Sea, whose diapason knells
On scrolls of silver snowy sentences,
The sceptred terror of whose sessions rends
As her demeanors motion well or ill,
All but the pieties of lovers' hands.

And onward, as bells off San Salvador
Salute the crocus lustres of the stars,
In these poinsettia meadows of her tides, –
Adagios of islands, O my Prodigal,
Complete the dark confessions her veins spell.

Mark how her turning shoulders wind the hours
And hasten while her penniless rich palms
Pass superscription of bent foam and wave, –
Hasten, while they are true, – sleep, death, desire,
Close round one instant in one floating flower.

Bind us in time, O Seasons clear, and awe,
O minstrel galleons of Carib fire,
Bequeath us to no earthly shore until
Is answered in the vortex of our grave
The seal's wide spindrift gaze toward paradise.

TO BROOKLYN BRIDGE

HOW many dawns, chill from his rippling rest
The seagull's wings shall dip and pivot him,
Shedding white rings of tumult, building high
Over the chained bay waters Liberty –

Then, with inviolate curve, forsake our eyes
As apparitional as sails that cross
Some page of figures to be filed away;
– Till elevators drop us from our day . . .

I think of cinemas, panoramic sleights
With multitudes bent toward some flashing scene
Never disclosed, but hastened to again,
Foretold to others eyes on the same screen;

And Thee, across the harbor, silver-paced
As though the sun took step of thee, yet left
Some motion ever unspent in thy stride, –
Implicitly thy freedom staying thee!

Out of some subway scuttle, cell or loft
A bedlamite speeds to thy parapets,
Tilting there momently, shrill shirt ballooning,
A jest falls from the speechless caravan.

Down Wall, from girder into street noon leaks,
A rip-tooth of the sky's acetylene;
All afternoon the cloud-flown derricks turn . . .
Thy cables breathe the North Atlantic still.

And obscure as that heaven of the Jews,
Thy guerdon . . . Accolade thou dost bestow
Of anyonymity time cannot raise:
Vibrant reprieve and pardon thou dost show.

O harp and altar, of the fury fused,
(How could mere toil align thy choiring strings!)
Terrific threshold of the prophet's pledge,
Prayer of pariah, and the lover's cry, –

Again the traffic lights that skim thy swift
Unfractioned idiom, immaculate sigh of stars,
Beading thy path – condense eternity:
And we have seen night lifted in thine arms.

Under thy shadow by the piers I waited;
Only in darkness is thy shadow clear.
The City's fiery parcels all undone,
Already snow submerges an iron year . . .

O Sleepless as the river under thee,
Vaulting the sea, the prairies' dreaming sod,
Unto us lowliest sometime sweep, descend
And of the curveship lend a myth to God.

CUMMINGS

[‘SOMEWHERE I HAVE NEVER TRAVELLED’]

SOMEWHERE I have never travelled, gladly beyond
any experience, your eyes have their silence:
in your most frail gesture are things which enclose me,
or which I cannot touch because they are too near.

Your slightest look easily will unclose me
though I have closed myself as fingers,
you open always petal by petal myself as Spring opens
(touching skilfully, mysteriously) her first rose

or if your wish be to close me, I and
my life will shut very beautifully, suddenly,
as when the heart of this flower imagines
the snow carefully everywhere descending;

nothing which we are to perceive in this world equals
the power of your intense fragility: whose texture
compels me with the colour of its countries,
rendering death and forever with each breathing.

(I do not know what it is about you that closes
and opens; only something in me understands
the voice of your eyes is deeper than all roses)
nobody, not even the rain, has such small hands.

GRAVES

FULL MOON

As I walked out that sultry night,
  I heard the stroke of one.
The moon, attained to her full height,
  Stood beaming like the sun:
She exorcised the ghostly wheat
To mute assent in love's defeat,
  Whose tryst had now begun.

The fields lay sick beneath my tread,
  A tedious owlet cried,
A nightingale above my head
  With this or that replied –
Like man and wife who nightly keep
Inconsequent debate in sleep
  As they dream side by side.

Your phantom wore the moon's cold mask,
  My phantom wore the same;
Forgetful of the feverish task
  In hope of which they came,
Each image held the other's eyes
And watched a grey distraction rise
  To cloud the eager flame –

To cloud the eager flame of love,
  To fog the shining gate;
They held the tyrannous queen above
  Sole mover of their fate,
They glared as marble statues glare
Across the tessellated stair
  Or down the halls of state.

And now warm earth was Arctic sea,
  Each breath came dagger-keen;
Two bergs of glinting ice were we,
  The broad moon sailed between;
There swam the mermaids, tailed and finned,
And love went by upon the wind
  As though it had not been.

NEVER SUCH LOVE

TWINED together and, as is customary,
For words of rapture groping, they
'Never such love,' swore, 'ever before was!'
Contrast with all loves that had failed or staled
Registered their own as love indeed.

And was not this to blab idly
The heart's fated inconstancy?
Better in love to seal the love-sure lips:
For truly love was before words were,
And no word given, no word broken.

When the word 'love' is uttered
(Love, the near-honourable malady
With which in greed and haste they
Each other do infect and curse)
Or, worse, is written down....

Wise after the event, by love withered,
A 'never more!' most frantically
Sorrow and shame would proclaim
Such as, they'd swear, never before were:
True lovers even in this.

BLUNDEN

REPORT ON EXPERIENCE

I HAVE been young, and now am not too old;
And I have seen the righteous forsaken,
His health, his honour and his quality taken.
    This is not what we were formerly told.

I have seen a green country, useful to the race,
Knocked silly with guns and mines, its villages vanished,
Even the last rat and last kestrel banished –
    God bless us all, this was peculiar grace.

I knew Seraphina; Nature gave her hue,
Glance, sympathy, note, like one from Eden.
I saw her smile warp, heard her lyric deaden;
She turned to harlotry; – this I took to be new.

Say what you will, our God sees how they run.
These disillusions are His curious proving
That He loves humanity and will go on loving;
Over them are faith, life, virtue in the sun.

DAY LEWIS

THE ALBUM

I SEE you, a child
In a garden sheltered for buds and playtime,
Listening as if beguiled
By a fancy beyond your years and the flowering maytime.
The print is faded: soon there will be
No trace of that pose enthralling,
Nor visible echo of my voice distantly calling
'Wait! Wait for me!'

Then I turn the page
To a girl who stands like a questioning iris
By the waterside, at an age
That asks every mirror to tell what the heart's desire is.
The answer she finds in that oracle stream
Only time could affirm or disprove,
Yet I wish I was there to venture a warning, 'Love
Is not what you dream.'

Next you appear
As if garlands of wild felicity crowned you –
Courted, caressed, you wear
Like immortelles the lovers and friends around you.
'They will not last you, rain or shine,
They are but straws and shadows,'
I cry: 'Give not to those charming desperadoes
What was made to be mine.'

One picture is missing –
The last. It would show me a tree stripped bare
By intemperate gales, her amazing
Noonday of blossom spoilt which promised so fair.
Yet, scanning those scenes at your heyday taken,
I tremble, as one who must view
In the crystal a doom he could never deflect – yes, I too
Am fruitlessly shaken.

I close the book;
But the past slides out of its leaves to haunt me
And it seems, wherever I look,
Phantoms of irreclaimable happiness taunt me.
Then I see her, petalled in new-blown hours,
Beside me – 'All you love most there
Has blossomed again,' she murmurs, 'all that you missed there
Has grown to be yours.'

EMPSON

MISSING DATES

SLOWLY the poison the whole blood stream fills.
It is not the effort nor the failure tires.
The waste remains, the waste remains and kills.

It is not your system or clear sight that mills
Down small to the consequence of a life requires;
Slowly the poison the whole blood stream fills.

They bled an old dog dry yet the exchange rills
Of young dog blood gave but a month's desires;
The waste remains, the waste remains and kills.

It is the Chinese tombs and the slag hills
Usurp the soil, and not the soil retires.
Slowly the poison the whole blood stream fills.

Not to have fire is to be a skin that shrills.
The complete fire is death. From partial fires
The waste remains, the waste remains and kills.

It is the poems you have lost, the ills
From missing dates, at which the heart expires.
Slowly the poison the whole blood stream fills.
The waste remains, the waste remains and kills.

AUDEN

1st SEPTEMBER 1939

I sit in one of the dives
On Fifty-second Street
Uncertain and afraid
As the clever hopes expire
Of a low dishonest decade:
Waves of anger and fear
Circulate over the bright
And darkened lands of the earth,
Obsessing our private lives;
The unmentionable odour of death
Offends the September night.

Accurate scholarship can
Unearth the whole offence
From Luther until now
That has driven a culture mad,
Find what occurred at Linz,
What huge imago made
A psychopathic god:
I and the public know
What all schoolchildren learn,
Those to whom evil is done
Do evil in return.

Exiled Thucydides knew
All that a speech can say
About Democracy,
And what dictators do,
The elderly rubbish they talk

To an apathetic grave;
Analysed all in his book,
The enlightenment driven away,
The habit-forming pain,
Mismanagement and grief:
We must suffer them all again.

Into this neutral air
Where blind skyscrapers use
Their full height to proclaim
The strength of Collective Man,
Each language pours its vain
Competitive excuse:
But who can live for long
In an euphoric dream;
Out of the mirror they stare,
Imperialism's face
And the international wrong.

Faces along the bar
Cling to their average day:
The lights must never go out,
The music must always play,
All the conventions conspire
To make this fort assume
The furniture of home;
Lest we should see where we are,
Lost in a haunted wood,
Children afraid of the night
Who have never been happy or good.

The windiest militant trash
Important Persons shout
Is not so crude as our wish:
What mad Nijinsky wrote
About Diaghilev
Is true of the normal heart;
For the error bred in the bone
Of each woman and each man
Craves what it cannot have,
Not universal love
But to be loved alone.

From the conservative dark
Into the ethical life
The dense commuters come,
Repeating their morning vow;
'I *will* be true to the wife,
I'll concentrate more on my work,'
And helpless governors wake
To resume their compulsory game:
Who can release them now,
Who can reach the deaf,
Who can speak for the dumb?

Defenceless under the night
Our world in stupor lies;
Yet, dotted everywhere,
Ironic points of light
Flash out wherever the Just
Exchange their messages:
May I, composed like them
Of Eros and of dust,
Beleaguered by the same
Negation and despair,
Show an affirming flame.

['LAY YOUR SLEEPING HEAD']

LAY your sleeping head, my love,
Human on my faithless arm;
Time and fevers burn away
Individual beauty from
Thoughtful children, and the grave
Proves the child ephemeral:
But in my arms till break of day
Let the living creature lie,
Mortal, guilty, but to me
The entirely beautiful.

Soul and body have no bounds:
To lovers as they lie upon
Her tolerant enchanted slope
In their ordinary swoon,

Grave the vision Venus sends
Of supernatural sympathy,
Universal love and hope;
While an abstract insight wakes
Among the glaciers and the rocks
The hermit's sensual ecstasy.

Certainty, fidelity
On the stroke of midnight pass
Like vibrations of a bell
And fashionable madmen raise
Their pedantic boring cry:
Every farthing of the cost,
All the dreaded cards foretell,
Shall be paid, but from this night
Not a whisper, not a thought,
Not a kiss nor look be lost.

Beauty, midnight, vision dies:
Let the winds of dawn that blow
Softly round your dreaming head
Such a day of sweetness show
Eye and knocking heart may bless,
Find the mortal world enough;
Noons of dryness see you fed
By the involuntary powers,
Nights of insult let you pass
Watched by every human love.

from NEW YEAR LETTER

O UNICORN among the cedars
To whom no magic charm can lead us,
White childhood moving like a sigh
Through the green woods unharmed in thy
Sophisticated innocence
To call thy true love to the dance;
O Dove of science and of light
Upon the branches of the night;
O Icthus playful in the deep
Sea-lodges that for ever keep

Their secret of excitement hidden;
O sudden Wind that blows unbidden
Parting the quiet reeds; O Voice
Within the labyrinth of choice
Only the passive listener hears;
O Clock and Keeper of the years;
O Source of equity and rest,
Quando non fuerit, non est,
If without image, paradigm
Of matter, motion, number, time,
The grinning gap of Hell, the hill
Of Venus and the stairs of Will,
Disturb our negligence and chill,
Convict our pride of its offence
In all things, even penitence,
Instruct us in the civil art
Of making from the muddled heart
A desert and a city where
The thoughts that have to labour there
May find locality and peace,
And pent-up feelings their release.
Send strength sufficient for our day,
And point our knowledge on its way,
O da quod jubes, Domine.

MACNEICE

AUGUST

The shutter of time darkening ceaselessly
Has whisked away the foam of may and elder
And I realise how now, as every year before,
Once again the gay months have eluded me.

For the mind, by nature stagey, welds its frame
Tomb-like around each little world of a day;
We jump from picture to picture and cannot follow
The living curve that is breathlessly the same.

While the lawn-mower sings moving up and down
Spirting its little fountain of vivid green,
I, like Poussin, make a still-bound fête of us
Suspending every noise, of insect or machine.

Garlands at a set angle that do not slip,
Theatrically (and as if for ever) grace
You and me and the stone god in the garden
And Time who also is shown with a stone face.

But all this is a dilettante's lie,
Time's face is not stone nor still his wings,
Our mind, being dead, wishes to have time die,
For we being ghosts cannot catch hold of things.

SPENDER

I THINK continually of those who were truly great.
Who, from the womb, remembered the soul's history
Through corridors of light where the hours are suns,
Endless and singing. Whose lovely ambition
Was that their lips, still touched with fire,
Should tell of the Spirit, clothed from head to foot in song.
And who hoarded from the Spring branches
The desires falling across their bodies like blossoms.

What is precious, is never to forget
The essential delight of the blood drawn from ageless springs
Breaking through rocks in worlds before our earth.
Never to deny its pleasure in the morning simple light
Nor its grave evening demand for love.
Never to allow gradually the traffic to smother
With noise and fog, the flowering of the Spirit.

Near the snow, near the sun, in the highest fields,
See how these names are fêted by the waving grass
And by the streamers of white cloud
And whispers of wind in the listening sky.

The names of those who in their lives fought for life,
Who wore at their hearts the fire's centre.
Born of the sun, they travelled a short while toward the sun
And left the vivid air signed with their honour.

ELEGY FOR MARGARET. VI

DEAREST and nearest brother,
No word can turn to day
The freezing night of silence
Where all your dawns delay
Watching flesh of your Margaret
Wither in sickness away.

Yet those we lose, we learn
With singleness to love:
Regret stronger than passion holds
Her the times remove:
All those past doubts of life, her death
One happiness does prove.

Better in death to know
The happiness we lose
Than die in life in meaningless
Misery of those
Who lie beside chosen
Companions they never chose.

Orpheus, maker of music,
Clasped his pale bride
Upon that terrible river
Of those who have died;
Then of his poems the uttermost
Laurel sprang from his side.

When your red eyes follow
Her body dazed and hurt
Under the torrid mirage
Of delirious desert,
Her breasts break with white lilies,
Her eyes with Margaret.

I bring no consolation
Of the weeping shower
Whose final dropping jewel deletes
All grief in the sun's power:
You must watch the signs grow worse
Day after day, hour after hour.

Yet to accept the worst
Is finally to revive
When we are equal with the force
Of that with which we strive
And having almost lost, at last
Are glad to be alive.

As she will live who, candle-lit
Floats upon her final breath
The ceiling of the frosty night
And her high room beneath,
Wearing not like destruction, but
Like a white dress, her death.

THOMAS

A REFUSAL TO MOURN THE DEATH, BY FIRE, OF A CHILD IN LONDON

NEVER until the mankind making
Bird beast and flower
Fathering and all humbling darkness
Tells with silence the last light breaking
And the still hour
Is come of the sea tumbling in harness

And I must enter again the round
Zion of the water bead
And the synagogue of the ear of corn
Shall I let pray the shadow of a sound
Or sow my salt seed
In the least valley of sackcloth to mourn

The majesty and burning of the child's death.
I shall not murder
The mankind of her going with a grave truth
Nor blaspheme down the stations of the breath
With any further
Elegy of innocence and youth.

Deep with the first dead lies London's daughter,
Robed in the long friends,
The grains beyond age, the dark veins of her mother,
Secret by the unmourning water
Of the riding Thames.
After the first death, there is no other.

FERN HILL

Now as I was young and easy under the apple boughs
About the lilting house and happy as the grass was green,
The night above the dingle starry,
Time let me hail and climb
Golden in the heydays of his eyes,
And honoured among the wagons I was prince of the apple towns
And once below a time I lordly had the trees and leaves
Trail with daisies and barley
Down the rivers of the windfall light.

And as I was green and carefree, famous among the barns
About the happy yard and singing as the farm was home,
In the sun that is young once only,
Time let me play and be
Golden in the mercy of his means,
And green and golden I was huntsman and herdsman, the calves
Sang to my horn, the foxes on the hills barked clear and cold,
And the sabbath rang slowly
In the pebbles of the holy streams.

All the sun long it was running, it … lovely, the hay
Fields high as the house, the tunes … m the chimneys, it was air
And playing, lovely and w… y
And fire green as g… ple stars
And nightly under the … re bearing the farm away,
As I rode to sleep the owl…

All the moon long I heard, blessed among stables, the nightjars
Flying with the ricks, and the horses
Flashing into the dark.

And then to awake, and the farm, like a wanderer white
With the dew, come back, the cock on his shoulder: it was all
Shining, it was Adam and maiden,
The sky gathered again
And the sun grew round that very day.
So it must have been after the birth of the simple light
In the first, spinning place, the spellbound horses walking warm
Out of the whinnying green stable
On to the fields of praise.

And honoured among foxes and pheasants by the gay house
Under the new made clouds and happy as the heart was long,
In the sun born over and over,
I ran my heedless ways,
My wishes raced through the house high hay
And nothing I cared, at my sky blue trades, that time allows
In all his tuneful turning so few and such morning songs
Before the children green and golden
Follow him out of grace,

Nothing I cared, in the lamb white days, that time would take me
Up to the swallow thronged loft by the shadow of my hand,
In the moon that is always rising,
Nor that riding to sleep
I should hear him fly with the high fields
And wake to the farm forever fled from the childless land.
Oh as I was young and easy in the mercy of his means,
Time held me green and dying
Though I sang in my chains like the sea.

ACKNOWLEDGEMENTS

ACKNOWLEDGEMENTS

Permission to use copyright material is gratefully acknowledged to the following:

Chatto & Windus Ltd for 'Wedded' by Isaac Rosenberg; 'Strange Meeting' by Wilfred Owen; 'Missing Dates' from *Collected Poems* by William Empson; J. M. Dent & Sons Ltd for two poems from *Collected Poems* by Dylan Thomas; Mrs Helen Thomas for two poems from *Collected Poems* by Edward Thomas; Macmillan & Co. Ltd and the Trustees of the Hardy Estate for nine poems from *Collected Poems* by Thomas Hardy; Macmillan & Co. Ltd, Messrs A. P. Watt & Son, and Mrs George Bambridge for 'Cities and Thrones and Powers' and 'Harp Song of the Dane Women' from *Puck of Pook's Hill* and 'Gertrude's Prayer' from *Renewals* by Rudyard Kipling (Canadian copyright permission *per* The Macmillan Company of Canada); Macmillan & Co. Ltd, Messrs A. P. Watt & Son, and Mrs W. B. Yeats for eight poems from *Collected Poems* by W. B. Yeats; Macmillan & Co. Ltd, Pearn, Pollinger & Higham Ltd, and Dame Edith Sitwell for 'Still falls the Rain' by Edith Sitwell; Cassell & Co. Ltd, Messrs A. P. Watt, and Mr Robert Graves for two poems from *Collected Poems, 1914–1947* by Robert Graves; Jonathan Cape Ltd and the authors, respectively, for five poems from *The Complete Poems of Robert Frost* (Canadian copyright permission *per* Henry Holt & Co. Inc. New York), and for a poem from *Word Over All* by C. Day Lewis; Random House Inc. New York for 'The Eye' from *The Double Axe and Other Poems* by Robinson Jeffers, copyright 1948 by Robinson Jeffers; Sidgwick & Jackson Ltd, and the literary executors of Rupert Brooke for 'The Soldier' from *The Collected Poems of Rupert Brooke*; the Oxford University Press for six poems from *The Poems of Gerard Manley Hopkins* and the extract from 'Contemplation' from *The Poems of Francis Thompson*; Messrs Shakespeare & Parkyn (as Solicitors for the Committee for Mr Ezra Pound) and Mr Ezra Pound for two poems from *Selected Poems* and an extract from *The Pisan Cantos*, by Ezra Pound; *The New England Quarterly* for 'Upon a Wasp Chilled with Cold' by Edward Taylor; Jonathan Cape Ltd and the Society of Authors (as Literary Representatives of the Trustees of the estate of the late A. E. Housman) for a poem from *Collected Poems* by A. E. Housman; the Society of Authors and Dr John Masefield for 'Upon the Downs' by John Masefield (Canadian copyright permission *per* The Macmillan Company, New York); William Heinemann Ltd for two poems and two extracts from *Collected Poetical Works* by A. C. Swinburne; Faber & Faber Ltd and the authors, respectively, for four poems from *The Collected Poems* of Walter de la Mare; two poems and 'Ash Wednesday VI' from *Collected Poems* by T. S. Eliot and for 'Little Gidding' from *Four Quartets* by T. S. Eliot; two poems from *Collected Poems* by Marianne Moore (Canadian copyright permission *per* The Macmillan

Company, New York); 'Sunday Morning' from *Collected Poems* by Wallace Stevens (Canadian copyright permission *per* Alfred A. Knopf Inc. New York); two poems from *Collected Poems 1921–1951* by Edwin Muir; two poems from *Collected Shorter Poems 1930–1944* by W. H. Auden and an extract from *New Year Letter* by W. H. Auden; two poems from *Collected Poems 1928–1953* by Stephen Spender; a poem from *Collected Poems 1925–1948* by Louis MacNeice; the Clarendon Press, Oxford, for a poem from *The Shorter Poems of Robert Bridges*; the Clarendon Press, Oxford, and Miss Helen Darbyshire for her text of Milton's 'Lycidas' and for extracts from her text of *Paradise Lost*; and to the same publishers for extracts from De Selincourt's text of the 1805 version of Wordsworth's *The Prelude*; Liveright Publishing Corporation, New York, for two poems from *The Collected Poems* by Hart Crane; Constable & Co. Ltd, for four sonnets from *Modern Love* and an extract from *The Thrush in February* by George Meredith; Alfred A. Knopf Inc., New York, and Pearn, Pollinger & Higham Ltd for 'Antique Harvesters' by John Crowe Ransom; Harcourt Brace and Company and A. M. Heath & Co. Ltd, for a poem from *Poems 1923–1954* by E. E. Cummings; A. D. Peters and the author for 'Report on Experience' by Edmund Blunden; the Macmillan Company, New York, and the author, for two poems from *Collected Poems* by Edwin Arlington Robinson; Charles Scribner's Sons, New York and the author for 'For a Dead Lady' from *The Town Down the River* by Edwin Arlington Robinson copyright 1910 by Charles Scribner's Sons, 1938 by Ruth Nivison; James F. Murray, Jr, New York and the author for 'Gulls' by William Carlos Williams.

INDEX OF FIRST LINES

AND

INDEX OF POETS

INDEX OF FIRST LINES

[First lines of extracts are printed in italics]

A numerous Host of dreaming Saints succeed 179
A slumber did my spirit seal 261
A sudden blow: the great wings beating still 409
A sweet disorder in the dresse 159
A widow bird sate mourning for her love 292
Absent from thee I languish still 189
Accept thou Shrine of my dead Saint 97
Adieu, farewell earths blisse 39
After a hundred years 368
After long stormes and tempests sad assay 21
After the pangs of a desperate Lover 184
Ah, did you once see Shelley plain 334
Ah fading joy, how quickly art thou past? 183
Ah! fair face gone from sight 400
Ah how sweet it is to love 184
Ah what avails the sceptred race 274
Alas so all thinges nowe doe holde their peace 4
All is best, though we oft doubt 155
All my past Life is mine no more 188
All's over, then – does truth sound bitter 327
All things that pass 365
Although I do not hope to turn again 434
And did those feet in ancient time 247
And if I did what then? 10
And slowly answered Arthur from the barge 319
And yet this great wink of eternity 446
Anear the centre of that northern crest 378
As I drive to the junction of lane and highway 397
As I in hoary Winter's night stood shiveringe in the snowe 30
As I walked out that sultry night 449
As imperceptibly as grief 369
As in a duskie and tempestuous Night 95
As virtuous men passe mildly away 81
As you came from the holy land 37
Aske me no more where *Jove* bestowes 162
At Sestos, Hero *dwelt*; Hero *the faire* 32

At the mid hour of night, when stars are weeping, I fly 275
At the midnight in the silence of the sleep-time 337
At the round earths imagin'd corners, blow 87
Away delights, go seek some other dwelling 91

Beautie, I know, is good, and bloud is more 74
Beautie, sweet love, is like the morning dewe 40
Beautiful must be the mountains whence ye come 391
Behold her, single in the field 263
Below me Trees unnumber'd rise 213
Blest be the God of love 107
Blows the wind today, and the sun and the rain are flying 390
Break, break, break 324
Bright star, would I were stedfast as thou art 300
But, hark, 'tis late; the Whistlers *knock from Plough* 132
But oh! o'er all forget not Kilda's race 224
But wherefore do not you a mightier waie 58
By the rude bridge that arched the flood 309
By what astrology of fear or hope 325
By what bold passion am I rudely led 139

Caged in old woods, whose reverend echoes wake 272
Call for the Robin-Red-brest and the wren 70
Calm is the morn without a sound 321
Calme was the day, and through the trembling ayre 22
Care-charmer sleepe, sonne of the Sable night 40
Care charming sleep, thou easer of all woes 91
Cities and Thrones and Powers 402
Cold in the earth – and the deep snow piled above thee 338
Come again to the place 393
Come down, O maid, from yonder mountain height 317
Come live with mee, and be my love 31
Come my Celia, let us prove 71
Come sleep, and with the sweet deceiving 92
Come spurre away 104
Complacencies of the peignoir, and late 423
Condemn'd to Hope's delusive mine 219
Crabbed age and youth cannot live together 65
Creep into thy narrow bed 353

Dark house, by which once more I stand 320
Dauncing (*bright Lady) then began to be* 42
Dear Cloe, how blubber'd is that pretty Face? 192
Dear Thomas, didst Thou never pop 193
Dearest and nearest brother 459
Death be not proud, though some have called thee 87
Deep in the shady sadness of a vale 298
Deere, why should you commaund me to my rest 47
Diaphenia like the Daffadown-dillie 31
Drinke to me, onely, with thine eyes 71

Eftsoones they heard a most melodious sound 17
Elysium is as far as to 367
Ere long they come, where that same wicked wight 14
Even as a child, of sorrow that we give 362
Ev'n like two little bank-dividing brookes 96
Even such is Time, which takes in trust 38

Fair hope! our earlyer heav'n by thee 119
Fair seed-time had my soul, and I grew up 266
Faire as unshaded Light, or as the Day 141
Faire Daffadills, we weep to see 160
False though she be to me and Love 197
Fames *Plant takes Root from* Vertue, *grows thereby* 133
Farewel, too little and too lately known 182
Farewell, Love, and all thy lawes for ever 3
Farewell, thou child of my right hand, and joy 72
Farewell ungratefull Traytor 185
Farr off from these a slow and silent stream 150
Fear death? – to feel the fog in my throat 336
Feare no more the heate o' th' Sun 69
Felix Randal the farrier, O he is dead then? 388
Fine young folly, though you were 103
Fix'd were their habits; they arose betimes 250
Follow a shaddow, it still flies you 73
Follow your Saint, follow with accents sweet 48
For Adoration seasons change 228
For, all that from her springs, and is ybredde 19
For his Religion *it was fit* 156

For though the caves were rabitted 342
For three years, out of key with his time 431
Forgot this rotten world; And unto thee 85
Fresh spring the herald of loves mighty king 21
From Dust I rise 127
From fairest creatures we desire increase 38
From Harmony, from Heav'nly Harmony 180
From these hie hilles as when a spring doth fall 1
Full fadom five thy Father lies 67
Full many a glorious morning have I seene 60

Gather ye Rose-buds while ye may 158
Gently dip: but not too deepe 26
Ghosts there must be with me in this old house 415
Give all to love 308
Gloomy and dark art thou, O chief of the mighty Omahas 326
Glory be to God for dappled things 388
Go, for they call you, Shepherd, from the hill 346
God made the country, and man made the town 238
Goe lovely Rose 171
Gorbo, as thou cam'st this way 45
Great is the folly of a feeble braine 57

Had we but World enough, and Time 135
Hail holy Light, ofspring of Heav'n first-born 151
Happy those early dayes! when I 120
He had been long t'wards Mathematicks 157
Hearke, now every thing is still 70
Helen, thy beauty is to me 311
Her voice did quiver as we parted 292
Here I am, an old man in a dry month 432
Here is the ancient floor 391
Here take my Picture; though I bid farewell 84
Here the crow starves, here the patient stag 435
Here where the wind is always north-north-east 406
Hereto I come to view a voiceless ghost 396
Him the Almighty Power 149
His Golden lockes, Time hath to Silver turn'd 27
How fresh, O Lord, how sweet and clean 112

How like a Winter hath my absence beene 62
How many dawns, chill from his rippling rest 446
How soon hath Time the suttle theef of youth 142
How sweet I roam'd from field to field 239
How vainly men themselves amaze 137

I am a parcel of vain strivings tied 341
I am: yet what I am none cares or knows 305
I caught this morning morning's minion 387
I do believ 128
I envy not in any moods 322
I got me flowers to straw thy way 106
I have been here before 363
I have been young, and now am not too old 450
I have desired to go 386
I heard no sound where I stood 316
I know the wayes of Learning; both the head 109
I looked for that which is not, nor can be 365
I love to see the old heath's withered brake 304
I met a traveller from an antique land 290
'I play for Seasons; not Eternities!' 384
I saw Eternity the other night 123
I see you, a child 451
I sit in one of the dives 453
I strove with none, for none was worth my strife 275
I struck the board, and cry'd, No more 110
I think continually of those who were truly great 458
I thought of Thee, my partner and my guide 265
I walk through the long schoolroom questioning 409
I walkt the other day (to spend my hour,) 125
I wander thro' each charter'd street 242
I was made erect and lone 343
I wonder by my troth, what thou, and I 77
I wonder do you feel to-day 333
If I should die, think only this of me 420
If ought of Oaten Stop, or Pastoral Song 222
If their bee nothing new, but that which is 61
If to be absent were to be 165
If yet I have not all thy love 78
In a coign of the cliff between lowland and highland 374

In a loose robe of Tynsell foorth she came 55
In Love, if Love be Love, if Love be ours 318
In Merioneth, over the sad moor 401
In such a *Night*, when every louder Wind 196
In the merrie moneth of May 11
In what torne ship soever I embarke 87
In Xanadu did Kubla Khan 255
Isled in the midnight air 414
It is not growing like a tree 76
It is not that I love you less 172
It is the evening hour 304
It seemed that out of battle I escaped 421
It was a Summer's night, a close warm night 270

Kinde are her answeres 50
Knowing the heart of man is set to be 41

Lastlie stode warre in glittering armes yclad 7
Lay your sleeping head, my love 455
Leave me ô Love, which reachest but to dust 13
Let me not to the marriage of true mindes 63
Let others sing of Knights and Palladines 41
Let the bird of lowdest lay 65
Let us go hence, my songs; she will not hear 372
Lift not the painted veil which those who live 290
Like as the waves make towards the pibled shore 61
Like the *Idalian* Queene 94
Like truthles dreames, so are my joyes expired 34
Lo! Death has reared himself a throne 311
Lo! in the mute, mid wilderness 301
Look in my face; my name is Might-have-been 362
Love bade me welcome: yet my soul drew back 113
Love born of knowledge, love that gains 384
Love heeds no more the sighing of the wind 401
Love in her Eyes sits playing 212
Love in her Sunny Eyes does basking play 132
Love in my bosome like a Bee 28
Love lives beyond 305
Love seeketh not Itself to please 241

Love still has something of the Sea 187
Love, thou art Absolute sole lord 114
Lovers rejoyce, your pains shall be rewarded 91
Loving in truth, and faine in verse my love to show 12

Man looking into the sea 427
Mark where the pressing wind shoots javelin-like 385
Methought I saw 302
Methought I saw my late espoused Saint 148
Midwinter spring is its own season 436
Minott, Lee, Willard, Hosmer, Meriam, Flint 306
Miss Danae, when Fair and Young 194
Much have I travell'd in the realms of gold 292
Must I then see, alas! eternal night 93
My father used to say 428
My heart aches, and a drowsy numbness pains 293
My heart leaps up when I behold 261
My life closed twice before its close 367
My Love is of a birth as rare 136
My love, this is the bitterest, that thou 329
My lute awake performe the last 2
My mother groan'd! my father wept 243
My silks and fine array 240
My townspeople, beyond in the great world 406
My true love hath my heart and I have his 13

Nature and Nature's Laws lay hid in Night 206
Never until the mankind making 460
News from a forrein Country came 130
Night came, but without darkness or repose 176
No coward soul is mine 339
No more – no more – Oh! never more on me 280
No more with overflowing light 404
No, no, go not to Lethe, neither twist 297
No one was with me there 414
No sound of any storm that shakes 405
No worst, there is none. Pitched past pitch of grief 389
Not *Celia*, that I juster am 186
Not, I'll not, carrion comfort, Despair, not feast on thee 389

Not in those climes where I have late been straying 276
Not marble, nor the guilded monument 60
Not with more glories, in th' etherial plain 205
Nothing is so beautiful as spring 387
Nothing so true as what you once let fall 208
Now as I was young and easy under the apple boughs 461
Now came still Eevning on, and Twilight gray 153
Now fades the last long streak of snow 323
Now hardly here and there an Hackney-Coach 199
Now once again the gloomy scene explore 248
Now, solitary, and in pensive Guise 214
Now that the winter's gone, the earth hath lost 162
Now the lusty Spring is seen 89

'O cruel Death, give three things back' 412
O Love, turn from the unchanging sea, and gaze 371
O mistris mine where are you roming? 68
O Rose, thou art sick! 241
O Time! who know'st a lenient hand to lay 253
O Unicorn among the cedars 456
O what avails the sceptred race 274
O wild West Wind, thou breath of Autumn's being 284
Obscurest night involv'd the sky 236
O'er desert plains, and rushy meers 217
Of all the causes which conspire to blind 201
Of Heaven or Hell I have no power to sing 369
Of Man's First Disobedience, and the Fruit 148
Oft has our Poet wisht, this happy Seat 181
Oft have I sigh'd for him that heares me not 50
Often rebuked, yet always back returning 340
Oh be thou blest with all that Heav'n can send 207
Oh! for some honest Lovers ghost 163
Oh happy shades! to me unblest 237
Oh thou that swing'st upon the waving haire 166
Oh, to be in England 329
Oh wearisome Condition of Humanity! 27
Old Father Ocean calls my Tyde 186
Old Yew, which graspest at the stones 320
On this lone Isle, whose rugged rocks affright 252
Once as me thought, fortune me kist 2

Once more the changed year's turning wheel returns 362
One ought not to have to care 416
One word is too often profaned 291
Onely a little more 161
Our birth is but a sleep and a forgetting 264
Out in the dark over the snow 420

Pale, beyond porch and portal 373
Past ruin'd Ilion Helen lives 274
Patience, hard thing! the hard thing but to pray 390
Peace, peace! he is not dead, he doth not sleep 287
Perhaps I may allow, the Dean 201
Poore soule the center of my sinfull earth 64
Pray but one prayer for me 'twixt thy closed lips 371
Presentiment is that long shadow on the lawn 367

Remember me when I am gone away 364
Romance, who loves to nod and sing 313
Romira, stay 169
Round the cape of a sudden came the sea 328

Say not, the struggle nought availeth 343
Season of mists and mellow fruitfulness 296
See! from the brake the whirring Pheasant springs 202
See the Chariot at hand here of Love 74
See, they return; ah, see the tentative 430
Set where the upper streams of Simois flow 345
Shall I come, sweet Love, to thee 50
Shall I compare thee to a Summers day? 59
She dwelt among the untrodden ways 261
She rose to his requirement, dropped 368
She smil'd, and more of pleasure than disdain 273
She walks in beauty, like the night 276
Since I am comming to that Holy roome 88
Since ther's no helpe, Come let us kisse and part 47
Skirting the river road, (my forenoon walk, my rest,) 353
Sleep, O Sleep 212
Slow, slow, fresh fount, keepe time with my salt teares 77

Slowly the poison the whole blood stream fills 452
So cruell prison how coulde betide, alas 5
So faire a church as this, had Venus *none* 33
So, we'll go no more a roving 283
So when the Shadows laid asleep 139
Soe well I love thee, as without thee I 48
Some had in Courts been Great, and thrown from thence 177
Somewhere I have never travelled, gladly beyond 448
Stand close around, ye Stygian set 275
Still falls the Rain 444
Sunset and evening star 324
Sure, It was so. Man in those early days 121
Surprised by joy – impatient as the Wind 265
Sweet, be not proud of those two eyes 159
Sweet day, so cool, so calm, so bright 109
Sweet is true love tho' given in vain, in vain 318
Sweet *Spring*, thou turn'st with all thy goodlie Traine 94
Sweet was the sound when oft at evening's close 230
Sweetest love, I do not goe 79

Tagus farewel that westward with thy stremes 4
Take, Oh take those lips away 92
Tawny are the leaves turned but they still hold 429
Tears, idle tears, I know not what they mean 317
Tell me not here, it needs not saying 398
Tell me not (Sweet) I am unkinde 166
Ternissa! you are fled! 275
Thames, *the most lov'd of all the Oceans sons* 170
That all should change to ghost and glance and gleam 444
That civilisation may not sink 413
That evening all in fond discourse was spent 251
That is no country for old men. The young 408
That time of yeeare thou maist in me behold 61
That which is marred at birth Time shall not mend 403
That's my last Duchess painted on the wall 335
The ant's a centaur in his dragon world 431
The Atlantic is a stormy moat; and the Mediterranean 428
The Bear that breaks the Northern blast 175
The *Curfeu* tolls the Knell of parting Day 225
The Dean, if we believe Report 200

Th'expence of Spirit in a waste of shame 64
The flower that smiles to-day 291
The Frost performs its secret ministry 253
The garlands fade that Spring so lately wove 252
The glories of our blood and state 101
The grey sea and the long black land 328
The house had gone to bring again 417
The irresponsive silence of the land 366
The isles of Greece, the isles of Greece! 281
The land was ours before we were the land's 418
The Lark now leaves his watry Nest 140
The last of last words spoken is, Good-bye 415
The lopped tree in tyme may grow agayne 29
The lowest Trees have tops, the Ante her gall 11
The moon now rises to her absolute rule 342
The moon was up, the Lake was shining clear 267
The river has not any care 399
The sea is calm to-night 344
The shutter of time darkening ceaselessly 457
The sky is low, the clouds are mean 368
The sounding cataract 262
The tide's at full: the marsh with flooded streams 380
The unpurged images of day recede 411
The waves come rolling, and the billowes rore 16
The wind flapped loose, the wind was still 363
The woods decay, the woods decay and fall 314
The World a Hunting is 95
The world is too much with us; late and soon 263
The world's great age begins anew 286
There are some heights in Wessex, shaped as if by a kindly hand 394
There came a wind like a bugle 367
There is a Garden in her face 51
There is a road that turning always 443
There is a silence where hath been no sound 303
There is none like her, none 316
There never yet was honest man 164
There was a Boy, ye knew him well, ye Cliffs 270
There was a sound of revelry by night 278
These market-dames, mid-aged, with lips thin-drawn 392
They are all gone into the world of light 124

They flee from me, that somtime did me seke 1
They leave their love-lorn haunts 421
They saw the sun looke pale, and cast through aire 53
They that have powre to hurt, and will doe none 62
They were approaching the region where reigns perpetual summer 325
Things Native sweetly grew 128
Thou hast made me, And shall thy worke decay? 86
Thou hast thy ponds, that pay thee tribute fish 73
Thou hearest the Nightingale begin the Song of Spring 247
Thou still unravish'd bride of quietness! 295
Three lovely notes he whistled, too soft to be heard 419
Thus by himself compell'd to live each day 249
Thus lovely, *Sleep* did *first* appear 188
Thus piteously Love closed what he begat 386
Thus was this place 152
Timely blossom, infant fair 198
'Tis hard to say, if greater want of skill 203
Tis the yeares midnight, and it is the dayes 80
'Tis true, no Lover has that Pow'r 157
To me faire friend you never can be old 63
To Mercy, Pity, Peace, and Love 240
To see a World in a Grain of Sand 243
To seeke new worlds, for golde, for prayse, for glory 35
To these, whom Death again did wed 119
To night the winds begin to rise 321
Tree at my window, window tree 413
Troop home to silent grots and caves! 301
Truly, My Satan, thou art but a Dunce 248
Turning and turning in the widening gyre 407
Twined together and, as is customary 450
Tyger! Tyger! burning bright 241

Underneath the growing grass 364
Up on the downs the red-eyed kestrels hover 418

Victorious men of Earth, no more 100

W. resteth here, that quick could never rest 6

We have bathed, where none have seen us 310
We saw the swallows gathering in the sky 385
Weepe with me all you that read 72
Weighing the stedfastness and state 122
Well dost thou, Love, thy solemn Feast to hold 382
Well I remember how you smiled 274
Well! If the Bard was weather-wise, who made 257
Were I (who to my cost already am 189
What care I, so they stand the same 309
What faire pompe have I spide of glittering Ladies 52
What is a woman that you forsake her 402
What then is love but mourning? 49
What though the field be lost? 150
When as the Rie reach to the chin 27
When Daffadils begin to peere 68
When do I see thee most, beloved one? 361
When first the College Rolls receive his Name 218
When God at first made man 111
When I consider how my light is spent 147
When in disgrace with Fortune and mens eyes 59
When in the Chronicle of wasted time 63
When Isicles hang by the wall 67
When lilacs last in the dooryard bloom'd 354
When Love with unconfined wings 167
When my devotions could not pierce 108
When rosy plumelets tuft the larch 322
When the hounds of spring are on winter's traces 376
When the Present has latched its postern behind my tremulous stay 398
When thou must home to shades of under ground 49
When to the Sessions of sweet silent thought 59
When we for Age could neither read nor write 172
When Westwall Downes I gan to tread 102
Whence thou returnst, and whither wentst, I know 154
Where do'st thou carelesse lie 75
Where, like a pillow on a bed 82
Where the city's ceaseless crowd moves on the livelong day 360
Where the remote *Bermudas* ride 134
Whilst in this cold and blust'ring Clime 173
Whither, midst falling dew 272
Who dreamed that beauty passes like a dream? 407

Who sayes that fictions onely and false hair 106
Who sees with equal eye, as God of all 207
Why cannot the Ear be closed to its own destruction 246
Winds whisper gently whilst she sleeps 171
Wintertime nighs 392
With a Whirl of Thought oppress'd 199
With all my will, but much against my heart 382
With how sad steps, ô Moone, thou climbst the skies 12
With that low *Cunning, which in fools supplies* 234
With thee conversing I forget all time 153
With youth, is deade the hope of loves returne 36
Woman much missed, how you call to me, call to me 395
Word over all, beautiful as the sky 361

Ye green-rob'd Dryads, *oft' at dusky Eve* 220
Ye have been fresh and green 160
Yes! in the sea of life enisl'd 344
Yet once more, O ye Laurels, and once more 142
You come to fetch me from my work to-night 416
You earthly Souls that court a wanton flame 168
Young and simple though I am 52
Your Beauty, ripe, and calm, and fresh 141

INDEX OF POETS

Arnold 344
Auden 453

Beaumont 89
Beddoes 310
Benlowes 132
Blake 239
Blunden 450
Bowles 253
Breton 11
Bridges 391
Brooke 420
Brontë 338
Browning 327
Bryant 272
Butler 156
Byron 276

Campion 48
Carew 162
Chapman 53
Churchill 234
Clare 304
Clough 343
Coleridge 253
Collins 222
Congreve 197
Constable 31
Cotton 173
Cowley 132
Cowper 236
Crabbe 248
Crane 446
Crashaw 114
Cummings 448

Daniel 40
Darley 301
D'Avenant 139
Davies 42
Day Lewis 451
De la Mare 414
Denham 170
Dickinson 367
Donne 77
Dowson 401
Drayton 45
Drummond 94
Dryden 176
Dyer, E. 11
Dyer, J. 213

Eliot 432
Emerson 306
Empson 452

Fletcher 89
Frost 415

Gascoigne 10
Gay 212
Goldsmith 230
Graves 449
Gray 225
Greville 27

Habington 103
Hall, John 169
Hall, Joseph 57
Hardy 391
Herbert 106
Herbert of Cherbury 93
Herrick 158
Hood 302
Hopkins 386
Housman 398

Jeffers 428
Johnson, L. 400
Johnson, S. 218
Jonson 71

Keats 292
King 97
Kipling 402

Landor 273
Lanier 380
Leigh 188
Lodge 28
Longfellow 325
Lovelace 165

MacNeice 457
Marlowe 31

MARVELL 134
MASEFIELD 418
MEREDITH 384
MILTON 142
MOORE, M. 427
MOORE, T. 275
MORRIS 369
MUIR 443

NASHE 39

OWEN 421

PATMORE 382
PEELE 26
PHILIPS 198
POE 311
POPE 202
POUND 430
PRIOR 192

QUARLES 96

RALEGH 34
RANDOLPH 104
RANSOM 429
ROBINSON 404
ROCHESTER 188
ROGERS 272
ROSENBERG 421
ROSSETTI, C. 364
ROSSETTI, D. 361
RUSSELL 252

SACKVILLE 7
SEDLEY 186
SHAKESPEARE 58
SHELLEY 284
SHENSTONE 217
SHIRLEY 100
SIDNEY 12
SITWELL 444
SMART 228
SMITH 252
SOUTHWELL 29
SPENDER 458
SPENSER 14
STANLEY 168
STEVENS 423
STEVENSON 390
STRODE 102
SUCKLING 163
SURREY 4
SWIFT 199
SWINBURNE 372

TAYLOR 175
TENNYSON 314
THOMAS, D. 460
THOMAS, E. 419
THOMPSON 399
THOMSON, J. 214
THOMSON, J.: (BV) 378
THOREAU 341
TRAHERNE 127

VAUGHAN 120

WALLER 171
WARTON 220
WEBSTER 70
WHITMAN 353
WILLIAMS 426
WINCHILSEA 196
WORDSWORTH 261
WYATT 1

YEATS 407

MORE ABOUT PENGUINS AND PELICANS

For further information about books available from Penguins please write to Dept EP, Penguin Books Ltd, Harmondsworth, Middlesex UB7 ODA.

In the U.S.A.: For a complete list of books available from Penguins in the United States write to Dept CS, Penguin Books, 625 Madison Avenue, New York, New York 10022.

In Canada: For a complete list of books available from Penguins in Canada write to Penguin Books Canada Ltd, 2801 John Street, Markham, Ontario L3R 1B4.

In Australia: For a complete list of books available from Penguins in Australia write to the Marketing Department, Penguin Books Australia Ltd, P.O. Box 257, Ringwood, Victoria 3134.

In New Zealand: For a complete list of books available from Penguins in New Zealand write to the Marketing Department, Penguin Books (NZ) Ltd, P.O. Box 4019, Auckland 10.